SOCIETY IN INDIA

Continuity and Change

DAVID G. MANDELBAUM

Society in India

VOLUME ONE

CONTINUITY AND CHANGE

UNIVERSITY OF CALIFORNIA PRESS

BERKELEY, LOS ANGELES, LONDON

University of California Press
Berkeley and Los Angeles, California
University of California Press, Ltd.
London, England
© 1970 by David G. Mandelbaum
ISBN: 0-520-01893-1
Library of Congress Catalog Card Number: 70-99952
Printed in the United States of America

4 5 6 7 8 9

To Ruth

Preface

The idea of this work began soon after I started my first field research in India in 1937. Like other students of the people of India, I was struck by the great diversity among them and yet I could sense the common qualities of society and civilization which they shared. These shared qualities have been noted by many earlier writers, but their observations lacked the detailed information available in modern field studies and were not guided by the concepts developed in recent years in cultural-social anthropology and in other social sciences. It seemed to me that a new general frame for understanding the Indian people and their society was possible; such a frame was clearly needed in order to understand particular groups and to grasp the trends of social change.

My military service in India, Ceylon, and Burma in 1943–45 brought me to a wide variety of places and considerably enlarged my knowledge of South Asian peoples. A period of field work in India in 1949–50 again stimulated me to thinking about the common ground of Indian social relations. In 1957–58 a fellowship at the Center for Advanced Study in the Behavioral Sciences enabled me to begin writing a general account of Indian society. A brief stay in India in 1958–59 gave me additional data for the analysis I had under way. The draft manuscripts of this phase of the work were read by several colleagues and friends; Cora DuBois' comments were particularly useful. These appraisals were encouraging but convinced me that in certain matters I needed to develop a different approach and a new set of concepts. For several years I turned to other projects and meanwhile tried to work out ideas that would help bring together in an orderly way the large body of data on Indian society, data that were rapidly being increased and immeasurably improved by the generation of fine anthropologists, both Indian and non-Indian, who began their field studies in India after national independence.

In 1963–64 I was Senior Fellow in New Delhi of the American School of Indian Studies and was able then to give more attention to this project.

This work has taken a long time to complete not only because of the size of the task and because of personal vicissitudes, but also because some of the key concepts were developed as the work progressed. As these new ideas took shape, some parts of what had already been written had to be recast.

Many of my colleagues at Berkeley have been helpful, particularly Murray B. Emeneau (companion in my first field experience in India) and Gerald D. Berreman. I have mulled over the nature of Indian society with anthropologists of several academic generations when they were students; among those from whose knowledge I have continued to benefit are Alan Beals, Henry Orenstein, and Surajit Sinha. Fellow anthropologists in India have been helpful over many years. I owe special thanks to M. N. Srinivas, N. K. Bose, and Mrs. Irawati Karve.

Support for the present work has come from several sources, including the Guggenheim Foundation, the Center for Advanced Study in the Behavioral Sciences, the American Institute of Indian Studies, the Committee on Research and the Center for South Asian Studies of the University of California, Berkeley. To them I express my grateful appreciation. Among the administrative officers whose efficient skills facilitated my work, I am especially obliged to D. D. Karve and P. R. Mehendiratta of the American Institute of Indian Studies and to Ralph Tyler and Preston Cutler of the Center for Advanced Study in the Behavioral Sciences. I am indebted to Mrs. Anne Brower, editor for the Department of Anthropology at Berkeley, for her editorial aid, her fine perception and patience. Hundreds of villagers have helped me toward some understanding of the people of India. Two who were among my first guides and friends were the late K. Sulli of Kollimalai village and M. N. Thesingh of Horanelli village, both in the Nilgiris district. To my family go the deepest thanks of all.

DAVID G. MANDELBAUM

Berkeley, California

Contents of Volume One

PART I: INTRODUCTION   1

1. Task, Concepts, and Scope   3
   The concepts of social system and of caste order, 4
   The nature of the evidence, 8
   The scope, the time, the focus, 9

2. The Basic Groups and Groupings   13
   Jati, 13
   Flexibilities in jati relations and, roles, 16
   Groups and groupings within the jati, 17
   Jati-cluster, 19
   Varna: villagers' theory and theorists' fallacy, 22
   Component groups and social concepts, 27

PART II: FAMILY AND KINSHIP RELATIONS   31

3. Family   33
   Ideal model and actual form, 34
   Hierarchy in family roles, 37
   Family functions, 41
   Changes in relations within a family, 45
   Economic factors in family form, 47
   Differences among regions, 54

4. Family Roles: Boy and Man   58
   As son: filial respect and its consequences, 58
   As brother to brother: partners and sometimes rivals, 63
   As brother to sister: durable bond, 67
   As mother's brother: supportive kinsman, 71
   As husband: social and personal gains, 74
   Other roles and social consequences, 78

5. Family Roles: Girl and Woman   82
   As daughter: the brief sojourn, 82
   As young wife: great transition and critical role, 84
   As matron: increasing influence, 88

The women of the family: expected friction and central importance, 90

6. Family Cycle: Formation and Maintenance   95

The recruitment of males and females, 96
Marriage as a test of status, 98
Explicit rules for marriage alliances, 101
Implicit rules and general procedures, 104
Precautions: astrology and pre-puberty marriage, 110
Marriage links and communication among villages, 112
The wedding, 115

7. Family Cycle: Growth and Completion   119

The growth phase: the rearing of children, 119
A cross-cultural study of child rearing, 123
The dispersal phase, 125
The family as module and as model, 130

8. The Wider Ties of Kinship   134

The lineage, 136
Lineage ties and ritual functions, 137
Lineage ties in economic and jural affairs, 139
The clan, 144
Gotra and other terms for kinship groupings, 145
Feminal kin, 148
Fictive kinship, 151
The uses of kinship, 152
Kinship bonds in North and in South India, 156
Résumé, 158

PART III: RELATIONS AMONG PEOPLE OF DIFFERENT JATIS   159

9. The Interdependence of Families and Jatis   161

Contractual and jajmani relations, 161
Specialized jatis and multiple functions, 164
Jajmani payments and obligations, 167
Supply, demand, and flexible payments, 169
Enforcement of jajmani relations: coercion and consensus, 172
Change and continuity in jajmani relations, 174
Solutions to the problems of interdependence, 179

10. Criteria for the Ranking of Jatis   181

Rank-free contexts of behavior, 182
Ritual criteria: personal pollution and purity, 184
Roles that require special purity, 188
Corporate pollution and jati rank, 189

11. The Social Relevance of Ritual Pollution and Purity   192

The contagion of pollution, 193
Extrapolations of the ritual criteria, 195
Ingestion as a ritual and social act, 196

The ritual and social bearings of sexual acts, 201
Means of purification and ideas about pollution, 202

12. Secular Criteria and the Attribution of Jati Rank   206

The application of secular influence, 207
The sources of power, 208
The reciprocal use of ritual and secular resources, 210
The attribution of rank according to jati blocs, 213
Consensus and dissention about rank order, 216

13. Cultural Variations and the Jati Order   222

Differences in religious practices, 223
Cultural contrasts and their social effects, 225
Résumé, 228

PART IV: RELATIONS WITHIN THE JATI   233

14. Alliances and Sections within the Jati   235

Hypergamy and hypergamous sections, 236
Alliances within a jati-group, 240
The bases of alliance strength, 244
Alliance cohesion, 247

15. Opposition and Cohesion within the Jati-group   253

Challenges and realignments, 254
Alliance development and variations in alliance formation, 257
Forces for jati-group cohesion, 265

16. Maintaining the Jati: Leaders and Panchayats   269

Leaders: tasks and motives, 270
Attributes of leaders and methods of leadership, 273
Panchayat as pattern of action, 278
Panchayat participants and procedure, 286

17. The Uses of Panchayats   294

Redress of ritual lapses, 295
Problems of enforcement and jurisdiction, 300
Dispute resolution and government courts, 305
The domains of court and of panchayat, 311

18. Jati Enterprises and Functions   316

Jati enterprises, 316
Variations in jati organization, 319
Jati as means of identity and as social unit, 321

BIBLIOGRAPHY   Bibliography-1

INDEX TO VOLUMES I AND II   Index-1

OUTLINE OF VOLUME TWO

Change and Continuity

PART V: VILLAGE, REGION, CIVILIZATION

19. Village: Separate Hearths and Common Home
20. The Village: Internal Regulation
21. The Wider Ties of Village: Centers and Regions
22. The Villager and Some Perennial Problems of Civilization

PART VI: RECURRENT CHANGE THROUGH SOCIAL MOBILITY

23. Jati Mobility
24. Cultural Adaptations and Models for Mobility
25. Mobility Tactics: Overcoming External Opposition
26. Maintaining Internal Cohesion: Fission and Fusion
27. Modern Means for Jati Improvement: Associations and
    Federations

PART VII: RECURRENT CHANGE THROUGH RELIGIOUS AND
    TRIBAL MOVEMENTS

28. Social Regrouping through Indigenous Religions
29. Social Aspects of Introduced Religions: Muslims
30. Social Aspects of Introduced Religions: Jews, Parsis,
    Christians
31. The Accretion of Tribal Peoples
32. Direction of Tribal Change

PART VIII: CONTINUITIES AND TRENDS

33. Psychological Forces, Social Processes, and Systemic Shift
34. Trends

APPENDIX: THE CONCEPTS OF SYSTEM AND OF STRATIFICATION

BIBLIOGRAPHY

INDEX TO VOLUMES I AND II

PART I *Introduction*

CHAPTER **I** Task, Concepts, and Scope

THERE was an observant Greek ambassador in India about 300 B.C., Megasthenes, whose account of the country and its people gives us our first general view of India as seen by a visitor. Megasthenes took note of the special way in which Indian society was organized. He observed that the people divided themselves into a number of occupationally specialized groups, that a person could marry only within his own group, and that no one could change affiliation from one group to another (McCrindle 1877, pp. 85, 212, 1901, p. 55; R. C. Majumdar 1960, pp. 224–226, 236–238, 263–268).

Many other voyagers to India after Megasthenes remarked upon this distinctive social order. It regulated a large part of public and private behavior; it was a most important concern of the people of the land. It seemed both familiar and quite unfamiliar to a visitor. It was familiar in that like tended to marry like elsewhere; sons commonly followed their father's occupation in the voyager's homeland; a hierarchy of society and privileges of rank were not strange to anyone. What did strike observers as unfamiliar was the rigor of these social divisions, the bases on which the divisions were made, and the thoroughgoing way in which they were applied to all aspects of life.

Because this kind of social order has been a central interest for a great civilization and a huge population, much has been written about Indian society. Both Indian and non-Indian writers have used the term "caste," originally from the Portuguese, for the prevalent social order in India as well as the component groups within that order. The very bulk of the literature has discouraged a good many readers who have sought a general understanding of Indian society. Some have been confused by the large tomes packed with details but devoid of clarifying concepts. Those writings that are more lucid and cogent generally cover only a limited part of the subject without making much attempt to trace how the various parts are fitted together. A good many readers, plunged into detailed descriptions of caste practices, come away with the feeling that Indian society is complex and inchoate beyond the hope of comprehension.

Indian society is indeed complex, but not necessarily beyond reasonable understanding, provided that the fundamental uniformities of caste behavior are grasped. Nor is it inchoate. Villagers use and manipulate their social organization in regular ways. They generally have no great difficulty in understanding the social arrangements of villages other than their own. One way of getting at the basic regularities in Indian society is to look at that society, and at its various components, as a system. Such a view directs attention to the whole social organization within which each component group functions. Emphasis on the whole helps to clarify the nature of the component groups because the function and definition of any group depends in large part on the relations of its members with members of other groups. Each person acts in more than one social role; he can take a number of different positions within his social system. The roles he is taught to assume and how he fulfills them often involve choice, strain, conflict, decision. The regular outcome of recurrent conflict and decision is also integral to the social system.

In taking this perspective, the student of society does more than observe the actors as though through the invisible fourth wall of a stage set. He must understand their actions in their own terms and incorporate the importance of their outlook and feelings into his larger view of their social system. In that larger view, it is possible to distinguish between the repetitive dynamic that is inherent in any social system and those changes that alter the nature of a whole system.

The Concepts of Social System and of Caste Order

A social system consists of a set of groups whose members together perform certain functions that they do not accomplish as separate groups. The groups are thus interdependent, and they are inter-

dependent in a particular arrangement. That is to say, the participants in each group act in regular, anticipated ways toward members of the other groups and toward the external environment.
When some participants do not carry out the kind of *interchange*
that others in the system anticipate, the others respond in regular
ways of *counterchange* to restore some systemic regularity to their
relations.

The boundaries of a social system are therefore defined by the
limits of interchange and counterchange among participant members and groups. The participants' awareness that they are interacting in regular ways is usually an important factor in the maintenance of any social system, but the description and analysis of a
social system is primarily the analyst's formulation of the regularities in the participants' actions.

The members of a single family and their relations with each
other can be viewed as comprising a system of social relations in
themselves. However, the social scientist's focus is on a wider scale
and so we have tried to formulate not only those systemic regularities that occur within and among the families of a particular place
and social level, but also those that we can discern among most village families in India.

In addition to family systems, Indian villagers typically maintain
lineages, the endogamous groups called *jatis*, and village communities, all of which may usefully be described and analyzed as systems.
When a system of lineage organization is discussed, the component
families are treated as subsystems of a lineage. Lineages can, in turn,
be viewed as subsystems of a jati. People of different jatis commonly work together (and sometimes compete) in their village; in
this sense, jatis may be seen as component groups of the system of
village-community relations. For certain purposes we can treat
villages as component parts of regions or of administrative units,
which in turn can be taken as subsystems within the whole society
of the people of India.

However, no living society, certainly not a vast and complex one,
actually works as smoothly and rationally as an abstracted flow
chart might imply. An individual fulfills many roles in various
systems. There are myriad interrelations among the roles and systems in which any one person takes part. What is attempted here is
to sort out several of the principal institutions of Indian society—

notably family, jati, and village—to understand them both as systems and as subsystems of the larger society, to indicate some regularities among a person's roles in various subsystems, and to formulate the social changes that people in India have made and are now making.

This conception of social system is an underlying premise of the analysis, but each part of the analysis is not closely structured after the definition of system. In each part component groups (or individuals) are noted, as are common patterns of interchange and characteristic ways of counterchange, but not necessarily in that order or in any complete way, mainly because adequate data on each subject are not yet available for such regular procedures.

There is a further examination of the concept of social system in the Appendix, together with a discussion of the concept of social stratification as it pertains to an understanding of caste organization in India.

The kind of social system that is called a caste system involves a special quality in the order of interdependence. It is a quality of pervasive inequality among the component groups. Inequality in privilege and reward, in dominance and subordination, is in one sense a universal characteristic of human society. Adults are not the equals of children. Each sex has its own spheres of privilege and dominance, even in societies where males are said to be all dominant. In most societies, whole groups have different degrees of dominance and privilege as against other groups; that is, most societies are stratified to some degree, either in the ranking of functioning groups or in class attributions. The term "stratification" emphasizes this hierarchical arrangement.

Human societies can be placed along a continuum of stratification. Some are very little stratified. For example, two tribal groups mentioned later, the Chenchu and the Paliyan, live by hunting and gathering; the people in these groups are so scattered and their social organization is so simple that there is little possibility for stratification. More stratified are those societies in which people sort themselves into classes, groupings differentiated in privilege but relatively open to recruits. Beyond such societies, at the other extreme of the stratification range, are those societies in which people group themselves into more sharply defined, more rigid and pervasive divisions with strongly regulated relations among the divisions. These are caste orders.

Though Indian caste society has often been depicted as a static social order, in reality the people of India have kept adjusting their social systems and at times have made fundamental changes in them. All social systems are used with some flexibility, if only because people have to cope with the dynamics of the seasonal round and of the life cycle. The biological stages of the human life cycle induce a cycle of family development, and the cyclical pattern of family growth, division, and reconstitution in India will be discussed in the chapters on family relations.

Another kind of repetitive change involves shifts in rank positions. Such shifts typically begin when lower groups become strong enough to challenge their superiors. They meet opposition and some are quelled, but others succeed in raising their rank. In so doing, they revise the previous order of precedence, though not the structure of the local order. Yet another recurrent process in India has typically been started when the followers of a religious leader form a sect; at first they deny certain features of the existing social system, but in time they become reabsorbed into that system. Tribal groups also have frequently been absorbed into caste orders.

In addition to these recurrent changes, there have also been systemic changes. The earliest literary sources in India, the Vedas, reflect a system of relatively open classes in which people carried on a culture and society that were basically different from those of later times, though the later forms were developed out of the earlier ones. G. S. Ghurye outlines four periods of social development. The Vedic period, which in his estimate ended about 600 B.C., was succeeded by a period in which the trend toward a thoroughgoing caste structure had begun. (Megasthenes observed Indian society in this second period.) During the third period a number of features of "classic" caste society became crystallized. Then, about the tenth or eleventh century, the system was developed that remained in operation with considerable consistency for about a thousand years (Ghurye 1961, pp. 42–111).

Within the past century the people of India have been strongly affected by the worldwide tides of change. The extent to which the technological and social-political innovations are bringing about systemic changes are noted throughout much of the following discussion and are reviewed in the final chapter.

The Nature of the Evidence

Social change, whether on a grand systemic scale or within a recurrent local cycle, flows from the choices, decisions, and dilemmas faced by individual men and women. Our study tries to include the individual's perspective, his understandings and motivations. To attempt to do this for so large a part of the world's population and for so complex a civilization, some writers have remarked, is to undertake a task of doubtful feasibility. Denzil Ibbetson began his extensive account of Punjab groups for the 1881 census with the statement that the only thing he knew about caste groups was that he knew nothing and he was not quite sure of that (1916, p. 1). In the opening passages of his book *Social Change in Modern India*, Professor Srinivas writes, "I am acutely aware of the difficulties and hazards involved in making statements claiming to hold good for Hindus all over India" (1966, p. 2).

Still, it is a task worth trying and one that has been made more feasible by the advances in research data and ideas during recent decades. Yet despite the notable improvement in research information, there remains the question of how adequate that information is as a basis for the generalizations that are drawn from it here. One answer is that though only a relatively few of more than half a million Indian villages have been studied or even surveyed, there are studies and surveys from all the major parts of the country, and the evidence so far seems to be consistent with the principles of social action that are formulated here. Moreover, the villagers among whom anthropologists and other social scientists have lived and from whom they have learned are aware of similarities and differences within their society; they can tell about those they see, and their generalizations can be tested against wider evidence. The generalizations presented here will be tested and undoubtedly revised as more data become available and sharper concepts are developed. But, obviously, no generalization can be proved, disproved, or modified before it is formulated. The formulations given in this study are offered more as working hypotheses to help grasp the nature of Indian society than as final facts about its total composition. A biologist once used the folklore motif of the magic well to describe the study of bees. It is also apt for the study of the people of India—the more one draws up, the more there is to draw.

Greater use is made of recent works by trained observers, both Indian and non-Indian, than of the older writings by scholars in the classic tradition or by officials and travelers. Much of the older thought and evidence has been absorbed into the newer studies, and although some of the older accounts are still useful for social as well as historical analyses, the newer studies are generally much better based. Yet good as the modern observers often are, they have observed certain aspects of Indian life relatively little. There are few studies of social relations in towns and cities. The emphasis here is on villagers, not only because the bulk of India's people are villagers, but also because we have so few good studies of town and city life. Although the roots of adult behavior and of personality lie in the common experiences of childhood, there are as yet only a handful of studies of childhood and child rearing in India that are based on close observation and informed research design.

In addition, there is a paucity of usable statistical data on significant matters. Outlines of behavior patterns can be drawn, but most questions of variation within a range and of distribution and deviation await more and better quantitative data. The present state of the evidence permits statements that something "often" or "characteristically" occurs when the present state of our inquiry requires additional information about how often and under what circumstances. Some good statistical data are available and have been used; but other published figures are difficult to use because it is not clear what was counted, in what manner, and for what purpose. So the case examples given here illustrate general conditions and concepts. They exemplify some part of the general range of behavior that is outlined; they do not necessarily indicate a mean or mode within that range.

The Scope, the Time, the Focus

Village society is the principal subject of this study. More than four-fifths of India's people are counted as villagers. Traditional urban society in India seems to have been basically similar to village society, insofar as we can tell from the studies that are available, though in recent decades educated city people have been in the forefront of social change. Because the village is the characteristic locale for the social relations discussed here, the term "villagers" is often used for the people whose activities are discussed. Much of what is said, however, applies as well to many town and city residents.

The geographic scope of this work includes mainly the people of present-day India. Examples from Pakistan villages are given for particular purposes, especially in the discussion of social organization among Muslims. But the civilization of India was developed over the whole subcontinent; every major linguistic region and major religion contributed to it.

The time is the present. The main period of observation is roughly the middle third of the twentieth century. Before that period considerable social change was under way, but during it the people of India have undergone especially marked changes. Some groups have been in the vanguard; they have changed far more than most of their countrymen. Others, not many, have been little affected. Most villagers try to hold firmly to some of the traditional ways while reaching for the benefits of modern ways.

This sketch of Indian social organization, then, does not apply in equal detail to all social groups or to all aspects of life at all times. It is intended as a general survey of basic social principles and patterns followed by most of the people of India. It is more a grammar of social relations than a dictionary of caste practices or a glossary of names. A sketch cannot show everything that is important at once. We begin with a discussion of the general nature of Indian society and of the customary relations among members of different groups. Then the chief components—family, jati, and village—are examined. The dynamic functions of these components are next considered as they have been adaptively used in the overall system of Indian society and as they are being evolved at the present time.

The focus is on the principal groups of village society and on the patterns of interchange and counterchange among them. An emphasis on religion, or economics, or politics would entail a different treatment. This societal emphasis is one that is made by many of the people themselves; the local social order is commonly a paramount concern of village life. The impact of other forces—economic, religious, political, demographic, psychological—is taken into account, but these forces are not the center of our inquiry.

The inquiry is meant for several kinds of inquirers. A reader seeking a general introduction to Indian society may find this work useful. Such readers will encounter a relatively limited number of technical and indigenous terms. The transcription of indigenous terms follows general usage rather than attempting strict phonological accuracy. Efforts toward such accuracy may become confusing or spurious, partly because there is no standard pronunciation throughout India for widely used terms and the pronunciation of a term usually varies within a linguistic region as well as among regions. It seemed better for our purposes to dispense with most diacritical marks and special typography. The term "caste" itself has often been used confusingly to denote the whole system as well as several of its components; here it is used mainly as an adjective, as in "caste system," rather than as a noun.

Some of the common geographic terms are not precisely defined in many of the works on India. What is meant by "South India" is relatively clear; the term refers to the regions in which the principal Dravidian languages are spoken, chiefly the states of Andhra Pradesh, Mysore, Madras, and Kerala. The term "southern India" refers to the same regions; "western India" is usually taken to mean most of the present states of Maharashtra and Gujarat. But "northern India" and "North India" are usually less well defined. "North India" is here used for the Hindi-speaking region centered in the state of Uttar Pradesh. The term "northern India" refers to a vast territory, the area from Bengal to Rajasthan, indeed almost all of India except for those regions included in southern and western India.

Specialists in the study of Indian society will find much here that they already know, though they may also find familiar ideas and data in unfamiliar contexts. Whatever may be usefully new to them has resulted in large part from the attempt to bring together the rich results of their research.

Those whose home is in India may find that the general description does not correspond at all points with their personal experiences. They may also feel a lack of those enlivening details and variations that make an abstracted view very different from the substance of reality. Analytical truth is rarely a good mirror for emotional truth, and the subject of caste relations in India is a matter of profound personal feeling for many.

In the opening sentence of a perceptive article on caste patterns, Surajit Sinha writes, "Social reformers and political leaders in India tend to regard the caste system as a major stumbling block to national integration, economic development and the moral regeneration of the nation" (1967, p. 92). Sinha does not contest the moral issues involved, but takes his first task to be that of showing the principles of interaction among caste groups. This is a commendable approach both for those who study Indian society and for those who want to improve it. It is most useful to have a clear understanding of what caste relations really entail in order to have a firm basis for evaluations and for programs of reform.

That understanding has been notably advanced in recent years by the work of both Indian and non-Indian scholars. Professor M. N. Srinivas has discussed the advantages and disadvantages of studying one's own society (1966, pp. 147–163). There are comparable benefits and drawbacks in studying a society other than one's own. In the study of Indian society there has happily been fruitful cooperation between both kinds of research workers. All students of Indian society have gained from the earlier work of scholars of various countries, among them J. N. Bhattacharya, L. K. Anantakrishna Iyer (Ayyar), and G. S. Ghurye of India; C. Bouglé and Émile Senart of France; Max Weber of Germany; L. S. S. O'Malley and J. H. Hutton of England. Each of these men has contributed to our knowledge from his particular perspective. Taken together, their works and those of similarly able observers have enabled us to view the Indian social scene from our present point of vantage.

At the beginning of a study of Indian society, two of its general characteristics should be noted. One is that certain basic ideas about society were, and are, shared by most people in the land. Yet social relations have been regulated locally, by the residents of a village or of a limited vicinity. The macro-themes for social behavior have been realized largely through micro-organizations.

Another characteristic lies in the difference between the common theory about social organization that villagers usually express and the ways in which they actually organize their social relations. A prime element in this discrepancy is their concept of *varna*. It is the popular theory, based on Hindu scripture, that society is composed of people in four ranked categories called varnas. In reality, not all Hindus are subsumed in those categories, and frequently there are differences of opinion in a village about who belongs to which category. Though insufficient as a sociological theory, this concept nonetheless is a significant factor in villagers' social perceptions and actions. They use it as a handy gross classification of others in their society, making much finer classifications for those within their own social groups. The jati is such a social group—a unit of great importance to the villager, and a basic component of the social system.

Jati

The answer a villager gives to the question, "Who are you?" depends, as it does everywhere in the world, on who is asking and on what the villager thinks the questioner wants or should know (cf. Mandelbaum 1956). Yet villagers throughout India are likely to include in their answer the information that they are members of the particular group to which both their parents and all their kin belong. To further questions they explain that each person is a member of this group by virtue of his birth into it; he may marry only within it; his (or her) children will also belong to that group.

The people of each endogamous group follow certain characteristic patterns of behavior and have certain assigned attributes—among them a specialized occupation—according to which the group is ranked in the local hierarchy. The criteria for ranking have to do, village respondents declare, with the ritual pollution and purity that are inherent in the group's practices. These ritual criteria are usually mentioned first. More closely questioned on this matter, a villager is likely to allow that considerations of power and wealth also enter into the ranking. Every member of the endogamous group shares in the rank position of the group and this affects his relations with members of other groups.

A villager from a low-ranked group may hasten to add that the defiling practices attributed to his group are imposed or inadvertent or nonexistent or unimportant. He will point out some groups in the locality that, in his opinion, should be ranked below his own and some supposedly superior groups to whom his own people are, at least, equal. Most villagers, however, assume that there should be a ranked hierarchy of groups, even though they may disagree about the particulars of the ranking. They also agree that members of their own group must keep themselves separate from those of other, especially lower, groups, not only in marriage but also in domestic intimacies such as eating together, and must observe a host of other prescribed distances.

The term *jati* is used here for this endogamous group. The word is common to a number of the languages of northern India, being derived from the Sanskrit root meaning "to be born." This word and equivalent terms in other Indian languages carry the connotation of one's social birthright as well as one's inherited group (cf. Karve 1965, p. 139; Ghurye 1961, pp. 48, 64).

Explanations of jati by villagers can be summarized in this definition. A jati is an endogamous, hereditary social group that has a name and a combination of attributes. All members of a jati are expected to act according to their jati attributes, and each member shares his jati's status in the social hierarchy of a village locality in India. Like all capsule definitions of fundamental social relations, this one begs many questions. If it did not, there would be little more to say on the subject.

The term "jati-group" refers to the members of a jati who live in the same village. They are likely to have more frequent communication with each other than with jati fellows in other villages. An Indian village typically holds several jati-groups, from two to more than thirty, each with its traditional rights and duties, its privileges and restraints, its special contribution in services or manufactures to the total functioning of the community. A complement of jati-groups may include landowning cultivators; tenants; priests; artisans such as carpenters, blacksmiths, and potters; service groups such as barbers and launderers; and menial workers such as sweepers and laborers. The people of each group in the village maintain marriage and kinship ties with their compeers in other villages. The endogamous group, the jati, includes members spread across a number of villages.

Every person is thus a member of his village and of his jati. The village, or a set of neighboring villages, forms a localized community of specialized, interdependent groups. The members of a jati, in their respective villages, form a set of actual or potential kin. A man depends on the village community for his livelihood and for services necessary to maintain his jati's style of life, but the position and the practices of his jati mold his career, define the range of his kinsmen and his closest companions, and affect a large part of his social relations.

Within a man's jati are those with whom he may have close and unquestioned relations. He may form a friendship with a man of different jati, but it is not usually as durable and unconstricted as a friendship within the jati. He may deal with others daily, but his closest links, those of marriage and kinship, are only with his jati fellows. His life and aspirations are intertwined with theirs. So a person's jati affects the nature of his relations with many other people. His family typically commands his most intense loyalties and efforts and his village encompasses much of his life, but his jati provides him with his circle of kin; it is usually a source of social support, and contributes much of his identity in village affairs.

Flexibilities in Jati Relations and Roles

Although considerations of jati are important, there are some activities in which the jati affiliations of the actors are not highly relevant. In work situations, men of widely different jatis may work side by side without keeping their usual physical and social distance. In play also, jati considerations are muted; two wrestlers, for example, may be from jatis whose men otherwise keep considerably farther apart. In some situations of devotional worship, devotees from different jatis may mingle in a closeness that is not allowed in other contexts.

Villagers commonly speak of a jati as though its members concentrated on one occupation and maintained rigid jati boundaries. The facts reveal more flexibility. A jati's traditional occupation does not necessarily restrict all members of the jati to that calling. A villager of a priestly jati often manages land or grows crops. Some in a carpenter jati are carpenters, but others may be farmers, or soldiers, or, nowadays, teachers or government officials. What the traditional calling did was to limit the possible range of a villager's occupations; for example, a man of priestly jati was not permitted by his jati fellows to engage in defiling work such as handling hides or leather.

Conversely, a leatherworker was not permitted by the higher jatis to enter the precincts of the high gods, much less to act as a priest in their worship. A leatherworker, however, may be a farmer, since agriculture is open to all. In one village of Kanpur district, U.P., men of the leatherworker jati now engage in seven occupations, including farming and masonry as well as leather work. There is no bar in this locality to their being cart drivers or tradesmen, but they do not have the capital for such enterprises (Sharma 1956a, pp. 122–123). The range of occupations open to men of any jati is now wider than it was at the beginning of the twentieth century, but many still follow their jati's traditional work, and many keep within the range of occupations open to those of their jati.

Marriage is the relation that demarcates each jati most clearly. All marriages are supposed to be between a bride and groom of the same jati; no marriage may be made outside it. Yet there is some degree of flexibility even in this. A wealthy man may not find a suitably prestigious bridegroom for his daughter among the families known to be of the same endogamous circle. In his search he may discover in a more distant village a desirable groom of a family of jati name and status position similar to his own. His task then is to uncover some previous marriage between the familial forebears of the couple. Given mutual desire and diligent ransacking of real or supposed connections, such historical precedent may be found and the marriage arranged. (Other means of reinterpreting jati boundaries will be noted later.) Most marriages do indeed take place within a limited cohort, from a few hundred to several thousand families in a given territory, but a villager tends to view his jati as a more firmly bounded, more clearly demarcated unit than it may actually be.

Groups and Groupings within the Jati

Each person belongs to certain groups within his jati. One such group is the family. Related families commonly act together as a lineage. The jati-group is another unit within a jati. In addition, some jatis have clan groupings. In some jatis families also are ranked in prestige groupings.

The best kind of family, in the common belief, is the joint family, a family in which two or more married men who are closely related —as father and son, or as brothers—live together in one household with their wives, sons, and unmarried daughters. All share a common kitchen and a common purse. This ideal form is actually realized, even if only for a short period, in the development of most Indian families, but at any one time there are also many nuclear families, consisting of one married couple, their unmarried children, and perhaps one or two other dependents.

A family usually cooperates with closely related families in a localized lineage. A lineage is a set of families whose men are related in patrilineal descent—perhaps as sons and grandsons of a set of brothers—whose households are commonly near each other in the village, and whose members exchange many kinds of mutual support. The tie that binds the men of a lineage is their descent from the same, known, patrilineal ancestor. (Some jatis of Kerala observed matrilineal descent, but as will be noted later, their jati organization followed the same broad principles used by patrilineal peoples.)

A larger grouping consists of those who trace their patrilineal descent from a remote and usually legendary ancestor. The members of such a grouping, here called a "clan," are dispersed among a great many villages and share in few or no joint functions. A clan is usually more of an attributive grouping than it is a corporate group. The most common function of the clan is to distinguish eligible from ineligible spouses. It is an exogamous unit within the endogamous jati; a man may not marry a woman of his clan just as he may not marry one of his family or lineage.

The members of a jati-group, those of one jati who live in the same village, unite in action on occasion, especially in defense of their joint rights in the village. They usually consider themselves to be sharply distinctive in the village. Even when two or more jati-groups in a village are culturally very close and are treated alike by others, they may keep themselves socially separate. For example, there are two jati-groups of carpenters in Dewara village (Adilabad district of Andhra Pradesh). The members of one speak Marathi and the members of the other Telugu. Dube notes that "the two may not intermarry; language, dress, customs, and beliefs separate them still further" (1955a, p. 182).[1] Two jati-groups in a village may use the same language, have the same traditional occupation, and follow much the same jati customs, yet the members of each will cherish some unique traits that distinguish them from other groups. Others in the village may lump the two jati-groups together; usually the members of the two do not.

A different kind of distinction is commonly made within a jati. Some families are recognized as being more prestigious than others, either because of wealth, education, ancestral honor, or for other

[1] There are a few jatis that include, in one endogamous unit, families from two different linguistic regions. Thus the Deshastha Rigvedi Brahmins include some families that speak Marathi and some that speak Kannada. A majority of the marriages within this jati are arranged between families of the same language, but there are some in which one spouse is from a Marathi-speaking family and the other from a Kannada-speaking family (Karve 1958b, p. 137). Such jatis, however, are exceptional and are usually groups that have been located along a linguistic boundary for centuries. It is far more common for all jati fellows to speak one mother tongue.

reasons. These classlike distinctions are not necessarily formalized, although as we will discuss later, such distinctions have sometimes led to the establishment of formal sections within the jati and occasionally to the formation of new jatis when the higher families split off from the rest.

In sum, a villager's interchange with others of his jati is largely through his roles as member of his family, lineage, and jati-group. But in his dealings with people of other jatis, a villager uses other social categories, such as jati-cluster, to define the roles and rules for interaction.

Jati-Cluster

A principal category used for dealing with people of other jatis is the jati-cluster. This is a set of separate jatis, classed together under one name, whose members are treated by others as having the same general status. It is easier to deal with many people, as one must in a complex society, by using jati-cluster categories rather than by regulating one's own behavior to each individual in terms of such narrower social distinctions as those of family or lineage or jati. The finer distinctions are necessary within the jati, not outside it.

The jatis that are classed together are usually similar in traditional occupation, jati practices, and relative rank. When people of different jatis classed together in a cluster live in the same village, the members of each generally hold themselves socially apart from other jati-groups of the same jati-cluster, though all members of the cluster may be considered very much alike by other villagers.

Some jati-clusters include only a few jatis and several thousand people; others cover dozens of jatis and millions of people. In a smaller cluster, especially within a confined territory, the members of the component jatis know about each other and do act together on occasion. The fact that they all are treated in like manner by others paves the way for some joint action, especially defensive action. In a larger cluster, few may know the full spread of the cluster and concerted action does not occur (cf. Karve 1961, pp. 11–12). Under modern conditions of widening communication the people of a jati-cluster, who may not previously have acted

together or have known of each other's existence, can now form
associations.

An example of a small jati-cluster is that of the Badagas of the
Nilgiri Hills in South India, who now number more than ninety
thousand and are mainly cultivators. They are divided into several
endogamous groups, each self-consciously different from the others,
though all speak the distinctive Badaga language. A Badaga villager
refers to himself, in his conversations and dealings with other
Badagas, by the name of his group, such as Wodeya. This division
within Badaga society is his main unit of self-identification among
the people collectively known to outsiders as the Badagas. It is a
unit of paramount importance to him, not only for marriage purposes, but also because much of his daily life is carried on with his
jati fellows rather than with any others who may be Badagas in
name and culture. There are some occasions, mainly ceremonial,
in which any Badaga irrespective of jati may participate, but in
other social contexts the various jatis remain as separate groups.

On the other hand, their neighbors, including the lower-ranked
Kotas whom I have studied, are little concerned with these distinctions among Badagas; they tend to view all Badagas as much of a
piece and refer to them as one. Kotas are indeed sensitive to individual differences, especially of wealth, among the Badagas
with whom they have dealings, but the ritual gradations among
Badaga jatis are of little concern to Kotas.

A much larger cluster consists of the many jatis of Maharashtra
known as Kunbis. These jatis have some cultural characteristics
in common. Villagers of this name work on the land and speak
Marathi. A jati called Kunbi is generally ranked below the farmer-
military jatis called Maratha. Beyond these similarities there are
wide differences among Kunbis in such matters as kinship arrangements, dress, and economic functions. Kunbis live in different parts
of the Marathi-speaking region, and those of one group may not
know of the existence of most of the others (Karve 1958b, pp.
126–127).

Two of the main jati-clusters in Gujarat are the Patidars and
the Barias. Both are cultivators by traditional occupation, but the
former are ranked higher than the latter. The Patidars tend to
ignore differences in status among the Barias. In one village, as
David Pocock reports, certain Baria families are superior in their

ritual practices to some Patidar families. But this does not perturb the Patidar villagers who "*include* the higher levels of the Bāriā with the lower level of the Bāriā and so exclude them from any claim to equality." Several of the Baria families are more strictly vegetarian than are some Patidars, but their Patidar neighbors "refer to them simply as Baria and include them in the general statement 'The Bāriā eat meat'" (Pocock 1957b, p. 28).

This gross, oversimplified classification is useful; dealing with people of other jatis is simplified. One does not have to calculate and adjust to all the actual gradations of ritual practice among members of large and varied groups. All are Baria or Badaga (or some other inclusive term) and are so treated.

A villager follows the common human tendency to make finer social distinctions among those who are socially more intimate with him than among those with whom he has more distant relations. A farmer of a village in Gujarat, for example, knows that a local shopkeeper is likely to belong to one of the jatis collectively known as Bania and that Banias belong to the third of the four scriptural categories. He can deal with the shopkeeper on the basis of this gross classification. If the farmer were fully informed about the social position of the shopkeeper, he would know such details as that the shopkeeper was of the Sarta jati, of the Visa subdivision of that variety of Banias who originated in Desawal (Toothi 1935, p. 125). Further, he would know the status of the shopkeeper's family and lineage within the jati. It is unnecessary for the farmer to know all this; indeed it would be impossible for him to adjust his relations with all others on the basis of such extensive knowledge.

However, for the shopkeeper himself, detailed information about his jati is supremely important. He maintains his bonds of kinship on the basis of such information and he is likely to recruit his business assistants and associates from among his closer kinsmen. Many of his religious duties are bound up with family and jati obligations. He uses these fine perceptions to guide his intimate relations, and in doing so he helps maintain his jati as a firm unit in the local social order. The shopkeeper, in turn, is quite uninterested in the precise social position of his farmer customer. All he needs to know is the general category of the customer's jati because it will not do to serve a menial sweeper as though he were a member of a high jati and, still less, to speak to one of the highborn as though he were a sweeper.

In his study of Ramkheri village, Adrian Mayer has discussed these classifications from the perspective of social function (1960, pp. 270–275). When a man performs services for others in his village, Mayer comments, he is classed by them in a broad category. When he interacts with jati fellows in other villages as a kinsman, he is classed by them as belonging to narrower groups and groupings.

The social vantage of the perceiver is another factor in social perspective. A landowner of high rank is not much concerned about the divisions among the lowest in his village. He lumps them all as untouchables or, to use the term that Gandhi preferred, *Harijans*, "children of God." Conversely, those of the lowest groups are usually not much interested in the detailed social differences among the highest in the village. These powerful people are all overlords to them and have to be so treated.

Such differences in social perception are necessary in all complex societies. The finer perceptions about one's social intimates make for firm, viable social units; the grosser perceptions enable people of different units to carry on effective social relations. The more detailed distinctions made by Indian villagers have mainly to do with their groups of close interaction—family and lineage, jati-group and alliance within the village. The broader groupings are mainly those of jati-cluster and varna, both are taxonomic groupings more than they are corporate groups, attributed categories rather than interactional units (cf. Marriott 1959b).

Varna: Villagers' Theory and Theorists' Fallacy

The most widely known social categories are the four varnas, the principal parts of society as given by the sage Manu in the law code of perhaps the second century A.D. (cf. Ghurye 1961, pp. 87–97; Dutt 1931, pp. 4–23). Most villagers accept the varna categories as the primordial makeup of their society. Into that scheme local jatis and jati-clusters are fitted.

The origin story, first noted in a hymn of the earliest scripture, the Rig-Veda, has it that the four varnas came into being from the body of the primeval man. From his mouth issued the Brahmins, who became priests and scholars. From his arms came the Kshatriyas, warriors and rulers; from his thighs came the Vaishyas, tradesmen, and from his feet rose the Shudras, cultivators (Basham 1954, pp. 240–241). Traditionally, those in the Brahmin category are supposed to manage the culture through their control of religion, Kshatriyas to manage the society through their control of armed might, Vaishyas to manage the distributive economy through their control of trade, and Shudras to produce the economic wherewithal for the whole society.

Similar versions of the proper division of labor and the assignment of rank in a society have come out of other civilizations. Plato, for one, propounded a comparable plan. In the Manu version, high as well as low lived in the villages; the high ranks were not concentrated at urban or court centers. Hence all four varnas could be represented in a village, although the actual village hierarchy did not necessarily follow the four-ply model.

There were, and are, considerable discrepancies between the scriptural plan and the real social order. The scheme omits from Hindu society the many jatis of so-called untouchables whose services are essential for a traditional village order. Further, all four categories were not everywhere represented. In much of South India, there seem to have been few indigenous Kshatriyas or Vaishyas, the martial and the mercantile categories. Historically, the varnas of the early texts were more like open classes than like fixed social strata (Bouglé 1908, pp. 28–29; Dutt 1931, pp. 58 ff.; Prabhu 1954, pp. 290–342).

Moreover, the scriptural scheme is highly oversimplified in some ways and quite misleading in others. M. N. Srinivas has noted the main distortions implicit in it (1966, pp. 2–12). One is that there is a single all-India hierarchy without any variations between one region and another. The many variations in ranking will be discussed below; sometimes the same jati will be ranked higher in one village than in another not many miles away.

Another mistaken notion is that the varna divisions are the functioning groups of the social order. The principal groups of social interaction are families, lineages, jati-groups, jatis, village communities, and other groups, but not the varna categories.

A third distortion is that the hierarchal order stands as clear and accepted by all, when in fact vagueness and disputes about ranking are common. Ambiguities and conflicts about precise rankings are indeed regular features of the system. Finally, the varna plan has been interpreted to mean that the groups and order of Indian society are immutably fixed. Historical evidence shows that there has been a good deal of social change.

To an Indian villager, however, these gaps in the folk theory are of far less consequence than the uses of that theory. With it he can sort out the principal parts of society and can readily place an unfamiliar jati within the general scheme. It provides a summary evaluation of jati rank. Rising groups take one of the higher categories as model and target for their mobility efforts. And the fourfold division offers a simple, hierarchical plan of society for villagers who assume that society is hierarchically arranged.

The varna scheme corresponds well enough to most villagers' social experience so that it can be used for preliminary sorting. A villager typically knows that Brahmins were decreed as the highest of four social layers as far as ritual affairs are concerned. That usually fits with what he finds in his own village; jatis of the Brahmin category are commonly in the topmost bracket of the ritual hierarchy, even though men of a local Brahmin jati may be neither scholars nor priests. It does not worry him that a jati claiming to be Kshatriya may seem to be more farmer than warrior or that a jati claiming to be Vaishya holds dubious credentials for such classification.

People of the three higher varnas, Brahmins, Kshatriyas, and Vaishyas, are supposed to conduct themselves in close accord with scriptural rules for purity. The three categories are collectively called the "twice-born" varnas from the initiation ceremony undergone by males of the jatis classed in these varnas. In that rite, a boy is invested with the symbol of the sacred thread. Each initiate is thenceforth and forever supposed to wear the thread over his left shoulder. The rite is deemed a second birth; those who wear the sacred thread are *dvija*, twice-born, in contrast to all others who do not undergo a ritual second birth. This rite is no longer so meticulously performed among "twice-born" jatis as it traditionally was, and some of their men no longer bother to wear the sacred thread. Nevertheless, the varna scheme still applies, in that jatis classed in the higher varnas are commonly the most respectable and powerful in a village. Their members, for reasons discussed later, usually do observe purity rules more rigorously than do other villagers.

Another use of the varna scheme is in providing a simple, handy approximation of complex evaluations of jati rank. In Ramkheri village (Dewas district of Madhya Pradesh) the varna classification can "be seen as the best assessment of a caste's various rankings" (Mayer 1956, p. 138). There, as in other villages, the varna divisions do not quite fit the facts of the social organization. Mayer lists the village jatis in rank order and appends this note: "The Vaisya *varna* has been placed below the Kshatriya in the traditional manner. In Ramkheri, however, the vegetarianism of the former is said by many to make the Vaisya equal to, if not superior to, the Kshatriya" (Mayer 1956, pp. 138, 141). But such discrepancies are not taken by villagers as serious objections to the four-part classification.

The varna outline also offers a convenient way of assessing jatis of different geographic and linguistic regions. When a villager encounters people of unfamiliar jati, he can make a quick appraisal of them by asking about their position in the scale of four. Most jatis can be fitted into the procrustean frame of varna.

The three higher varnas also are taken as reference categories, that is as models for conduct, by aspiring people of lower jatis. Each model is also a target in the sense that a rising group tries to become accepted as legitimately belonging to one of the higher varnas. When its people become so accepted, they have achieved a principal aim of their mobility efforts.

Finally, the varnas provided a neat outline of social relations, which villagers like to think of a trimly hierarchical but which characteristically involve ambiguous positions, disputed rank, and overlapping jurisdictions. The precise rank of a jati-group in its village may be nebulous, and jati rankings are often differently given by different residents of the same village. But the varna outline assures villagers that there really is a changeless, India-wide hierarchy. "More important, perhaps," Mayer comments, "it helps to distinguish the hierarchy in the area of greatest obscurity, the middle reaches, where statements about varna membership are almost the only verbalizations of general status" (1956, p. 143).

The classical varna plan is a series of binary divisions (Leach 1967, pp. 10–11). Human beings are either within Hindu society or outside it. If they are within that society, Edmund Leach observes, they are either "twice-born" or ordinary persons. If they are twice-born, they are either religious or secular specialists; if they are secular, they are either warrior-rulers or merchants. If they are ordinary persons (Shudras), they are either "clean" or "unclean," depending on whether people of the "twice-born" varnas can accept water from their hands or have similar interchange with them.[2]

A society, like music, exists in time; it develops, changing yet formed, through time. Indian music flows with great spontaneity, but against the formed background of the tonic notes of the drone, the *thanpura*. Indian society has been full of changes and improvisations, but also against a background frame, the tonic themes of varna hierarchy. As the drone is an essential element in Indian music, so has the varna idea been essential in Indian society. Srinivas has commented that it is a matter for wonder that, in spite of the distortions of reality implicit in the varna model, it has continued to survive (1966, p. 4). Perhaps it has been used for so long just because of its distortions. People in complex societies tend to use some simple—indeed oversimple—theory of their society. The varna scheme has been such a theory, one that reflected and reinforced the basic attitude about social relations.

Students of society are familiar with theorists who, often unwittingly, shape their reports of a people's behavior to fit their theory. In this case, the people have provided the theoretical conception and have not been abashed by the lack of fit between fact and theory. That theory, we should note, has served its purposes for a long time.

Varna is frequently mentioned in Sanskrit scripture—jati less often. Émile Senart warned that the two terms are confused in the literary tradition, which, he wrote, "is less concerned with the faithful record of facts than with their arrangement in systems conforming to the tendencies of a strongly biased group" (1930,

---

[2] Anthony Wallace has observed that folk taxonomies require about four binary discriminations, perhaps the minimal level of cognitive capacity required to sort out such complex arrangements as kinship terminologies or military rank (1961, pp. 146–147). The varna scheme, with its four categories and with the distinction between clean and unclean Shudras, requires four binary discriminations.

p. x). K. M. Panikkar has similarly noted (the emphasis is his) that "this four-fold division *is only ideological* and is not in any manner based on the facts of the social system. It is what Hindu sociologists wanted their society to be—a theory of caste-idealism unrelated to actual practice" (1956, p. 7).

Panikkar, a historian-statesman who successfully engaged in practical political affairs, underestimated the influence a popular theory can exert. The varna scheme may not have been well based on social facts but its long reign has certainly influenced the facts of Indian society.

Component Groups and Social Concepts

The main social locale is the village. Each family depends on families of other jatis in the village and its vicinity for certain essential goods and services. High-ranking landowners must have the services of the menial sweepers. If any one of the landowners' jati should take pay to perform menial services for others, the status of the whole jati would be jeopardized. The families of sweepers depend on the patrons for their livelihood, for emergency help, and for aid in their ceremonies. The mutual dependence is woven of many strands.

More will be said later about the nature of the village community or village locality. A village is usually a clear social and territorial entity, not only in the records and accounts of governmental administration, but also in the view of its inhabitants. But the people who take part in the community activities of a village, that is in the joint functions carried on within the village, are not so clearly bounded. A village family typically uses goods and services provided by people from a number of surrounding villages. Its washerman may live in one, its carpenter in another, and the family itself may provide services or goods to others in a circuit of villages. Its kinship relations will extend to jati fellows in a number of villages. So the actual village settlement is more the center of the community functions of its residents than a neat package for these functions.

Villagers have maintained important ties with people at urban centers since the beginnings of the civilization. At these centers they have carried on trade, religious acts, governmental contacts. A village is not, and never was, an isolated entity. Characteristically, its people have many ties with other villages in the locality and with specialists at centers.

Other components of village society have become increasingly important in recent times. Government agencies used to carry on police and tax-collecting functions principally; they had little direct effect on social relations among villagers. Voluntary associations were few in number and limited in purpose, consisting largely of gatherings for religious devotion. But with modern developments, governmental programs have had some impact on village relations. Voluntary associations, whether for political purposes or to promote civic welfare, have grown in number and influence. Nonetheless, the traditional social components discussed in this chapter are still the fundamental social realities in a villager's life.

The terms that villagers use for these groups and categories have sometimes seemed confusing to observers. The meaning of a term may vary depending on the social position of the speaker, or the context of use, or the functions that are being emphasized. Indeed, the field of societal analysis in India is strewn with pitfalls of terminology. A villager's style of expression can seem literally self-contradictory to an overliteral listener or reader.[3] Further, some of the common terms used by professional students of Indian society are not unambiguous.

In the U.P. village of Kishan Garhi, for example, the people of the high jatis use the classical term, *gotra* or *got*, for their exogamous clans and the same word is used to mean the endogamous jati by villagers of the lower ranks (cf. Karve 1965, p. 124). In Ramkheri village all villagers use the same word, *kutumb*, to mean either lineage or clan. The meaning conveyed depends on the

[3] G. M. Carstairs discusses such seemingly contradictory statements, which he heard in the course of his study in a town of Rajasthan. He comments that his respondents were not at all disconcerted by the juxtaposition of opposites and indicates that this is different from Western modes of thought. But the difference may well exist more in conventions of expression than in canons of logic. One man told Carstairs emphatically "I never see ghosts, I'm not that kind of man." Almost in the same breath he went on to tell how he had seen a ghost in the jungle quite recently (1957, pp. 52–53). This apparently contradictory statement may instead have been meant to convey emphasis rather than logic. Perhaps this man should be understood as telling Carstairs that he is not at all the kind of person who looks for ghosts around every corner, but in this episode he *did* see a ghost.

context of use, as we shall note in the discussion of these groups (Mayer 1960, pp. 167–168).

When Mayer asked in this village about jati relations, many of the replies indicated "there is no caste left" (1960, p. 48). This is obviously not so, as Mayer's study, drawn from some of the same respondents, clearly shows. But the purport of such answers is to say, in an emphatic if hyperbolic way, that there are now state laws against discrimination (not necessarily strictly enforced), or that the former condition of jati relations has changed.

As for the ambiguities in observers' terms, we have mentioned the varying usages of the word "caste." The inadequacy of this term as it is often used in the literature is put succinctly by H. N. L. Stevenson, "It is difficult to pin the term caste to any sociological reality" (1954, p. 49). It has been pinned to too many social entities —endogamous group, a category of such groups, a system of social organization. It seems best to use the term, apart from direct quotations, as an adjective that refers to the highly stratified social system. The term "subcaste" has been used by some writers to refer to the endogamous group, the jati, but the definition of this word tends to be blurred if "caste" is concurrently used in several different senses.

The phrase, "the caste system of India" is best taken to refer to that set of ideas about society that many people of India share and that they use systematically in governing their social relations. Salient among these ideas is the view, implicitly held and sometimes explicitly expressed, that most social relations should be hierarchically arranged (cf. Dumont 1966).[4]

Hence villagers tend to establish rankings among the families of a lineage, among the lineages of a jati, among the jatis of a locality. The commonly held criteria for ranking will be discussed in later chapters, as will the behavioral consequences of these criteria. The shared ideas include some about the makeup of society that are not, as we have noted, objectively accurate, but are nonetheless subjectively powerful. All these central understandings form an important part of the overarching frame of Indian civilization.

The India-wide precepts were enacted in a multitude of village

[4] Louis Dumont's able and detailed exposition of this concept appeared after the present volume was well along and so the analysis in that work was not incorporated in this.

localities with little or no supervening control. Because government agencies now have increasing influence on village society, social controls and regulations are not as completely in local hands as before. But a large part of villagers' interchange and counterchange still takes place among the people of a locality as they act in the component groups of the local system. Our survey of these groups begins with the most intimate, the family.

PART **II** *Family and Kinship Relations*

CHAPTER **3** Family

As the jati is fundamental to village society, so is kinship fundamental to the jati. All of a person's kin by descent and marriage, both actual and potential, are within his jati; none are outside it. The boundaries of his jati are continually revalidated through marriage; his closest interactions are typically with his kinsmen. A man's responsibilities to his kin are important considerations in the social enterprises he undertakes. So we must understand how villagers act as kinsmen in order to understand how this social system works.

Kinship begins with the family. In one sense the whole society begins with the family because a society is a living entity that must continually be replenished. The system of a whole society cannot be stopped and started again like a mechanical device. If replenishment is halted, the society ceases to exist. This imperative of replenishment for every society is met by its smallest social component, the family.

Everyone is born, not of a collectivity or into a full-fledged social system, but of parents into a family. In societies of all types, the family is the fundamental multipurpose organization for many of the principal life functions of the individual and of society. Moreover, as Eric Wolf has written, the family is the bearer of virtue and of public reputation; a man's reputation is linked with that of his family and with his own relations to his family. Although the standards used for social ranking vary widely, Wolf notes, the rankings in each society define whom one can trust and whom one may marry. "Invariably, they refer back to ways in which people handle their domestic affairs" (1966, p. 8). Domestic patterns establish the nature of the relations between the sexes and among the generations. They teach the fundamental lessons of who "we" are and who "they" are; how we may link with others; whom we may marry and whom we must not marry. Such patterns instill motivation in the young so that, in time, they will bring up their own young to seek similar life goals and follow similar cultural patterns.

These common functions of families across the world are carried out through a great variety of family forms, that is, of particular definitions and alignments of family roles. Yet each form of family structure is grounded in the biological constants—in the relation of parent and child, of husband and wife, of sibling and sibling. Another constant feature is a recurrent cycle of family development, in which a family is formed through marriage and mating, expands with the arrival of children, disperses as the children marry and eventually separate to establish new households, and sooner or later is totally replaced after the parents die (cf. Fortes 1958, pp. 4–5; Collver 1963, pp. 86–87).

Among village families in India these general features bear a characteristic Indian stamp, partly because of the widely shared ideal model for family relations and partly because of the common perspective of hierarchy. There are, to be sure, many differences in family organization according to jati, regional, and economic variations. Yet underlying the variety there is also a notable degree of similarity in family relations.

Ideal Model and Actual Form

The common ideal is that of filial and fraternal solidarity, which prescribes that brothers should remain together in the parental household after they marry, sharing equally in one purse and in common property, helping each other according to need and each giving according to his best abilities. Brothers should not only cleave to one another, but, even more important, they should remain with their parents and be steadfast to them. This ideal has strongest sway while the father is alive and influential, and fades after both parents are dead and the brothers' children marry (cf. Gore 1965, pp. 211–213). It has more influence among those who are higher and wealthier than among the low and landless. It applies to the men of a family but is a central concern for women also. In most jatis, high and low alike, daughters customarily leave their natal family on marriage. A bride goes to live where

her husband lives (which is with his father) and does not share in
her own father's and brothers' property. Women, especially as
mothers, uphold the ideal at least as vigorously as men do, but they
themselves are not implicated in it in the same way.

Indian village society is patrilineal and virilocal except for a few
matrilineal groups, notably the Nayars of Kerala who are discussed
below. The patrilineal principle defines those men who are expected
to cooperate most closely in a family and lineage group. The family
ideal governs the relations between close male kin. It is a motif
that holds constant interest; villagers hear it told over and again
in tales from the *Mahabharata* and other classical sources. It is
celebrated in popular song and is a common background of village
gossip.

This ideal of filial-fraternal solidarity has been reinforced by
being built into the chief textbook of Hindu law, the *Mitakshara*
of the twelfth century. Under this code each male is entitled to an
equal share of the family property from the moment of his birth;
hence all brothers are coparceners, each entitled to the same share
his father and brothers have. Joint ownership is assumed by law,
and the assumption usually implies, though it does not require, joint
residence and joint social and economic activities (cf. Desai 1955,
p. 110; Mandelbaum 1948). Women, whether in the status of
daughter, wife, or widow, are entitled to maintenance by their
male kin, but under the ancient law they had no other vested rights
in the family property.

No voluntary act is required to establish a close life partnership
among brothers that binds them together in a firm legal entity.
But the act of legal separation of family property does require
voluntary action. When brothers or brothers' sons separate their
households and property, as eventually they feel forced to do, they
must petition to some formal authority in order to divide the joint
property. This family law for Hindus was enforced during the
British regime.[1] Though post-independence legislation has changed
the inheritance laws, there is still a strong inclination among vil-

---

[1] The administration of Hindu family law by British courts, according to
K. M. Kapadia and others, undermined the traditional family organization
because it made rigid and inflexible a law that had been dynamic and adaptable. (See Kapadia 1958, pp. 250–251; Cohn 1965, pp. 111–113; Derrett 1961,
pp. 251–252.)

lagers, men and women alike, to follow the ancient mode of property rights and inheritance. There were regional variations in legal tradition, notably the *Dayabhaga* code of Bengal, but essentially all the regional codes and local customs postulate that it is desirable for married sons to live, work, and share property with their parents and to remain together after their parents have died.

This kind of family cannot go on indefinitely; there are both physical and social limitations to its continuance. If sons and sons' sons keep adding their wives and children, there is a physical limit to the number that can be fed and housed in one household. Brothers' sons are not under the same obligation to stay together as are true brothers. The fission of the larger family is an inevitable step in the cycle of domestic development.

Taking that step results in the hiving off of smaller family groups, usually nuclear families, each consisting of a married couple and their children. When the sons grow up and a new bride is brought in, the family becomes what is known as a joint family, one that includes two or more married couples. The distinction between nuclear and joint families is one that is made by outside observers and census officers rather than by the villagers themselves. Family members do not consider that they have merged disparate nuclear families when there are two married couples in a family rather than just one; they regard this change as a natural and much desired growth of the original family. Nor do they use different terms for a single-couple and a multicouple family; there is usually only a single basic term for both. Each son is expected to bring his wife into his natal household. All eat from the same kitchen, live in the same house or compound, and share income. The males pool all property, support each other closely in the village and advance each other's cause in the world—and even into the afterworld.

The inducements to maintain close filial-fraternal relations are considerable. To begin with, most newly wed couples are barely into adulthood and have neither the material nor psychological resources to start a household of their own. Later in their married life, when they have more resources, they may still stay on in the household because the disadvantages of separating are greater than the annoyances of living together. Brothers are expected to help each other whether they live together or not. I knew two brothers in a village who became bitter enemies, yet when one grew so deranged mentally that no one would care for him, his estranged brother took him into his own house and nursed him until he was well enough to earn his living again. Then the mutual enmity was promptly resumed. Though brothers who live separately may still feel mutual obligations, living together in a joint household makes these obligations more automatic and compulsive.

In the joint family there is immediate aid to tide a member over illness; there is the increased efficiency of pooled labor and the economies of a single kitchen and household; and there is greater strength to ward off encroachments from others. Domestic rites and celebrations can be staged more elegantly by a large family, and the resulting prestige enhances all within the family. Each person is seen by others in the village in the light of his family's reputation. When he comes to a major life transition such as marriage, the reputation of the family weighs heavily in the decisions that are made. He is much advantaged if his family is large, harmonious, and joint, thus demonstrating that its members are reliable, worthy people.

Despite these advantages, centrifugal forces inevitably build up so that every family sooner or later breaches the ideal. Among the very poor the breach typically comes not long after the new bride is brought into the family. Early separation also occurs among families at the other end of the economic scale, those with men in the modern professions. Those families who own and cultivate their land are likely to keep up the ideal pattern longer. The ideal is acknowledged by almost all villagers and this tends to prolong fraternal cohesion. Cohesion and cooperation are not completely severed when a family splits into smaller households. Though the partition may have taken place in bitterness, family ties are often repaired and some degree of mutual support resumed.

Hierarchy in Family Roles

Hierarchical authority within a family rests on the biological facts. Parents have to exert authority to socialize their children and human offspring must remain dependent on their parents for years. Human males, if only because they are larger and stronger than females, possess a certain, if limited, authority in their families.

Indian villagers tend to place special emphasis on hierarchy within the family as part of their general presumption that interaction takes place, unless otherwise defined, between a superior and a subordinate.

Age and sex are the main ordering principles in family hierarchy. "The men have the more decisive authority in the traditional Indian family as compared with women," M. S. Gore notes, "and elders have greater authority as compared with young persons" (1965, p. 216). He adds that difference of a year or two in age is sufficient to establish firmly who is the formal superior. As between the authority of an elder woman and a younger man, sex is the more important determinant. Men have the formal property rights, and so the formal authority of a younger man—not necessarily his actual influence—is higher than that of his older sister, though he is expected to respect and cherish her.

The spheres of men's and women's activities tend to be sharply separated, especially among those in North India who observe *purdah*, the custom of keeping the women of a family close to the household. Women secluded in this way can have only very limited visits and contacts outside the kinship circle. Only a small proportion of Indian families ever wanted or could afford to practice purdah, but the principle of restricting women much more narrowly than men has been common.

A husband is expected to be his wife's superior and to receive symbolic and actual deference from her. There is no great expectation that the couple should share thoughts and tastes. This is not to say that conjugal love and devotion are any less than in other societies. Indeed the devotion of the Indian wife, both in legend and in fact, is one of the proud values of family life. It is to say that the roles of man and woman are markedly segregate. A woman moves about within her household and perhaps in those fields and households where she may work, not often going beyond these limits. A man has a much wider ambit in space and among people.

A married couple may not meet often in the course of the daily round. At meals the women customarily serve all the men first and eat only after the men have finished and risen. A wife, in all her relations with her husband, should adhere to the scriptural ideal of being a *Pativrata*, one who follows her husband's will and

authority in all respects (Karve 1953, p. 78). And while many
villagers know very little about scripture and less about this particular term, the ideal is exemplified, at least in formal ways, at all
social levels. Thus a wife customarily follows behind her husband
when the two happen to walk together; she scrupulously avoids
uttering his personal name lest this be taken as a disrespectful
liberty; she greets him ritually with gestures of respect and deference.

A woman is deferent as wife, but not as mother. Children owe
permanent deference to both parents. Parental authority is unceas-
ing as an ideal and is sustained in fact, though the actual duration
and degree of this authority are affected by economic circumstance
and jati tradition. Within a household a son or daughter must not
flout a parent's will, especially not the father's. If grown sons do
not wish to follow a parental mandate, they usually find ways to
circumvent rather than to contradict it. A widowed mother may
wield considerable influence on her son and his family, as one
educated woman of an eminent family has testified: "When I was
growing up, Father was the chief authority in the house on all
official and financial matters. He was a district commissioner and
practically ruled the district like a king, and yet he would always
go to his mother, who was nearly illiterate, for her final decision
in any important family matters. Grandmother was the authority
too in all household matters and Father left everything to her.
In such matters as settling weddings Father and Mother did the
preliminary choosing, then Father would ask Grandmother for her
final approval." (Ross 1961, p. 96.) The ideal of deference to
parents is rarely questioned, and in practice it endows the elders
with an authority that is not lightly ignored by their children.

Among brothers, authority rests with the elder. Some of the
same respectful compliance that a son gives to his father, a younger
brother should give, in formal terms at least, to his elder brother.
When an eldest brother succeeds as head of the joint family, his
younger brothers, and their wives and children, are supposed to
give him the kind of allegiance and obedience that the father com-
manded. Within the realm of women's activities, a woman's authority usually depends on the position of her husband in the
household. The wife of the senior man is the paramount authority

in women's affairs subject only to the presence in the household of his mother, who must be heard out patiently and respectfully (Ross pp. 55, 132).

As in any human relationship, the weight of influence in a family may be wielded by a forceful personality, say a youngest brother, even though he does not have an acknowledged position of power in the family structure (cf. Sarma 1951, p. 52); however, the formal hierarchy is clear and influential. All understand that a man should have authority over his wife and children, that a woman should exert control over her unmarried daughters and her daughters-in-law, that a senior brother has legitimate authority over his younger siblings in the family. Each person's dominance yields to the presence of higher family authority. The eldest brother should give ear to the wishes of the mother; the mother should defer to the wishes of the father; the father should give way in family affairs if he is overruled by his father or by the senior male of the joint family. People do not always behave in this way; personal inclination and particular circumstance may induce them to act against these expectations, but the hierarchical norms are usually powerful influences on family conduct.

With family authority goes responsibility. The superior is also obliged to look after the welfare of his charges so that they will not suffer, either by their own misjudgment or because of untoward circumstances. The general ideal, as related by a villager of Poona district, is that a man should respect and obey his elder brother as he would his father and should treat his elder brother's wife as an elder sister. "The oldest male of the highest generation is supposed to receive the most respect and obedience, the female at the opposite pole, the most protection and care" (Orenstein 1965, pp. 47–48).

One quality of family life among villagers has been particularly noticed by some observers. Thus T. N. Madan writes of the Pandit Brahmins of a Kashmir village, "What strikes the observer is the extreme restraint which characterizes relations between adult men and women in Pandit society" (1965, p. 76). Adrian Mayer (1960, p. 214) makes a similar comment about a village in Madhya Pradesh: "The dominant note in the formal pattern of relations in the household is that of restraint. There is restraint between people of differ-

ent age and restraint between those of opposite sex." Mayer adds
that while his characterization may make the household appear (to
one from a different tradition of family life) as a place full of
restrictions and autocratic authority, "Yet, in a happy household
this is patently not the case. Authority on the one hand, and respect
on the other mix in an easy carrying out of duties, and the reticence
of the women is one of modesty, not fear." Restraint and hierarchy,
it should be noted, are also characteristic of relations among people
of different jatis as well as within the family.

Family Functions

A family in India, as elsewhere, is a corporate group whose members act together to meet their common purposes. Typically they
live in the same house and eat food prepared in the same kitchen;
they work together, pool their income, expenditures, and property,
and perform religious rituals as a family.

These functions are scarcely distinctive; similar functions are
performed by family groups through much of the world. But in
village India a great many of a person's activities are carried
out with his family throughout his lifetime. In the larger joint
families, in which several adult men and women and their children live and work in closest proximity, lines of authority must
be made plain lest disagreements about them escalate. In such joint
families, the nature of the family as a system, with its regular,
expected interchange and redressive counterchange, becomes more
readily apparent.

Each person learns the fundamentals of his culture and society
from his family; he experiences his main satisfactions and shares his
personal achievements with other family members. In his jati-group
he is primarily identified as a member of his family, and he assumes
the reputation of his family in the village. His whole life experience
is embedded in his family relations. The main transitions of the life
cycle are family celebrations, and the grand occasions of a person's
life are mainly those that occur in the context of the family (cf.
Kapadia 1958).

In a village, the family is the principal unit of economic production as well as of consumption. Land is owned and worked by fam-

ilies. The exchange of goods and services in the traditional manner is largely between families of different jatis. Property is tradition-ally held in common by the men of the family and it was not until the Hindu Gains of Learning Act of 1930 that a man could legally lay claim to the economic returns of his own skill and enterprise.

A family is a unit before the gods. In almost every house there is a special place for the holy things that help guard all in the house-hold. That place may be no more than a lithograph tacked to a wall or it may be an elaborate shrine in a separate room; in either case all in the family come under its protection. Religious observ-ances entail much participation by family groups. In Senapur village of U.P., for example, Opler found some forty calendrical rites being observed, twenty-five of which revolved mainly around fam-ily needs and purposes. He concluded that "a large part of the religious system is an elaborate apparatus for putting family mem-bers and family interests under the protection of benign super-naturals, and for defending the family from unfriendly supernatural attacks" (1959a, p. 273).

Priests do not usually have much to do with these rituals, which are planned, directed, and carried out mainly by members of a family for the family's welfare. The women of the family have the greatest responsibility for this sphere of religion (cf. Minturn and Hitchcock 1966, pp. 67–68). Life cycle observances are mainly family affairs, each of them marking an occasion when the family, helped by its other kin, delivers up to society a person in successive stages of social completion, from newborn baby to ancestral soul. It is in the name of his family and on their behalf as well as his own that a man pays ritual homage to the ancestors, thus linking each person with the remembered and with the infinite past.

Rites for the family's ancestors are particularly important in fam-ilies of the higher varnas and in these families the father acts on behalf of all. If he is gone and the grown brothers live together, only the eldest need perform the memorial rites. Among Kashmiri Brahmins, if the family has separated the eldest brother still must conduct these rites for all, but among Brahmins in Tanjore district each household head must separately carry out this ritual duty (Madan 1962b, p. 14; Gough 1956, p. 839). The crises of death and birth affect all who live together in a family; all must observe proper seclusion and cleansing to rid themselves of their common defilement. The whole ritual purity and pollution of the jati rests largely on conduct in the family context as in eating, in mating, in ritual observance.

A family is not only a reproductive unit and a socializing agency; it also provides each person with his main link to the wider society. Kinship ties are generally taken to be the most durable, reliable, worthy, and moral of all social relations (cf. Madan 1965, p. 222). Kinship begins with the family and is extended through the family. The family is also a principal unit in village organization. When labor or money or participation is needed for a village purpose, one man or one amount is levied from each family household. When gifts are given as part of the stringent competition for family status, they are given and received as from one family to another, even though the immediate recipient may be a bride or new initiate.

All these functions are met by people acting in family groups, whether the group is large or small. The number of people in a family varies according to the phase of the developmental cycle, being greater when there are coresident sons, their wives and children, and smaller when the couples split to set up separate households. A good part of the discussion of family life in India has assumed that there is a basic discontinuity between the single-couple family, called the nuclear or elementary family, and the larger family of more than the one couple and their children, called the joint or extended family. Some commentators have further assumed that a joint family is a merger of nuclear families. Neither assumption is valid, as we have noted, from the villagers' point of view. Nor was a distinction made between nuclear and joint families in the *Mitakshara* or in the more recent interpretations of Hindu law. Only for modern income-tax purposes is the distinction legally recognized (Shah 1964a, pp. 11, 18, 32; Madan 1962b, pp. 13–14).

Yet the number of people in a household and the nature of their family roles do make a difference in the way in which a family functions. When the first bride joins a previously single-couple family, only one person is added but several new role relations are established. She is not only a new wife for the son, she is also daughter-in-law to the father, daughter-in-law to the mother, and perhaps also sister-in-law to a younger son and to a younger daughter. The relations between parents and children are affected if the children's grandparents live in the same household because the younger couple must be more restrained toward their own children in the presence of elders. A couple with one child considers the family incomplete if that child is a girl, but if it is a boy, they are likely to see their family as unduly small yet in an important way complete (Shah 1964a, pp. 7, 33). The number of men in a family is economically significant because the pooled labor and wealth of several men may give them advantages over a smaller family.

Many classifications of family form are logically possible because there are hundreds of combinations of kin roles, including widowed mothers or father's sisters, resident sons-in-law, and orphans who may be related quite distantly. Although detailed classifications by role composition have been made, it is not always clear what useful purposes such typologies serve. The joint family has been defined in different ways, depending on which of the common features is selected as essential.

Some scholars have followed the traditional legal definition, which takes the joint ownership of property as an indispensable feature of the joint family (Madan 1962b, p. 13; Bailey 1960a, p. 347). But a man and his infant son are coparceners in the traditional legal sense, and a household group that contains only one couple and one child is scarcely a joint family. Moreover, under modern land tenure legislation, it has become profitable in some places for fathers and sons to separate their property legally while continuing to share residence, kitchen, and the rest of joint family living. The legal definitions are necessary for legal purposes, but they seem less useful for understanding actual behavior.

The Census of India procedure has been to take the household as a principal unit of enumeration, defined as a group whose members take food from a common kitchen (Gopalaswami 1953, pp. 48–50). That definition, however, is not suited for general analyses because a set of married brothers may set up separate kitchens to avoid domestic ruckus while they continue to share the same house, property, and work (cf. Mayer 1960, pp. 177–182).

While fine classifications of family forms in India have not so far been very fruitful, some useful distinctions have been indicated. The differences between a family that is felt to be incomplete and one that is more nearly complete have been noted by A. M. Shah (1964a, pp. 3–4); family striving and family goals are probably

quite different in the two types. A distinction has been made by
T. N. Madan between patrilineal and paternal extended families, the
former consisting of the parental couple and an only son and his
wife, the latter including parents and two or more married sons.
In the former there will be no partition of family property accompanied by the usual tensions; in the latter, partition and domestic
friction are quite probable (1962b, p. 14). One difficulty in some
discussions of family forms is that the term "family" is used too
loosely, including a wide range of lineal kin or kindred as well as
the coresidential, tightly knit, and closely related domestic group
(cf. Dumont and Pocock 1957c, pp. 48–49).

Any cogent analysis of Indian family life must include the concepts shared by most Indian villagers—of patrilineal ties and virilocal residence, of proper relations between father and son, between
brother and brother. The family members are expected to form one
solidarity, living in one household as long as possible, supporting
each other in the round of their days and in the cycle of their lives.
A family may be physically separated, even legally split, yet the
brothers may continue to act as a functioning family. This happens,
not infrequently, when a brother from a village family moves to a
city with his wife and children. He and his dependents return to
the village home as often as they can; he contributes to the income
of the village family; he rallies to their help and they to his whenever there is emergency need or ceremonial occasion. Before arranging a marriage or taking any decisive measures affecting their
careers or fortunes, the members consult with each other, giving
due deference to the views of the elders among them. This traditional spirit of the family is frequently upheld in both village and
city (cf. Agarwala 1955, pp. 141–142; Desai 1955, p. 103; 1956, pp.
147–148; Kapadia 1959, pp. 74–75; Ross 1961, pp. 9, 39).

Within these general characteristics of Indian families, there are
three broad types of variation—within a family over time, within
a village and region, and among regions.

Changes in Relations within a Family

Within a family the constellation of relations changes in the course
of the family cycle. Within a village and region there are differ-

ences in family relations according to wealth, occupation, and jati rank. Finally, there are differences among the linguistic-cultural regions.

The way in which any family role is carried out changes over time even though the same persons are involved. A girl of fifteen, newly arrived in a family as a bride, owes and gives deference to her mother-in-law. Twenty years later, as the mother of sons, she still is a daughter-in-law and still owes deference to her husband's mother. But the quality and the mode of deference alter a good deal over the years. Her relations with the wives of her husband's brothers, as Madan has observed in a Kashmir village, shift from friendliness or indifference to a competitive attitude (1965, pp. 132–135).

A woman's change of role behavior can be quite great. Mrs. Karve writes that "it is not rare to see women who were nothing but meek nonentities blossom into positive personalities in their middle-aged widowhood, or boss over the weak old husband in the latter part of the married life" (1965, p. 136).[2] And the wife who urges her husband to separate from the joint family, Desai comments, is commonly the same person who later, as mother and mother-in-law, is most unwilling to see her joint family split (1955, p. 104).

The relations between father and son normally change as a boy grows into adolescence. A father is expected to act more sternly toward his adolescent son than he did when the boy was a young child. Later still the relations shift again, as is illustrated in Mayer's account of Ramkheri village in Madhya Pradesh. A boy there begins to be held responsible for his actions at about the age of ten. From this age through adolescence his father is expected to be more of a disciplinarian than at any other stage. After the son marries, and certainly when he begets a son of his own, he can become somewhat more independent, though he must always observe great respect for his father. Some men of the village carry

---

[2] Occasionally an aberrant person will violate the proprieties and nothing much will be done about it, perhaps because only extreme measures are needed and are not easily taken. Thus D. N. Majumdar tells of one village family in which the daughter-in-law, who ought to have conducted herself with the most circumspect bearing toward her father-in-law, fell into a quarrel with him and beat him over the head with a piece of iron (1958a, p. 217).

this respect to the point where they will not even smoke in front of their fathers. Should the father become infirm, another shift in the son's role behavior takes place. He continues to give formal respect to his father but takes over actual authority and the direction of the household (Mayer 1960, pp. 214–219).

The context of behavior also affects family conduct. In the context of public behavior a wife should not challenge her husband's formal precedence and authority. But inside the house, as Mrs. Karve has indicated, domineering women are not unknown. For young married couples, public behavior is that carried on in the presence of *any* third adult. Alone they may chat, laugh, tease, but as soon as one other adult can see or hear them, they must lapse into quiescence. In the presence of the husband's father or mother they must be exceedingly restrained in their communications with each other to the point of seeming to ignore each other, and they must refrain from paying much attention to their own children. It is this contextual factor in particular that makes relations within a three-generation family different from those in a two-generation family. The presence of the husband's parents in the joint family intervenes between husband and wife and their children.

Economic Factors in Family Form

Within a village, there are differences in family relations according to jati rank, occupation, and wealth. These are well illustrated in the studies of Kumbapettai village in South India (Gough 1956) and of Senapur village near Banaras in North India (Cohn 1961a). Kumbapettai, in the Tanjore district of Madras, had been dominated by Brahmin landowners since it was founded in the 1780s.

During 1951–1953, when Dr. Gough studied the village, the Brahmins were still paramount. At the bottom of the village order there are three jatis of landless laborers, who are now called Adi Dravidas, "original" Dravidians. Among the Brahmins a father's authority is strong and enduring. Among the Adi Dravidas a son becomes a wage earner shortly after puberty, usually moves into a separate house a few years after marriage, and as an adult is expected to work independently with his siblings and peers rather than to be submissively dependent on his father. Adi Dravida women are much more independent, economically and socially, than are Brahmin women. They may divorce easily and frequently; widows can remarry; these women are not so isolated from their natal families as are Brahmin women, and they can earn wages as field workers.

Economic factors bolster the differences in family roles. The Brahmins are landowners and farm managers who do no manual labor. Since their whole economic resource is land, and the land is owned jointly, a young man can scarcely afford to leave his paternal family after marriage. Joint ownership and common management require a structure of authority; the head of a Brahmin joint household can effectively be the manager of the lands and can thus wield decisive authority in his family until he is quite old. Their women own no land in their own right and make no contribution to the household income. Adi Dravida women, by contrast, are quite self-sufficient economically and can therefore be more independent in family matters. The son of an Adi Dravida family quickly comes to earn as much as his father does and thus a father has no economic hold over the young man. Hence paternal authority does not last long as compared with the authority of a Brahmin father.[3]

The Adi Dravidas do not believe, as do the Brahmins, that the fate of a woman's soul depends on lifelong union with and service to one husband. An Adi Dravida father does not have to bind his son closely to him, since he does not consider, as does a Brahmin father, that his own fate in the hereafter depends on the son's performing memorial rites for him. Despite these differences, both groups share the same family ideal. The Adi Dravidas do not disparage Brahmin values in secluding women or in prohibiting the remarriage of widows. Families of lower rank who become prosperous and can afford to keep their women out of the fields often try to adopt the kind of family relations they see maintained by the local Brahmins (Gough 1956, p. 827).

In Senapur village the Chamars, traditionally leatherworkers and mostly landless laborers, share the ideal of family relations held by the dominant landowners, the Thakurs. Chamars would like to

[3] In commenting on Gough's account, Louis Dumont states that, at least on the basis of his experience with South Indian villagers, the disparities are not so great as Gough depicts them. He does agree that there are certainly differences in familial relations as between the two social levels (Dumont 1961b, p. 83).

follow the same model as do Thakurs, having three generations living in one house and eating from the same *chula* (hearth). "Those who take food from one *chula* form the commensal group, which means to a Chamar the sharing of property and rights, a common pocketbook, a common larder, common debts, common labor force, and usually one recognized head" (Cohn 1961a, p. 1052). A good many of the Chamars do succeed in maintaining joint families for a time; in 1953 there were 42 joint families out of 122 Chamar households in the village. But the Chamars' poverty militates against long-lasting joint families. One consequence of poverty is the short life span. Only a few Chamar males live long enough to be the head of a three-generation household. At the time of the study only about 6 percent of the Chamar males in the village were more than fifty years old. When the father dies before his sons have children, a binding influence on the joint family is eliminated.

Moreover, every year most of these Chamars must live through two to four months in which they have little food and are frequently hungry. In eight of twelve instances of family partition among Senapur Chamars, quarrels over distribution of food and income caused the split. "A brother with one small child does not see why he should share his meager earnings with a brother who has three small children and hence gets a larger share of the household food supply" (Cohn, p. 1053). Such quarrels are not readily suppressed by the father's authority, even if he is alive, in part because he has little economic power. A man's earnings as a laborer decline sharply after age thirty-five and a grown son may earn more than his father does. Among the Thakur landowners, older men retain their economic influence because they can, like the Brahmin elders of Kumbapettai, wield managerial functions into old age. Brothers among the artisans and middle-rank farmers of Senapur may keep together because of the greater efficiency of pooled labor. Since Chamars have little land or joint enterprise, they cannot gain much from such economies.

Nor do the Chamar wives contribute to fraternal and filial solidarity. Women's explosions in a Thakur household can usually be controlled short of fission, but a Chamar woman is neither as submissive nor as secluded. She earns almost as much as a man does and earns it for a longer period. If she decides to leave her husband's family and goes back to her father's house, she is welcomed there because she brings food and money into whatever household she chooses to join. If she does not want to live with a mother-in-law, she does not have to do so. A young Thakur wife has no such choice.

Chamars are not rooted to a particular locality, as Thakurs are, and readily leave their parental families to go where economic opportunity may be found. When a Chamar man goes to the city to work, his wife and children usually remain with his family. This brings advantages of added income for the joint family. Each of the three Chamar schoolteachers in the village grew up in a joint family. Only through the combined resources of a multicouple family can Chamars generally afford to let a child acquire some education.

All Chamar families in which there are sons become joint families for at least a few years. A young man brings his bride into the household when he is between the ages of fifteen and seventeen and usually does not set up a household of his own until he is over twenty (Cohn, p. 1052). To maintain joint living for a longer period requires both higher income and higher aspirations. Income alone is not enough; some of the richer Chamars do not choose to live in joint families, but those Chamars who have some education usually aspire to the family standards of the higher jatis. Here, as in the South Indian example, those who want to raise themselves socially emulate the prestigious family model.

Family occupation affects family form throughout the land. Village surveys from different regions show that families who own and cultivate their own land tend to remain together longer as multicouple families than do noncultivating landowners and still longer than do landless laborers of the same locality. Hence at any one time owner-cultivators tend to have a higher proportion of joint families. In a survey of four villages of West Bengal, Sarma found some correlation between higher jati status and a higher proportion of joint families but found a more marked relationship between occupation and family form. In a sample of 111 families of owner-cultivators, 35 percent were nuclear and 65 percent were joint families. In a sample of 126 families of agricultural laborers, 75 percent were nuclear and 25 percent were joint families. Share-croppers and noncultivating landowners came between, with nuclear families making up 45 percent of a sample of 148 and 58 percent of a sample of 53 families respectively (Sarma 1964, pp. 198–

201; 1959, pp. 104–105; other tabulations from this survey in Burd-
wan district in 1953–1954 are in L. K. Sen 1965).

Similar differentiation by occupation is indicated in other sur-
veys, although the results are not directly comparable because the
several authors do not use the same categories or definitions. In
Senapur, for example, among the families of the landowning
Thakurs 19 percent are nuclear but among the largely landless
Chamars 59 percent are nuclear. In Rampur near Delhi, the families
of the Jats, who are the main landowners, are 70 percent joint, of the
Chamars 19 percent are joint. In a sample of high school students in
Baroda, 65 percent of those from Patidar jatis, who are mainly
owner-cultivators, lived in joint families, while 37 percent of those
from Bania jatis, traditionally tradesmen, lived in joint families
(Kolenda 1968, pp. 363, 368; Shahani 1961). The lower proportion
of joint families among tradesmen indicates a shift in their family
form. Merchants commonly have a relatively high proportion of
joint families, in the economic and legal if not in the residential
sense. There are considerable economic benefits from having joint
family ownership and management of a string of shops even though
the separate households may come together only for family convocations (Desai 1964, pp. 177, 186, 189, 194, 208, 212; Agarwala
1955, pp. 140–144). But the Bania families represented in the
Baroda sample were giving up trade and their men were seeking
professional and government occupations. Among them, the occupational rationale for keeping joint families intact over a long period
was no longer so important as it had been (Shahani 1961, p. 1827).

Owner-cultivators are likely to maintain joint families longer
than do others in the same village, but different jatis of owner-
cultivators vary in this regard. In Ramkheri village, for example,
both Rajputs and farmers (Khati) are owner-cultivators, but the
joint families of farmers continue longer on the whole than do
those of Rajputs. This is the case, Mayer explains, because the
farmers are true husbandmen and are much concerned with the
greater efficiency of farming by a joint family, whereas the Rajputs
are more interested in land as a means to wealth and status (1960,
p. 181).

Another variable that affects family form has been discerned by
Pauline Kolenda in her comparative study of families in six places
(Senapur, Khalapur, and Sirkanda in U.P.; Rampur in Delhi State;

Ramkheri in Madhya Pradesh; and the Pramalai Kallar in Madras). This variable depends on the contribution that a woman and her natal family make to her husband's livelihood. When the husband and his family provide much social and economic support and when the wife and her family offer little, then married couples stay longer in the joint family. Conversely, when the wife is an important earner and her natal family contributes to her conjugal family, then the agnatic joint family tends to be of shorter duration. Kolenda finds that the key difference between the three communities in her sample with many joint families, on the one hand, and the three with few, on the other, is that in the former "the *husband* does not develop important economic bonds or continuous social bonds with his wife's kin" (1967, pp. 173, 211).

Agricultural technology also can affect family form. In a survey of fifty-nine villages of Poona district, Orenstein found that there were proportionately fewer joint families in those villages that had the most acreage per family under irrigation. Families with more irrigated land, he suggests, get more of their income in cash. Their members are likely to separate more quickly because the disposition of money income leads to arguments, and both the cash and the irrigated lands are readily divisible. Perhaps also the managerial function and the authority of the family head is lessened under small-scale irrigation farming (Orenstein 1960, pp. 318–319).

Yet the presumed general decline of the joint family in India, the subject of much discussion, both popular and scholarly, is not apparent from census returns. To take one possible indicator, the average number of people in a household has not changed markedly since the Census of 1891 (Gait 1913, pp. 46–47; Goode 1963, pp. 239–240; Sengupta 1958, pp. 387–388). A close study of the census data for eleven states between 1911 and 1951 shows a net increase rather than a decrease in average household size. But this may be a result of increased population and insufficient housing rather than indication of a rise in joint family living (Orenstein 1961; Lambert 1962, pp. 126–127).

The passing of joint families is supposed to be particularly marked in cities, but the evidence so far available shows no great rejection of joint family living among urban people. A study of 201 families in Calcutta, 100 from an old and poorer area and 101 from a new, wealthier section, showed that 80 percent of the families in the wealthier part and 57 percent in the poorer neighborhood were joint. An over-all sampling of Calcutta families showed 42 percent to be joint (J. Sarma 1964, pp. 201–205). A survey of Poona in 1937 showed 28 percent joint families; a resurvey of 1954–55 showed 32 percent. In a narrower sampling in Poona, of 182 fathers with married, employed sons, 66 percent had sons living with them. Two-thirds of those in the sample who could do so, actually fulfilled the ideal for multi-couple residence (Sovani and others 1956, pp. 95, 450; Sovani 1961, p. 207; Dandekar and Dandekar 1953, pp. 127–129).

As this survey shows, it is useful to find the ratio of multi-couple families to *possible* joint families. Couples who have only daughters or are childless cannot readily develop into joint families. Such a calculation was made in a 1958 survey of 2314 couples of Nagpur district. Of the total sample, 30 percent lived in multi-couple families. But when the proportion was calculated of those who had "eligible primary kin," that is, those who had some choice in the matter, the percentage of joint families was 41.8 percent. Among those who had such a choice 49.6 percent of the village couples, 39.5 percent of the town couples, and 32.2 percent of the city couples were living in joint families (Driver 1963, pp. 41–44). The main purpose of this study was to assess fertility; no significant differences were found in fertility as between single and multi-couple families. Other studies have also shown no greater fertility in multi-couple families (*ibid.*, p. 82; Bebarta 1966).

Surveys of two towns in Gujarat reveal that joint family living there also is far from defunct. In Mahuva, a town in South Gujarat, 21 percent of a sample of 423 families were joint in the full traditional sense, and 95 percent maintained some kind of family cooperation with related families (Desai 1964, p. 69). In the town of Navsari 56.5 percent of a sample of 246 families were joint by the author's definition; they included 66.6 percent of the population in the sample. A survey of families in 15 villages in the same area showed 49.7 percent joint families (Kapadia 1956, pp. 112–115).

One student of family organization has concluded that the changes in India are not yet great but that the direction of change is clear (Goode 1963, p. 247). But from the evidence he summarizes, it seems that such directional change, even as reflected in attitude and opinion surveys, is also not great or at least not yet very great. The filial-paternal ideal is still strongly respected in cities as well as in villages and is quite often observed in practice, though insufficient housing has probably forced added joint-family living. The conditions of urban life may ultimately make for a decreasing proportion of joint families, but so far we must agree with the conclusion reached by N. V. Sovani, that urban living must have some effects on family relations but what they are has not so far been made clear (Sovani 1961, pp. 206–207).

In sum, people tend to remain in joint families longer when economic factors favor such families. The poorest and the lowest groups tend to have fewest joint families, but even at these social levels, most families become joint for at least a time after a son marries. When families of low jati acquire enough economic substance to be able to aspire to the higher model and enough education to want to do so, they are apt to take on the more esteemed family patterns including longer duration of the joint family. Joint ownership of land and close dependence on the land help keep joint families together. Among merchants and artisans the economies of scale of a large household are reasons for upholding joint families. When land income is mainly in cash, or when newer occupations bring in money earnings, the economic basis for a joint family is weakened and the family tends to exist for a shorter duration. But, as the urban figures show, the joint family is not by any means totally eliminated nor is the ideal of filial-fraternal solidarity abruptly abandoned.

Differences among Regions

A third kind of variation in family style is by region. Although the available studies of this kind of variation are quite preliminary, certain differences among linguistic-cultural regions can be noted. Thus the recruitment of wives differs between Hindus of the Hindi and adjacent regions, on the one hand, and, on the other, Hindus of South India, who speak Tamil, Telugu, and Kannada (cf. Marriott 1960, pp. 40–42). In the northern parts, wives are usually taken from beyond the village and beyond the closer kin. In the south, a man is expected to marry a girl from among his closer kin. In some southern jatis there is preference for marriage to a mother's brother's daughter or an elder sister's daughter. We shall consider this difference later in our discussion of marriage rules and kinship practices.

The most divergent region of all in matters of family and kinship was—and to some degree still is—Kerala. The Nayars and some of the other jatis of this region were matrilineal; they counted the tie between mother and daughter to be the durable relationship. Nayar women stayed in their natal household—their mother's house—after marriage. Inheritance was from mother to daughter, from brother to sister's children, rather than from father to son. Men also continued to live with their natal, matrilineal families; a Nayar man was a visitor in the household where his wife and children lived. Yet despite this reversal of patterns followed elsewhere in India, Nayar families were quite like the patrilineal families in other respects. Their kinship terminology follows the basic Dravidian pattern used by the patrilineal societies of South India (Yalman 1967, pp. 359–372). The joint family of several married sisters, their children, their mother and her sisters, occasionally their sojourning husbands, was the ideal type and seems to have been the common type. The permanent bonds were between mother and daughter, among sisters, and between brother and sister. A Nayar man in his role as father had no legal rights or authority over his own children. He would play with them, give them gifts, offer friendly counsel. As the male head of a family, his authority was over his sisters' children.

Father-son relations were more complicated if the boy was the child of a union of a Nambudiri Brahmin man and a Nayar woman. Only the eldest son of a Nambudiri family was permitted to marry. A younger son would have an alliance with a Nayar woman in a union that was regular and approved, but was not full marriage. Colonel Unni Nayar (who was born in 1911) has described his boyhood in a Nayar joint family and his Nambudiri father whom he greatly admired. Neither he nor his mother would eat with his father or even watch him eat. He could not touch his father during the day, between the father's morning bath and until the time after his dinner when he was in a more relaxed state of personal purity. Here also the context of behavior influenced the nature of permitted relations. "If I touched Father during the day, he had to bathe afresh and change his clothes. In point of fact, Father, although undemonstrative, did not object to being touched when he was by himself. If others were present he had to observe the decorums, and we got thrashed, not for polluting a Brahmin, but for being tactless" (1952, p. 56). It was not so much the children's violation of propriety that mattered, but the fact that they did so in the presence of others, in the context of the public view.

Whether the father was a Nambudiri or a Nayar, his relations with his children were quite like those which, in much of India, a boy has with his mother's brother. Among the Nayar the mother's brother, especially if he were the head of the family, was expected to carry authority and enforce discipline over his nephew. A Nayar boy had to give the same deference and instant obedience to the head of his mother's family that the patriarchal elder receives in families of patrilineal jatis.

Though roles were reversed, a Nayar family resembled the usual patrilineal joint family in that it was the basic unit of economic activity; its members were coparceners; its male head managed the external family affairs while the senior woman managed the home economy. The family members united in the ritual of the household deities. Just as brothers of a patrilineal family are exhorted to stand fast together and to rise above the divisive influence of their wives, so in a Nayar household the sisters and their brothers were expected to remain united and impervious to divisive arguments from spouses and children. In recent decades special external pressures, legal, economic, and social, have made the traditional matrilineal family rare among the Nayars, but matriliny is still a force among them. The Nayar family is a kind of mirror image of the usual Indian joint family. It provides an important example of one extreme of human family organization, in which the social role of father is minimal. It also demonstrates that so radical a variation as matriliny could be accommodated within the general Indian family and jati framework (cf. Gough 1961c, pp. 298–370; Unni 1956, pp. 45–46; Karve 1965, pp. 291–308; Kapadia 1958, pp. 273–280; Dumont 1961a, pp. 32–33; Dumont 1964a, pp. 85–86; Mencher 1965).

That framework of assumptions and expectations about family life includes the ideal of filial-fraternal solidarity, the emphasis on hierarchy, the pervasive scope of family functions, and the tight identification of person with family. How these assumptions and expectations are actually carried out depends on how individuals act in their family roles.

CERTAIN characteristics of family roles are common to families throughout the land. Some common features, to be sure, are biologically given. As in other human societies, the major roles are those of husband and wife who are also father and mother, of son and daughter who are siblings to each other. And as in other societies, people use broad stereotypes of proper family behavior to guide and judge family conduct. These formulas mask as well as explain; they gloss over some recurrent tensions and ignore other regularities of family life. In the following descriptions of family roles the popular stereotypes must be taken into account, but the descriptions themselves are to be taken not as revised stereotypes but rather as broad outlines of actual behavior within which much variation occurs. Some major variations are those noted in the preceding chapter, by family wealth and ritual rank and by region.

The family roles to be considered are first those of a boy and man, then those of a girl and woman. Not every family has a full complement of members and roles but there is a strong tendency to fill in a missing major role. If a child's father dies, one of the father's brothers, his own elder brother, or another man suitably related, able and willing to do so, acts as father to him. When a girl has several brothers, there is often one in particular (perhaps the one closest to her in age) with whom she shares the essential brother-sister relation and who later is foremost in the important role of mother's brother to her children.

As Son: Filial Respect and Its Consequences

Some of the main features of the family roles of a male have already been mentioned. As boy and man he should treat both parents with great respect. Respect entails obedience and the avoidance of any behavior that might indicate a contrary will or wayward desires not under firm parental control. In the ideal depictions, a son devotes himself completely to the welfare as well as to the will of his parents. This ideal is graphically presented in Mahatma Gandhi's autobiography when he tells how, as a boy, he was deeply affected by a drama about a son's self-sacrificing devotion to his parents. A picture of that devoted son carrying his blind parents on a pilgrimage by means of slings fitted to his shoulders left an indelible impression on Gandhi's mind. He goes on to tell of his marriage at age thirteen and of his great preoccupation with his wife. But nothing in his role as husband could be allowed to conflict openly with his devotion as son. "I dared not meet her in the presence of the elders, much less talk to her" (1940, pp. 11, 17).

At the moment of his father's death, Gandhi was with his wife rather than devotedly caring for his sick father, as he thought he should have been. This marked a crucial point in his career; the experience turned him more firmly toward asceticism. He said that the unfilial deed remained "a blot I have never been able to efface or forget. . . ." (S. H. Rudolph 1965, pp. 86–89).

Not every young man has such an experience or responds so sensitively; Gandhi was then of an age, from a jati, and in a region where filial respect was required in utmost degree. Yet similar deference to parents is seen in parts of India far from Gandhi's birthplace and at the lower as well as the higher reaches of a local hierarchy (e.g., Sarma 1951, p. 55; Dumont 1957b, pp. 212–214).

Parents also owe a certain respect to their children; they should not behave in ways that make it difficult for their children to respect them. This is even more important when a son is grown and his parents are, or may soon be, dependent upon him. In Dr. K. Gnanambal's account of a village in northern Mysore, she tells of old men who would be "gabbing away gaily about their old days, but shutting up like clams when their sons appeared on the scene." A woman of this village, of a cultivator jati, often amused the other women with song and dance imitations of actors. One day while she was doing a lively step her son passed by and happened to see her. Seeing him, she stopped and left abruptly. When Dr. Gnanambal later asked her why she had fled, she said, "Now that my son is married, he is my protector. My husband is alive; but who knows at what time I may have to depend on my son for a cup of gruel?" (1960, p. 58). Her blithe deportment was unseemly for a grown man's mother and could diminish the son's social stature in the village.

Between father and son, relations are supposed to be formal and restrained and are often so in reality. Each may have great affection for the other, but after the boy becomes adolescent there should be little familiarity, intimacy, or demonstrativeness between them. This holds especially true among landowners of high ritual rank. Thus among the Brahmins of a Tanjore village, a father gives a good deal of attention to his sons in their early childhood, being particularly concerned with giving them food. Later, when a boy is eight or nine, he comes under stricter training; he and his father must keep physically more distant from each other. The boy does not touch either parent and he should prostrate himself in obeisance before each of them daily. After the son's marriage he may be given some economic responsibilities but while his father is alive and while the son is in the same village as his father, he does not attain to the full responsibility of an adult. "I am only a young boy, madam!" one man of thirty-five, a husband and father, replied to Kathleen Gough's questions about his responsibilities. "My father is alive—what is my responsibility?" (1956, pp. 835–838).

Such long dependence of son on father is reversed after the father's death, when the fate of his soul depends on his son's ritual observances. The imperative need for sons and the long dependence of son on father is sanctioned and sanctified in scriptures. The father-son relation and duties constitute the essential legal bond of the classic Hindu family (Kapadia 1947, pp. 83–92; Derrett 1960, p. 311).

In families of lower jatis, as has been noted, a son's dependence is not typically so intense or protracted, yet even among them a father is expected to maintain an aloof authority toward his son. Thus among the Pramalai Kallar, a cultivator jati of the Tamil area, a father is generally indulgent with a young child. But as his child grows up, Dumont observes, the father becomes a more distant person, isolated in his authority. The son takes orders from his father but scarcely dares to discuss anything with him, even to clarify important matters on which the father has given orders. The father's authority is so great yet so sensitive of challenge that the two have very little direct communication (1957b, pp. 212–213). A similar relationship is noted in the account of the Balahis, a Harijan jati of Madhya Pradesh. Firm and formal authority is exercised by the father of a Balahi family; he is expected to keep a considerable social distance between himself and his adolescent and grown sons (Fuchs 1950, p. 21). In other jatis and regions as well, an adolescent boy is usually subjected to much stricter authority than he felt as a child; his father is supposed to become more reserved and distant.

The father-son relation is not without personal strain even among those who extol the ideal. In one Rajasthan town the men of the high jatis insisted to the inquirer that it was unthinkable to disregard a father's command, but they also gave him reason to think that the tension between father and son was very strong (Carstairs 1957, pp. 68–69). A grown man may resent his father's strong authority, but open defiance is rare.

Whenever such defiance does erupt, the son can stand on his legal rights and demand partition and his equal share of the family property. One such case was still talked about in a Maharashtrian village years after the event. Among Brahmin landowners of a Kashmir village this occurs only in rare circumstances; normally a son behaves as if his father were the sole owner of the estate. So is it also in a Mysore village, save that there the possibility of a demand for partition is said to soften the father's stern control (Orenstein 1965, p. 57; Madan 1965, pp. 63, 168; Harper 1963, pp. 169–170).

A questionnaire on family relations was given in Bangalore to 157 men and women, mainly educated and of high jati origin. There were many more spontaneous mentions of affection between sons and fathers than of dislike and hostility. Only 16 mentioned antagonism as against 74 references to affection. Yet this was the highest incidence of hostility mentioned for any family relationship. Several respondents noted that there was a marked drawing apart of the two when the son was a young man but was not yet independent. In the words of one respondent, "The father is always a little like a stranger to the son and the mother acts as intermediary between them" (Ross 1961, pp. 101, 137, 144).

The mediating function of the mother is depicted as a central factor in family organization among the Pramalai Kallar, where the social distance and incipient rivalry between father and son make mediation necessary. This circumstance, Dumont comments, helps explain the extremely strong position of the mother of a family in the Tamil country. If she is competent she can manipulate the affairs of the family into which she originally came as a lowly stranger. She can wield decisive influence, if not formal authority, through her sons (1957b, pp. 212–213; see also Orenstein 1965, pp. 56–59).

Between mother and son there is everywhere in India a strong, tender, unchanging, dependable bond. The bond is celebrated in sacred writing, romanticized in popular tale, upheld in the actuality of family life. A mother is respected; motherhood is revered. Sons give abundantly of both the tokens and the substance of esteem. She is not the aloof person a father is supposed to be. She is everlastingly loving and caring, certainly in ideal, often in reality. This is particularly true of a woman in a wealthy family who has little more to do than to care for her children. In that care lies her greatest fulfillment as a person.

Her authority over her son's domestic life continues after he brings home a bride, and sometimes includes the regulation of his sexual relations with his wife (Karve 1965, p. 12; Gough 1956, p. 838). In his autobiography, Rajendra Prasad, first President of India, tells of his visits to his village home in Bihar while he was a student. His was a landowning family of a Kayasth jati and the women, including his young wife, were kept in the strictest kind of purdah seclusion. He met his wife only during his school holidays and then he had to sleep apart from her. "In the middle of the night, my mother would send a maid-servant to wake me up and she would take me to my wife's room." He had to be back in his own bed before others woke in the morning. Later in his life he saw to it that some of the more extreme family practices were changed in his own joint family and he pressed for similar reforms in wider circles (1957, pp. 22–23, 238–239).

Women of the middle and lower jatis who work outside the home are not usually as totally centered on their children. Their control over their sons is not as ubiquitous and prolonged, but in all jatis the mother-son relation is a pivotal one. The principal strain on it commonly comes when the son's wife feels securely enough established in the household to assert some independence, if only by a gesture. As quarrels burst forth, a man is apt to feel himself torn between irreconcilable adversaries—between his mother whom he cannot cross and the mother of his sons whom he really does not want to make unhappy (cf. Dube 1955b, p. 143).

A test of these opposing pulls was made in a questionnaire given in the Delhi area to 590 Aggarwal men and women. Their traditional jati occupation is that of merchants and shopkeepers. Each man was asked whether he was closer to his mother or to his wife or equally close to both. A majority of the men, 56 percent, replied that they were closer to their mothers; only 20 percent said that they were closer to their wives; 19 percent replied that they were equally close; and 5 percent gave other replies. However, only 17 percent of the wives of these men thought that their husbands were closer to their mothers; 57 percent said that their husbands were closer to them. The author comments, "It seems obvious that men's own experience of their relationship to mother and wife is different from the image the women have of these relationships" (Gore 1961, p. 102). The majority of the men in this sample followed the traditional pattern, in the questionnaire reply at least, of holding the maternal bond above the marital one.

As Brother to Brother: Partners and Sometimes Rivals

Among brothers the ideal of unity, solidarity and mutual support is better realized when brothers are under the firm authority of their father or when they rally against a threat from outsiders. But when paternal authority is weak or absent and when they are not defensively united, grown brothers often rub each other the wrong way and find reasons for argument. However, if one brother is considerably older than another, say by ten years or more, their relationship is less likely to become strained. Then the elder more easily assumes some of the responsibility and respect that the father commands, and if the father dies while the younger is still a boy the elder brother usually fulfills the duties of a father.[1]

All agnatic relations tend to be formal, Mayer says of Ramkheri

[1] This happened in Jawarhalal Nehru's family. His father, Motilal Nehru, was a posthumous child who had two brothers much older than he was. One of them raised Motilal. Nehru writes that the relation between his father and his uncle was a strange mixture of the brotherly, the paternal and the filial (1941, p. 17).

villagers, and this holds widely true (1960, p. 219). A major ambiguity and common cause of strain in the fraternal relation is that brothers are equals and yet are not equal. They are all equal in property rights, all equally representative of the family, all equally bound in with the family's social status and fortunes. Yet an elder brother is also vested with some authority over a younger and the younger should, in some degree, be submissive to his elder brothers. But sooner or later the question arises of the degree and nature of deference. The uncertainty as to when equality should be paramount and when inequality should prevail tends to rile their relations.

Men of lower jatis are more likely to emphasize the equality of brothers—the peer rather than the unequal relationship. The Kotas of the Nilgiri Hills were formerly a low-ranking tribal group, traditionally artisans and musicians. Their traditional occupations fostered the peer relationship, since a man could not work a smithy alone or be a one-man band. A man had to have the cooperation of other Kotas in making a living, and the cooperation was best accomplished by a band of brothers, if not real brothers then classificatory ones. Fraternal equivalence is assumed in Kota ritual. One brother can substitute for another in such rituals as that of divorce; if a man does not want to face his wife's father, before whom he must formally divorce his wife, he can send his brother to stand in for him at the rite. Just as brothers shared equally in work, property, and ritual so they shared rights in each other's wives. Each brother had the right of sexual access to another brother's wife (Mandelbaum 1938).[2]

In contrast to this Kota example, people of most jatis in northern India (and of the higher in the south), give formal expression to inequality among brothers. An elder brother must avoid direct com-

[2] Similar rights used to be held by brothers among Nayars of Travancore (Gough 1965, pp. 9-11). This pattern of fraternal equality is still followed by some of the hill people at the Himalayan edge of India. It is the basis for tacit wife sharing in some groups as well as of institutionalized polyandry among others in this region (Berreman 1962c). Another practice that involves the substitutability of brothers is the levirate under which a widow is expected to become the wife of her deceased husband's brother (Srinivas 1965, p. 41; Karve 1965, pp. 19-20, 224). This obviously cannot occur among those who prohibit widow remarriage, but it is a custom of some middle-ranking jatis.

munication with his younger brother's wife; when he approaches she must veil her head and face. A younger brother, on the contrary, may have familiar and easy relations with an elder brother's wife (cf. Karve 1965, pp. 19–20, 136; Sarma 1951, pp. 66–68; Lewis 1958, pp. 191–192; Mayer 1960, pp. 220–221). In some groups an elder brother must proclaim, through ritual act at the younger brother's wedding, that thenceforth he will not so much as touch the garment of the bride (cf. Planalp 1956, pp. 507–508; Freed and Freed 1964, p. 153). Should he do so, even accidentally, the woman will resent it and is likely to make her resentment known.

So different is the relation of a younger brother to his elder brother's wife that the two joke with each other, even tease each other on sexual matters.[3] She may discuss his future wife with him. Gandhi wrote of his nuptials, "My brother's wife had thoroughly coached me about my behaviour on the first night" (1940, pp. 14–15).

Among some of the cultivator jatis near Delhi this joking relationship was customarily allowed to extend to sexual relations as well, although those with some education in the jati have learned that such practices are uncouth by both Sanskritic and modern standards. The case of a young wife, sorely troubled on this account, is told by K. D. Gangrade (1964). She had recently been married to a man considerably older and less educated than herself. Her husband was employed in the city and in his absence her husband's younger brother began to claim his fraternal rights. When she realized that his joking had become pointedly serious she took her troubles (her fifth-standard education was probably a factor in this) to a social worker. The welfare worker advised her to put the matter tactfully to her husband and to her mother-in-law. Both the client and the social worker (who was of a Brahmin jati) were taken aback when the other members of the family indicated to the young wife that she had no cause for complaint and that she should do her proper duty as wife and sister-in-law.

The mother-in-law plainly said that, "after all the children be-

[3] This difference between the roles of elder and younger brother is generally more marked in the north, but some south Indian jatis also maintain similar patterns, particularly in the permissive relations between a man and his elder brother's wife (cf. Dube 1955b, pp. 153–156; Reddy 1952, p. 232).

long to the household" and that sexual relations with a husband's younger brother are not tabooed (*ibid.*, p. 252). The account of this case ends happily for wife and welfare worker; they convinced the mother-in-law that following the traditional practice now leads to the break-up of a joint family. What transpired in this family later, the published record does not reveal. Though the people of this jati gave unequal privileges to brothers, an elder being vested with more authority, a younger endowed with sexual rights not held reciprocally by his elder brother, they nonetheless share the characteristic concern for fraternal unity and condemnation of fraternal discord.

The bond between brothers is taken ideally as a durable and cohesive relationship for cooperative action, second only to the tie between father and son. In actuality the fraternal bond tends to become unstable in time. Brothers of a poor family of low jati may have little to quarrel about. If they are all laborers or heavily dependent on an overlord, they have little cooperative enterprise of their own. But those brothers who together manage and work the land or jointly provide goods and services are likely sooner or later to fall out.

Such estrangement among adult brothers is noted as a salient feature of the family system in a Kashmir village (Madan 1965, p. 169). Similarly, an account of a village of Poona district mentions that brothers commonly quarrel after their father has died, each viewing the others as rivals. Their quarrels sometimes become bitterly vindictive (Orenstein 1965, pp. 45, 48). The same fraternal conflict is reported from a village near Bangalore in Mysore. There the incidence of brothers' quarrels is not a large proportion of all village conflicts but "it is the most shocking kind of conflict and the most contrary to traditional values" (Beals and Siegel 1966, pp. 130–131). In most places and jatis, brothers are expected to be allies; they are so exhorted by parents, kin, and neighbors. But as they become husbands and fathers they tend to become rivals within the one household and they may be abetted in this by their wives. They usually want to be friendly and mutually supportive, yet the younger may find himself irked by the elder's arrogation of undue authority, and the elder by the younger's flaunting of unwonted independence.

As Brother to Sister: Durable Bond

No such uneasiness mars the usual relations of brother and sister, which are typically more stable, durable, and affectionate. A man can be giving and protective to his sister, open-handed and open-hearted, without formal reserve or inward calculation. He gives more to her than he receives from her and feels rewarded just to do so. He keeps up the relation after his sister has married and has left her original home. This entails special responsibility toward her husband and particularly to her children, and the relationship is of major importance for the individual and for the jati. So in acting as brother to his sister a man also assumes the duties of brother-in-law and of mother's brother. In discussion of the one role, it is well to consider the extensions of that role as well.

Rivalry figures little in the brother-sister bond, nor is there rivalry between mother and daughter for the affection of son and brother. Because the daughter must soon leave her natal home, her mother is eager that the girl's brother be fond of her. Then the family will be able to keep closely informed about the girl's fate among those people in whose household she must live. A girl's brother is often the mother's emissary to her. Should she need help and protection in that house, he tries as best he can to give it (Karve 1965, p. 131; Dumont 1957b, pp. 206–207; Carstairs 1957, p. 70; Sarma 1951, p. 54; Mayer 1960, pp. 219–223; Ross 1961, pp. 110, 163–165; Rowe 1960, p. 304).

The moment when a bride leaves her natal home is commonly a poignant one in the wedding ceremony. Then the brothers of the bride (often it is a particular brother) are apt to demonstrate great grief and not only because the occasion demands it. Srinivas tells that he has seen a Coorg man, from one of the proudest warrior traditions in South India, break down with grief at that moment (1952a, p. 147).

A boy's elder sister may be his special childhood companion. Though just barely older, she may care for the boy child, lugging him about on her hip and treating him as her playmate as well as her main chore. If all others in the household are too busy or too constrained to look after him with continual loving care, at least she is neither distracted nor inhibited from treating him as a real person rather than as a container of urgent biological needs or a carrier of future social status. A younger sister does not tend him in the same way but she may also be more companionable and relaxed with him than a preoccupied adult is apt to be.[4]

Though a study of child care among the Rajputs of Khalapur village north of Delhi indicates that girls do not usually take care of younger children, this may be exceptional (Minturn and Lambert 1964, p. 234). Certainly it is common in villages to see small girls taking care of even smaller tots. Carstairs makes the point, on the basis of his observations in a Rajasthan town, that a growing child experiences a continuity of physical and emotional contact with his sisters of a kind that is denied to him by his parents. Even his mother is constrained with the child when the mother-in-law is about and she also is engaged in other work. A sister's care is not diminished for these reasons (Carstairs 1957, p. 71).

There is ritual recognition of the special bond between brother and sister in an annual rite observed in northern and western India. The sister gives her brother a charm, often a thread which she ties around his wrist, as symbol of her solicitude for him. He gives her a gift in return, token of his role as benefactor. On this day (called *Raksha Bandhan* or some variant thereof) a man may receive charms from several donors, from his wife, from a Brahmin with whom he has dealings, or from others who can give him ritual protection. But usually the principal charm is that given by his sister, and the occasion is one when sister and brother should meet. If they cannot meet, a man's sister may send him the charm through the mail. In South India this affirmation occurs as part of other rites. In the region of Dharwar in Mysore, brothers and sisters are expected to meet in the festival of Naga Panchami and Deepavali.

---

[4] Nehru's recollection of the birth of his next younger sister when he was eleven years old illustrates how people outside the family can help set the scene for relations between siblings. "One of the doctors came and told me of it and added, presumably as a joke, that I must be glad that it was not a boy, who would have taken a share in my patrimony" (1941, p. 26). Nehru remembered that he had been bitter and angry at the thought that anyone should imagine that he would harbor so vile a notion. The implications of the doctor's little joke, that brothers were rivals and one should be glad at the birth of a sister because she was not a brother, were angrily rejected in this instance but would hardly be lost on other boys in like circumstance.

The brothers give gifts in kind, the sisters mainly in blessings (Gupte 1919, p. 178; Lall 1933, p. 147; Underhill 1921, p. 134; Marriott 1955b, p. 198; Orenstein 1965, p. 59; Lewis 1958, p. 208; Ishwaran 1965, p. 84).

When a man's sister marries, he too takes on a new and different set of relations. Over much of northern India he becomes inferior to his sister's new family. To her he remains one of the closest of the dearly beloved in her childhood home. To her new family he becomes one who, by definition, is to be taken lightly. As she is subordinate to her husband, so is her whole natal family in some degree subordinate to that of her husband. A family that takes in a girl as bride considers itself superior to the family that gives her in marriage. Her family acknowledges this, though sometimes only grudgingly.

In South India this kind of rank differential is not built into marriage alliances. In some Tamil groups the bride's family is thought inferior to the groom's but, as Dumont comments, the difference in rank at the marriage ceremony fades away in time, "so that there is no suggestion of the wife coming from a lower-ranking lineage." The superiority of one family line over the other is continued only if matrilateral cross-cousin marriages are consistently made between the two (Dumont 1961b, p. 84; see also Dumont 1953; 1957a, pp. 33–37).

No inferiority at all attaches to the bride's family in other parts of South India. In the Kannada-speaking village of Gopalpur, for example, a woman's new family receives her brother as an equal and her father as an honored guest because he has conferred on them the boon of a bride (Beals 1962, p. 27).

Yet whatever formal status may be applied to each family, a brother throughout most of India is expected to keep giving gifts and ritual services to his married sister, perhaps also to her husband and certainly to her children. His benefactions are not requited in any equal measure. There is little calculation of reciprocity; the giving is supposed to be its own reward. Moreover, in the process of being benefactor he gets little glory. Since he is a chief link between his family and his sister's conjugal household, he bears the brunt of their superior airs. In North India and Bengal, the very word for wife's brother is a common term of abuse which a man flings at a cursed ox, which he uses for a shoddy tool, and by which he refers to the affinal kinsman who periodically appears bearing gifts (cf. Nicholas 1965, p. 33). For all that, a brother does not usually flinch from going to visit his sister if he thinks she needs to see him. And, of course, he gives the same kind of treatment to his own wife's brothers and to all the brothers of his brothers' wives. Receiving such treatment does not sap a man's regard for his sister nor does it block a real, as well as ritual, devotion to her children.

In many South Indian jatis, brother and sister are important figures in the marriage arrangements for each other's children and even, in some groups, for their own marriages. Thus in some of the southern jatis an elder sister is expected to urge her younger brother to marry her own daughter.[5] In one Mysore village about 7 percent of 518 marriages studied were between actual maternal uncle and niece, about 3 percent more between classificatory uncle and niece (McCormack 1958b, p. 39). A university professor who came from one of the cultivator jatis of Tamilnad once recounted to me how fortunate his marriage had been. The children of his elder sisters had not been well educated but luckily for him only the boys survived to adolescence, so he was not under pressure to "preserve the family" by marrying an elder sister's daughter and was able to marry an unrelated, educated girl of his jati. The marriage of a man to his elder sister's daughter, Yalman points out, is one variation on the main theme of South Indian kinship, that brother and sister have close relations (1967, pp. 351–352).

Much more common in the south is the preference for marriage between cross-cousins, that is, the children of a brother and sister. It is a preference rather than a firm prescription; most matches are actually contracted outside this preferred range of kin. Thus the percentage of marriages made outside this range is 60.4 percent in one Mysore village, 70 percent and 80 percent for the dominant cultivator jatis in two other Mysore villages, 82 percent in an Andhra Pradesh village, and 88 percent among the Brahmins of a village in Tanjore district, Madras (McCormack 1958b, p. 36; Epstein 1962, pp. 168, 297; Dube 1955b, p. 119; Gough 1956, p. 844).

[5] Marriage to a younger sister's daughter is commonly forbidden in the north and west. But it is permitted in one jati of Marathi-speaking Brahmins, who have apparently taken up the southern custom (Karve 1953, p. 233).

Nevertheless, a sister in these villages is generally expected to have the right of first refusal for her child in selecting a spouse for her brother's child. A brother has a similar right, which in some jatis is formalized in ritual. Thus among the Nadar of the Tinnevelly district in Madras there is a special rite before a wedding in which the mother's brothers of a bride publicly disavow their claims to her if she is not marrying either a mother's brother or his son (Raj 1959, pp. 104–105). Similarly at weddings in Morsralli village in Mysore the bridegroom's sister is especially honored with gifts and she is later honored again at the weddings of his children as a token of her rights in him and in his children. In Morsralli, McCormack observes, the brother-sister relation is the main basis for cordial relationship among relatives (1958b, pp. 44–46).

As Mother's Brother: Supportive Kinsman

A man is expected to take his sister's children as his special charge and in almost every jati and region, he does so. He takes particular interest in her sons. In the northern regions he is not, as he is in much of the south, a potential father-in-law; but in all regions his attitude toward a sister's son is one of benevolent concern. Toward this boy he can be both happily attached and conveniently detached. He can have the satisfaction of giving freely of his bounty to a beloved youngster without also having the duty of molding him into a proper member of society. That responsibility is upon the father and the agnatic relatives of the patriline. The people of the mother's natal family (and later of the wife's) are more sympathetic and supportive of him as an individual, as will be noted again below, and among them, the mother's brother is a main source of support (cf. Dumont 1957a, p. 36; 1961b, pp. 86–87). A child typically looks forward to the exciting, happy visits to his mother's first home. There both mother and son are welcome guests, and her brothers are chief among those who welcome and cherish them.

The mother's brother is an important figure in life cycle ceremonies from birth to marriage. Thus at the initiation ceremony of a Pandit Brahmin boy in a Kashmir village, one of his mother's brothers performs rites designed to help and protect him, while his father's siblings remind him of his new duties and responsibilities. In this region a busybody who takes undue interest in the welfare

of others is sarcastically called a mother's brother, but the image of
the truly benevolent and affectionate mother's brother is a repeated
theme of song and folktale (Madan 1965, pp. 213–215). At the
other end of the social scale and of the subcontinent from this
highest jati of the northernmost region, are the Nayadis, traditionally beggars and the most polluting of jatis in Kerala. Among
them also, special ritual services are performed by the brother of
the mother at a child's life-cycle rites. In turn, the nephews take a
special part in his funeral rites (Aiyappan 1937, pp. 62, 68–70).

Though the precise ritual varies by jati and region and the
reality of the relationship varies by personality and domestic circumstance, yet a man commonly does perform special ritual services
for the children of his sister and generally gives them help and care
as well. If several brothers are eligible to perform the rites, the
senior or most suitable among them does so. The marriage of a
sister's child usually calls forth the brothers' best efforts and they
may then cooperate willingly even if otherwise they are cool to
each other.

This is not to say that there is no strain in relations between any
brother and sister or that the ideal is regularly enacted to the full.[6]
In his account of Shamirpet village near Hyderabad for example,
Dube notes that "family histories recorded for the purpose of this
study do not reveal any permanent tender emotional ties between
brothers and sisters." And in Gamras (Kanpur district) Sharma
found that the cordial and intimate relations between brother and
sister tend to change after the brother's marriage, when his wife
begins to intervene. But in both places a mother's brother is still
the giver of gifts and ritual services whenever his sister's child is

___

[6] Among the Nayars of Kerala, the brother-sister relationship was different
from that in patrilineal India because both lived in the same household
throughout their lives. Yet this, also, was a strong and supportive relationship. This was not so among the Nambudiri Brahmins, the neighbors and
ritual superiors of the Nayars. Only the eldest son in a Nambudiri family
could marry a Nambudiri girl. There were many spinsters, and since they
were kept in seclusion, they contributed little to the family. "Relations between brother and sister were never close; indeed there was a tendency to
regard sisters, both elder and younger, as simply a drain on the family resources" (Mencher and Goldberg 1967, pp. 95, 101). The patrilineal Nambudiris, in this regard, diverged more from the Indian norm than did the
matrilineal Nayars.

the subject of ritual observance (Dube 1955b, pp. 157–159; Sharma 1956a, pp. 282–284).

The more common sentiment is illustrated in a proverb heard in Ramkheri village. "One hundred Brahmins, one sister's son." That is, one gains more spiritual merit when he helps his nephew than when he gives lavishly to Brahmins. The brother-sister relation and its extensions in this village are like those in many jatis and villages. Mayer notes that the one-sided giving by the mother's brother to his nephews and nieces is really an extension of a brother's protective, beneficent relation to his sister. A man takes more interest in the nephew while the sister is alive. "The primary interest thus lies in the sister rather than the people of her conjugal household" (1960, p. 223). A sister, in turn, performs important ritual services for her brothers' children. But she does not have as firm an attachment to her brother's children as he has to hers, perhaps because she is more recipient than donor and, being less mobile and independent, she is less able to give either of goods or services.

The relation of a boy to his father's brother, Mayer continues, is an extension of the relation to his father and of that between brothers which is "correct" and restrained as often as it is warm and cooperative. Since the mother's brother lives in another place, he need not be concerned with daily affairs or rivalries; he appears only as a gift-giver and helper. "His is either a positive or a neutral, but not a negative role; and distance enables him to cast a cloud of excuses over his actions if they contradict the ideal pattern" (1960, p. 224). A boy's father's brother is usually a kind of secondary father, perhaps less aloof and more approachable than his own father, but nevertheless a figure of similar authority. One's mother's sister may be sentimentally close, but she is physically remote in her own married home, less free to visit and to give to her sister's children than is their mother's brother.

The ancient literature attests to the protection a man gives to his sister's children; the mother's brother is the one to whom a character turns when he is in dire straits (Kapadia 1958, p. 219). So is it today; when a boy or man feels oppressed by home pressures, he is apt to turn to his mother's people for refuge and help. Later in life, when the mother's brothers are dead or declining, he may similarly turn to his wife's brothers.

The social consequences of these ties with feminal kinsmen will be discussed later. The solidarity of a jati across villages is continually reinforced by the brother-sister relation and its ramifications. Children come to know quite early in life that there are kinsmen and jati fellows in other villages who are friends and protectors. When a man's sister marries into another village, he is obligated to maintain good relations with his jati fellows in that village for his sister's sake, just as his wife's brothers keep up relations with him and his family. Cohesion within the jati is thus strengthened because of the loyalty and affection which men have for their sisters and the sister's children.

As Husband: Social and Personal Gains

In his role as husband, a man should always be the superior, the initiator, the receiver of deference from his wife. A village wife rarely flouts these expectations openly. Commonly she renders the expected gestures freely, spontaneously, and in full, as part of her womanhood, not out of feelings of duress. The man is expected to make clear demonstration of his husbandly authority at the beginning of a marriage and never to relinquish it, at least not publicly. Moreover, a young husband's personal, conjugal interest in his wife should in no way interfere with his duties to his parents, his siblings, or to other elders of his household.

A marriage begins with the newlyweds as the most junior couple in a multi-couple household. In private, alone together, the new husband may be playful, passionate, argumentative, affectionate. The physical arrangements are usually such that privacy can be attained only briefly, hurriedly, and in darkness. In fine weather, the fields offer some haven. But in the presence of other persons, especially elders of the household, the two must keep their distance and the husband's aloof precedence must prevail (cf. Dube 1955b, p. 142; Mayer 1960, p. 220; Sharma 1956a, p. 272). In later life they need not ignore each other quite so studiously in public, but a husband's formal superiority must always be duly acknowledged by his wife.

This prescription of the husband's role is held at almost all social levels and regions. A husband's authority is more durably imperative among the higher and wealthier jatis than among the lower and poorer, where women can earn on their own and therefore are less totally dependent. Yet it is also upheld among the lowest jatis, as Fuchs' account of an untouchable jati, the Balahis of Nimar district of Madhya Pradesh indicates. A Balahi husband, Fuchs writes, takes no notice of his wife in the presence of strangers, and does not talk to her unless they are alone or with near relatives or neighbors. But after some years, the two become easier with each other, and a clever woman learns how to lead her husband without his becoming aware of it. Her range of influence is limited, but she can exert some influence; and her husband is restrained from mistreating her beyond the conventionally acceptable limit lest she be taken back by her natal family (Fuchs 1950, pp. 165–167).

Husband-wife relations, as described for the highest jati of Kashmir, are broadly similar. One informant illustrated them by describing the return of a Pandit Brahmin traveler to his home. The men, women, and children of his household flock around him. Men and women embrace him, kiss his forehead. The women weep with joy, the children run about and shout. Even the neighbors, Muslims as well as Brahmins, join in the joyous welcome. But there is one woman who does not join in, who continues to do whatever she was doing before the commotion began. She may go into the kitchen, ostensibly to work there. In any event she will take no overt notice of the returned man or he of her. She is his wife.

One reason for this formal aloofness, Madan explains, is that any display of special interest between the two is taken as a sign of a bond that may disrupt the man's filial and fraternal duties and so is highly disfavored. For this reason a young wife may not prepare any food especially for her husband. If she wants to do some household task for him, she must do it for the whole family. Another reason for the display of indifference is the elders' view that a young couple should have only one interest of their own apart from the rest of the family—in sexual relations and those only in order to beget children. "Consequently there is a sense of shame which surrounds the wife-husband relationship for many years after marriage when sexual drive is held to be the main interest which a man and his wife have in one another" (Madan 1965, pp. 134–135).

Such shame is generally much less strong in middle and lower jatis. Although a young wife among them is supposed to be exceedingly shy and demure and the couple may have to make clan-

destine arrangements to have sexual relations, others in the family
do not necessarily decry their sexual interest in each other. In all
jatis the formal superiority of the husband must be diligently mani-
fested, and in all it may covertly be directed by his wife. So among
the Balahis, "the formal domination of husbands over wives, though
true, conceals the fact that women are able to exert a far greater
influence over their husbands than even they care to admit" (Fuchs
1950, p. 136).

When a youth becomes a husband, not much in his daily life
seems altered. He lives in the same household, does the same work,
acts in much the same family roles. But the marriage does typically
make a difference in his social potential and in his concept of himself. He now has a woman of his own whose whole being is directed
to him even if she must not show it openly. He knows that he is
receiving an intensity of attention from her that he may not have
experienced since infancy. His social potential has been enhanced;
an unmarried man in most groups is not considered to be a complete person, and in some he does not even rate a full funeral
ceremony when he dies.

The personal impact of the marriage on the young man is dramatically begun with the wedding ceremony. He becomes a king
for those days, a being so exalted that even his elders give deference
to him. That lofty feeling, usually coming at a time of adolescent
restiveness, is made possible by the girl as bride and is reawakened
daily by her covert ministrations as his wife. Her presence thus
assures him that he truly is a superior individual, no matter what
his jati rank or personal capacity may be.

This is sensitively shown in the Wisers' account of Karimpur
village in Mainpuri district of Uttar Pradesh. The authors observe
that no matter how humble a man's position in the village, he
becomes a personage when he enters his own courtyard. His wife
is ready to do his bidding with head bowed and voice subdued and
so are other women junior to him. A young husband finds this
most pleasant. He has been dependent on others, now he has a
human being under his control. Mrs. Wiser tells how she and some
of the village women were sitting together one day when a young
man, not long out of boyhood, appeared delivering a storm of
abuse. She was momentarily puzzled and then noticed that the girl

at her side was smiling under her scarf. It was the young man's new wife whom he was ordering about. She hurried to do what he ordered and returned, all smiles. He had shown that he was a proper husband, she that she was a proper wife; both were satisfied (1963, pp. 79–81).

Later in a marriage, there may well be quarrels in which the wife gives as well as receives. In the Andhra village of Shamirpet, Dube observes, almost everyone will verbalize the ideal of husband-wife relations in similar words, but the reality of family life is not quite as the ideal formula would have it. "The husband is, without doubt, superior and has, in most families, the upper hand; but practically nowhere do we find him a completely dominant, authoritarian, and patriarchial figure" (1955b, p. 142).

A woman then is not without certain powers. For one thing, she is in charge of domestic ritual purity. If she feels vexed and vengeful, she may be careless about the purity of food or of her own person. She need not go to the length of traffic with other men, she need only be a bit lax about her own menstrual seclusion. Furthermore, a wife is readily seen by her husband's family as an active temptress. A man is supposed to have only a limited amount of life-giving fluids and rapid loss is believed to weaken a man drastically. Women are not so debilitated by frequent intercourse (Beals and Siegel, 1966, pp. 43–46; Berreman 1963, p. 170; Carstairs 1957, pp. 83–88).[7]

The rhetoric of marital quarrels in a Mysore village has been noted by Alan Beals. Certain actions, such as "salutary beatings" lead to reconciliation, others quite surely to divorce (Beals MS. 1965). There are probably similar patterns of domestic discord in other villages and regions. Generally the elders who are most closely related to the quarreling pair try to prevent a serious break. Each marriage bond is permanent among those higher jatis in

[7] The common men's notion that women make aggressive sexual demands is attested in the account of the Balahis. This account also mentions the women's view, which is rarely noted. Many Balahi men complain, the author tells, that their wives would run away if they omitted intercourse for three consecutive nights. "Balahi women maintain that the nights with their husbands are their only pleasures in a hard and dreary life, for, so they say, a woman has nothing else to think of, while a man may have many other interests and distractions" (Fuchs 1950, p. 165).

which divorce and the remarriage of widows are forbidden. A woman of these jatis, once married, is linked to her husband with the finality of birth and death. As we have previously noted, divorce and widow remarriage are permitted in many of the other jatis, but even where divorce is very common, as it is among the Kotas of the Nilgiri Hills, the parents of each spouse typically hope for a durable marriage for their child. Marriage among the Kotas is a simple matter, quickly arranged and consummated. It is often a brittle arrangement for young people. Divorce is readily contrived and frequently accomplished. Most men and women have a history of a number of marriages and divorces. After a couple has a child or two, their marriage is more likely to settle into the lasting relationship that their elders urge them to have (Mandelbaum 1938).

Divergent as these Kota marriage practices are from those of the high jatis, the Kotas hold quite similar notions about the desirability of a stable marriage and of the formal superiority of the husband in such a union. At all social levels, a man may take additional wives, especially if the first produces no children. This right has been curtailed by recent legislation but in any event polygyny was not common. A particularly wealthy or powerful man might take more than one wife. A widower could always remarry. In some jatis the sororate is preferred or mandatory; that is, a sister of the wife is taken as additional or substitute wife. Where widows can remarry, the levirate is commonly preferred; a brother of the deceased husband becomes the next husband or at least he has the right of first refusal. Generally a second marriage, whether for a man or a woman, is marked with a much simpler wedding than was the first and is not as prestigious an arrangement as the first might be (Srinivas 1965, pp. 40–41; Dumont 1960; Karve 1965, p. 134).

Other Roles and Social Consequences

When a man marries he acquires not only a wife but also a new set of relatives, his wife's close kin. To them, as was mentioned earlier in this chapter, he is a respected person, the recipient of their good will and gifts. Among the Pandit Brahmins "his affines

are his well-wishers and sympathizers." In the early years of a
Pandit Brahmin's marriage his relations with his wife's kin are not
close, but when his children are growing up they induce closer ties.
A man's affines typically support him both in word and in substance. Their gifts are for his entire household as well as for him
personally, given partly for their daughter's benefit, to help better
her lot in her husband's family, and also as a means of building and
maintaining their own family's status in the jati. The families rated
highest are those who are most lavish in their gifts to their daughters' marital families (Madan 1965, pp. 137–140). Similar relationships between a man and his affines have been noted in a wide
spread of jatis and regions (e.g., Mayer 1960, pp. 225–227; Harper
1963, pp. 171–173).

Another aspect of the husband's role in the Kashmir village may
also be of common occurrence, though wider evidence is not as yet
on record. Madan notes that a man with adult children is rather a
lonely person in his household. His sons must keep a respectful distance from him and their wives even more so. A woman in her old
age can more easily shift her interests to others in the household,
but the older a man grows the more dependent he is on his wife
since he cannot readily be on familiar terms with the younger
people in the household (1965, p. 137). Apparently the pivotal,
mediating role a mother often takes between her husband and her
sons when they are adolescents, continues when they are mature
men with children of their own.

To those children their father's father is part of the paternal
authority and the agnatic discipline. Even more than their own
father, he must be respected. While they are in his presence, levity,
horseplay, demonstrations of parental affection are unsuitable. Relatively few poor men survive long enough to be grandfathers for
any considerable length of time. Those who do are often in separate
households from their grandchildren and, in any case, they may
be enfeebled or senile.[8]

In the joint families of high-ranking landowners, however, the
paternal grandfather is often a figure of some consequence to his

[8] The retirement of an elder from paramount influence in a household
occurs at all social levels. In Driver's sample of 2314 multi-couple families
in Nagpur district, the elder couple occupied a subordinate position in 26.3
percent (Driver 1963, p. 41).

grandchildren. He is expected to exert his authority in instructing and disciplining the children and so should be strict with them. Hence among the Pandit Brahmins he does not favor frequent visits by them to their mother's natal family and frowns on the loving attention they are likely to get from the mother's parents and brothers there. "They complain that children get spoiled during such visits and by the time they return they usually become undisciplined" (Madan 1965, p. 212). But the same man who may make such complaint about his son's children may well act as the benevolent admirer of his daughter's children when they come to visit.

A Pandit child's attitude toward each of his grandmothers is similarly divided. He may sense some of the characteristic strain between his mother and his father's mother. But his mother's mother welcomes him most fondly as the darling son (or daughter) of her beloved and sorely missed daughter. A Pandit Brahmin's ties to his mother's first family are most important to him when he is young. After he marries and especially after his mother dies, his principal home of affection is with his wife's rather than his mother's natal family (Madan 1965, pp. 210–213; see also Sarma 1951, pp. 62–65; Mayer 1960, p. 220; Ross 1961, pp. 92–98).

This Pandit example illustrates general themes in the family roles of a man at most social levels and regions. He works with the other men of the household, as their assigned life partner, to achieve many vital purposes—food, shelter, socialization, defense. With them his roles are cast largely as a member of a cooperating group. Cooperation among the men is continuous in daily tasks and grand events but there is commonly also an element of rivalry or strain in these relations.

A man's relatives through his mother and wife do not contribute much to the daily maintenance and cohesion of the family group, but they are a fundamental resource for him as a person. Our later discussion of feminal kin will note that men who are related through women need not deal with each other as responsible members of a group but more as persons worthy of support. A man gets respect, affection, and sympathy from his mother's and wife's natal family and he gives of the same supportive currency to his sister's and daughter's conjugal family. In his roles as an agnate, a man supports the residential household group and the local lineage, but in his relations through the women of his family he also contributes to identification and cooperation within the jati. Hence these individual, affectionate, affective aspects of a man's family roles do much to foster the cohesion of the larger social group, the jati.

CHAPTER 5

Family Roles: Girl and Woman

THE break between being a daughter and sister in one family and becoming a wife and daughter-in-law in another is sharp and, as many women recall, sorely difficult. Their recollection of the sweet joy of girlhood is not merely a construct of nostalgia; girls are commonly under less stern discipline than are boys, especially as their puberty and time of departure approaches.

As Daughter: the Brief Sojourn

Formally and manifestly the birth of a daughter is a much less auspicious event than the birth of a son. When a choice must be made between the needs of a young son and a young daughter, a son is far more likely to get the better food, clothes and care. This is eminently so in the Kashmir village that Madan describes, and yet the girls themselves do not seem resentful of any discrimination. Their parents admit and justify discrimination but also insist that they do not love their daughters less than their sons (Madan 1965, p. 78). Similar favoring of sons is common elsewhere in India, as is a similar lack of strong resentment by daughters, either as children or in their later recollection.

One clue to the reason for this response is offered in the study of child-rearing among Rajputs of Khalapur village in Uttar Pradesh. Rajput mothers of this village, as observed and as questioned, are less warm and more hostile to their sons than to their daughters. "This hostility to boys is particularly interesting in view of the fact that these Rajputs, like most Indians, want to have sons rather than daughters" (Minturn and Lambert 1964, p. 232). A possible explanation offered by Leigh Minturn is that women prefer daughters on emotional grounds, partly because a daughter must soon leave her mother, partly because a woman must never directly express hostility or resentment of her husband. These emotions, Dr. Minturn suggests, are expressed in the coldness with which these women treat their sons (Minturn and Lambert 1964, pp. 232–233; Minturn and Hitchcock 1966, p. 97).

These Rajputs may be exceptional among Indian villagers in this and, as was mentioned in the previous chapter, their girls are given less work and responsibility for domestic chores than are those in many other jatis and regions. Nevertheless, it is quite typical that a girl's place in her original family involves less restraint and permits more open affection than she enjoys after her marriage. Her father usually sees no great need to assert strong authority over her. Among the Havik Brahmins of a Mysore village, a girl is said to be "like a flower," which needs to be cherished and cared for because she will soon marry and come under the stern discipline of another family (Harper 1963, pp. 171–172). Similar sentiments are expressed in families from a wide array of levels and places (e.g., Madan 1965, p. 77; Gore 1965, p. 227).

A girl, especially one who is a younger child, may have a particularly affectionate relation with her father. Such a relationship is described by Mrs. Ranade in her autobiography. When her elder siblings were young, their father's mother was still in the house. Her father could not talk to his children in the presence of his mother, and she was always present: "But Grandmother died the year before I was born, and so, for the first time, my father was free to follow his own desire. He made much of the baby daughter. . . . I dared take liberties and be familiar with him in a way that quite scandalized my older brothers and sisters" (1938, p. 3). This was in a Brahmin family of Maharashtra toward the end of the nineteenth century; similar affection between father and daughter is noted in more recent accounts (e.g., McCormack 1958b, p. 44).

Such fond relations cannot well be carried on after the daughter goes to her new house. A father, especially in North India, rarely visits his daughter in her married home. His position in that household is an ambivalent one. As an elder he should be respected and given food, but as one who has given a girl to the other family, he must not take anything from them, not even a cup of tea. The donor of a bride must not receive anything at all from those who have taken his daughter (Karve 1953, p. 130; Dumont 1961b, pp. 84 ff.). Despite such ambivalence or disadvantage, a father may greatly benefit from a daughter's marriage. One important way in which a prospering man can demonstrate his power and enhance his family's status is through arranging a prestigious marriage for his daughter. She thus helps translate his secular gains into the more durable and desirable gain of higher status within his jati.

The responsibility for rearing a daughter, for molding her into a proper social person, rests with her mother. Her father may pamper her or remain aloof, but her mother must train and discipline her. That training is mainly aimed at turning her into a good daughter-in-law, obedient, skillful, demure. The girl's chances of a fine marriage are much improved if she gives evidence of these qualities (even more are her chances damaged if she displays contrary inclinations); the family's prestige is enhanced if she demonstrates these virtues after she is married, and her own happiness hinges on making the best of her roles as daughter-in-law and as wife. As a daughter approaches puberty her mother tends to draw closer to her and to remember poignantly that this child of hers will soon be cast beyond her mother's help. This thought softens discipline and leavens training with maternal compassion (cf. Srinivas 1942, p. 195; Ross 1961, pp. 61, 104, 150).

As Young Wife: Great Transition and Critical Role

The nuptial rites mark the great divide in a girl's life. She is physically transferred from the familiar intimacy of her childhood home to a strange place and new people, some of whom are, by reason of their roles, either distant or disciplinary. The transition is not easy and the bride has been prepared to find that it is not easy. Describing the lot of a bride in Senapur village, Opler writes that "In story, proverb, and song, the society has from her earliest years reminded her of the sharpness of the transition at marriage, and of the possible hostility of the mother-in-law and sisters-in-law" (1958, p. 561).

The sad parting scene, when the bride is taken away from her parents' home, touches onlookers' hearts when it is enacted in reality as it does when described over and again in drama and story. The modern relevance of one classic version of this scene has been remarked by Mrs. Karve. It occurs in the fourth act of Kalidasa's drama, *Shakuntala*, of about the fifth century A.D. Mrs. Karve comments that this act well portrays "the situation in every Hindu household." The parents are happy about the match, yet apprehensive about their daughter's future. The girl is eager to join her husband, but tremulous about leaving her beloved family and friends. The father gives advice to the girl on how she should behave in her new home. Mrs. Karve writes that this situation has been depicted in song and drama, in religious poetry and in proverbs, in almost all languages of India as far back as literary records exist; "and a study of these illumines the present situation as it is enacted before our eyes" (1953, p. 20).

In the parting scene, Shakuntala's father advises her to obey her elders, to be very kind to her rivals, and not to be perversely blind and angry with her husband even though he should prove less faithful than a man might be. He adds that when she brings forth a son, she will not any longer miss her father (Kalidasa, 1959 edition, pp. 48–49). In this advice there is the assumption that she will encounter personal rivals in her husband's household and that the husband may not actually behave like the revered figure she must take him to be. Still, she must keep her emotions in check, for "self-willed women are the curse of life." And there can be a redeeming event, the birth of a son.

Some fourteen centuries later, a Brahmin woman of western India, Mrs. Ranade, recalled her father's advice when she was about to leave her home as a bride. He told her to endure silently whatever trouble might come. She was not to talk back even to a servant and should control herself even if something seemed utterly unendurable. He warned her that he expected her behavior to enhance his family's name and that if it did not he would never allow her to visit her mother's house. "Already I was beginning to sense that the discipline in this new home would soon make my carefree life in my mother's home seem like heaven itself" (Ranade 1938, pp. 20–21).

Her forebodings were soon realized. She found herself separated from her mother for the first time in her life and surrounded by a chattering, inquisitive group of women of her new home, who let her hear their cool, unflattering appraisals of her appearance and prospects. This was in nineteenth century Poona. Writing in mid-twentieth century, Mrs. Karve depicts a similar atmosphere in which a contemporary bride of North India finds herself. When her affinal kin take their first look at her face, she must keep her glance demurely lowered or her eyes entirely shut. After marriage she must be self-effacing, neither seen nor heard too much. Whatever misfortunes come to the household within a year or so of her arrival may well be attributed to her inauspicious qualities (1965, pp. 135–136).

A young wife, of any jati and region, usually has lowest status in the family and is given the more onerous chores. Whatever goes awry, she is apt to be called the culprit. Whenever the finger of blame is pointed, it somehow swings toward her. A common saying is that a pot was golden if a daughter-in-law has broken it, only earthen if the mother-in-law broke it. The Pramalai Kallar have a version of this saying. They put a new daughter-in-law in a similar position, even though their women are relatively independent and a new couple usually lives with the parents for only a brief time (Dumont 1957b, p. 207).

The young woman must keep out of the way of the male elders. Communication with her husband's father and elder brothers is minimal; in some jatis it is entirely prohibited. These men may give warning coughs when they come into a room where she is, but the responsibility for avoidance behavior, whether it is covering her head or leaving the room, is hers (cf. Sarma 1951, pp. 57, 67; Karve 1953, p. 134; Dube 1955b, p. 155; Fukutake et al. 1964, pp. 43–44).

Her greatest responsibility is to bear a child, preferably a son. Barrenness is a fear, a curse, an unending reproach. Among Kannada-speaking women, not only is the word for barrenness, *banje*, forbidden, but the word for the root of a certain plant, *baje*, is also taboo because it sounds like that fearsome term (Srinivas 1942, p. 171). Everywhere in the land a newly married wife can hardly escape constant reminders of this ominous possibility. An unfortunate who must at last conclude that she will bear no child may well urge her husband to adopt a son or to take another wife so that there may be a child to his name. In any event, the biological facts are such that relatively few young women become pregnant in the first months after the start of their marital life. For those who join their husbands immediately after first menstruation there is an even longer average interval before conception takes place than among those who begin married life a few years after menarche (Mandel-baum 1954a). So a great many young wives undergo harrowing months or years before they know that they are pregnant and feel blessed.

During this period of stringent responsibility, a young wife is also more isolated than ever before or again. Her mother-in-law is supposed to be more of a disciplinarian than a comforter. The other women in the household are not allies. The male elders must keep their distance; the husband's younger brother, who is eligible to be her friend, may not yet have established really easy relations with her. And her husband, her life's mainstay and the whole reason for her presence in the house, cannot appear to take an interest in her. She, in turn, should not show special interest in him though all know that she must perforce pin her hopes and fasten her thoughts on him alone. She does not address him directly and never uses his name. Only his seniors and close friends may do that, not his wife (cf. Bharati MS. 1966).

Where village exogamy is the rule, a young wife is physically iso-lated from her childhood home and companions. But even in those places where she can see her mother every day, she must be care-ful to show that she is under the hegemony of her mother-in-law. An incident told by Gerald Berreman illustrates this. A young wife who lived near her parents in Sirkanda village had stopped to talk with her mother when Berreman came by. The two women asked him to take a photograph of them sometime, but when he offered to do so then and there, the younger woman quickly declined. She had been sent by her mother-in-law to gather fodder and the mother-in-law would not like it if she dallied to be photographed. The women suggested that he approach the mother-in-law and offer to take the photograph without mentioning their conversation (1962a, p. 282). Reflected in this small incident is a major precept of Indian family structure, that on marriage a woman comes under the authority of the husband's family, that the authority is mainly exerted by her mother-in-law, and that nothing, neither her rela-tions with her husband nor those with her parents, should impair that legitimate authority or her willing submission.

The situation of a young wife can easily be depicted in more somber tones than is the common reality. She is relatively isolated within the family structure, but she is not in solitary confinement.

She can maintain a joking relation with some in the family, perhaps with her husband's younger sister, as well as with his younger brother, or with another brother's wife (cf. Sarma 1951, pp. 67–68). This banter may well be, as joking relations often are in human society, an expression of ambivalence about the true nature of the relation, yet it also relieves the strained tautness of her conduct. She is usually quite a young girl and has the resilience of girlhood. A chore such as getting water from the well can be used as a refreshing relief from the presence of the elders; in the new home there is the excitement of new sights, new people, and the discovery of the person and personality of her husband. She may get to visit her parents' home even before she is pregnant.

But the real relief comes when she becomes pregnant. Her mother-in-law can afford to relax a bit in her role as taskmistress; her husband is pleased; the men of the household are glad; there is an awakened interest in seeing that she eats well and rests easily. This first burgeoning also marks her first upward move in the family status hierarchy.

Before the birth of her first child a woman in some regions returns to her parents' home.[1] Even where birth takes place in the husband's household, as it often does in Hindi-speaking regions, she goes to her parents for a lengthy visit after the childbirth (cf. Karve 1953, pp. 154, 163; Mullick 1882, p. 112; Lewis 1958, p. 49). There in her familiar home she is a favored, freer person. She is a daughter of the house and a daughter of the village, the very terms have a benign ring. She is apt to use quite a different mode of conduct when she visits her old home—less restrained, more outgoing—and in a few places she may even assume different standards of personal morality (Karve 1953, p. 129; Majumdar 1944, p. 163).

As Matron: Increasing Influence

On her return with the child, the young wife's status begins to change. She is no longer the lowly probationer she was at first. If the child is a son, she has proved herself in the most important way

---

[1] For one Indian woman who was to give birth to her third child, this required a trip from New York to Moscow. Her husband was an official of the United Nations, her father was India's Ambassador to Moscow (Bacon 1956, pp. 257–258).

of all and her confidence is the more secure. The son is her social redeemer and thenceforth her importance in the family tends gradually to increase. In Ramkheri village the change in her position is symbolized in the eating pattern. When she first arrives in the household, she eats last of all, after the other women. Later she eats at the same time, but turned away from the other women as a sign of respect and of her diffidence before them. Finally, when she feels quite secure, she will face the other women, even those of the elder generation, while eating or eat side by side with them, a sign of equality inside the house as it is at public feasts (Mayer 1960, p. 220).

A young wife, once past the initial stage of her marriage, can enjoy the advantages of her wifely role. She is now a full person, capable of joining as a needed ritual partner in her husband's domestic rites, having certain jural rights in her married home and contingent rights in her original family. Now that she lives away from her girlhood home, she is free of the strains of everyday living together there and may be emotionally closer to her natal family than she was before (cf. Yalman 1967, p. 350; Madan 1965, pp. 79, 124–125, 224).

In some domestic matters she can have her own way. For example, a woman's ritual stringency is largely her own affair. She may be, and often is, more stringent about domestic purity than is her husband. Among the Rajputs of Khalapur, men commonly eat meat but their wives will not. The men must cook their own meat on separate hearths because the women will not touch it or have their kitchens defiled by it (Minturn and Hitchcock 1966, p. 44). In South India I have known of women of vegetarian sections of the Badaga of the Nilgiri Hills who were married to men of non-vegetarian sections. Although among the Badagas as among most other Indian villagers a bride is socially assimilated into her husband's household, these brides do not give up their purer diet. And when such a bride becomes first lady of the house, no meat is ever cooked in her kitchen. If her husband and sons want to eat meat, they must cook it themselves, outside.

In South India generally, a woman's activities are not so closely restricted as they are in the Hindi-speaking North. "A woman in the South," Mrs. Karve observes, "lives and moves freely in her father-in-law's house" (1965, p. 242). She does not usually have to cover her face in the presence of elder males as she does in the Hindi region, nor is she so cut off from her natal family. Yet women of the highest jatis in the south are also quite restricted. In Kumba-pettai village of Tanjore district, women of the lowest groups, the Adi Dravidas, remain in close touch with their mothers after marriage; young women of the Brahmin jatis are far more isolated both spatially and socially from their mothers. Sisters of the Adi Dravidas usually are in more frequent and close relations with each other after they are married than Brahmin sisters of this village can possibly be.[2]

One feature that is consistent across jatis and regions is the great concern of the husband's family about the conduct of the young wife. Should she deviate from the prescribed obedient, complaisant conduct, the corrective forces are, as it were, already poised, and the family elders are quick to bring redressive pressures. Counterchange is on a hair trigger in respect to the behavior of a newly married woman.

The Women of a Family: Expected Friction and Central Importance

Another constant feature is the disciplinary role of the mother-in-law and the gradual resistance of the daughter-in-law. As the younger woman comes to feel more self-assured, as she grows more mature physically and psychologically, she becomes less complaisant and less automatically yielding to the directives of her mother-in-law. Quarrels tend to erupt with increasing frequency and with escalating acrimony.[3] Women do not feel as constrained in venting

[2] Because sisters are likely to be separated after their marriage, with little opportunity for visiting each other, relations between sisters are not central to family structure. Yet the errant behavior of one can affect the whole life status of the other. An educated woman in Bangalore told that when she was studying for the M.A. degree her family arranged a marriage for her to which she objected so violently (and ultimately successfully) that she was about to commit suicide in the traditional way by jumping into a well. "My mother found out and stopped me at the last minute. She told me I had no right to commit suicide, for it would interfere with my sister's marriage, for people would think I had an affair with someone" (Ross 1961, p. 272).

[3] A young wife, pushed to desperation, may take extreme measures. In Senapur village near Banaras she may become possessed by an evil spirit (Opler 1958, pp. 560–566). Among the Havik Brahmins of Mysore she may

hostility against other women as do the men in a family and their quarrels are not taken as seriously as are struggles among the men. The degree of verbal hostility varies by jati practice as well as temperament. Among Kumbapettai Brahmins little open hostility can be shown within the family and within the jati. Among the Kotas of the Nilgiri Hills differences of opinion can quickly blossom into loud, vituperative argument. But whatever the permitted level may be, the women's quarrels in the household generally exceed those of the men both in frequency and volume.

The women of the family are not expected to get along well. As a Kannada proverb puts it, a thousand moustaches can live together, but not four breasts. The hostility between mother-in-law and daughter-in-law is both proverbial and a frequently observed fact. Thus among one of the very lowest of low jatis, the Nayadis of Kerala, the stereotype appears in their expression for crocodile tears, "like a daughter-in-law weeping for her dead mother-in-law"; and the reality is summarized by Dr. Aiyappan's statement that there is always considerable friction between a mother-in-law and her daughter-in-law (1937, p. 37).

The Wisers tell of loud quarrels in Karimpur village and add that to intrude in affairs between husband and wife is futile, but to interfere in a quarrel between mother-in-law and daughter-in-law is to invite the verbal obliteration of one's self, one's forebears, and one's descendants (1963, p. 83). Such quarrels may flare up on almost any pretext but the root causes are generally the same everywhere. The daughter-in-law wants to strengthen the interests of her husband and children; the mother-in-law looks to the interests of the household. The elder woman finds that the younger is disrupting unity among the brothers; the younger finds the elder to be intolerably demanding and domineering (cf. Nicholas 1961, p. 1059; Madan 1965, p. 132).

This opposition between mother-in-law and daughter-in-law is graphically shown in an account of a Mysore village in which uncle-niece marriages occur. When a girl marries her mother's brother, her maternal grandmother then becomes her mother-in-law also. Her maternal grandfather, who would not otherwise have

similarly fall prey to malevolent intrusion, or she may starve herself or attempt suicide (Harper 1963, p. 173). Throughout village India, instances are graphically told of women who drowned themselves in wells.

much to do with her marriage arrangements, assumes some authority in his capacity as prospective father-in-law. "The same amount of suppressed hostility and ill feeling seems to exist between a grandmother and granddaughter when their relationship becomes one of mother-in-law and daughter-in-law" (Gnanambal 1960, pp. 54–55).

Nor are relations among women of the same generation more amicable in the family. One example is given in Sarma's depiction of family life in Bengal. She notes that a young wife can have very friendly relations with the girls, her husband's sisters, in her new home. She is anxious to please and they are quite pleased to accept her. But when they marry and leave the family, the relation alters. Each of them becomes more and more cut off from their father's household, and each can hardly help being envious of her brother's wife, who is, or will be, mistress of her former happy home. The wife of the brother, on her part, is not overjoyed by her husband's aid and gifts to his sister. Even while the sisters are unmarried and on close, friendly terms with their brother's wife, they can be her severest critics if they think that she is not behaving properly. In folk songs of many regions the two, a man's wife and his sister, are characterized as natural enemies (Sarma 1951, pp. 68–69; Karve 1965, pp. 129–130; Madan 1965, pp. 132, 171; Srinivas 1942, p. 193).

The women who have married into the family, the wives of the brothers, must live in very close proximity. A description of their relations as observed in Shamirpet village tells of the common situation. Dube writes that the brothers' wives have rivalry, jealousy, and suspicion for one another. "There is always considerable backbiting and telling of tales. Alliances are formed and broken periodically. . . . The intrigues and jealousies among the womenfolk in a joint family are the despair of men" (1955b, p. 155).[4] No doubt there are some families in this village as in other villages whose

---

[4] Traditional family life in China was characterized by quite similar relations among women. Maurice Freedman thus summarizes the usual situation in traditional China: "Mother-in-law, daughters-in-law, and unmarried daughters formed a battlefield on which any one daughter-in-law must fight for herself and, later, for her children." As in India, there was a difference between the higher and lower social-economic levels. "In a family of low status and simple structure . . . each brother stood close to his wife, so that while a wife might be made miserable by poverty and hard work, at the

womenfolk live together in smooth harmony. But whatever tensions are built up, and some tensions inevitably arise in all family life, they tend to be readily expressed in women's intrigues and jealousies. These often lead to the dissolution of the joint family but they support the people's notion that men are inclined to live in amicable partnership but are riven apart by their women (cf. Srinivas 1952b, p. 30). This notion is well worth protecting because the men should continue to cooperate as members of the lineage and jati-group even after they separate the household. So attributing the split to the women helps the men break an uncomfortable solidarity and then to resume cooperative relations.

The popular stereotypes omit important aspects of a woman's family roles. Though boys are indeed favored over girls within a family, yet girls generally seem to suffer little emotional deprivation on that account. And after a girl's marriage the favoring among siblings is reversed. Then her brothers give in to her; she gets much more from them than she is ever expected to give. Furthermore, a young woman is expected to feel the shock of transfer from daughter to daughter-in-law and typically she does feel it keenly. Her low status as young wife is part of the systemic separation between agnatic and affinal bonds. But though the young wife is taken to be a person of little consequence in the family, her role is one of great importance. Few family roles are subject to such close scrutiny or so liable to such quick redressive action.

The formal subordination of women in the household does not bar an elder woman from dominating her domestic scene nor does it hamper a younger woman from competitive struggle with other women of the house. Though a young woman may have the lowliest place in her conjugal family she nevertheless may be a main vehicle for a rise in status of her natal family. And although a marriage must be between two who are ritual equals in the local jati system, the two may be from families that are unequally en-

---

lower levels of society she had greater strength as an individual." Freedman indicates that solidarity among brothers in families of higher status was strengthened by their mutual opposition to the powerful father who controlled their economic fate and social relations (1962, pp. 328–329). In India, brothers in a family of higher rank are not so united by mutual opposition to their father.

dowed within the jati. A principal lever in the competition for family status is the prestigious marriage of a daughter.

Villagers fulfill their family roles in a cycle of family development that is vital for all of village society and economy, as well as for the maintenance of the jati.

CHAPTER **6** Family Cycle: Formation and Maintenance

The characteristic stages of the family cycle in village India are less clearly demarcated than they generally are in urbanized, industrialized societies. In a demographic comparison of family cycle in India and in the United States, Andrew Collver points out that the stages in America are quite distinct. The American cycle begins with two relatively short phases, one from marriage to first birth and the second comprising the childbearing period. Then follows a longer period, mainly of child-rearing, and a shorter one during which the children marry and leave the parental home. Next is a long period in which the parents live alone, often followed by several years of widowhood.

Among Indian families, as we have seen, there is much greater overlap of successive stages. The marriage of a couple and the period to first birth typically take place as part of the growth phase of the husband's natal family. Often the childbearing years occur in the same milieu; sometimes, although it is not approved, a woman may still be bearing children after she has become a grandmother. The phase after the childbearing years tends to be brief or absent because of the short life expectancy. Collver notes that more than half of all marriages in India end before the wife reaches age forty-five because of the death of one of the pair (1963, pp. 86–87).

Nonetheless, family development throughout village India does occur in several stages, distinguishable to the observer and demarcated by the villagers. Marriages, deaths, and formal partition are the main marking events. The marriages of the children are the grand events of a family's career. The new union is only potentially a new family. The potentiality may be realized in short order, as among the lowly poor and the professional elite, or the pair may remain an incipient new family for many years. The stage during which children are born to a couple may cover much the same years as those of child-rearing. The subsequent marriage of sons is seen as part of the family's growth rather than as the harbinger of dispersal. The actual dispersal, through death or partition or both may take a long time in coming to pass, but it finally comes, sometimes with traumatic tension.

Each incipient new family begins through the efforts of an old family to maintain itself. Family members feel obligated to assure the input of new members and to cope with the output of former members. The inflow is of infants and of brides; the outflow is of departing girls and departed souls.

The Recruitment of Males and of Females

Males come into the family at birth and remain until separated by death or partition. If husband and wife find themselves unable to bring forth a son biologically, or if no son survives childhood, they may bring one into the family socially through adoption. The need for adopting a child is indicated in one survey in which over a fifth of the older couples in the sample had no living son. Out of a sample of 626 married women over 50 years of age in Banaras district, 22 percent had no son. About 30 percent had one son alive; less than half enjoyed the security of two or more living sons (Collver 1963, pp. 95–96).

Adoption is firmly rooted in formal law and customary practice. An adopting father takes a boy from his own jati, preferably one who is from his lineage. Among the Pandit Brahmins of Kashmir a man may adopt a boy of his wife's kin if no suitable child of his agnatic line is available (Madan 1965, pp. 82–86).

The incidence of adoptions can be stimulated by economics. In one Mysore village where irrigation has made land far more remunerative than before, the orderly transmittal of an estate is of high importance. Among the landowners, 10 percent of all the males had been adopted. But in a nearby village, where the lands are not irrigated and economic opportunities are not so bound in with the land, only 2 percent of the men of the same jati had been adopted (Epstein 1962, pp. 179, 306). But whatever may be the rate of adoption, it is everywhere in India an approved method of maintaining family development when parturition does not do so.

Another alternative, less commonly taken because of considerations of cost and temperament, is that the husband take another wife, or several, in order to beget a son. Still another alternative is open to a prosperous landowner who has a daughter but not a son. He can arrange a marriage for his daughter to a man who will join his family. The son-in-law helps work the family lands which eventually pass to the daughter's children. This is an inferior kind of marriage for a man, to go to live on the bounty of his father-in-law. Yet there are some such marriages in most places, since an impoverished young man will reckon that the attractions of the estate make up for whatever stigma for him may be involved in the marriage (cf. Klass 1966, p. 960; Madan 1965, pp. 62, 127–128; Fukutake et al. 1964, p. 139).

Whatever means are used to assure the inflow of males, the family members do not usually have to ponder difficult choices or manipulate touchy social considerations. They have only to celebrate a birth with proper ritual or, being convinced that a birth is not forthcoming, to secure a suitable alternative with main dispatch and little fuss.

Marriage, the transfer of a female from one family to another, is commonly a matter of transcendent concern and much activity in both families. It is an inescapable choice point and usually brings into the balance every aspect of the family's status, resources, and social relations. It cannot be avoided, because the person of a pubescent daughter in a household, unwed and unclaimed, is uncomfortable, even ritually dangerous for the other members of the family. It is uncomfortable, because her continuing presence betokens either neglect of duty on their part or grave personal defect on hers. It can be dangerous because her untethered sexuality may bring social disgrace, perhaps supernatural retribution, on the whole family unless she is promptly bound in marriage (cf. Kapadia 1958, p. 140).

The need for marrying off a grown son is not quite so urgently felt as that of marrying a daughter. This is in part because there is not the same spur of fear about his unbespoken sexuality and in part because his status and the reputation of his family do not suf-

fer so much if he remains unmarried. Still, his family should do
their duty by him and do justice to him by getting him married.
Marriage is a sacrament, ordained and imperative, which every
normal man and woman should undergo.

A marriage mobilizes the family's social resources. Through marriage the members renew their kin ties or establish new bonds of
kinship. Celebrating a marriage requires that all who can be genu-
inely counted as kin or allies participate through giving gifts, performing services, or just being present for the occasion. The closest
kin must take part in all these ways. Other related families should
send at least one representative if only to keep alive the kinship
bond. The family's jajmani associates contribute their goods and
services: the barber often acts as go-between and ceremonial assist-
ant, the potter, washerman, and other clients fulfill their roles
in the ritual and receive gifts in return. In a village near Lucknow,
for example, client families of ten different jatis must perform ceremonial roles in the marriage of a landowner's child. In a village of
Mysore, clients of seven jatis assist in marrying off their patron's
child (Majumdar 1958a, pp. 43–49; Epstein 1960, p. 230). A patron
family, in its turn, need not attend the wedding of a child of their
sweeper's family, but that wedding elicits some gifts from every
patron of the sweeper family.

Marriage as Test of Status

On all social levels, a marriage is a test of a family's status. Then
more than at any other time a family's alliances stand forth proven
and personified by gifts and attendance; its status hinges on its
strength in allies and clients. Hence a marriage provides the prime
opportunity for demonstrating and validating family status. A family, like other social units in this society, is hierarchically appraised,
judged by jati fellows and by fellow villagers as superior or inferior to other families.

Such judgments frequently differ on specific rankings but usually
agree on the general position of a family, whether of landowners
or of sweepers, as being among the more eminent or among the
more negligible in its sector of the community. There are some villagers who may not be particularly concerned, in the ordinary
round, with their family's status, but they can scarcely avoid some

such concern when a marriage is to be arranged. A comparative weighing of status factors is built into the process. Even when a marriage takes place within the close circle of kin, as when a man in South India marries his sister's daughter, the family elders must consider the relative advantage of strengthening the family by inner reinforcement as against bolstering its status by external connection.

In the marriage negotiations, the achievements of each family's forebears are weighed, as are the current assets, such as the wealth and power of its members and the personal charm of the principals. Temporal assets do not automatically bestow higher status. They must be used in ways that confer status, and one of the main avenues is through establishing a marriage alliance with a family of unquestioned higher standing. The alliance does not at once make the lower family the absolute equal of the higher, certainly not in those parts of North India where inequality is stipulated through the formal inferiority of every bride's family to that of her groom.

What an advantageous marriage accomplishes for a status-ambitious family is to put its members into the same bracket of rank as the higher family. If previously that higher family had not deigned to take brides from the lower family because it was too poor or undistinguished—though since both were of the same jati they could have done so—the marriage demonstrates for all to see that the lowlier family has risen far enough for the higher to accept one of its daughters. The higher family, in North India, gains by this match through the lavish gifts that the lower gives to its daughter in her married home. The bride's family, in a Muslim village of Punjab where this gift flow has been closely studied, gives about ten times as much in gifts to the groom's family as they receive from them (Eglar 1960, pp. 108–115; Marriott 1962, p. 265).

In some other parts of India, no such formal disparity is required and the two families are expected to be of about the same status. Even in such places there is close examination of the respective status of each to assure that they are really on equal footing. Thus in Ramkheri village of Madhya Pradesh, marriages are arranged between families that are about equal in reputation and wealth. Gift-giving is not heavily one-sided; the groom's family has somewhat greater expenses at the wedding although after the marriage it receives more from the bride's kin. Here, also, a wedding involves great expenditure, much gift-giving, and large attendance by kin and allies of the two families (Mayer 1960, pp. 227–235). Each of the families must be able to contribute an amount appropriate to their mutual, equal status.

A family's status is tested whenever one of its children is married, whether the regional pattern is one of relative equality or of built-in inequality between the contracting families. Status mobility, for a family as for a jati, requires a solid economic base. Wealth is not a sufficient condition for attaining a higher rating, but it is usually a necessary precondition. A very poor family cannot begin to indulge in fancies about raising its status; its members can only marry off a child as best they can.

Under some conditions, economic considerations are given more importance than direct status gain. This has been so in Dalena, the Mysore village whose lands are not irrigated but those of surrounding villages are. Dalena men have nevertheless prospered through the purchase of irrigated lands and through work in a nearby town. They have also increased their marriage alliances with nearby irrigated villages. "As Dalena farmers bought wet lands in neighbouring villages they wanted to strengthen their foothold in these villages by marriage ties" (Epstein 1962, p. 296). Dalena girls, in turn, are sought as wives because families of these other villages like to establish affinal ties with the entrepreneurs and town workers of Dalena.

Experience in the town has become an asset for a prospective groom. This was demonstrated when the daughter of a wealthy traditionalist of Dalena was married to a man of an inferior lineage and from a very poor household of that lineage. The man is a factory worker and is familiar with town ways. When the girl's father appeared uncertain about the match, the suitor got his town friends to convince the father of the suitability of the marriage. For the young man it meant a marked rise in status. His work in the factory enabled him to achieve higher prestige in the traditional social system of the village (Epstein 1962, pp. 296–301; 1960, p. 199). Town and factory affiliations are becoming recognized here as economic assets along with the more traditional economic holdings.

The advantages for the two principals as well as for the two families are not ignored. A family will hesitate to give its daughter in marriage into a village in which there is much conflict or into a family in which the work wlll be extraordinarily hard. But the girl and the boy are not expected to take much part in the family deliberations because their youthful fancies are not very relevant to the serious, long-range considerations that have to be kept paramount in negotiating a marriage alliance.

Explicit Rules for Marriage Alliances

Two kinds of rules are followed in marriage negotiations, explicit structural rules such as those of endogamy and exogamy, and the implicit rules of the game of maneuvering for family advantage. The structural rules require that the couple belong to the same endogamous group, the jati, and also that each spouse come from a different exogamous category within the jati. Each jati defines these categories in its own way and there are myriad elaborations on these rules, but in fundamental outline they are quite similar throughout the land.

Exogamy means that husband and wife may not be related to each other before marriage in ways that are prohibited, quite as incest is prohibited. The tabooed relationships are those of kin position, of kin grouping, and, in some of the northern regions, of locality. Two people in certain specific kin positions are forbidden to marry, as, for example, a man and his mother's sister. Prohibited also are unions within kin groupings, such as between two who are patrilineally descended from the same real or mythical ancestors. In jatis which follow Sanskritic usage, the prohibited kin positions are collectively known as the *Sapinda* relations and are traced through both father and mother. The kin grouping of Sanskrit scripture called *gotra* will be discussed later, as well as similar groupings noted here under the generic term clan. People of all jatis observe some exogamy by kin position and, in many jatis, by clan groupings also (cf. Srinivas 1942, pp. 32–49, 57–65; 1965, pp. 42–46).

Exogamy by locality as well as by kinship is observed in some regions. Over a large part of northern India, husband and wife must not come from the same village or cluster of villages. This local exogamy is found from Bihar to eastern Punjab, in Rajasthan, Gujarat, and into Madhya Pradesh. It does not hold for some of the Himalayan hill people (Berreman 1962d) and its southward limit is reached about the Malwa region of Madhya Pradesh, where marriage within the village is allowed but is uncommon and not very well regarded. An argument sometimes given against intra-village marriages is that children who were reared in the same village may have called each other brother and sister as children and are, in a vague way, related. But the more cogent reason is that such marriages conflict with the proper relationship between spouses and between affinally related families.

The practical reasons for village exogamy are shown in Morton Klass' account of marriage in a West Bengal village. Marriage alliances within the village are permitted there but most marriages are made between families from different villages. The father of a girl knows that she will want to come back for visits as often as possible after her marriage. If she can easily carry her complaints back to her original family and if they can readily attempt to intervene, there may be more tension between the two families than would otherwise occur and more than will be good for the newly married couple and the two affiliated families. Hence a father is reluctant to make a match within the village. "For a number of reasons, which he assesses quite correctly, such conflicts are more likely between families of the same village and less likely between families of different villages" (Klass 1966, p. 966).

The same arguments against intravillage matches are given by the Brahmins of a Kashmir village, even though some 20 percent of their marriages are of this kind. Not only is the assimiliation of a bride to her husband's family impeded if her natal family is in the same village but also the proper superiority of her conjugal over her natal family is awkwardly disarranged if the two are fellow villagers (Madan 1965, pp. 111–112). So also in a hill village of Orissa where village exogamy is not mandatory but is usually practiced. Marriage there "almost always is outside the political community" (Bailey 1960b, p. 168).

Where village exogamy is strictly mandatory, the men who live and work together as agnates are quite insulated from any influence from their respective affines. Harold Gould has noted this in villages of Lucknow district, where only a woman's brother will customarily come to visit her in her conjugal home, and where she must meet him in an outbuilding or in some other place that is separate from the family's main house. These villagers hold that an affine should not make even an occasional intrusion into the place of agnatic solidarity. "The wife ceremonially wails on her brother's shoulder when he comes, an act which announces the continuation of affective ties between a woman and her natal family, and I have observed the considerable strain that crosses the faces of the husband and his agnates on such occasions" (Gould 1961a, p. 298; see also Gould 1960b).

Village exogamy seems to be an outcome not only of a special need for filial-fraternal solidarity, but also of special fear for the fragility of those bonds. The wives in a family and their natal kinsmen are apparently perceived as potential sources of family disruption. Hence the wives should be isolated from their original kin, which also means that their husbands, in their roles as brothers, are equally isolated from their own beloved sisters.

That isolation is additionally marked in those parts of North India where another rule (noted later in the discussion of hypergamy) is added to village exogamy. There, if *any* family of Village A has taken a bride from Village B, a girl of Village A, of *any* jati, must never be given in marriage to Village B. As between any two villages, all in one must be the marital superiors to their respective jati fellows in the other (Karve 1965, p. 125). I have seen an old woman of a village in Delhi State, senior enough not to have to veil her face before men, do so nevertheless when a young man of another village came in, because he had married a daughter of her village. All in her village were obliged to show respect to one who had married a village daughter. Another kind of village exogamy is that exemplified in Rampur village also near Delhi, where a bride may not be taken from any contiguous village or from those in which the bridegroom's clan is well represented (Lewis 1958, p. 161; Karve 1965, pp. 119–120).

Where marriage within the village is permitted, the villagers are not necessarily less concerned with filial-fraternal solidarity but, rather, more influenced by other factors. In the Himalayan village of Sirkanda, as Berreman explains, in-village marriage seems to be preferred because a woman is an economic asset and relatively independent, and marriageable women are quite scarce. A young wife can readily leave her husband and return to her natal family if she does not like her marital home, a possibility not usually open to village women in the Hindi-speaking area. A woman of this hill region is more apt to stay with her husband if her own parents are nearby. Hence marriage within the village helps a family keep a young wife (Berreman 1962d).

In South India also, marriages within a village are permitted, possibly because of the importance of strengthening existing kinship ties. This will be noted in the later discussion of the extensions of kinship. The differences in exogamy and other kinship patterns between North and South have been described by Mrs. Karve who postulates four zones, each characterized by certain family and kinship usages. In addition to a northern and southern zone, she delineates a central zone culturally and geographically intermediate between the two, and also an eastern zone, mainly of tribal groups (Karve 1953; revised edition 1965). Mrs. Karve's pioneering work has opened the way for further studies of kinship and marriage practices in India.

Jati endogamy is the other part of the explicit rules for marriage, on which, as has been noted, the whole system is seen to rest by those who maintain it. We need only repeat here that a village couple must stem from two families that have historically belonged, because of their common attributes, to the same set of intermarrying families. That historical nexus is usually accounted for in myth, bolstered by ritual, manifest in daily practice, and maintained by forces within and outside the jati. Yet there are ways of reinterpreting the history and of readjusting the boundaries of the endogamous group. Those boundaries are more inviolate in the villager's notion of their society than is sometimes the case in actuality.

Implicit Rules and General Procedures

Rules for exogamy and endogamy are quite explicitly expressed, other rules for marriage are usually less explicitly stated. Within each jati's code of exogamy and endogamy, marriage negotiations follow a complex series of stylized maneuvers and spontaneous manipulations. Among very poor families the preliminaries are brief, the matter quickly settled. But with families of any jati who have something to bargain about, who can afford to aspire to better place, or who strive to maintain their traditional position, the negotiations are typically intricate. They follow an unwritten game theory that is well understood by the participants, certainly by the adept marriage brokers and go-betweens. Each family attempts to maximize its gain through the marriage and to minimize any loss, either in status, wealth, or the welfare of its child. Each brings to bear whatever resources it has; if it is deficient in one kind of resource it plays up its other strengths. A family with a dim-witted, torpid son uses its wealth and influence to secure a passable bride for him. A family whose son has a research degree and a foot in the higher civil service can arrange a match that bejewels the family with dowry, prestige, and the comely person of the bride.

The negotiations are usually initiated by the family of a girl. This is in accord with traditional prescription and with the fact that a girl's family feels under pressure of time as a boy's family does not. A girl has only a short period during which she is properly eligible for marriage. After that, as has been noted, her unmarried state raises questions and dark suspicions. In the quest, the searchers look for a boy with suitable family and personal attributes. His family should be of somewhat higher status within the jati (or certainly not lower), of the proper exogamous group, and a family that is not likely to inflict undue hardship on a young wife. In his person the boy should be active, healthy, somewhat older than the girl, not unusually disfavored in appearance, and of a suitable level of education. The family of the boy looks for counterpart attributes in the girl; her demeanor, health, and diligence are politely but firmly ascertained. Fairness of skin is a decided boon as is also her general attractiveness of appearance.

The wealth of the bride's family is particularly important among northern jatis, because her natal family must be perpetual donors. Among many of the jatis of the South, there is some notion that the groom's family should be the wealthier, but this is mitigated by the concurrent idea that the bride should be from a closely related family and that her family should be the principal givers after the wedding (Beals and Siegel 1966, pp. 43–46; Klass 1966, pp. 960–962; Orenstein 1965a, pp. 48–50; Lewis 1958, pp. 159–195; Madan 1965, pp. 112–113).

These are some of the premises for negotiation; all are in some degree negotiable. Each side is alert to its own advantage and the family's long-run gain, but this does not mean that one side must lose in the transaction. The mutually desired outcome is that both sides should feel that they have gained. To advance this end there are ritual devices by which, once the collective bargaining is over and agreement reached, the two sides ritually signify their present and future amity (cf. Epstein 1960, p. 204).

Ordinarily both sides do gain, though not the same things. When a family has wealth but low status in the jati, its members will usually try to make an alliance with a family that needs the wealth and can impart better status. The drive for social mobility, which animates the social system and which, as will be discussed later, has made for recurrent change in it, is typically expressed by villagers when they act as members of their smallest social unit, the family, as well as when they act as participants in larger groups and groupings. A family's status, like the ritual purity of its members and the ranking of its jati, requires continual revalidation. Family prestige can, in some degree, be transmitted through a marriage alliance, unlike ritual purity and jati rank, which cannot be imparted across families. Families that have no great imbalance between resources and respectability, tend to seek alliances with families that are about equal, or, under hypergamy, as nearly equal as the hypergamic rules permit.

A marriage alliance always entails some redistribution of wealth as well as of persons. The rules for that redistribution vary among regions. In a good many jatis of South India, the family of the groom pays bride wealth at marriage to the family of the bride (Karve 1965, p. 180; Srinivas 1942, pp. 14–21). After marriage, however, the woman's family continue to give gifts to her and her children. In most of North India it is the family of the bride that gives a dowry to the groom and his family, with little or no return from them. In all regions, the negotiators must reach agreement on the exact amounts of gifts in money and kind that are to be given before, during, and after the wedding. The principal payments, whether dowry or bride wealth, are intended to stabilize the marriage, to benefit the girl, and, if magnanimous, to enhance the prestige of the donors.

Dowries are usually given by those who maintain marked status differentials within their jati and who assume the bridegroom's family to be superior to the bride's family (cf. Yalman 1967, pp. 172–177, 352). Bride wealth rather than dowry is given where women are strong economic assets to a family, where they are relatively independent, and where they are relatively scarce. Thus among

some of the Pahari-speaking people of the Himalayas a bride price
is paid at marriage and the transaction is initiated by the groom's
family. Women there are more independent socially, more valuable
economically, and proportionally fewer than they are in the plains
below the Pahari villages (Berreman 1962d, p. 57).

The type of marriage payment which is customarily given may
vary among the jatis of a village. In Gaon village of Poona district,
the higher jatis pay dowries, while bride price is customary among
the Harijan jatis. But even in the higher jatis of Gaon the family
of a man may pay bride wealth if their son has personal defects and
if the maiden is especially attractive (Orenstein 1965a, p. 50).

Arranging for the marriage of children is a critical responsibility
for the head of a family, and many men come to find themselves
under severe pressure on that account both from inside and outside
the family. An example of a particularly difficult series of choices
occurs in a study of a village near the city of Baroda in Gujarat.
The landowners are of the Leva jati of Patidars. Each Patidar jati-
group belongs to one of the ranked, hypergamous sections of its
jati. The Patidars of this village, though landowners, belong to one
of the low sections. Their girls can marry into a higher section but
their boys can only marry a girl of an equally low Patidar level. As
a result there is a shortage of girls for the Patidar boys of this village to marry because many of their girls have married into higher
sections. The shortage is aggravated by the higher ratio of males to
females and by the fact that widowers—though not widows—may
remarry, and some of these take young girls (Poffenberger and
Pandya, MS. n.d.; see also Fukutake et al. 1964, p. 60).

Consequently a Patidar father of this village must give a dowry
in order to get his daughter suitably married into a higher section
and must pay a bride price in order to get a Patidar girl for his son
at all. A few men remain unmarried, more marry girls of lower,
non-Patidar jatis. When this occurs the family tries to convince the
other villagers that she is a Patidar and their neighbors are willing
to go along with that fiction publicly. But they well know which
of the village wives were born Patidars and which were not. Of
twenty-seven Patidar couples mentioned in the study, two-thirds of
the wives had been taken from a lower jati.

In one family with three sons and two daughters, the father
steadfastly refused to sacrifice his daughter's marriage prospects for

those of his sons. He tried to arrange for a Patidar bride for his eldest son but the bride price needed was more than he could muster and he finally had to get a bride of lower, carpenter, jati for his first-born son. He could have secured a large sum by marrying his daughter to a family of low section but refused to do so since that would have been a greater blow to his family status than was arranging an inferior match for his eldest son. So he married his elder daughter into a higher village and had to give a large dowry. This drain meant that there was no capital available for the marriage of his second son who, at age thirty-four, was still unmarried and kept protesting until he reached the point of refusing to work the family lands.

The youngest son, interestingly, gave his father no trouble in the matter of marriage. He is both physically handsome and able enough to have done a year of college work and to have secured a post as a teacher. He was a good enough match to marry into a Patidar family of equal status, and after his first wife's death, to marry again and even to obtain a token dowry. This case illustrates several factors in marriage negotiations: the different circumstances under which dowry or bride wealth may be given, the covert transgression of jati endogamy under dire necessity, the weight of personal attractiveness, and particularly the greater importance for a family's reputation that is often attached to the proper marriages of its daughters than to the marriages of its sons.

The education of his daughter may present a knotty problem to a father. If she can read and write there may be no difficulty and some advantage on that score in getting a daughter married. But if she has gone through secondary school, it may be hard to find a groom for her whose family will be willing to take in an educated girl. They may fear that she will not make a proper, dutiful wife because of her schooling. If there are a good many educated men in her jati, education can be an asset to a marriageable girl, but if there are few she may have been educated beyond her marriage bracket.

The situation in some village families is all the more difficult for college-educated girls. The village father who encourages his daughter to take a college degree when there are few male college graduates in the jati may be accused of sacrificing his daughter's chances in life to a mistaken whim intended to glorify his own name. Moreover, a family whose sons and daughters are educated beyond the usual level of their jati and village may be thought to be presumptuous. Unless they are skillful in mollifying their kinsmen and neighbors, they may become a target for opposition.

Yet education is now seen by villagers as a generally desirable asset, for the sake of one's child as well as for the good of a family. Educated boys and their families increasingly, as we shall note again later, insist on a bride with an education suitable to the education of the groom. Thus, as more boys receive high school or college education, the incentive to educate girls also increases.

Providing a suitable dowry for a marriageable daughter is a common problem for families. It is often a difficult, burdensome matter, but it is an imperative of the system of family and jati. To skimp on the dowry is not only to put one's own child at a disadvantage but also to demean the whole family. So although social reformers have long opposed the payment of large dowries and legislators have tried to limit dowry size, a father faced with the problem rarely has the heart to heed the reformers' arguments (with which he may agree) rather than to promote his daughter's welfare. Nor does he usually have the fortitude to follow the law rather than his wife's urging. And the payment of the dowry is only one part of the total expense of a marriage.

The redistribution of wealth affects many more people than just the members of the two principal families. A wedding can be used to activate a network of gift-giving involving families of different jatis as well as kin. A newly prosperous villager can give generous gifts at a wedding to people with whom he could not previously have afforded to exchange gifts or favors. Establishing a wider range of gift-giving brings returns in power as well as in prestige to a magnanimous donor because, as we shall discuss below, the recipients are more apt to support the gift-givers in the perennial contentions of village life. The distribution of wealth, like the alliance itself, entails both explicit and implicit rules. Which family gives more, what kinds of gifts are given and to whom, are explicitly stipulated by village and jati consensus. The amounts to be given to jajmani associates are sometimes stipulated in a written code (cf. Lewis 1958, p. 163). But just how much is given, in what proportions and under what circumstances, is finally determined only after playing the serious game of negotiating a match.

Precautions: Astrology and Prepuberty Marriage

So momentous is the occasion of marriage that several kinds of precautions may be taken to minimize the uncertainties involved in the decision. Astrology is one such means; arranging prepuberty marriages is another.

All marriage plans must reckon with the supernatural forces that affect the course of every critical venture—auspicious and inauspicious days, favorable and unfavorable omens, the horoscopes of the couple and their astrological congruence. Through astrology man's uncertainty about his personal fate is made more tolerable. One's fate is seen as linked in a grand mechanism of astral spheres, which move in preordained and predictable cycles across the firmament of time. The fortunes of persons and societies move in conformity with the celestial cycles. Each person—better, each soul—becomes geared into the cosmic movement at the moment of birth. The nature of his entrainment is forever determined at that moment when his personal fate latches into the grand apparatus. One's horoscope reveals how his life fits into the celestial progression to which all life attaches. The fate so ordained for one person may be forecast as being utterly incompatible with that of another; if the two join their lives in marriage only disaster for them can ensue, and so any plans for their union must be abandoned.

Yet astrology is a flexible art, not entirely impervious to manipulation. It is always possible for determined matchmakers to seek another, more favorable reading from a different astrologer. Conversely, should one side want to withdraw tactfully from a proposal, it is sometimes possible to locate an astrologer whose examination of the two horoscopes will find an insuperable bar to the match.

Astrology, as part of the Sanskrit tradition, is used for planning marriages by those who guide their rituals according to Sanskrit scripture. A person's horoscope among such families is consulted at every juncture of his career, sometimes with far-reaching results.[1]

---

[1] A former Chief Justice of India, Mehr Chand Mahajan, tells in his autobiography that immediately after his birth the family astrologers declared that the moment had been so disastrously inauspicious that the infant's father would surely die if he saw the face of his son. So the infant was taken away

In the middle and lower jatis, especially in South India, there are many who make no use of astrology. But peoples of all jatis believe in auspicious and inauspicious days and in favorable and unfavorable omens. These beliefs postulate a similar, though simpler, view of grand, impersonal mechanisms, which affect each life and through which each person must thread his fate.

There is a certain parallel between these beliefs and the people's theory of a caste society. In both instances the universal structure, of fate and of society, is seen as absolutely decreed and, in the large, immutable. Yet within both these fixed frames men try hard to better their position and that of their kin.

Another way of reducing the uncertainties of a complex marriage negotiation is to make a definite agreement before the prospective bride reaches puberty. Then all can proceed according to a clear schedule without pressure of the problem of the girl's sexuality. She begins full marital life soon after menarche. In some jatis the exact interval is prescribed, thus for certain Brahmins the nuptial rites that mark the start of sexual relations traditionally took place sixteen days after the onset of first menstruation. This firm calendar is not the only advantage of celebrating the formal wedding before the bride's—or even the groom's—puberty. Another advantage is that each family can immediately benefit by whatever advantages it has achieved through the alliance. This status capital can then be used to push its ranking still higher in other negotiations.

Prepuberty marriages have been forbidden in a series of legislative acts of both the British regime and the independent government of India. But there is still great pressure on the head of a family to make suitable arrangements for a girl's marriage as soon as it is feasible to do so. Though the median age of marriage for girls in India has been rising in recent decades and has gone up dramatically in some places, it is still relatively low. The system of village family life militates against any general rise in age at marriage substantial

---

to be raised in an isolated hamlet by a family of a different jati. After seven years his father succeeded in getting a new reading from a council of astrologers, that the boy had been born under a very lucky conjunction and that he would become a great man, a judge or a minister (Prime Minister of princely Kashmir as it turned out, as well as Chief Justice of republican India). His mother and grandmother took him back, but it was not until five years later that his father mustered enough courage, amid lavish ritual precautions, to look at the face of his son (Mahajan 1963, pp. 3–7).

enough to affect the fertility rate significantly (Srinivas 1965, pp. 38–40; Goode 1963, pp. 232–236; Karve 1965, pp. 73–74, 126–127; Mandelbaum 1954a).

Marriage Links and Communication among Villages

A family with both ambition and means is likely to search as far afield for a prospective spouse as it can, because a wider radius of search produces more alternatives from which to select the best alliance. Families of the higher and wealthier jatis usually bring in brides from a wider territory than do lower groups. Thus the average distance of the bride's village is 37.5 miles in the highest bloc of jatis of a village in Faizabad District (U.P.) while the average distance for the next lower blocs is 6.4 and 7.5 miles (Gould 1960b, p. 486).

A similar spread can occur within a jati, as it does among the Noniyas (earthworkers by traditional occupation) of Senapur in U.P. In that village, the average distance of Noniya marriage alliances is 12 miles, the nearest affinal link being 3 miles and the farthest 55 miles. But among the educated people of the jati who live in towns as professional men or government officials, there is a different marriage network, mainly with similarly wealthy and elite families. This net has a much broader range, extending for a few families to as far as three hundred miles. But for families whose wedding parties and visitors must come by oxcart or local bus, no such extensive and expensive range is possible; the bulk of their marriage alliances are made within a quite compact territory. The shape of that territory is defined as much by the main travel routes and by the existence of previous alliances as it is by physical distance alone (Rowe 1960, pp. 301, 307; Gould 1960b, pp. 481–482; Miller 1954).

Other influences on the radius of matrimonial alliance are geographic distribution and jati power. Thus in Rampur, near Delhi, two of the lower groups have a much greater average distance for matrimonial alliance than do the two highest jatis. The dominant Jats and the Brahmins bring brides from an average of about 12.5 miles while the low Chamars average 20 miles and the Nais, barbers, average about 24 miles. The Nais have only a few families in any one village and so must sometimes reach far to find an eligible bride or groom. The Chamars have long struggled against the overlord Jats and have recently found good jobs away from the village. With more resources and rekindled hope they are probably seeking a broader base of power beyond the close neighborhood of their village (Lewis 1958, p. 161).

The outer limits of search for a spouse are set by the boundaries of the linguistic region. Very rarely is a village girl married into a family which uses a language different from her own. Within the linguistic bounds, each jati-group of a village has its own usual range of intermarriage. Their jati fellows within this range are known to them, relationships with their families are easily traced, ancestry and familial characteristics can be ascertained, marriage customs are mutually shared and understood.[2]

These families and jati-groups, as Klass notes of a West Bengal village, constitute the villagers' effective jati. A family does not like to marry its daughter beyond that circle because visits will then be infrequent and expensive, so most marriages in this village are arranged within a radius of from five to ten miles (Klass 1966, pp. 960–966). Here also a wealthy, ambitious family can afford the greater expense of a more distant marriage and may seek such a match for the prestige it will bring.

Within a jati's geographic spread, some areas may be more prestigious than others. Among Rajputs, for example, the more westerly or northerly are the higher and there is a general tendency to marry daughters to the west and take brides from the east. This is the way it is often put, though the phrasing more consistent with Rajput

[2] Calculations of average marriage distance are available for a few villages. Thus in Haripura in Mysore, 21 percent of 397 marriages of villagers are within the village, 57 percent within a radius of five miles, and the rest mainly within 15 miles (Dhillon 1955, pp. 75–76). In Wangala, also in Mysore, 50 percent of existing marriages are within 4 miles, 82 percent within 10 miles, and 9 percent outside a radius of 20 miles (Epstein 1962, p. 169). A much wider range is given for Shamirpet in Andhra Pradesh. Of 380 marriages, 68 percent are within a radius of 35 miles, 30 percent were farther, up to 60 miles, and 2 percent even more distant that that (Dube 1955b, p. 54).

In Ramkheri in Madhya Pradesh, the average distance village girls go is 12.8 miles for Rajputs and 12.5 miles for Farmers. Brides are brought in for these two jati-groups at an average distance of 17 and 11.8 miles respectively. Cotton-carders go a bit farther afield, 18.6 and 19.7 miles (Mayer 1960, p. 210).

practice is that girls are married into families that live in the direction of upstream on the main rivers, and girls are taken from the downstream direction (Karve 1965, p. 125; Mayer 1960, pp. 211–212).

One important outcome of this seeking for family and jati advantage in marriage is that every person is tied into a network of social relations extending across many villages, and each person's network is linked to innumerable other networks. For all the social avoidance and segregation inherent in a local caste system, there is no sharp break in communications and relations among the local systems of Indian culture and society. "This small village of 150 households," Lewis says of Rampur, "may therefore be seen as forming the locus of affinal kinship ties with over four hundred other villages. . . . This rural cosmopolitanism provides a striking contrast with the characteristic village isolation found in rural Mexico" (1958, pp. 161–162).

It is a salient fact of Indian society that the people of one village are in touch with kin in scores, often hundreds, of other villages. An analysis of 446 marriages in Ramkheri showed affinal relations with 219 villages (Mayer 1960, p. 208; see also Rowe 1960, p. 299; Mayer 1962; Cohn and Marriott 1958). The multiple interlacing of villages is primarily a function, not of polity or economy, but of jati and of family. In their totality these lively networks profoundly influence the whole culture and society, but each link is fashioned with an eye to the welfare of a little domestic group, its status, its economic advantage, and, by no means the least, the future well-being of its child.

This is true even where marriages within a village are permitted, as they are in Wangala in Mysore. There 85 percent of the couples studied come from different villages; the couples were of the dominant peasant jati, traced over four generations.[3] A village is far from

_____

[3] In recent years there has been an increase in marriages within this village because of a special economic influence. The whole range of the villagers' social relations has been narrowed because their energies are concentrated on growing sugar cane and under the quite exceptional local conditions of sugar production, in which a state-owned factory takes care of marketing and managerial functions, they do not need wide social contacts. Hence when only the currently existing marriages are tabulated, 42 percent are within the village and 58 percent between villages.

A different trend has occurred in the nearby village of Dalena. As noted being an isolated and insulated community; each has been continually affected by influences from beyond the village bounds. Not the least of these outside influences is brought in by the wives.

The Wedding

After the negotiations are completed, the wedding is solemnized and enjoyed. A wedding not only confirms a particular couple's union and the alliance of families, it also affirms the centrality of marital union in the universe of man and God (cf. Hsu 1963, pp. 31, 185–186). It proclaims the alliance so that all people in each family's social orbit may know of it. The immense importance attached to weddings throughout village India is reflected in the example of wedding expenditures in two Mysore villages where these costs have been studied.

A wedding is the largest single expense that most families have to bear. Weddings in Wangala, Mrs. Epstein notes, provide a principal step in the struggle for status. The groom's family in this region bears most of the wedding costs. A family of the very poorest level spends (in 1955 prices) about Rupees 272 to marry a son, a relatively poor farmer family Rs. 1,218, a richer farmer Rs. 2,110, and one of the very richest, "magnate" families Rs. 2,866. The very poorest family, with exceedingly little to spare, still manages to pour out three or four months' income on the marriage rites. The relatively rich families devote close to a year's total income to marry each son.[4]

When the total cash expenditures, those made by everyone in

---

above, their lands did not get irrigation as did the villages all about them and Dalena people had to enlarge their social relations if they were to benefit from the prosperity of the region. Hence the proportion of intervillage marriages rose from 44 percent in the four-generation record to 69 percent in existing marriages (Epstein 1962, pp. 167–169, 296–297).

[4] Mrs. Epstein estimates the average monthly income per consumption unit in Wangala at Rs. 33. Men older than fourteen are counted as one consumption unit, women and children at given fractions of a consumption unit. The poorest households have a monthly expenditure per consumption unit of Rs. 10 to 15 (1962, p. 342). I have based the estimated proportion of income devoted to weddings on rough extrapolations from these figures. A similar estimate, that between six months' to more than a year's income is spent on a wedding, is given for weddings in Ramkheri in Madhya Pradesh (Mayer 1960, p. 227).

Wangala during 1955, were calculated, it was found that 4 percent of that total was spent on weddings. Savings in this prospering village came to 16 percent of the average monthly budget. "Most of the savings are spent on weddings when economic differentiation displays itself in lavish feasts" (Epstein 1962, pp. 101, 108, 110). That is, when family wealth is translated into family prestige.

In the contrasting village of Dalena, where people have been impelled to turn outward while the Wangala villagers were turning inward, the struggle for prestige among middle-farmers is differently expressed. They think it more important to have a bicycle or a watch and similar possessions than to give a lavish wedding feast. Such personal possessions bring prestige both in town and village, while wedding expenditures impress mainly one's fellow villagers. Hence weddings are less expensive in Dalena than in Wangala and are one-day affairs rather than three-day celebrations as is normal in Wangala. For all that, Dalena people still spend a very sizable sum on weddings. A typical wedding expenditure budget for one of the poorest families is Rs. 225, for a poor farmer Rs. 712, for a rich farmer Rs. 895, and for a "magnate" Rs. 2,402. Despite the partial eclipse of weddings as occasions for prestige gain, the chief lender of money in Dalena attempted to improve his social status by staging a very costly wedding for his son. And Dalena farmers whether of the richer or the poorer class, still lay out a good part of a year's income on the wedding of a son (Epstein 1962, pp. 263–266).

As will be noted again in discussing social mobility, marriage remains a chief means of social rise for a family within its jati and a costly wedding is a main feature of a prestigious alliance. This holds through all social levels. Magnates and maharajahs have been known to impoverish their fortunes by grand marriages for their children. At the other pole, the Harijans may keep themselves in economic servitude, as they do in one Mysore village, mainly because of their passion for expensive marriage celebrations (Harper 1965).

Among the vast majority of India's people, a wedding is at once a culmination and a beginning, a demonstration and a test, a stage and a theater, an affirmation and a consolidation. It is the climax of the negotiations and the formal beginning of the new relationship. It is the grand occasion demonstrating the family's social worth through the participation of kin, jati fellows, village neighbors, and prestigious friends. Certain measures of their esteem are quite precise, as when the size of each gift and the name of its donor are loudly announced to the assembled guests.

It is both a demonstration and a test of status. Here, best of all, a family's claim to eminence can be gauged by the wealth, power, and purity that its members mobilize for the event. Also tested and demonstrated in the festivities are the relative standings of the guests: Who is accorded precedence by the hosts, who sits near whom, what courtesies are extended to which guests? All these proclaim relative rank among individuals within a jati as they do also among jatis. For this reason a wedding may be shot through with factional bickering and may become a scene of high tension.

For the principal actors the wedding provides the stage for a supreme pageant. It is an exalted occasion for the bride and groom; both are temporarily transfigured into a regal or divine pair and "the aura which shines around them also touches the members of their families" (Dumont 1959, p. 519). It is a theater for aesthetic enjoyment of many kinds—of the quality of the musicians, of the munificence of the bride's jewels and costumes, even of the elegance of the groom's equipage. A counterpoint of humor often sparkles through the solemnities, as in the chorus of bawdy songs sung by neighbor women and in the more private but equally ribald jokes made by the guests.

All major rites affirm, in a kind of metalanguage, a people's leading values: as principal nodes of social life in India, weddings are used to affirm a number of values. Some of these affirmations are in the ritual itself, others in what appears as byplay. There are certain ritual patterns by which the hopes and expectations for the marriage are expressed. Typically these include symbolic expressions of the couple's unity (as in taking steps together), some ritual action to show their new relation to each other and to their respective families, and ritual acts done together before the deities to invoke divine blessings and at the same time to proclaim the new social fact before society (cf. Lewis 1958, pp. 162–195; Madan 1965, pp. 117–121; Srinivas 1965, pp. 47–50).

In addition to such formal avowals, unscheduled assertions may crop up at a wedding. Just as tensions about disputed rank or village factions often intrude into the occasion, so also may the tensions between the newly allied families. Thus Mrs. Tilak in describing her wedding in a Maharashtra village about 1880 notes that "On those occasions the bridegroom is encouraged to have a fit of the sulks." Her bridegroom was instructed to ask for the gift of a ring and to sulk until he was promised it. But he tired of the tactic quickly, joined the wedding party and so forced his family to come along with him to the wedding feast. "There was none of the usual quarrelling and ill-feeling from beginning to end" (1950, p. 12). Such trials of strength between the two families at the time of marriage are still common. Where the two families are about equal, members of each want to make sure that the other does not arrogate undue superiority. In those regions where one is formally inferior to the other, its members want to show that there is a limit to the inferiority they will accept. A main theme of village drama, as Beals notes for Gopalpur village, concerns this tension (1962, p. 24).

Yet a wedding is a force for social consolidation. The alliance is formed; despite bickerings and other signs of tension, the bond is sealed. Each family, in rallying its kin and supporters, revitalizes its ties with other families of jati and village. It also keeps going, through the wedding and all the rest of the marriage complex, the endless cycle of family life and thus of society itself.

CHAPTER 7 Family Cycle: Growth and Completion

THE advent of brides and the birth and rearing of their children constitute the growth phase of the family cycle. A common turning point occurs with the death of the family head. If several married brothers then remain in the household, there usually follows a period in which divisive strains mount. In time these strains lead to formal partition. The brothers separate into nuclear families and then as their children reach marriageable age, the cycle returns to the growth stage. Though daughters leave the household, sons' wives and sons' children come into the family. These cyclical phases, described by Gould for North India, occur in families of the other regions as well (Gould 1965a, pp. 39–41; 1965c, pp. 182–184).

The Growth Phase: the Rearing of Children

The bride settles in and in time brings forth her child, the family's child. Within the family circle the child learns the fundamentals of his culture and society; he is taught to become the kind of person who will, in his turn, fulfill the appropriate roles of family and society. This process is shown in a study of child rearing in Khalapur village, some ninety miles north of Delhi. The authors of this study observed family life in a sample of families from the dominant Rajput jati of the village (Minturn and Hitchcock 1963; paperbound edition 1966). These Rajputs take great pride in their warrior tradition and many of the men still uphold the traditional mode of family relations.

Among them, as elsewhere in village India, the way in which childbirth is managed foreshadows the expectations that the family has for the newly arrived member and the fundamental cultural lesson that the child will later be taught (cf. Gideon 1962). The notion of pollution is inherent in these practices. The newborn infant arrives in a highly polluting state and must be carefully and gradually brought into a safer ritual and social condition. Physiological processes have produced the baby, but it is only after the family performs the proper ritual that the infant becomes a member of society. Society, not nature, has the decisive word in adding a new person to its number.

The sharp difference between the status of male and female, a difference that runs through all social relations, is presaged by the kind of welcome given to a newborn son—with drumming, singing, and proud public announcements—in contrast to that accorded to a new daughter, whose advent is more quietly observed. The formal inferiority of girls to boys seems mitigated in this village, as was noted before, by the mothers' attitudes; in any event girls show little suffering on that score. But one result of this differential interest is that fewer girl babies survive, not because they are deliberately neglected but rather because much greater medical efforts are usually made to cure a sick baby boy than a sick infant girl. The infant mortality rate for boys in one Khalapur sample was 25 percent, for girls 41 percent (Minturn and Hitchcock 1963, p. 284). A similar mortality differential has been noted in successive reports of the Census of India and the same reasons, the relative favoring of boys rather than any deliberate neglect of girls, have been adduced for it (Gait 1913, p. 218; Blunt 1939, p. 70; Goode 1963, pp. 235–236).

As a Rajput child in this village begins to speak and can be trained, the most common form of punishment is scolding. A usual form of scolding is to call the child by a "derogatory but not obscene name"; that is, by the name of either of the two lowest jatis, the leatherworkers or the sweepers (Minturn 1963, p. 327). What he must not touch and who he should not be are inculcated as soon as the child can understand anything. The training repeatedly reinforces the idea that there is a hierarchy of relations, inside and outside the family, and that a proper child carefully observes the proprieties of subordinate and superior roles.

The domestic arrangements drive home this lesson. In Khalapur, as in many North Indian villages, men and women have virtually separate quarters; the women of the family usually do not enter onto the platform where the men spend most of their leisure time, asleep and awake. The men typically come into the women's quarters for some specific purpose, and, having accomplished that purpose, leave. Young children scoot fairly freely between the two, and they early become aware of the women's quick covering of the face when an elder man of the family enters and of his warning cough before he comes into the women's area. Social distance, respect avoidance, and hierarchical calibration of action are daily made manifest to the child in his own home.

The child, as junior in the household, must soon be taught deference and obedience. The virtues that Rajput parents in Khalapur most emphasized in interviews were obedience, politeness, peaceableness. But Rajputs pride themselves also as being a martial, dominant people, so while obedience in the family is emphasized, dominance over social inferiors is tacitly encouraged. Perhaps because of these conflicting injunctions, that the child must be quite deferent to some and quite imperious toward others, the Khalapur children did not seem to the observers to be particularly well trained. They were not quick to obey their mothers, nor were they closely attentive to the orders of their fathers (Minturn 1963, pp. 338–340).

The ways in which adults discipline and reward children in Khalapur, as everywhere, vary among individuals, between men and women, and according to kinship roles. But all agreed on one principle of child training: a child should not be praised to his face lest this make him disobedient. One Khalapur man summed it up in these words: "If we praise, the child will think that we love him too much and then he will not be under our control" (*ibid.*, p. 325). This explanation can be interpreted to mean that control of the child is of paramount importance. He must be trained to be properly deferent, suitably observant of the hierarchy of family relations. Yet his deference and his adherence to the hierarchy cannot be taken for granted; they are jeopardized if the child hears himself praised, "loved too much," and so gets an overweening sense of his own importance. And a child, or anyone, who comes to feel so important will not easily accept subordinate status and the deferent demeanor that must go with it.

These men tend to blame the women for disregarding this

principle. Although the observers "almost never heard a woman praise a child, the men complained that women lost control of children because of too much praise" (Minturn and Lambert 1964, p. 232). A child is indeed praised sometimes and held up as a model for other children, but not in his presence. Nor should parents praise their own children in any company lest the evil eye be attracted. Excellence, immoderately flaunted, draws envy if not malevolence.

Similar testimony about not praising children comes from a study by Joan Mencher of child rearing among the Nayars of Angadi village in Calicut district. (Khalapur is within sight of the Himalayas; Angadi is on the tropical coastal strip of Kerala.) In both places the views on this fundamental aspect of child rearing are alike. In Angadi all praise is suspect. It is taken either as untrue or if true as dangerous. The danger lies partly in encouraging the praised one to "take advantage." The latter explanation was given by everyone who was interviewed on this question. As one Angadi villager commented about praising children, "We won't say anything nice to them, feeling that if we say it out like that they will take advantage. So praise and affection will be in our mind only. . . ." All through a villager's life in Angadi this attitude prevails. People have a natural desire to be praised and also a fear of praising. It is almost impossible to accept praise easily as being well deserved (Mencher 1963, p. 62).[1]

There are other parallels in child rearing between these two villages at opposite ends of the subcontinent. In the southern village as in the northern, a child "should, above all, be obedient and respectful to elders." The Nayar child in Angadi is not encouraged to assert himself, not rewarded for being self-reliant or innovative; much the same is true for the Rajput child in Khalapur (Mencher 1963, p. 57; Minturn 1963, p. 359).

The pressures on these Rajput boys change as they begin to

---

[1] The taboo on praising children is not equally observed everywhere in India (cf. Kennedy 1954, p. 168; Cormack 1961, p. 62). Urban, educated mothers, possibly because of acquaintance with Western child-rearing practices, do not observe it as do mothers in the two villages that have been cited. And yet in interviews with eighteen such women, mothers of children in the Baroda University nursery school, five said that a child should not be praised to his face because it would make the child "too proud," two that a child should not be praised at all, and two that a child should not be praised when others are present (Poffenberger 1964).

spend more time in the men's area. As early as six years of age and no later than twelve or fourteen, they move out of the women's quarters entirely. They are then under stricter discipline and are exposed to masculine values, particularly in respect to aggression and quarrels. Women do not try to pass on their personal quarrels to their children; a woman will usually allow her child to play with children of a mother with whom she is at odds or whose family is antagonistic to her own. But the men take care to instill their posture of loyalty or hatred. They warn their boys not to play with boys who belong to a hostile lineage. They are equally careful to point out the family's allies and the neutrals as well as the opponents. Men feel that they cannot afford to be passive about antagonisms. Each family has enemies in the village; any one of them may in a fit of temper, drink, or zeal, decide to settle a grievance with a "conversation of sticks." A youth must be ready to defend himself and his family in physical combat (Minturn 1963, p. 332).

There is a marked change in what is expected of these boys and girls as they grow into adolescence. The shift is more gradual for the boys and takes place within the roles they have had all their lives, as sons, nephews, brothers. But the girls, in Khalapur as in other villages, must change more abruptly from one set of roles to another, from being daughter and sister to becoming daughter-in-law and wife. Both changes bring on a sharp stiffening of discipline after a relatively permissive childhood.

A Cross-Cultural Study of Child Rearing

The study of these Rajput families is part of a comparative study of child rearing in six societies. The data from Khalapur have been compared with similar data from villages in Mexico, the Philippines, Okinawa, Kenya, and from an American town in New England (Whiting 1963, pp. 1–13). Among the six, the sample from Khalapur village was low in training for self-reliance; it was also low in training for responsibility in domestic and farm tasks. The latter is congruent with the actual social situation of the Rajputs of this village; their associates and servants are responsible to them for providing goods and services. Their pride is in their warrior virtues and overlord position rather than in the skills and purposes of cultivators.

Another comparative analysis was made in respect to training about aggression. The Rajput mothers are unusual among the groups studied in the degree to which they allow their children to aggress against them. As boys join the men's groups they learn to extol fighting in defense of honor. Yet there are countervailing pressures against aggression. Mothers discourage fighting among the children, older men discourage fighting within the kin and jati-group. More than in the other five societies, aggression is allowed and prized by these Rajputs in certain contexts and vigorously disapproved in others (Minturn and Lambert 1964, pp. 230–239).

In a further comparison of the six case studies, Beatrice Whiting has noted that the Khalapur people engage in more physical assault, more litigation, more violent in-group quarrels, than do the people of the other societies, except possibly those of the Kenya sample. She suggests one of the reasons for this may be that Rajput males have to make a difficult transition in identity when they move during childhood from the female sphere to the separate, segregate world of the men. Among the six societies the two in which there is greatest violence are also the two in which there is greatest separation between the men and the women.

A Rajput woman of this village, during the years when her children are young, is mainly confined to the household and to the women's locale within it. With few exceptions, she never sleeps or eats with her husband. Their sexual relations are surreptitious and hasty. A very young child rarely sees his father and mother interacting at all. One man from a jati of similar tradition said that he grew up without ever hearing his father and mother talk to each other (Whiting 1965, pp. 128–135).

When a Rajput boy in Khalapur moves from the one realm to the other, he learns that his earlier home among the women is most inferior. It is then, Beatrice Whiting suggests, that conflict about sex identity may occur. He has previously identified mainly with women, now he must make a sharp change in identity and characteristically feels impelled to make a brave show of the masculine virtues. There seems to be a circle of causation. "The separation of the sexes leads to a conflict of identity in the boy children, to unconscious fear of being feminine, which leads to 'protest masculinity,' exaggeration of the difference between men and women, antagonism against and fear of women, male solidarity, and hence to isolation of women and very young children" (Whiting 1965, p. 137).

This is a tentative interpretation based on a sample of families in one jati-group. It provides an idea to be tested, not a conclusion to be accepted. As in any large population, there is a broad range of personality characteristics among Indian villagers.[2] Anthropologists and others who have known Indian villagers well know many who are outgoing, independent, enterprising persons, even though the prevailing emphasis for young children seems to be more on passivity, dependence, defense. The reciprocal relationship between child rearing and social organization among Indian villagers has yet to be clearly formulated and tested, but these first approximations open a wide range of interesting questions.

The Dispersal Phase

The whole constellation of family relations shifts in a characteristic way, as we have noted, as the children grow up. There comes the time when the daughter must be married and sent off, when the son must receive a wife. The necessary growth through incoming brides also guarantees eventual dispersal, because there follows a time when the household becomes too cramped, psychologically and socially if not physically, to hold the brothers, their wives and children. Even if the brothers manage to stay together as one joint family through their lives, their sons almost certainly grow restive when they, in turn, become fathers, and then they separate to establish families of their own.

Herein lies an inherent contradiction and continuing strain in family life. The partitioning of the joint family, typically the separation of brothers, is in fact inevitable. But the ideal belief is held through most of the society that fraternal solidarity should not be breached and when it is, someone is at fault and should be

---

[2] To cite just one example, a study of achievement orientation among trainees from one Orissa village showed a considerable differentiation in this personality trait. A similar study of Orissa school children showed that those whose fathers were in "entrepreneurial" activities (the sale and production of oil and of milk) had higher achievement orientation than children from jatis of weavers and cultivators (McClelland 1961, pp. 271–273, 380–381).

blamed. Hence family separation is frequently perpetrated in quarrel and accusation. Amicable separations do occur, and, in any event, kinsmen and village elders usually try to restore friendly relations among brothers after a stormy parting (cf. Kapadia 1956, pp. 125–126). But quite often long echoes of recrimination leave a legacy of bitterness into another generation. Thus in a Kashmir village most of the landowners complain that they failed to receive their just share of the joint estates because of the dishonesty of their former coparceners. Even voting behavior, as studied in a Sikh village near Ludhiana, is largely influenced to the third generation by the enmities generated through family partition (Madan 1965, p. 162; Izmirlian 1964, pp. 34–36, 122–125).

The more property there is to divide, the more protracted are apt to be the throes of parting; the more touchy each brother's honor, whether from jati tradition or personal bent, the more bitter the aftermath. Those whose education or job sends them forth from the household are often spared this fraternal fracas; an only son is also exempt. Among the poorer families of lower rank, as was noted, the divisive quarrel tends to come earlier, usually between father and son. The son and his wife leave quickly; whatever rancor flares then, soon dissipates.

But among families of some substance, of the middle and higher echelons of local rank, the division does not usually take place all at once, in a clean decisive break. The strains mount, but at every stage there are countervailing forces and people urging continued cohesion. The first step in the process of family fission is usually that of establishing separate hearths within the household; all no longer eat from the same kitchen, food stores are divided, cooking and eating are done separately (cf. Bailey 1957, pp. 88–89; Sengupta 1958, p. 384; Minturn and Hitchcock 1963, p. 232). New walls may next be built inside the house as a physical partition foreshadowing the economic and legal partition to follow. The brothers may then separate their farming or craft activities and thereafter formalize the split in a legal act of joint family partition.

At any of these stages, the presence of the father tends to slow the process; the death of the father, and even more of both parents, tends to hasten the legal division. An examination of fifty instances of family partition in a Kashmir village showed that forty were among brothers, only four among fathers and sons. The rest were among relatives of different degrees of relationship. Similarly, a survey of married brothers in a village of Poona district showed 65 percent living together while their father was alive (a number had moved away from the village for economic reasons), but only 16 percent continued to live together after their father had died (Madan 1965, p. 165; Orenstein 1965a, p. 39; Fukutake *et al.* 1964, p. 50).

Frequently, married brothers act as if their father were the sole owner of the family property. Under the traditional code of Bengal, a married son was in fact not ordinarily entitled to claim his separate share until after the death of his father. Among the wealthier families in Bengal, Sarma notes, the possession of a substantial house delays family partition. It is awkward and expensive to separate living units within the home, and though the building could be sold and the proceeds divided, this is an unpalatable solution because of the pride and prestige in having an ancestral dwelling. In time, however, this pride is usually relinquished and the house is sold (Sarma 1964, pp. 194–198).

The causes of family strain, as has been noted before, are commonly said to be quarrels among the women. And commonly women do quarrel; theirs is a kind of accepted quarreling relation as other dyadic relations are accepted as joking or as solidary relations. Whatever may be the reasons for any particular argument, there are some general predisposing factors. Most village women spend a great deal of their lives within a narrow courtyard. The space is cramped and opportunities for friction abound. A woman, after she is a mother and a secure matron, does not hesitate to defend her rights in the household vigorously and loudly. She has come from another family, often from another village; she harbors no special loyalty or affection for her sister-in-law who is usually from yet another village and family.

This also holds true in South India, where there is preference for arranging marriages closer to home. It is so in Namhalli village, near Bangalore, in which about one third of the wives are from the village. In another village of Mysore, Ishwaran studied the break-up of joint families. "I was invariably told by my respondents that the arrival of the new wives was the main cause for it." They said that the women from unrelated families brought in new values and interests which led to conflict and the separation of the family.

Hence they were convinced that brides should not be brought in from distant families, even though bringing them from closer areas did not seem to guarantee family cohesion (Ishwaran 1965, p. 86; Beals and Siegel 1966, p. 43).

Money in the common purse, whatever a family's rank or region, is usually in short supply for each woman's needs. Food in the common larder runs low in the lean seasons and doling out food to the children of the family can easily become a daily source of tension. As each wife pours out her trouble to her husband when he comes home, he is apt to remember how one of his brothers or another has not done his proper share in getting the family's livelihood or has shirked a clear responsibility. A younger brother is then likely to find the elder more insufferably overbearing than before, the elder finds the younger more incorrigibly impertinent than ever. The brothers seek and usually find support in different directions, from their respective wives' relations. Both brothers find the idea of separation attractive, all the more so if a man's mother and his wife are constantly at each other, placing him in the uncomfortable and hopeless middle (cf. Karve 1953, p. 79; Srinivas 1952b, p. 29–31; Mayer 1960, pp. 178–179; Minturn and Hitchcock 1963, p. 261; Nicholas 1961, p. 1059).

"As long as the brothers stay united, the social personalities of the younger brothers do not attain completion," Srinivas writes of Rampura, in Mysore (1952b, p. 30); younger brothers elsewhere in India as well, find this a constant irritant as they come into manhood. Each brother has an equal right, as legal coparcener, to change this state of inequality by demanding the formal assignment of his share of the family's property. If the father is alive, vigorous, and forthright, he brooks no nonsense about family separation. He can only lose by it, in power, comfort, prestige, and wealth. The mother, who may have helped set off the outburst now tries to calm it; she scolds, reasons, weeps, bemoans her cruel fate and ungrateful sons.[3]

[3] In a broad comparison of family life in India and China, Francis Hsu concludes that a main difference is that the father-son relationship is central in Chinese families while in Hindu families the mother-son bond is the central, satisfying relationship. Hence social cohesion and cooperation are greater in China because the core relationship of trust between men is a continuous one. In India there is not the same continuity or trust. The mother-son relationship is not a link in a continuous mother-son line because, as Hsu puts it, no mother is a son and no son is a mother. The father-

The elders and leaders of the family's lineage and jati-group counsel patience and unity. They too can only lose if their kinsmen and community come to be known as quarrelsome, irascible people. Parents will think twice before betrothing their daughters to a fractious lot. A council of the lineage or even of the jati may be assembled to hear out the case. In it the elders point out to the brothers what they already know, that each will lose by the division.

They will lose economically by the immediate expenses of setting up a separate household and in the long run by the dispersal of their land and labor. And there is the danger—for which ample precedents are quoted—of long lawsuits, which sap energy and drain away resources.

They will lose socially. The name of each one in the family may be diminished by their separation. The brothers hear eloquent arguments against separation. One elder in a Gujarat town, defending joint living, said that the five fingers are not of equal length, but the loss of any one makes the hand ugly and defective, so each member must allow for the shortcomings of the others for the good of all. Moreover, "even if the family is very poor, if all live jointly and there is unity among them, you will receive offers of marriage for your children as soon as they are born" (Desai 1964, p. 170).

Even more, no man can hope to stand alone and defend himself singly in the village. Each will go down before enemies, for enemies are immanent, unless they can unite in strength of arms, of wealth, of patrons, and of clients. Each will lose as an individual. Who will look after the children, if the foodwinner falls sick? Indeed, who will look after the livelihood of the sick man himself? The elders may suggest various healing moves. Perhaps one brother may go off to find work in a city. Among some groups a younger brother is encouraged to find personal freedom in the army (Ross 1961, p. 47; Gould 1961c).

Brothers who cultivate their own land together, whose pride, strength, and security lie in their land, are usually ready to see the disadvantages of dispersing the ownership. Brothers whose income is in cash or who can raise cash crops as well apart as together are

son relationship, moreover, is one of mutual dependence and so lays the basis for cooperation within a group while the mother-son relationship is one of unilateral dependence. It does not enhance group solidarity because it is primarily a dyadic relationship (Hsu 1963, pp. 48–52). Compare, however, a different view noted in footnote 4, pp. 92–93 above.

less likely to delay the parting (Bailey 1957, p. 92; Desai 1964, p. 103; Epstein 1962, pp. 176, 306). Yet whatever their economic circumstances may be, there is usually some delay in separating after the first restless signs because the parting goes against the grain of the ideal and is contrary to the pattern of domestic authority in which they have been reared. This keeps the restive ones quiescent for a time.

But only for a time. The smoothing measures repair cleavages only temporarily. Before long other cracks in family solidarity appear and the pacifying devices only paper them over until finally no devices can hide or stop the split. The limits of this kind of counterchange are reached. The old family can no longer be maintained and new ones are established to succeed it.

The Family as Module and as Model

Relations within a family are in certain important ways similar to relations within a jati and in a community. We should scarcely expect it to be otherwise; no society can long endure a clashing incongruence between its smaller and its larger social groupings. But in India there is a particularly close nexus between family and jati, and it is necessary to understand family life well in order to grasp the nature of jatis.

What a person does in his role as family member underlies his behavior as jati member. His family serves both as model and as module for his jati relations. It provides the matrix for the beginnings of his conduct and contains the ends, the purposes, of his social striving. It is his fundamental corporate group, the locale of much of his social action, and it is also a main unit of attribution, from which expectations about his behavior are projected and judgments of his activities are made.

The family is a module, a regular structural segment of the jati, just as the jati is a module of the community. Every person is born both into a family and into a jati, and not into one only. He cannot readily opt out of either family or jati. As his jati is the field of actual and potential kin, so the family is the actual field of closest kin. All in a jati are taken as ritual equals by the community primarily because they are considered to interact as equals in their family capacities.

The village family is also the fundamental module of production and of reproduction. Most economic activities—cultivation, crafts, services—are performed by people operating in family groups or acting as representatives of their families. The interchange of goods and services according to jati specialization is, as has been seen, an interchange between families of different jatis. And the interchange among families of a jati in marriage is the basis of jati integration, of much of the cultural communication, and of a good deal of the economic distribution.

As a reproductive, socializing group, the family provides the primary model of social relations for the child. He first learns the expectation of hierarchical order in society through the hierarchy of the family. Respect, deference, avoidance, are all inculcated as part of family roles (cf. Dumont 1957b, pp. 7, 11; Carstairs 1957, pp. 63–76; Sarma 1951, p. 53). Inside the family, deference to elders is essential in family relations. Among families, each must strive to keep up and, if possible, to improve its prestige among other families of its jati.

A child learns about pollution and purity in the daily round of household tasks, in the preparation of food, in the various degrees of purity of the separate precincts of the house, in the daily avoidances brought on by one's biological functions, and in the periodic avoidance brought on by his mother's menstrual cycle. The touch taboos observed between family members because of temporary pollution set the style for keeping permanent distance between members of different jatis. The household is the scene of stricter purity observance than is the village outside, the women are the most careful guardians of domestic purity, hence the child's earliest experiences are with the more rigorous observances of the purity-pollution theme (cf. Mayer 1960, pp. 51–52).

The importance of matching conduct to context, of switching role behavior as the social situation changes, is daily illustrated to the child in the household. Thus he feels the restraint that descends upon his relations with his mother or father, who may have been playing gaily with him a moment before, when his grandfather enters the room. He sees his mother joking with his younger uncle, withdrawing demurely from the presence of his elder uncle. Even in their quarrels, members of a family are likely to affirm the ideal of family solidarity, each charging the other with dereliction of family duty and loyalty. Such quarrelers implicitly agree—through their vehement disagreement—that loyalty to family ought to be put above all other personal and social considerations.

The basic patterns of social control, of systemic counterchange, are learned and are used in family relations. In Gopalpur village of Mysore, for example, the giving or withholding of food is a main means of control. "The individual is brought to feel that the major securities and satisfactions of life are to be found in the acquisition of a large number of friends and supporters and in the control of them through the use of food. The most important supporters of the individual are the members of his family" (Beals 1962, p. 22).

In much of his day-to-day activity a villager acts in the capacity of family member and is so perceived to act by others. In extraordinary situations of stress, a person's first loyalty inclines to his family, above all other considerations (cf. Cohn 1961a, p. 1055). It is scarcely possible to single out and deal with one person in a village. As one man is called forth, his family comes forth with him. Often enough this is physically so; typically it is symbolically and figuratively true.

Yet in the expansion of the family, cleavages regularly appear. It is part of the process of family growth, part of a family's natural, inevitable, yet disapproved development. The pattern of family fission, with each couple setting up a social space of its own, resembles the pattern of jati fission, which will be considered later.

A family can usefully be seen as a structure of roles and as a system of structure maintenance. So viewed, the similarities and recurrent crises of family life throughout a vast population can be formulated. But family life in any real family is much more than role structure and counterchange, just as a house is much more than the set of blueprints and a home infinitely more than a dossier of behavior patterns. In an actual family there are decisions, choice points, exigencies, rewards, sorrows. A villager's emotions, motivations, conflicts, achievements are chiefly played out within his family and with other families. The central themes of traditional drama and story have to do with family affairs. The scenes from the *Ramayana* that are dramatized in the annual pageant of Ram Lila in northern India, are mainly concerned with family problems. They show, for example, how a woman caused great difficulty by seeking to promote the interests of her own son above those of the others in the joint family. They depict the grief of a mother when her son is exiled, the devotion and virtue of a wife, the loyalty of a younger brother (Opler 1959, p. 28a).

Scenes from the other epic, the *Mahabharata*, are also staged, told, and retold in villages of every part of the land. In Mrs. Karve's words, "It is simply the story of a huge, big joint patri-family and illustrates the interrelations, the personality development, the feuds, the strength, the weakness, the ethos of the joint families" (1953, p. 21; see also Sarma 1964, p. 198).

Family battles there are in plenty, but their very intensity and the interest they elicit testifies to the importance of family to the individual and to society. For the family is at the core of a man's allegiance, of his loyalty, his identification. It is his own gauge of his success in life, it is a main standard used by others to measure his earthly achievement. All the more is it so for a woman. A man may have outside interests and achievements, a village woman cradles them all in her family.

However, caste society is not just the family writ large, nor is a family only a jati in miniature. There are other groupings, other bonds, other traditions within a jati and among jatis that together make up village society.

Beyond his family, a villager carries on much of his life with other kinsmen. A good part of his daily round, most of his visiting, all domestic ritual are typically done with relatives. A village family reaches out for help from its related families in an emergency, on ritual occasions, in the work of the field or the struggle of the feud. And those families turn to them for help when sudden necessity or regular occasions require.

A man relates to several classes of kinsmen beyond his immediate family. His most frequent interchange is usually with those families closest to him in patrilineal descent and in residence, a group that may be called a localized lineage. The men are brothers who have set up separate households or the sons of brothers or patrilateral cousins. All in these households, including wives, adopted children, and resident sons-in-law, are considered part of the group even though they are of different patrilineal descent from the related men. There may be as few as two families in such a localized lineage or as many as from twenty to thirty. The families belonging to one lineage usually perform formal ritual functions together, especially in mourning observance, and such joint observance helps to define the boundaries of the group. They also cooperate in many other activities. The lineage is regarded as an extension of the family and so it is an exogamous unit. There can no more be a marriage between a boy and a girl of the same lineage than of the same family.

A larger exogamous category is known in many jatis, though not in all. For our purposes it may be called simply the clan. It is usually a grouping rather than a group, a taxonomic category rather than the basis for joint action. Each person inherits the clan of his father, and marriage within the clan is forbidden because all in it are considered to be descended from the same progenitor. The common ancestor of lineage members is usually an actual, remembered person, but the common progenitor of fellow clansmen is typically a legendary, supernatural character. The members of a clan tend to be too dispersed and their kin ties too remote for them to share much in the way of common interests or joint action. Occasionally the clan does provide a basis for cooperative activity, as in the worship of a clan deity, but the clan grouping is mainly used to classify jati fellows into eligible and ineligible spouses.

Another class of kinsmen does provide a basis for some joint action. In this class are the families of the jati-group, those of the same jati who live in one village. They are kinsmen in the sense that all are either actual or potential relatives with the added bond of village residence. They may observe rituals together, they may aid each other economically, they normally come to the defense of any jati fellow whose welfare and status may be threatened by others. This group will be discussed in the following chapter, in the context of jati organization.

Another class of kin includes those related to a man through the women of his family, particularly through his mother and his wife. These kinsmen are concerned about him as a person rather than as the representative of his family or of any other corporate group. They are expected to sustain and protect him and commonly do so. He, in turn, does the same for the husband and the children of his sister and, later in life, for those of his daughter. The term "feminal kin" is used here for this class of relatives. A woman's feminal kin are mainly those through her mother, that is her mother's brothers and others of her mother's natal family.

A man shares the same lineage, clan, and jati-group with a good many other men. But only rarely do two men share the same feminal kindred. Even brothers have different relatives through their respective wives, unless they marry sisters. Further, a man belongs to only one lineage, one clan, one jati-group, but he may have a wide array of feminal kin who may not have any particular relationship with each other aside from their common jati.

Finally, there is the class of fictive kin. Because villagers consider kinship bonds to be the best basis for reciprocity and allegiance, people who are not actually related by descent or marriage can establish fictional bonds of kinship with each other. In that way a person can secure for himself the benefits of a wider circle of kin than biology can provide for him. These relatives, like all kinship relations, can be deployed in a man's quest for power and status or, as he might prefer to put it, in his striving for the security of his family.

The Lineage

A man's lineage fellows are literally and figuratively close to him for they are, after all, the brothers who have separated their fields and hearths but who continue to sustain their fraternal allegiance. Once the trauma of parting is past, they tend to honor the brotherly bond. Their sons and grandsons carry on the relationship with some of the fidelity that the fraternal ideal requires, and also with some of the friction that fraternal relationships often involve.

That ambivalence is the greater because the ideal of lineage solidarity is not so strongly proclaimed as is the fraternal ideal, and moreover it is not always clear who should be counted as a full lineage member. Lineage ties lapse after several generations, but the number of obligated generations is not usually specified clearly. A father's brother's son who moves to a distant village is a full lineage member for ritual purposes but he can hardly be a full participant in corporate activity (cf. Mayer 1960, pp. 182–183).

Hostility sometimes encroaches on lineage unity. This is recognized clearly in a village of Poona district, where one man commented that just as brothers always fight, so do their sons and grandsons (Orenstein 1965a, pp. 85–87). In a Kashmir village, lineage fellows help each other, and yet conflict among them is a prominent feature of kinship relations. "The sibling rivalry which leads to partition of the household is later revealed in more intense form in the relationship between cousins" (Madan 1965, p. 201).

Nevertheless, lineage fellows do commonly cooperate in ritual, in economic enterprise and in general rights and procedures. Thus they often participate together in life-cycle rites even when they are at odds on other matters. Lineage members who share jural rights may put up a common front in order to keep the rights but may also quarrel about who is to get greater advantage from them. As close neighbors they usually exchange economic aid, from fire for a cold hearth to the labor pool at harvest. In dispute settlement, the court of first appeal in domestic quarrels is commonly an assembly of the men of the lineage. They usually try to settle such an affair quickly and smoothly, lest the reputation and status of the whole lineage suffer. When a man gets into a quarrel with a villager of another lineage or a different jati, he generally finds immediate defenders and close allies among his lineage mates. His other kinsmen are mainly in other villages; his agnates are right there with him (cf. Mayer 1960, p. 239).

Such cooperation is continually reinforced because lineage families commonly live close together, in the same village street or in the same ward or hamlet. They are near each other because brothers set up their new households not far from the old one. This is in part because they must—their lands and homesites are there—in part because it is well to have close relatives nearby. So when one falls ill, the others cannot easily ignore his need; when there is a death in one house, the others will not plead ignorance; when emergency help is required by one family, the others cannot well be elsewhere (cf. Lewis 1958, pp. 22–23; Minturn and Hitchcock 1963, p. 237; Berreman 1963, p. 176; Epstein 1962, p. 174; Nicholas 1962, p. 174).

The strand that binds the lineage is that of patrilineal descent but the actual cooperation includes all those who reside with the related families. Notably this includes the wives, each of whom was born into another lineage, and also the adopted children and the occasional man who has come to live with his wife's relatives. When a bride joins her husband's family, she becomes a member of his lineage for most purposes, ritual, economic, and legal, but she also retains some affiliation with her original lineage and some rights in it. Only rarely is a woman totally cut off from her natal lineage.

Lineage Ties and Ritual Functions

A main link among the families of a lineage is the joint performance of ritual functions. They observe pollution seclusion together and participate together in each other's life-cycle observances. In some places they worship the same lineage deities; all the families of the lineage share the tutelary spirit who watched over the founding family and all think of themselves not only as wards of the same deity but also as descendants of the same ancestor.

In Totagadde village of western Mysore, for example, offerings are made to lineage deities who are believed to live near the house and to protect its people and animals from the depredations of other supernaturals. Vegetarian food is placed for the household deities of Brahmins, blood offerings for the guardians of lower ranking households.

The Havik Brahmins of this village observe lineage pollution to an exceptional extent (Harper 1964, pp. 161–167). After the death of a Havik Brahmin, every man and woman of the deceased's lineage must remain in seclusion for eleven days. During that period they may perform no rituals nor may they approach closely to other Brahmins. They are then like untouchables to the others of their jati. The touch of a Brahmin in mourning defiles another Brahmin. Moreover, their lineages are of unusually great depth, including all men who are patrilineally descended from a common ancestor up to the seventh ascending generation. Haviks say that even beyond that degree of kinship some mourning seclusion, though of progressively diminishing length, should be observed among men even more distantly related, up to the twenty-first ascending generation.

Women keep the full mourning period of their natal lineage so long as they live in one of its households. When they marry and move to another house, their seclusion on the death of a person of their original lineage is much curtailed, but they undergo full seclusion for a death in their husband's lineage.

These Brahmins also observe the happier restrictions because of a birth in the lineage. When a child is born to one of the lineage families, all men and women in it may not attain the highest state of ritual purity nor participate fully in ceremonies until the mother emerges from her eleven days of deepest avoidance (Harper 1964, pp. 167–169).

There are not many jatis whose people maintain such strict seclusion for all in a lineage nor who trace lineage connections back so far, but very commonly lineage relatives do share death pollution and contribute to the funeral expenses. They contribute also in money, goods, and by their presence to all the life-cycle observances of their lineage fellows (cf. Mathur 1964, pp. 43–44; Orenstein 1965a, pp. 75–79, 84–85; Madan 1965, p. 198).

Some of the limits to such reciprocal aid are illustrated in the account of Bisipara, a village of highland Orissa. Lineage fellows within each of the several jatis do help each other, especially with ritual and for a ritual emergency. But if one of them suffers a personal misfortune, as when his oxen die, he looks more for help to his relatives through his mother and his wife than to his supposedly closer agnatic kinsmen. The reason for this, Bailey writes, is perhaps indicated in the local proverb which says that the brother is the enemy. There is potential hostility among brothers, in Bisipara as in other parts of the land, at least when the family estate is to be divided. This does not mean that brothers hate each other. They often cooperate in the fields and aid each other in sickness or in ritual crises, but they may not be so responsive to a personal economic crisis. It is as though partition sets the pattern for their future relationship. "In sickness, or against outsiders, the brother is an ally and a friend. But if he mismanages his part of the estate, let him look after himself" (Bailey 1957, pp. 83–84).

Here as elsewhere the men of a lineage may fall out in a factional dispute and their factional enmity may reduce or even wipe out any effort at mutual assistance. However, lineage fellows do generally side with each other in village encounters, even though all do not necessarily become involved in each other's personal quarrels unless the name and fame of the lineage is involved. Among the Pramalai Kallar, for example, a man may act as a substitute in ritual for a lineage fellow when his lineage relative has had a quarrel with someone else involved in the ritual exchange (Dumont 1957b, p. 176).

Lineage Ties in Economic and Jural Affairs

Lineage fellows also cooperate for economic and jural purposes. For example, in Gaon village particular jatis render services for the whole village. This public service work is allocated according to lineage and lineage segment within each jati of the scavengers, Brahmins, temple priests, potters, leather workers, and rope makers (Orenstein 1965a, pp. 64–90). Such service to the village rather than to patron families is common in this part of Maharashtra.

Though the localized lineage is an important unit in Gaon, the villagers do not set precise, formal boundaries to it nor do they have a single word for it. A common term is *bhāuki*, which is used to refer both to those who are descended from a known patrilineal ancestor, wherever they may live, or to the cooperating, related families, who usually live in neighboring houses within a village. In most jati-groups of Gaon there is only a single lineage or one is highly dominant. Some of them keep no genealogical records and the families who hold themselves to be of one lineage may not really know which patrilineal ancestor they have in common; they assume that there has been at least one. Contiguity of residence is a more potent cause for collaboration than is exact genealogical history. For this reason and also because the group includes wives and others, Orenstein believes that these localized groups are not quite lineages in a technical sense of the term. For our present purposes they can be termed localized lineages, despite some lapses of genealogical record.

Two of the twenty-four jatis of Gaon do not have any lineage groups. One is the basket weaver jati, which is divided into exogamous moieties rather than into lineages. The other is the goldsmith jati. Orenstein points out that there are typically only one or two families of goldsmiths in a village, and kinsmen so dispersed cannot well cooperate in corporate lineage groups (1965a, pp. 62–65). Within the localized lineages in Gaon, a set of two to four households is taken as a segment which is "formed out of or inherits brothers' tensions and brothers' ties" (*ibid.* p. 84). A still larger segment of a lineage is the unit for rotating village work. Among the scavengers, for example, each such segment cleans the village for its allotted part of the year.

Since the boundaries of the lineage are not rigidly specified, questions arise as to whether, for example, a brother's son who has moved to the city should be considered a member of the lineage group. The test is whether he is invited to marriage and funeral ceremonies and participates fully in them. On occasions when lineage members foregather, decisions on lineage affairs and adjudication of lineage quarrels usually take place and lineage membership is then demonstrated (*ibid.*, pp. 70–71, 85).

Among some groups, major economic functions are assigned to the lineage. This is so among the Jats of Meerut and other

districts around Delhi. The men of a lineage have sole rights to
a certain portion of the village lands and none of that portion can
be transferred out of the lineage. This customary law of the jati
has been recognized and enforced by the government courts. For
these Jats and other landowners of the region it is continued as a
main principle of social organization (Pradhan 1965). Such unity
of land and descent is a common feature among tribal peoples in
India, as will be noted later.

The great emphasis on the patrilineal line in North India made
the jatis of genealogists very important. Their services were especially crucial among Rajputs, Jats, and similar groups whose lineages were wedded to land and where power could hinge on fine
calculations of inheritance rights. As Shah and Shroff note for
Gujarat, "a Rajput's status in society depends on his position in
the genealogy of his lineage," and that position can only be vali-
dated by the genealogists' records (1958, p. 263). The genealogist
does more than keep the pedigrees of lineage and clan. He is
commonly also a bard who extols the feats of the patriline, tells
of the glorious accomplishments of the ancestors, and not only links
the living members to the shining past but also traces their descent
from the deities themselves. Those whose patriline was thus kept
fresh in memory and green in glory, have been inclined to form
their action groups with their patrilineal kinsmen more commonly
than in South India. There are few professional genealogists in the
South while in North India some of the artisans, merchants, and
even leatherworkers have acquired professional genealogists (Shah
and Shroff 1958; Mayer 1960, pp. 194–201; Baines 1912, pp. 85–
89).

In earlier centuries the nexus of land and lineage was the basis
of state as well as of village organization in many parts of India.
In the late eighteenth century, Bernard Cohn notes, dominant lineages in what is now eastern Uttar Pradesh acted as rulers of little
kingdoms. A lineage of overlords was responsible for the payment
of land revenue and for the provision of troops to the suzerain
power. These lineages were far larger than they are now, sometimes comprising more than a thousand families, because men who
could maintain lineagelike solidarity for a larger number were
stronger economically and politically (Cohn 1959a, pp. 79–80;
1961c, pp. 616–619; Srinivas 1966, pp. 33–35).

When the British first took control, they too made the lineage or its headman answerable for land revenue and for the maintenance of order. In 1789 the British began to change the system of land tenure and revenue in this region and impaired the power of the ruling lineages, but it was not until the settlement of 1880–1882 that the little kingdoms of the ruling lineages were drastically altered.

The political functions of lineages are now mainly confined to village alliances and factions; land rights in few jatis are still vested in the lineages, but it is still common for lineage elders to act in the settlement of disputes among the families of their lineage. In eastern Uttar Pradesh this is so not only among the descendants of the former rulers but also among the Chamars, the traditional leather-workers and laborers. In Senapur village, disputes within a Chamar household that cannot be quelled by the family head are taken to the leader of the lineage. Since he lives in the same part of the Chamar hamlet he knows about the quarrel from its beginning and can usually suggest some solution. When the quarrel is between two families of the lineage, the lineage headman similarly tries to smooth over the eruption. If he cannot do so he calls a council of the Chamar hamlet, at which all the lineage leaders should be present together with other family heads in the hamlet.

The same kind of council is brought together to settle disputes between whole lineages with the addition of eminent Chamars from outside the hamlet. Quarrels between lineages can be serious affairs, which may even lead to the penalty of outcasting if they involve major defections of social obligations or irregularities in marriage or occupation.

The failure of a family to invite all its lineage relations to a wedding can precipitate a turmoil. All adult males from both lineages should attend a wedding and also at least one adult male from every other household in the Chamar hamlet. If one of the households is not invited, whether by error or intent, the insult will be resented and formal redress through the hamlet council will be demanded. And when one family suffers an insult from another Chamar family, its whole lineage may rise in wrath (Cohn 1959a, pp. 82–84; 1960, pp. 422–424).

Rights and privileges within a jati are often held by a lineage rather than by a particular family. The office of headman of a jati-group or of council elder may be in the keeping of particular lineages (cf. Reddy 1952, p. 243; Epstein 1962, pp. 127–128). Where lineages are shallow in depth and limited in function, there is usually not much difference in rank among them. But where important functions are assigned to the lineage as a unit, there are likely to be marked status gradations within and among lineages. Thus in one Gujarat village, a Rajput's status is commensurate with the rank of his lineage and also with the seniority of his branch within the lineage and of his family within the branch (Steed 1955, p. 127).

In general, then, a villager's next larger group for cooperation, beyond his family, is the set of families who are close in both descent and residence (cf. Dumont 1964b, pp. 75–76). Descent provides the rationale for cooperation, propinquity the opportunity. Coresidents of other descent lines participate with the men who stem from the same patrilineal ancestor. But identification with one's natal descent line can never be abandoned in matters of marriage and sexual intercourse. No man may have sexual relations, in or out of marriage, with a daughter of his own patriline on pain of the penalties of incest. No matter where she has lived, no matter how long she has been away from her childhood home, she remains until death a part of her natal line in this respect.

An example of the distinction between the ties of descent and of residence is given in the account of Ramkheri village in Madhya Pradesh. Three different words (*kutumb, bhaibandh, khandan*) may be used for lineage by these villagers. Each of them can also refer to yet another kind of grouping, the intended reference depends on the context of use. Thus the term *bhaibandh* means either lineage or clan. When a man is asked to which *bhaibandh* he belongs, he will give the name of his clan because he understands the question as referring to his patrilineal category. But if he is asked where his *bhaibandh* is living, he will reply with reference to his lineage, because that is his group of common residence as well as of common descent.

Close residence favors the continuation of the closer ties of lineage, distance makes for forgetting them. One man in this village said that he had *bhaibandh*, here referring to lineage fellows, in two nearby villages and while he was not sure of his exact relationship with them, he still invited them to his ceremonies. But he also had

lineage relatives in a village some thirty miles away with whom he
did not keep up the reciprocal exchange. Lineage connections with
people in a village as distant as that are dropped after five or six
generations. "Then the lineage passes into the clan (*bhaibandh
gotra men jata hai*), and the people become clan mates (*gotra bhai*)
only" (Mayer 1960, pp. 167–168).

The Clan

The lineage passes into the clan. This comment indicates a recurrent process in kin relations. A lineage, like its component families,
develops through a cycle of growth and separation (cf. Madan
1965, pp. 225–227). But the separation of a lineage is usually a
gradual process and comes about through the slow, piecemeal
relinquishing of mutual exchanges—sometimes under protest, sometimes mutually accepted—rather than in an abrupt, explosive break.
Just as a family, after partition, passes into the lineage, so does the
lineage in time separate into the clan.

The exogamous principle is never relinquished. People who have
abandoned lineage cooperation with each other still inherit affiliation in the same clan. They and their patrilineal descendants
through all of time presumably remain in the same exogamous
category. Lineage relations are limited in time and space; the clan
endures through time and across space.

In that sense the clan is an affirmation that the incest taboos of
patrilineal exogamy are immutable and eternal. The members of a
clan usually have an origin story linking all of them to the same
supernatural source. In Ramkheri there is a clan goddess for each
clan of a jati; worship of the same goddess is the main test and
affirmation of belonging to a particular clan. If a stranger comes to
a village and claims to be of a certain clan, he is not allowed to
worship with the other members until they have been assured of his
claim by finding mutual, known kin or through the guarantee of
someone whom they can trust (Mayer 1960, p. 184).

Cooperation within a clan depends in good measure on demographic and economic factors. Where the families of a jati are scattered and only one or two exist in a village, as among the goldsmiths
of Gaon and in some of the Ramkheri jatis, there may be too few
families to form a lineage cohort in any one locality. In that case,

each family may establish close, supportive relations with families of its clan as well as of its lineage (Mayer 1960, pp. 168–169).

There are some jatis, mainly the lower and poorer, among whom lineage is little elaborated and clan ties are vestigial or absent. The potters of western Maharashtra, for example, do not have clans nor do the earthworkers of eastern U.P. (Karve 1958b, p. 131; Rowe 1960, p. 300). But in most regions the general pattern of lineage and clan relations that we have sketched is known, though the terms used by both villagers and anthropologists vary considerably. Thus in the Himalayan village of Sirkanda, related families group themselves as a lineage (Berreman uses the term clan for this unit) because of their common patrilineal descent and residential propinquity. A clan ("sib" is the term used by Berreman) has ritual functions in Sirkanda as it does in Ramkheri. Clan fellows in Sirkanda feel a certain allegiance to each other, so that there are few factional disputes in which men of the same clan are pitted against each other (Berreman 1963, pp. 176–187).

In Totagadde in the south, as we have seen, the Havik Brahmins maintain lineage connections among people linked to a quite remote ancestor. In actual practice the more distant kin ties are often sloughed off by being conveniently forgotten. But even in the long kinship reckoning of the Haviks, the descendants of a common ancestor are no longer lineage mates after a number of generations but only *sagotra*, members of the same clan or *gotra* (Harper, 1964, p. 163).

Gotra and Other Terms for Kinship Groupings

The Sanskrit term "gotra" is very widely used. A Brahmin must specify his gotra affiliation in his daily devotions when he makes an exact identification of himself before the gods. But this word refers to different kinds of grouping in different jatis and it is used by jatis at all social levels. Even in the Vedas there seem to be different meanings attached to it and there has been a lively difference of opinion among Indologists as to its central or original meaning (Madan 1962c, pp. 60–63; Kapadia 1958, pp. 124–130).

Gotra is most commonly used to mean what we have called a clan, that is an exogamous category within a jati. Its principal use, often the only one, is to regulate marriage matches. All members of a gotra are presumed to be descended from or associated with the same supernatural source. People of different jatis may carry the same gotra name and claim descent from the same legendary sage or deity. But this implies no special connection between them. Gotra names have been taken over by many who were adapting their ways to the Sanskritic norms and so the Sanskrit labels appear in jatis of various sorts (Hutton 1961, p. 55; Dumont and Pocock 1957c, p. 52; Madan 1962c, pp. 72–73; Mathur 1964, pp. 47–49).

The functions attached to the grouping called gotra vary by jati and region. The usage in Sirkanda is quite exceptional because the gotra category is used there only for ritual identification in the marriage rite and is not an exogamous unit. The Pandit Brahmins of Kashmir use the gotra category in more typical scriptural fashion for both exogamy and ritual identification but, less typically, they allow some marriages within a gotra to be arranged through the use of a legal fiction or by the performance of expiatory rites. In a West Bengal village, by contrast, gotra exogamy is said never to have been violated. In Ramkheri, as we have noted, the clans or gotras not only are exogamous but also have common deities and rites (Berreman 1963, pp. 187–191; Madan 1965, pp. 103–105; Klass 1966, pp. 957–958; Mayer 1960, pp. 184–188. See also Hutton 1961, p. 56; Karve 1965, p. 118; Karandikar 1929, p. 76).

In earlier times a band of Rajput warriors who conquered a territory and founded a state were sometimes related as clan brothers. In some of these princely states, even under British rule, there was a constant struggle between the prince and his clansmen, the nobles. He wanted to keep them in their subordinate place as his vassals; they claimed higher privileges as his clan brothers (Cole 1932, p. 135; Shah and Shroff 1958, p. 260).

A particular clan of a dominant jati sometimes wields leading influence in a set of villages. Thus in Rampura, near Delhi, one of the clans gives its name to a unit of some twenty villages because these villages accept the leadership of the members of that clan even though other clans are represented among them (Lewis 1958, pp. 29–30). Generally, however, clan functions are now minimal, and those villagers who do maintain clan divisions do so, whether under the term gotra or some other, mainly as categories for exogamy.

Exogamy may be extended beyond one's own clan. Some, especially in the higher jatis of north India, prohibit marriage into four gotras, namely: one's own, that of the mother, the father's mother, and the mother's mother. This is called the "four-gotra rule"; if strictly observed it forbids the marriage of a prospective bride and groom if they share any two of their combined eight gotra links (Karve 1965, pp. 115–125; Mayer 1960, pp. 202–203). Other North Indian jatis extend the prohibition less widely—only to one's mother's clan or to those of mother and of father's mother.

Clan exogamy may also be extended by clustering several clans into an exogamous bloc, called a phratry in kinship analysis. Among the Marathas, each clan has a totemic symbol, a javelin, or a kind of grass, or the leaves of certain trees. At the time of a marriage each family worships the clan symbol, but at other times it plays little part in family ritual. Several different clans have the same symbol and there may be no marriage between two persons who share a clan symbol. The clans of the Marathas are also ranked in a hierarchical order for purposes of marriage alliance. Mrs. Karve depicts the hierarchy as capped by the "five-clan" division and descending in five layers to the division of the "ninety-six clans" (Karve 1965, 176–179; Orenstein 1965a, pp. 62–63, 124–126).

One of the most complex clan arrangements of all is that of the Rajputs, who are widespread across northern India. Rajputs agree that an order of clan rank exists, but often disagree as to the ranking of a particular clan. Each Rajput clan is part of a larger grouping, the branch. Several branches make up one of the main lines and all in one line consider themselves descended from the same primordial progenitors such as the sun, the moon, serpents, or fire (Karve 1965, pp. 165–171; Mayer 1960, pp. 164–165).

In sorting out the groups and categories of kin at any level or region, it is especially important to recognize what was previously noted, that local terms can be misleading. A student who concentrates on the particular terms rather than on social structure and social function soon finds himself bogged down in a hopeless morass of seemingly conflicting usage. Villagers, like those in Ramkheri and elsewhere, apply the same term to quite different groups, distinguishing one meaning from the other by the context of use. Further, a term that in one context may refer to a group may mean a kind of kin linkage in another context. In discussing an account of a Punjab village, Marriott notes that "the term 'biradari' refers not to just one concrete structural unit at the village level, but rather to patrilineal connection, real, putative, or fictional, at any level of segmentation" (1962, p. 264; also see Honigmann 1960b, p. 836).

The same unit may bear different labels. In Sirkanda, for example, the exogamous grouping is called either jati or *biradari* (Berreman 1963, pp. 149, 182). But jati is also used by some Sirkanda people in the usual sense of the endogamous rather than the exogamous group. Nor, as has also been mentioned before, are the technical terms in the anthropological literature on India well standardized. The term "lineage" is used here instead of Murdock's "compromise kin group" for the group that combines unilineal descent with residential unity (Murdock 1949, pp. 65–78). There really is no "compromise" in the formation of such a group; rather the group shows the complementary effects of patrilineal descent and local propinquity.

In village practice, each of the larger social categories, the jati and clan, is usually known by a distinctive name to distinguish it from the others of its kind. But the smaller interactional groups, the family and lineage, do not have separate labels and are referred to usually by the name of a prominent member. These smaller kin groups operate mainly within a village community, while other kinship relations tie together people of different villages.

Feminal Kin

One important linkage across villages is that between a man and the relatives for whom we use the term feminal kinsmen. They are related to him through his mother, his married sisters, his wife, and his married daughters. A continuous flow of gifts goes on between a man and his feminal kin, as well as periodic visiting, regular communication, mutual bolstering of status, and reciprocal support in personal emergencies. A man gives to his married sisters and daughters and to their conjugal families; in turn, he receives from his wife's and mother's natal families. Central to these relationships are the perduring ties between parents and daughter, and especially between brother and sister. It has been noted that the mother's brother is an especially supportive kinsman because he cares deeply for the child of his sister. As a brother, a man characteristically wants to help his sister in her married house in every way that he can, by aiding her husband, by backing his family, by giving gifts and favors to her children. A father also seeks to help his married daughter in the same ways, but he usually leaves the direct participation to his sons.

In his family and lineage a man has to cope with the daily tasks of livelihood, with maintaining the kin group, defending its status and extending its power. His feminal kinsmen, through his mother and wife, are more concerned with him as a person than as a member of a group, with the special occasions of his life and of their lives rather than with the daily round, with support in personal exigencies rather than with the regular maintenance of a group. They live elsewhere than in his village—by reason of village exogamy in the North, by common occurrence in the South—and so they are not part of any local rivalry among brothers or power contest between families. Dumont describes how a Kallar of Madura district feels when he visits one of these kinsmen in their home. A change in his attitude is soon noticed, "there is no more etiquette, fun and jokes immediately appear: he feels released; it is a pleasure to go, even for some work, to such a place" (1950, p. 13). The same sentiment is expressed in a Muslim village of Gujrat district in West Pakistan. A man cherishes his mother's natal family throughout life. As a young child he learns that visits to them surround him with affection and return him with fine gifts (Eglar 1960, p. 80; also see Madan 1965, pp. 209–217). Women in all parts of the land also feel freer when they visit their father's house or their mother's brother's house, but women do not go about as readily and so these relations are more actively carried on by the men.

These feminal relationships, as has been noted, help to integrate each villager and each village into a social network of villages that affect many aspects of village life. One incidental effect is that a man's economic standing can be made known through these channels. Beals gives the example of a villager of Gopalpur who needs to be vouched for in order to do some business in a village in which he is a stranger; if a daughter of Gopalpur is married there, she can attest to his reputation. "The existence of marital ties facilitates all economic transactions, both on a village and on an individual level" (Beals 1962, p. 28).

The importance of affinal ties is documented in William Rowe's study of marriage networks among the Noniyas, who were traditionally the earthworkers of Senapur village near Banaras. In a sample count of visits by Noniyas from different villages, 86 percent were between households that were affinally related. Few of these visits were from jati fellows in the villages closest to Senapur because the Noniyas of these villages belong to the same exogamic locality as do the Senapur Noniyas and so they do not carry on the more intensive interchange that goes on among affines. It is intensive because a family must invite as many affinal relatives as possible to share with it in all its celebrations. Moreover, families related by marriage help each other in many ways. They exchange labor; they borrow farm equipment, animals, and cash from each other. When a Noniya wants to consult a shaman secretly, he goes to an affinal village. When he gets in trouble in his home village, especially if it is with the dominant landowners, he flees for refuge to his mother's brother or to his wife's brother (Rowe 1960).

The Chamars of this village cherish these ties in the same way. Their visits to feminal kinsmen are frequent and may be long. A Chamar child may spend two or three years with his mother's natal family. A Chamar, like a Noniya, flees to his mother's or his wife's people if he gets into trouble with one of the landowners in his own place. This is one reason why a number of men of the lower jatis in a village (15 percent in the case of Senapur Chamars) have come in from other villages. Some are attracted as resident sons-in-law, but others find haven or livelihood with relatives (Cohn 1955, pp. 57–58).

Men of higher as well as lower jatis turn first to a mother's brother or wife's brother for shelter. When it became known that a young Rajput of Khalapur village had become attached to a girl of lower jati, such great pressure was brought to bear that he could no longer remain in his village; he fled to his mother's brother. Among these dominant Rajputs, as among subordinate groups, a man's relations with his feminal kinsmen are quite different from his relations with his agnates, being "comradely and without strain" (Minturn and Hitchcock 1963, p. 239). These easy, comradely relations may be extended even to the fellow villagers of one's feminal kinsmen.

Such extension is evident in Bisipara in Orissa. There is hardly a man in Bisipara, Bailey writes, who cannot trace an effective kinship link with at least one household in every other Oriya village of Kondmals subdivision. Some of these links are agnatic, more often they are affinal or uterine—that is, through the mother's brother. And they are extended to all in the related village, even across caste lines. Thus a herdsman of Bisipara had visitors from his wife's natal village from time to time. Some were untouchables. "The welcome they received depended on their importance and the closeness of the tie, but at least they would be allowed to sleep in the courtyard" (Bailey 1957, p. 248).

Fictive Kinship

The range both of feminal kin connections and of agnatic bonds can be extended in some regions through establishing fictional ties of kinship. In Shanti Nagar, near Delhi, every villager customarily uses a kinship term for another resident of his village, irrespective of caste lines. The common terminology does not confuse villagers at all; they know quite well that a man of another jati whom they call father's brother is not in a relationship identical with that of the real father's brother. Nevertheless, the use of the term connotes some of the flavor of the real relationship (Freed 1963a, pp. 86–87; see also Marriott 1955b, pp. 177–178).

The link of fictive kinship between any two villagers is usually established first through two prominent men of their respective jatis. If these two call each other brother on the basis of generation and reciprocal aid, this provides a bridge for extending kinship terms across caste lines for others. Each person can trace the links between his family and the prominent man of his own jati. He then traces kinship affiliation to all in the other jati as though through a brother of that prominent man. Freed tested this and found that 81 percent of the total of 1543 terms he elicited were correct according to this procedure. Most of the other replies had been adjusted to minimize great incongruity between the fictive kinship term and the actual generational or status positions (1963a, pp. 97–102).

When kinship terms are similarly extrapolated to the fellow villagers of a mother's brother, the number of people who are subsumed within a person's kinship terminology is vastly expanded.

There is a great difference between actual cooperation and the mere use of kin terms, but the terms do provide a potential beginning for the building of profitable reciprocity if a man chooses and is able to do so.

The Uses of Kinship

There is considerable scope for choice in kinship relations. In the sharp competition for status and livelihood, a man and his family must have kin as allies. A villager's staunchest supporters are his kinsmen, or, better stated, the most dependable allies are those linked by some kind of kinship bond. An ambitious man, seeking power and the status lift that power can bring, must enlarge and strengthen the circle of his kin. Any man who is anxious to protect his family's social position must constantly see to consolidating his defenses of kinship.

To be sure, not all persons feel the same pressure or have the same latitude of choice in establishing kinship relations. A child has no option about the close environs of kin into which he is born. A woman has little choice until she gains some influence in the household and then her influence in the wider spheres of kinship is exerted mainly through the men of her family. But a man, especially the head of a family, does have some freedom of choice. The choices are presented so insistently and the need for decisions is so demanding that to many the option seems more a slavery to obligation than freedom of choice. How much to give at the birth of a second sister's third son? How many guests to invite, from how distant villages, to the eldest daughter's wedding? What to do for a deceased brother's importunate son?

Certain obligations permit little leeway. A man's responsibilities to his father and mother cannot be accepted or rejected at will, nor do most men consciously want to reject these duties any more than they want to avoid responsibility for their own children. As brother, a man characteristically wants to help and protect his sister, although he may have to decide which of his sisters to help more and how much to help any. As brother to his brothers, he feels compelled, inwardly and outwardly, to come to their aid when dangers to life or name threaten, but beyond that a man may fulfill fraternal obligations either formally and frugally or lovingly and lavishly. A Gujarati saying has it that "a useless brother is a stranger," thus combining the ideas that even the brother bond is subject to differing interpretation and that a kinship relation is valid only to the extent to which it is activated.

The more kinship ties a man activates with others, the more gifts he invests in each relationship, the more the others are likely to reciprocate with whatever they have to give—with allegiance even more than with goods—and the more his power grows. The scope and the limitations of that growth are sketched by Beals for Gopalpur in Mysore (1962, p. 32) and the description holds true over much of India. The Gopalpur man who extends his chain of relationships is able to arrange marriages for others even of different jatis, because he is known through the region and has relatives in many villages. A man who has made a great name constantly feeds and entertains his many relatives and for this he must have wealth. Once he has established a wide circle of kin, their help and influence enable him to keep and increase his wealth. But in acquiring wealth he competes with other men of Gopalpur, for their land if for nothing else, and he also competes with eminent men of his jati and locality for prestige and influence. He must somehow mollify or overshadow them or else they may unite to stem his advance. His success depends a great deal on his ability to recruit unwavering supporters from among his kinsmen.

A villager has scope for such recruitment because he can usually trace some kinship connection with many more of his jati-fellows than those with whom he actually keeps up kinship exchanges. This is the difference between the kinsmen of recognition and the kinsmen of cooperation, as Mayer calls them in his study of Ramkheri in Madhya Pradesh. There as elsewhere in village India a rich man invites many more relatives to a wedding, for example, than does a poor man. "Thus kinship largely depends on wealth and ability to invite and 'keep kin from growing cold' as the Ramkheri people say" (1960, p. 249).

In general, however, it is only the wider extension of kinship that depends on wealth because even a poor man must entertain his close relatives at the main life-cycle rites in his family. Also, even quite close relatives may not take great offense if they are not invited to the festivities of a poor man, but if they feel they have been snubbed by a man of wealth and prestige they must object vigorously or their own status and self-esteem will be by so much diminished.

Yet, as Mayer reports, kinship ties do lapse. In all classes of relationship there are instances in which the interchange has "grown colder," mainly by mutual abandonment. One man does less and then the potential partner in the reciprocity does less also. It was noted above that lineage bonds in Ramkheri are loosened with the passage of generations and with physical dispersal. The linkage, if not the precise ancestral links, tends to be remembered long after the interchange has lapsed. In Ramkheri the lineage of recognition is remembered about ten generations from the founder. The lineage of cooperation tends to last at the most for five or six generations. Among feminal kindred there is a similar difference between the cooperating kindred and those who are kindred of recognition only. Hence a rich man of Ramkheri is likely to include his wife's mother's brother among his kindred of cooperation and invite him to a wedding in the family, but a poor man is likely to omit such an invitation (Mayer 1960, pp. 169–172).

The villagers themselves, Mayer relates, make a clear distinction between those kin ties that exist only in theory and those that are maintained by coactivity. Many of them consider that kinship is defined more by social interchange than by remembered connections through descent or marriage. The ideal is to maintain as wide a kinship circle as wealth and energy will permit, and a successful family is one that keeps up a wide network of kin relations, that extends its kinship of cooperation as far as possible into the kinship of recognition. At the level of lineage and especially through the more expansible feminal kindred there is room for extension of relations. The feminal kindred provide a large field for maneuver; lineage mates are limited to the descendants of a founding ancestor, but the marriages of the several women of his family enable a man to establish bonds with a good many people of different families, kindreds, and lineages.

Among a man's fictive kin, also, there is a difference between those merely of recognition and those with whom he maintains close, friendly, supportive interchange. An ambitious man can create levers of power by transforming potential allies among his fictive kin into actual associates, just as he changes formal lineage kinsmen into close allies.

There is quite a different kind of fictive kinship that must be distinguished from the type just described. A man may establish an individual bond with another man as brother or with a woman as sister. Sometimes the pair may be of different jatis and usually the tie is created when the two take the same guru, the same mentor, and so become "guru" brothers and "guru" sisters (cf. Orenstein 1965a, p. 164). In the account of Ramkheri, these are called "ritual kin" and the other type of fictive bond is called "village kinship." The ritual tie provides a means of bridging differences of jati and neighborhood but little joint activity is entailed. Ritual kin treat each other as friends but not usually as close allies or working partners (Mayer 1960, pp. 139–146). Ritual kinship seems less motivated by considerations of power gain than by personal friendship and its effects are generally limited to the dyadic relationship.

The fact that kinship and power are often closely connected in village affairs should not lead us to view kinship as just a means to power. Quite apart from the other uses of kinship that we have noted—in the socialization of children and in the economic and religious spheres, for example—the chief environment in which a villager lives as an individual, in which he is cared for and cherished as a person, is the environment of kin. Such fundamental experiences in human relations as the private joys of husband and wife, the rearing of a child, the pride in children, the frolicking interplay among young brothers, the deep affection between brother and sister, the joyous welcome given to a sister's son, the happy visit of a mother's brother, the lively sojourn of a father's sister, the pleasure in grandchildren and the comfort of having grandparents —these and much else in kinship are apart from questions of power and are, in their way, as important for individual and society. But in the round of village life questions of power characteristically keep coming up, partly because social hierarchy is assumed yet the specific order is often contested and becomes an issue in a power struggle.

There are some men and families, even whole villages—who are relatively aloof from power struggles. Very many are not; they feel that they dare not be lest they sink shamefully to the lowest depths of their society. A villager's road to power is typically cleared first by mobilizing kin allies and by deploying them effectively. Nor can a villager shed his kin after he achieves a position of eminence. Thus, in the account of Khalapur, it is noted that a prominent man cannot afford to ignore his own kinsmen and friends. If he does to any marked degree, he is no longer a prominent man, no longer considered strong in village affairs (Minturn and Hitchcock 1963, p. 257). A powerful man, by definition, is one who sees to the welfare of many kinsmen. If he does not, whatever his resources of wealth may be and whatever connections he may have with higher sources of influence, villagers reckon that he cannot be a really powerful person.

To be respected, a man should accrue and support a wide range of kin; the pursuit of this ideal helps to explain and to rationalize his quest for power. A wealthy man can approach the ideal far better than can a poor man, and those jatis whose families are the wealthier in a community are better able to do so than are the poorer jatis. Any useful social relation among villagers is likely to be couched in the idiom of kinship because kinship relations are presumed to be more durable, stable, unconditional, and pervasive. Contractual and other kinds of relations are more limited in time, more constricted and conditional in use, fluctuating by occasion and context.

Kinship Bonds in North and in South India

Marriage alliances are the principal means by which new kinship bonds can be forged and, as has been noted in discussing family roles and maintenance, there is a fundamental difference in this regard between North and South India. Broadly put, in the South a family tries to strengthen existing kin ties through marriage, while in the North a family tends to affiliate with a separate set of people to whom it is not already linked.

The system of kinship terms used by most Dravidian-speaking people of South India is congruent with closer marriage. It dichotomizes all descent lines into those with whom one may marry and those with whom one may not. The terminology provides that in a man's own generation males are either brothers to him or brothers-in-law, and females are either sisters or potential spouses. Morgan long ago noticed that the Dravidian terminology is beautifully consistent and symmetrical (1871, p. 394). Its structure can be derived from a few postulates, a principal one being that the children of brother and sister should marry. The term used for cross-cousin of the opposite sex (a man's mother's brother's daughter and usually also his father's sister's daughter) has the connotation of prospective or possible spouse. By extension all potential mates are called cross-cousin. The kin of cooperation are periodically reconsolidated by marriages within that circle (cf. Dumont 1953; 1957a; Dumont and Pocock 1957c, pp. 58–64; Karve 1965, pp. 243–252).

In his analysis of South Indian kinship, Nur Yalman concludes that there is always emphasis on the connections and reciprocal rights between brother and sister. "Brother and sister must be separated, but their offspring must also be united." Yalman states that the preference that husband and wife should also be the children of a brother and sister is a close expression of the principal of jati endogamy (1967, pp. 374–375).

Ties of fictive kinship may be established in this pattern. Two jati fellows who are not actual kinsmen may arrange to become as of one kindred. Yalman cites an example of two newly rich men in a village in Ceylon (similar cases occur in South India) who found it expedient to join forces. One of them began to call the other mother's brother, and after the proper reciprocal terminology had been taken up by all in their respective families, he then married the other man's daughter. She had now become his cross-cousin and was a suitable spouse in Dravidian terminology (Yalman 1962, p. 554). Yalman also points out that the Dravidian-Kariera type of kinship terminology is used by the Sinhalese, by Ceylon Muslims of the East Coast who are matrilineal and matrilocal, and in South India by such very diverse peoples as the Todas, Coorgs, Pramalai Kallar, among many others. In his view, these varied societies share more than the system of terminology. They have in common a tendency to form close, intermarrying kindreds that are also centers of power (1962, pp. 567–569).

In most of North India, by contrast, there is a centrifugal rather than a centripetal tendency in making marriage alliances. A prospective match is seen more as an opportunity to ally two different sets of kin than as a way of strengthening an existing set. Each spouse is taken, in terminology and in practice, as a representative of his set, while the Dravidian terminology and practice is focused more on the person as an individual. In northern India, unilineal kin are often linked to a particular locality, either in fact or by implication, so that village exogamy is common. In the southern usage, the emphasis is more on bilateral connections, and there is little or no territorial exogamy. Affines in the south may cooperate and are involved in each other's affairs in a way that is not tolerated in northern jatis (cf. Karve 1965, pp. 104–138; Marriott 1960, pp. 40–43, 52–53; Yalman 1967, p. 348).

Résumé

The several echelons of kinship begin with the family as the primary multipurpose group. Family members provide for each other's biological needs and social care. The family is the main unit for reproduction and socialization, for consumption and production; it is a principal focus of interaction and attribution. Families develop through a cycle, with the major variations that we have noted.

In time, a family typically disperses into the local lineage, the next echelon of kinship cooperation. This consort of families, close both in agnatic descent and in residence, is usually close also in cooperation within the village. As a group, these related families form a unit for attribution as well as interaction within the jati. The clan, the larger kinship category, is used mainly to sort out potential spouses as possible or impossible. Another class of relatives, a person's feminal kin, interact importantly with him and he with them, but in a personal, dyadic way rather than as a corporate group.

A person's jati encompasses all his kin; its limits are the limits of his kinship relations both actual and potential. Kinship ties thus characterize and bound the jati. Relations among people of different jatis are fundamental in each local social system. These relations are examined in the next part of our inquiry.

PART III *Relations among People of Different Jatis*

CHAPTER 9 The Interdependence of
Families and Jatis

To CARRY on any civilization, men must specialize
their work in complex ways and exchange their products and services in a regular manner. That is, they are interdependent and they
follow a characteristic order of interdependence. This is scarcely a
new revelation, but in studying the peoples of India it is especially
important to clarify the actual as well as the purported interdependence.

The traditional specialization of a villager, as we have noted, follows the specialization assigned to his jati, which covers preferred,
permitted and forbidden occupations. The traditional modes of exchange are the counterparts of this specialization; in village society
they entail both contract and status relations, as Maine first used
these terms (1861).[1] That is, they involve a range of relationships
along a scale from purely contractual, individual, impersonal, temporary, limited transactions at one end to broadly supportive,
group-oriented, long-term, multiple bonds at the other.

Contractual and Jajmani Relations

The broader, more durable relations are essentially those between
a food-producing family and the families that supply them with
goods and services. These are called "jajmani" relations, the Hindi

[1] Students of Indian society can benefit, not only by Sir Henry Maine's
still useful writings, but also by the example of his life. In 1856 he was offered an appointment in India as legal member in council. His doctors told
him then that if he went to India "his life would not be worth three months'
purchase." But after a few years' delay he accepted the appointment and
went to Calcutta. He stayed for seven years and returned "a much stronger
man than he had been at his departure" (Stephen 1921).

word for them as used in William Wiser's study of the subject (1936). While contractual exchanges have become increasingly important in almost all villages, usually displacing some of the jajmani arrangements, commercial transactions have been part of the traditional economy for many centuries. Villagers in the region of Totagadde in western Mysore, for example, have been engaged in the production and export of a commercial crop, areca nuts, for at least six centuries (Harper 1959b, p. 776). Local, regional, even overseas markets have existed throughout the course of Indian civilization (cf. Thapar 1966, pp. 109–135); markets of a traditional kind are still important, as we shall note in a later chapter, for village economy and society.

Moreover, certain traditional occupations were, in many places, on a contractual rather than a jajmani basis. The weaver, Baines observed, "is not entitled to a customary share of the harvest, but is paid for what he makes and sells" (1912, p. 62). Finally, even in jajmani relations there are some products or services that have to be contracted and paid for separately. Thus in a village of Poona district, the ropemakers supply the farmers, under jajmani arrangements, with all necessary rope manufactures except for well ropes, which are specially long and thick and for which special payment must be made (Orenstein 1962, p. 304). I have known village barbers who provided their services in the traditional jajmani ways, except when a young man wanted a haircut in the city style. That had to be paid for in cash (cf. Sharma 1956a, pp. 128–130).

Cash or barter transactions have long been integral elements of village economy. Yet the traditional jajmani relations are more conspicuous in village life because they entail ritual matters and social support as well as economic exchanges. The whole of a local social order, the people and their paramount values, are involved in such jajmani links.

These links are between families rather than between jatis. Thus a family of farmers gets its metal tools from a particular family of the blacksmith jati and in return the blacksmith family gets a share of the farmer's crop at harvest. The relationship is supposed to be— and often is—durable, exclusive and multiple. It is durable in that the link may be inherited on both sides. A blacksmith serves the same farmer family that his father and grandfather served, and the farmer family gets its tools and repairs from the descendants of the blacksmith family whose men made tools for their forefathers. If one of the associated families dies out, another of its lineage may take its place in the relationship. If a blacksmith family has more sons than its clientele can support, some seek other associates in places where there is a shortage of smiths. Some take up other employment, often in farming, since men of any jati may work on the land.

Jajmani relations are exclusive in that the farmer family is supposed to carry on such relations with only one blacksmith family, and those blacksmiths should make tools only for their own farmer families. They may make some things for sale at a market as well, but they may not poach jajmani associates from other blacksmiths. Jajmani ties are multiple in that more than economic exchange is involved. There is much more to the association than just the exchange of shaves for rice or sickles for wheat.

The families of village officials or village servants, the watchman for example, maintain jajmani relations with the whole village rather than with particular families. Each watchman family gets a contribution at harvest time from every farmer family's crop. The village officials and servants may also have the tax-free use of village land. In some parts, especially in the Maharashtra region, the artisan and service families maintain jajmani relations with a segment of the village rather than with individual families. Such families there have rights to serve all who live in a particular section of the village, or who cultivate a certain section of land (Orenstein 1962, pp. 310–314; Baines 1912, p. 28).

In all jajmani relations, the right to provide goods or services to particular associates is vested in the family, inherited through the family or lineage, and enforced by the jati. If one blacksmith family attempts to take over the farmer associates of another, then the injured blacksmiths appeal to the council of their jati to call off the intruders. And if the blacksmiths of a village believe that the farmers are unfair to them, they may try to have all blacksmiths of the locality boycott the farmers until they give up their unfair practices.

The term "jajman" originally referred to the client for whom a Brahmin priest performed rituals, but it is generally used to refer to the patron or recipient of specialized services and the term "jajmani" refers to the whole relationship. The provider of goods or services is called by a variety of terms, "kamin," "parjan," "pardhan." "Balutedar" is the Marathi word (cf. Beidelman 1959, pp. 6–7).

Specialized Jatis and Multiple Functions

A patron family must carry on jajmani relations with those whose services are required for ritual purposes, especially concerning the family's pollution, and also with those whose services and products are materially useful (Pocock 1962, pp. 82–87). A family requires the services of a priest, often of a Brahmin jati, to maintain or restore the state of ritual purity suitable for its members. Even more, it must have the services of specialists of lower jatis to perform those necessary tasks that pollute those who do them—the washing of dirty clothes, the cutting of hair, the delivery of the newborn, the sweeping away of excreta, and similar defiling chores. All such tasks fall within the basic notion of pollution; all are ritually required in the traditional order.

The ritual specialists do not work for everyone in the village. Although washermen and barbers are not ranked among the higher jatis because their jati occupation involves work polluting to those who do it professionally, they will not ordinarily wash the clothes or cut the hair of the lowest villagers. Even they would be defiled and their jati status degraded by doing so.[2]

This is also true of a Brahmin jati of priests, whose services villagers see as on an entirely different plane from those rendered by the ritual specialists who absorb pollution (M. S. A. Rao 1961). They will not usually minister to families of the lowest jatis. Hence most Harijan families cannot get the services of these ritual specialists and so some of them perform these tasks for their jati fellows. When low-ranking families prosper, however, and are able to discard defiling practices, they try to get ritual specialists to serve them and, as we shall see later, they often succeed.

[2] In some places, there are different jatis of washermen to serve different blocs of the local hierarchy. In the south of Kerala, there is a special jati of barbers who serve Harijans (1931 Census, Vol. 28, Part 1, p. 382). Among the lowest of Kerala jatis are the Nayadis whose jati occupation is begging. The right to beg within a certain territory is held by a Nayadi family which can mortgage or sell this right to another Nayadi family (Aiyappan 1937, p. 29).

The other kind of jajmani workers are the artisans and the un-skilled laborers. Artisans generally exchange their products with anyone in the village (cf. Harper 1959b, p. 772). They tend to be more independent of the patrons than are the laborers, because a laborer family usually has its jajmani relations with a single family of landowners or cultivators, while artisans deal with a number of patron families and so are not totally bound to any one of them (cf. Bailey 1960b, p. 169).

Economic exchange is only one facet of jajmani relations. A land-owner family may have only occasional transactions with some of its associates, as with a goldsmith family in another village, but with others there is more frequent and many-sided interchange. A family of cultivators expects help on its ceremonial occasions from most of the associated families. There is also an expectation of mutual per-sonal support in family emergencies or factional quarrels. Some-times the specialist families are pressured to support the jati of their patrons when that whole jati is embattled.

Such reciprocal services are often formally stipulated, especially for life-cycle rites. In a village of Lucknow district, for example, a marriage in a family of Thakurs, the dominant landowners, involves the formal participation of families from ten of the fourteen jatis represented in the village (Majumdar et al. 1955, pp. 197–204; Ma-jumdar 1958a, pp. 43–49).

A principal ceremonial role is taken by the associated family of the barber jati. The barber's wife cleans and refurbishes the house; she massages the bride, helps her bathe and dress. She joins in the wedding songs and in the stylized derisions with which the groom's party is met. The barber himself accompanies the marriage party in the ceremonial round, doing for the members of the wedding what-ever tasks need to be done. He is present through all the ritual, help-ing the priest, performing such bits as the formal tying of the groom's shirt to the corner of the bride's dress. In return, the barber and his wife are given a sum of money and tips of a rupee or two when they perform some special service in the course of the rite.

At the birth of a Thakur child, the associated families also help. The household priest prepares the child's horoscope to guide in aus-picious planning for its development. A woman of one of the low jatis helps with the delivery, cuts the cord, cleans and attends the mother for several days after the birth. Then the barber's wife takes over as attendant, bathes and massages the mother, cleanses the room, helps with the household tasks.

A man of the barber's family hurries about, delivers invitations to the birth feast, helps with the chores at the feast. The household servants of the Pasi jati also carry the good news to friends and relations. Iron bangles for the baby and other metal requisites are provided by the blacksmith family. The washerman family launders the clothes of mother and infant, a special task because these have to be cleansed of the extraordinary defilement of childbirth (Majumdar et al. 1955, pp. 193–195). All who help receive gifts in return—of food, of money, of clothes. The amount given is partly set by custom and partly by considerations of the donor's affluence and the recipient's entreaty.

Jajmani associates are expected to be, and some are, broadly supportive of each other, with the quality of ready help that close kinsmen are expected to show. Villagers tend to be nostalgic about such supposed support in the past. One farmer of Shamirpet village near Hyderabad reminisced about his family's relations with their barber family. As Dube translates his comment, "In many cases they were just like members of our family, and although both parties maintained the traditional caste distance, we could always take each other into confidence even on matters of a delicate nature" (1955b, p. 61).

Barbers often do have a privileged relationship, for one reason because they frequently are used for reconnaissance and to make preliminary feelers in arranging a marriage. They are commonly the stage managers and technical assistants at ceremonies. Their women act as midwives. Because their nonbarbering functions are so useful, there are even jatis of Sikh barbers in Sikh villages where the cutting of hair is forbidden but where the traditional managerial, midwifery, and communications functions of a barber jati are needed (Patnaik 1960b; I. P. Singh 1958, p. 481).

Even when a patron's jati is at odds with a client's jati, personal relations between the two families may well remain friendly, even covertly supportive, despite the antagonism between their groups (cf. Bailey 1960b, p. 138). In personal emergencies, as when a farmer needs help quickly to save his crop, he is likely to call on his jajmani associates for help. And when a worker is in dire need, he expects his patron to do something to help him, whether by loans or by supporting him before government officials or in the village council (Wiser 1936, pp. 112–116).

In factional contests each side usually tries to rally its jajmani associates. This occurred in Senapur, a village not far from Banaras, in 1957. The Noniyas, traditionally low-ranking earth workers, had prospered enough by then to build a primary school in their hamlet. The dominant landowners, the Thakurs, viewed this as a threat to their dominant position. When the Noniyas tried to get the village carpenters, tile-makers (potters), and bamboo workers to help in constructing the school, they failed because the Thakur patrons put pressure on these jati-groups. The Noniyas next tried to hire such workers from other villages and again they failed, because the Thakurs of Senapur had enlisted the support of the Thakurs in these other villages. In the end, the Noniyas did succeed in building the school by buying construction materials from a place adjacent to Banaras city and hiring carpenters from a distant village (Rowe 1963, p. 44).

Jajmani Payments and Obligations

The relation usually involves multiple kinds of payment and obligations as well as multiple functions. This is illustrated in a study of an artisan jati, the Lohars, of the same village of Senapur in Jaunpur district of eastern U.P. (Reddy 1955). The traditional work of the Lohars is with iron as blacksmiths. In Senapur they also work in wood, because there are no carpenters in the village. They make and repair agricultural implements for the landowner-farmers, the Thakurs.

This work is apportioned among the Lohars according to hereditary shares. Each family has an exclusive and inalienable right over its share of work, which is not encroached upon by others. The Thakurs too are bound by the same fixed tenure. "When a Lohar family multiplies and divides the work, each share comes to compass the work of fewer agriculturists unless they also multiply at the same rate" (Reddy 1955, p. 130).

A Lohar family's right to a certain set of clients is treated as a property right; at the father's death, his clients are divided among his sons or his sons-in-law. Should one family have more clients than it can handle, its men may—after proper consultation with other Lohars and with the patrons—transfer some of their clientele to another family. As in other kinds of property, there is uneven distribution among Lohar families. One may have a larger, more lucrative practice than does another.

Lohars cooperate to maintain adequate service for all patrons. When one of the Lohars fell ill during a busy season, another took on the sick man's work in addition to his own. He asked for no recompense for the extra work, either from his jati-fellow or from the Thakurs. In the 1950s, there had been no encroachment within living memory by one Lohar on another's jajmani rights. When there was such a case in a nearby village, the jati council "came down with a heavy hand and fixed the offender in his former place" (Reddy 1955, p. 138).

The amount of work a Lohar family is expected to perform for an associated Thakur family is reckoned according to the amount of cultivated land. A standard measure is called a yoke of cultivation, the land which can be cultivated with one pair of bullocks. This is about fifteen *bighas*, some ten acres. For a Thakur family of one yoke cultivation, the Lohar family puts in about sixty to seventy man-hours of work each year and receives about 40 *seers* (about 80 pounds) of grain.

Certain kinds of work, as on new types of agricultural implements, are not clearly included in the customary arrangements. Some patrons own mechanical chaff-cutters and sugarcane presses. Minor repairs on these are treated as part of the jajmani work, but a patron who adds extra payment for these jobs is apt to get better service (Reddy 1955, pp. 138–139).

Lohars also make ritual accessories for their clients—bridal seats for weddings, tables for household worship, litters for funerals— and receive suitable gifts in return. When minor repairs are needed in a patron's house, his Lohar makes them—without charge if it takes a matter of minutes, paid with extra foodstuff if he must spend a few hours at it.

Here end the obligations of jajmani relations; work of other kinds is a matter of daily hire and wage competition. When a Lohar works at building a new house, or making a cart, or on major repair of a sugarcane press, he works for an agreed daily wage or at a piece rate. Some Lohars are known for special skills. Two brothers of Senapur are good at press repair; another Lohar specializes in making carts. A Lohar who takes on a large job shares the work with his jati-fellows. They share capital equipment too. "It is also a day-to-day occurrence that the few Lohars who have installed bellow furnaces freely offer their equipment to be made use of by other Lohars" (Reddy 1955, p. 138).

The distinction made by these Lohars between work in the jajmani relation and that in a more contractual context is often made in village economy. It is the difference between regular services in the traditional round and work on occasional jobs or on new varieties of equipment and service. Sometimes, as has occurred in Senapur, work on new equipment begins to merge into the regular jajmani account.

The traditional method of payment, in all regions, is made dramatically at harvest time when each farmer family hands over some newly cut sheaves to its jajmani families, or measures out a pile of grain on the threshing floor for each of them (Wiser 1936, pp. 65–67; Srinivas 1955b, pp. 14–15; Neale 1962, pp. 20–27). These harvest payments are only part of what the worker family receives. Where the cultivators own most or all the land of the village, all sorts of rights are under their control. An artisan or service family may be dependent on a landowning family for their house site, for places where their animals may graze, for wood and cow-dung fuel, for the loan of tools and draft animals, even for a plot to use for funeral pyres. In addition, the patron family gives them clothing and other gifts on ceremonial occasions, gives small tips for special service, and may help with loans of money in emergencies and with protection against predatory neighbors (cf. Wiser 1936, pp. 10–11).

Supply, Demand, and Flexible Payments

In some areas, the administrative land records for the village, through the British period, stipulated the precise obligations and payments that were to be met under jajmani arrangements. Even the gifts each associated family was entitled to receive at a wedding in the patron's family were specified (Wiser 1936, pp. 14–15; Lewis 1958, pp. 60–61, 163). But whether there were such officially recorded codes or not, the actual exchange varied with the bounty of the harvest, the respective claims of the associates, and conditions of supply and demand.

This still obtains where jajmani relations are kept up. During a lean year a farmer simply cannot share out as much as he normally does, but when the sheaves are heavy and the granaries full he does not begrudge some extra measures to those who have given good service. But even in the best of years, a farmer is not likely to parcel out more than the minimum amount to, say, a carpenter who has repeatedly put off doing the farmer's repairs or to a washerman who has lost and torn clothes beyond ordinary endurance.

Similarly, a worker family adjusts the measure of its service according to the payment and treatment its members receive. In Rampura in Mysore, for example, those who pay in grain are favored over those who pay only in money; grain payments imply enduring, reliable relationships. "The quality of the service rendered by the Smith, Potter, Washerman, and Barber depends on whether the customer pays annually in grain or not, on the quantity of grain paid, and on the customer's general social position" (Srinivas 1955b, pp. 11, 13).

There seem to be villages where jajmani payments are made quietly, without demur or harangue by any party. But in my own observation, at least some of those who pay feel themselves bedeviled by their importunate workers and they proclaim so loudly. And some of those who are paid argue vigorously against the miserable, miserly amounts that they say are offered; they may not feel strong enough to voice their complaints loudly, but they do so frequently, as though to accept the patron's payments too meekly and silently might invite a smaller payment next time.

Payments also fluctuate according to the available supply of skills and labor and the demand for them. If there is a shortage of blacksmiths, the farmer who is most liberal with extra gifts is likely to get the best service from a blacksmith family. Specialists are imported into a locality where there is need for them. Brahmins have been enticed to settle in places where previously there were no Brahmins, when some of the residents had become prosperous and ambitious enough to require their services. Leading villagers of Totagadde in Mysore recruited a barber from another village when their village barber died and left no successor (Harper 1959b, p.

770). In another Mysore village, all the local sweepers had taken other employment at the time I visited the village. The village leaders brought in a family of a Harijan jati from another linguistic region to do the sweeper's menial work.

Another means of alleviating a local shortage in a particular craft is to have men of another, similar jati do it in addition to their traditional profession. The Lohar blacksmiths of Senapur do carpentry because there is no family of a carpenter jati in the village. Conversely, when there are too many men in a jati-group for employment in their traditional occupations, some of them have to migrate or turn to work on the land. Agricultural labor is open to all, insofar as such work is available.

Supply-and-demand adjustments in traditional jajmani relations are, to be sure, less flexible than those provided through contractual and market transactions. A jajmani patron cannot abruptly discharge a superfluous or inefficient worker or quickly hire new workers, but there was and is a considerable degree of economic adjustability even in the traditional arrangements (Beidelman 1959, pp. 53–56; Orenstein 1962, p. 313; Pocock 1962, p. 91; Kolenda 1963, p. 22; Bose and Jodha 1965, p. 117).

The actual amounts paid to each participating family in a jajmani relation can vary according to differences in size of clientele. In a village of Poona district, the largest amounts are received by carpenters, blacksmiths, and menial workers of the untouchable jatis. A family of Brahmin priests gets lesser amounts from each patron (Orenstein 1962, p. 305). But though a Brahmin priest may get less from any one family, he may collect from more families and may have other sources of income.

In some Mysore villages that Alan Beals has studied, men of the lowest jatis are employed as village servants, as watchmen and irrigators. This gives them a more assured income than that enjoyed by families of several other jatis which rank higher in the local hierarchies. But overall, men of the higher jatis generally receive a higher rate of pay for their services than workers of the lower groups. Unskilled workers are most dependent on the good graces of patron families and are usually least able to exert leverage to better their condition. In Gould's tabulation of actual jajmani payments in Sherurpur village (Faizabad district, U.P.) "the washermen received the lowest average remuneration, the barbers next lowest,

and the carpenters and blacksmiths the highest—an order of precedence which accords perfectly with their relative traditional sta-
tuses" (1964, p. 20).

Those who provide specialized skills and services themselves need
the goods and services of others. A carpenter family requires a
barber, a shopkeeper family needs its washermen and other service
workers. In Senapur, the landowner family tended to manage the
whole set of their workers; the carpenter, barber, and washerman
families who served them also served the Noniyas who were their
tenants, and each of these provided services for the others (Rowe
1963, pp. 42–43). But landowners in most other places did not
manage their associated families so tightly; each specialist family
made its own jajmani arrangements, either through direct exchange
of labor or by paying in cash or kind (cf. Gould 1964, pp. 33–34).

Few villages hold a complete array of specialist families. The
people of Sherurpur, for example, use the services of thirty-five
households of specialists who live in a number of the nearby villages. Each of these villages has its own network of jajmani affili-
ates. Thus jajmani ties establish a web of relationships among villages across the land in which there are few complete breaks.
Gould comments on jajmani affiliations radiating from Sherurpur,
"Taken to its logical conclusion, therefore, such a network as
this ultimately reaches to the borders of a linguistic region and
perhaps to some extent even beyond" (1964, p. 34).

Enforcement of Jajmani Relations: Coercion and Consensus

Jajmani interchange is between families of a locality; jajmani
counterchange, however, devolves on the jatis. The enforcing of
jajmani rules rests with the jatis that are involved in an issue about
them. These rules can be flexibly interpreted in various ways but
certain minimum standards are maintained at any given time in
each jajmani relation. Thus a shift in service arrangements between
a blacksmith and a landowner family in Senapur village could not
be done only by the families involved, but had to be approved by
the elders of each jati-group. And when a blacksmith usurped
clients from another blacksmith family, their jati council punished
the offender.

If the dominant landowners of a village become convinced that one of their service or artisan groups is derelict in its obligations or threatens the power and status of the landowners, the patron families are likely to bring collective pressure on them by withholding payment, by beating their men, or through any number of other means of harassment. The attacked jati-group may retaliate through a boycott, refusing to provide their services until the landowners retract or compromise.

Such clashes are apt to spread from one village to others in the locality where jati-fellows of the opposed groups live. Both sides have the general village audience to their quarrel very much in mind because what is often at stake is not merely a demand for higher pay or fewer duties, but the insignia and prerogatives of higher rank within the whole local order.

Collective action by either side has to overcome loyalties to jajmani associates in favor of the interests of the jati (cf. Gough 1960, p. 27; Orenstein 1962, p. 710). Yet when jati fellows really become convinced that their jati status is in danger, jati solidarity prevails. Then the united strength of the landowners is usually greater than that which any artisan or service jati can muster. Historically, however, some artisans have maintained their stand quite well. We shall note later that a loose confederation of five artisan jatis pressed their claims for higher status over much of South India for several centuries until the present time. They did not overcome the resistance of higher jatis, but by the same token they were not beaten down. Landowners could not dispense with their services nor shatter their general unity.

But jatis whose men are mainly landless laborers have no such resources and can wage no such struggle. The vast differential in power between the richest and highest in a village and the lowest and poorest has been taken by some authors as the central element in jajmani relations. It is the main reason for their scathing critiques of jajmani relations (Beidelman 1959; Lewis and Barnouw 1956). These authors excoriate jajmani arrangements as the means by which the rich and powerful exploit the poor and coerce the workers into sustaining the power of those who have the upper hand and the higher rank.

Other students of Indian village life have replied to these critiques, saying that there is consensus as well as coercion in jajmani relations, that jajmani exchanges bring solidarity and mutual benefits as well as conflict and exploitation. These observers note that, in their own observations of jajmani interchange, artisans and service workers are not totally helpless against the landowners; all jatis seek to maximize their gains, all wield as much power as they can, all villagers want to avoid pollution insofar as they can, and some coercion and exploitation are inevitable in all societies. They argue that to condemn jajmani arrangements as brutally exploitative is too sweeping and obfuscating a generalization (Rao 1961; Orenstein 1962; Berreman 1962b, p. 393; Kolenda 1963, pp. 21–29; Gould 1964, pp. 29–39).

This exchange among anthropologists parallels the controversies among sociologists about stratification in which some writers stress the conflicts and disruptions that are involved in a stratified order and others emphasize the integration and effective action that orderly stratification makes possible.

Clearly, however, all these forces and elements are involved. At one stage in the development of a society conflict and disruption may be in the ascendant and at another period internal concord and unity will be more characteristic. Those who now decry jajmani arrangements as exploitative may be justified in doing so in order to arouse remedial action. But objective understanding of a traditional relationship is not much advanced through the use of polemical terms.

Change and Continuity in Jajmani Relations

The jajmani relationship has by now been largely supplanted in many villages, although in relatively few has it completely disappeared. It has been supplanted mainly because more money is now used in village economy and because modern transport makes market transactions more feasible. Cash crops are usually not included in jajmani arrangements. A worker or artisan who is paid with a load of sugarcane can only try to sell it, and he prefers to get the money in the first place. Where food grains are raised for sale, as in irrigated villages in Maharashtra, the cultivators who have money may prefer to pay for their shaves and pots with cash at a market center. Many artisans and specialists have moved to market centers and towns and do their work there (Orenstein 1962, pp. 313, 316; Karve and Damle 1963, p. 37).

Moreover, the power of a local dominant jati has been reduced in many places because their village dependents can move away more easily than was formerly possible, can get some income from outside the village, and can better summon political help for their complaints. With less isolation and reduced concentration of political power, the coercive element in jajmani relations has also been reduced (cf. Orans 1967).

Yet the advantages of jajmani for economic stability and security are still sufficiently great that many villagers want to continue with at least some such arrangements. The cultivator gains from them in that he gets better credit and a more certain labor supply than he usually can through cash transactions. Artisans and service families work for him through the year without much pay and then are given a large payment at the time when the farmer can best afford to do so, at harvest. At times of peak demand for labor, a farmer is more likely to get help from jajmani associates than from those who can charge whatever the market will then bear. The workers, in their turn, get more assured employment, and a variety of gifts and concessions, which together may amount to more than money wages could buy in the village. In recent decades, when grain has regularly been scarce and the value of the rupee whimsical, payment in grain is often preferred.

In a questionnaire survey in five Maharashtrian villages, over two-thirds of the respondents (222 of 326) answered that they thought the *balutdari* (jajmani) arrangements were convenient, mainly because of the credit facility. Only some 10 percent of the respondents thought that these arrangements were unprofitable. Others approved of them either because they were traditional or because of the general security they provided (Karve and Damle 1963, pp. 28, 151–152).

In addition to the economic benefits, the ritual services that jajmani associates provide are still in demand. Some landowners in villages of Poona district keep up jajmani relations mainly so that they may have ritual services readily available, as when a washerman must cleanse polluted clothing after a death, or when a messenger of low jati must be sent around to relatives with the news of a death, or when a goldsmith must purify the household deities (Orenstein 1962, p. 312). Presumably all such services can be obtained for hire but hired persons may not readily be available when needed nor can they be trusted to do their ritual work thoroughly if they do not have long-standing ties with the family served. Further, in villages where factional struggles are common, a landowner likes to have dependable support from at least some in other jatis, and worker families like to have a patron's protection.

This is not to say that jajmani relations are on the increase, but rather that this mode of traditional interdependence still has its uses as is shown in three villages where jajmani relations have been studied, one in Mysore, one in Rajasthan, and one in Uttar Pradesh.

Totagadde, in Shimoga district of northwestern Mysore, is the village in which the growing of a cash crop, areca nuts, has been the main productive enterprise for centuries. The relations between a landowner-horticulturalist and those who work for him are more limited, temporary, and contractual than are traditional jajmani relations where subsistence agriculture is the mainstay. Yet even in this village many persistent relationships exist between cultivators and workers. Some service workers serve for a year; some artisans keep the same customers for many years; many workers and artisans are under obligation to a landowner for the kinds of favors that are in his gift, such as lending money without interest, helping in litigation, lending tools, giving building materials and garden produce. In this village "the concept of obligation gives a greater measure of stability and permanency to economic relationships than otherwise might exist" (Harper 1959b, p. 773).

Jati separation is as sharp in this village as it is elsewhere in the region. The commercial economy did not undermine jati organization or the ranking of jatis. It did affect the nature of interdependence, but did not cancel out the inclination toward relationships more durable than monetary market dealings alone.

In a village of Barmer district in western Rajasthan, there have been notable changes, but when Bose and Jodha studied the villagers in 1963, many of them still maintained some jajmani relations. This is a village where subsistence agriculture is carried on under semi-arid conditions. Before independence, it was part of a princely state and the demesne of a feudal overlord. His departure opened the village to new influences and in their train jajmani relations have become more voluntary. Families that prefer to do so may contract for services, and some service families no longer perform their traditional occupations. But many keep up certain jajmani relations. Of a sample of 129 households out of a total of some four hundred, about 75 percent maintained jajmani ties with families of the low leatherworker jati. About 60 percent maintained such ties with carpenter families (Bose and Jodha 1965, p. 111).

Leatherworkers do the ritually polluting work of preparing hides and making leather goods; they also do such defiling chores as removing dead animals from the fields and such menial tasks as collecting fuel and carrying messages. Because the jati council of these leatherworkers had ruled against such degrading work, thirteen of the seventeen households of this jati in the village had stopped doing it. But four families have ignored the council's ruling and gain most of their income from carrying on their jati's traditional service. Of the fourteen carpenter families in the village, eight participate in jajmani relations but get only about half their income in that way. Both the blacksmith families maintain jajmani arrangements but get less than half their income from them (Bose and Jodha 1965, p. 117).

Not much of the village economy is now carried on through jajmani arrangements; however, we do not know whether very much more was so managed in earlier years. Some ritual services are still carried on within jajmani arrangements, especially in matters concerning death pollution. Many express favorable opinions about jajmani. Of 129 patrons questioned in this study, 126 replied that jajmani relations were useful in providing cheap and dependable labor and 111 agreed that another benefit was in cheap and assured ritual services. Only 24 agreed that social support was one of the benefits of jajmani relations.

Among those who provide jajmani services, 12 of the 14 questioned replied that assured income was one benefit and 10 agreed that gifts and concessions were important. Payments are made in both cash and kind but most patrons (76 percent) replied that payment in kind gave better returns to the workers (Bose and Jodha 1965, pp. 118–123).

The situation in this village is repeated in many others. Villagers are generally favorable toward the real and supposed benefits of jajmani, but relatively few carry on complete jajmani relations. Those who provide services are now reluctant to accept any overall stigma of inferiority, those who receive services hesitate to take on multiple obligations. But many carry on some jajmani relations and even more give a jajmani-like quality to their economic and ritual exchanges with people of other jatis, gaining some stability of relations without the full roster of jajmani obligations.

Similar conclusions emerge from Gould's close study of contemporary jajmani relations in Sherurpur-Naktipur, adjoining hamlets in a densely populated area south of Faizabad city in U.P. Families of six specialist jatis maintain regular jajmani relations with the cultivators and other villagers. Washermen have the largest proportion of their clientele, 77 percent, on a fixed grain-payment basis. Here also it is the ritual, pollution-absorbing aspect of the service that is important.

Carpenters and blacksmiths are next highest in jajmani clientele with 69 percent and 67 percent respectively of their custom in such arrangements. This is not only because of the importance to a cultivator of having secure relations with these artisans but also because "the capacity to retain traditional ties with carpenters and blacksmiths marks a household as socially important" (Gould 1964, p. 18). The barbers in the village have 62 percent of their clientele on a jajmani basis; despite the easy availability of commercial barbering and its lucrativeness for barbers, this jajmani arrangement tends to be maintained because of the ritual importance of the barber. Two other specialist jatis, potters and plowmen, have only minor jajmani ties.

Among patrons of Sherurpur, the two highest jati-groups, Thakurs and Brahmins, have the highest proportion (70 percent) of jajmani relations. These families maintain "no relationships that do not retain at least some traditional flavor" (Gould 1964, p. 19). Even the families of "menial-impure" jatis carry on a considerable proportion (43 percent) of their dealings with the service jatis through jajmani arrangements. Among all jatis, families with the greatest proportion of cash income tend to rely least on jajmani arrangements while those who have grain but little cash use jajmani services most (Gould 1964, pp. 19, 35).

Though jajmani relations are clearly important in the eyes of these villagers, they are of minor consequence in the village economy. The most valuable and productive crop is sugarcane and this cash crop does not enter into jajmani. The harvest of grain and peas in 1960 for the 70 households that engage in jajmani relations came to 221 tons. Of this production, a little over three tons was disbursed as fixed payments to jajmani specialists. Only about 1.5 percent of the relevant harvest was distributed in the jajmani pattern (Gould 1964, pp. 30–31).

This figure does not include the many exchanges that are not fully on a jajmani basis but that are also not completely contractual or commercial. Thus the people who do the polluting tasks of removing dead animals, of working in leather, of assisting at childbirth are here paid in both cash and kind, with both wages and gifts, for a single job and over an extended period. But even if these payments were taken into account, they would add up to only a small part of total village production.

In the past, a greater part of village economy in this region was probably carried on through jajmani arrangements, but it is not at all clear that a major part of production and distribution was so channeled. What is clear, however, is that jajmani relations were and, to a degree, still are important for the ritual and social order. The jajmani pattern, Gould concludes, "arises from a religious dichotomy between pure and impure whose implications work themselves out as a complex system of religious and economic relationships embracing, and indeed in large part defining the dimensions of a locality" (1965, pp. 17, 38–39). Jajmani interchange, in this and many other villages, still provides a measure of economic credit and stability; even more, it helps to define the local social order by defining those who can secure ample ritual services.

Solutions to the Problems of Interdependence

All peoples who maintain a civilization must establish effective interdependence among specialist groups. Such relations should be reliable, enduring, and trustworthy, but they should also be flexible, manipulable, and adaptable. The two kinds of qualities militate against each other. If a relationship is easily begun and readily terminated, it is not likely to be enduringly reliable. If it is endowed with an aura of durability, it cannot readily be adapted to changing circumstances.

Indian villagers have traditionally included both kinds of interdependence in their societal repertoire. Some relationships have been contractual, limited, and flexible through the use of money, barter, and markets. The other relationships have been broad and durable. Villagers define kinship relations as more broadly supportive and enduring than are most others and see jati as a unit whose members are or could be kinsmen. Jajmani relations provide for nonkinship interdependence in ways that nevertheless have some of the same qualities of reliability and perdurance. These relations are guided and enforced by villagers acting in their capacities as jati members, but the actual exchanges are made between villagers acting as members of their respective families.

We shall note later that tribal peoples in India remained in smaller, less productive groups because, for one reason, they did not have as effective ways of relating to nonkinsmen. The solution that was developed in Indian civilization remained in use for many centuries, until the impact of modern influences became felt. One response to these influences was to shift more exchanges to contractual relations and so to amplify that traditional side of economic activities. But villagers have been inclined to continue with at least some jajmani-like relations for the broader, more personal and supportive bonds that many villagers want to keep.

Villagers, moreover, tend to see social relations as hierarchically ordered. In those jajmani relations that involve ritual services, underlying ideas about hierarchical relations are symbolized. These ideas provide a rationale for the order of village society; they indicate who should be higher and who lower, and why it should be that way. We next examine the criteria that villagers use in explaining and calibrating their social order.

INTERDEPENDENCE among families and jatis is more than an order of precedence for particular transactions: it is taken as an order of life. In each person's dealings with his neighbors of other jatis, their rank relative to his prohibits some kinds of interchange and sets limits on others.

The social order is made manifest in a thousand and one details of daily life. For the most part, these details are so commonplace that a villager is hardly aware of them. Thus, when men gather to talk, whether in gossip session or serious council meeting, they generally seat themselves with consideration to jati rank. A cot is often used as a bench; some sit on it, others sit on the ground. The upper part of the cot, the part where a sleeper puts his head, is reserved for those of higher rank in the assemblage. The seating order described for a village of Kanpur District is this: Brahmins must precede all others on the upper cot, Thakurs precede all but Brahmins. Those of next higher rank sit at the foot of the cot, those of quite inferior status sit on the ground. When only men from the lowest jatis are present, say Chamar leatherworkers and Dhanuk pigkeepers, men of the two jatis may sit on the same cot, but a Chamar will allow a Dhanuk to sit only at the lower part (Sharma 1956a, p. 259).

Seating arrangements are more than polite distributions in space, they symbolize authority arrangements and power relations. The Brahmins sitting at the head of the cot and the Thakurs next to them are expected by all to take the lead in the talk and then to express for all whatever consensus may be reached. The Dhanuk pigkeeper, from his place on the edge of the ground-sitters, is not expected and does not usually expect to be heard prominently, whether the talk is banter or deliberation. In some villages the Brahmin jati-group is small and relatively insignificant; it is given precedence but does not possess power. The Brahmin who speaks from his place at the head of the cot in such villages may have an influential voice only in matters of minor ritual performance, not in questions of weighty secular decision.

Separation in seating is but one detail of the permitted interchange and forbidden contacts among jatis. In some matters, notably marriage, there should be no interchange outside the jati. For other activities, such as smoking together, there may be a larger circle of permissibility. Those in the highest ranks are usually quite rigorous about avoiding close contacts with those of the lowest; they insist that the lowest groups use separate water sources, separate residential areas, and various other means of ensuring physical as well as social distance between the lowest and the highest jatis.

Rank-free Contexts of Behavior

Powerful and pervasive as is the order of jati rank, there are limits to its application. It does not enter equally into all activities; it is not constantly in the forefront of attention; it is not an itemized, ironclad code for interaction.

In certain activities, as has been mentioned previously, the relative rank of the participants is of less consequence than it is in others. Work in the fields, for example, is far less involved with ritual avoidances than is work in the kitchen. During the bustle of the harvest, people of widely different jati rank may work side by side and may come in physical contact in ways that are tabooed in the houses and streets of the village. People of every jati rank may work on the land, and they work together more closely there than elsewhere (Jagalpure and Kale 1938, pp. 393–394; Mathur 1958a, pp. 51–52; Silverberg 1959; Gould 1964, p. 32).

In play as in agricultural work, jati restrictions tend to be mitigated. Thus in wrestling matches between village teams in Mysore, young men of all jatis, except the very lowest, may lock arms in competition (Beals 1964, p. 107). The dramatic troupes that tour villages in western U.P. can include actors of different jatis (Gumperz 1964, p. 94). In some contexts of worship, especially in the devotional *bhakti* worship, differences of jati rank among the devotees are supposed to be irrelevant and to some extent actually are overlooked. Such latitude in work, sport, drama, and worship is old in India; the generally freer conduct outside the village, as at markets or fairs, is also of long standing. With the modern expansion of villagers' experiences with towns, commerce, government, and new forms of work, there has been an extension of the traditional leeway to these new activities.

Wide difference in rank does not preclude informal personal relations. A woman of a sweeper jati may come into a wealthy household of high status to do the menial cleaning, to remove ordure and the like. Her movements in the household are strictly bounded; she may not enter the kitchen or touch persons or come too close to the household shrine. But her daily visit may be most welcome to the women of the household who, being of high rank, are much restricted in their movements outside their house. Though their movements are restricted, their avid interest in the private lives of their neighbors is not. The sweeper woman goes about the village freely and visits different homes. She can be a prime carrier of gossip, a center of human interest, and she sometimes is a source of lively amusement.

In households that employ full-time servants, as Jyotirmoyee Sarma describes in a Bengal village in Hoogly district, the servants become members of the household even though they must keep to jati avoidances. Such servants of the low Bagdi jati cannot enter the inner rooms, must not touch or handle the water to be used for bathing or drinking, and must observe many other taboos. Yet the children of the household use terms of fictive kinship with them and such servants may be trusted with considerable responsibility (Sarma 1960, pp. 192–195).

Despite such limitations, jati rank does impinge directly on many aspects of village life. The tokens of rank often indicate real differences in power as well as in symbolic precedence, great differences in privilege as well as in forms of address. One villager's expectations about another's behavior are framed by the other's jati rank and customs. Their dealings with each other are constrained by the relative positions of their jatis in the local order.

On what grounds then, do villagers assume that there is a ranked order and how do they explain the rankings they make? The higher jatis, as is the way of the powerful everywhere, explain it on the basis of their inherently superior worth. Those of lower jatis are not always sure about that, but they are usually quite sure that their own jati is worthy of higher place than it presently enjoys. Villagers generally agree that the rankings involve ritual purity and pollution. The ritual criteria they note are indeed important; secular forces are also important factors in jati ranking, as will be discussed in Chapter 12.

Ritual Criteria: Personal Pollution and Purity

The traditional explanation is that people of higher jatis are less defiled and keep themselves more pure for purposes of religious ritual than are those of lower jatis. The lowest jatis are the most polluted and least able to have close relations with the higher gods and the higher jatis. Both pollution and purity are linked to a person's biological and physical acts; they are especially related to the bodily processes of men and animals. Perhaps explanations of social superiority and inferiority in all societies are ultimately linked to personal, corporal experiences. Certainly these experiences have been related to religious concepts in many. In Indian civilization these links are explicit and have been explicitly applied in the ordering of village society.

The main emphasis of the ritual criteria is on pollution rather than on purity. Becoming polluted bars a person from ready relations with man and god. He must keep his distance from people who are not so polluted as he is, lest his defect disable them also; he may not perform acts of worship because, in his defective state, he is repugnant to the deities. Any serious pollution entails avoidance and isolation.

There is, however, a vast difference between the two main kinds of pollution. One kind is temporary and personal pollution, to which every mortal is subject daily. The other kind is that permanent and corporate pollution ascribed to all in a jati, which is a main criterion in sorting out the social order (cf. Kane 1941, pp. 165–179).

The sources of pollution are many; the most potent of them are contacts with death and with bodily emissions such as blood and excreta. Every person is impaired by these defilements both regularly and sporadically. When a person defecates or urinates, he is thereby unclean. He must avoid ordinary relations with humans and must not approach the supernaturals until he has cleansed himself, if only by a token wash and perhaps a token prayer.

Every secretion and excretion that is separated from the body— as well as any separated growth of hair and nails—becomes a defiling object; by the act of severance a person puts himself in an impure state. "Faeces, urine, semen, menstrual blood, spittle, and parings of nail and hair are all ritually impure" (Srinivas 1952a, p. 104; see also Mathur 1964, pp. 103–105). These are not all charged with equal pollution potential. After touching one's own saliva, only a wash of the hands is necessary; at menstruation a woman must undergo much more prolonged purification.

Each person must put himself in the state of purity suitable to whatever activity he undertakes. A householder, in the Bengal village studied by Sarma, must wash and change clothes before touching cooked food, especially rice. Once having touched food, he is not in a fit state to turn to other activity until he has washed again. The act of ingestion puts a person in a state of mild disability; he must discharge himself from that state by a ritual wash before going on (Sarma 1955, p. 171). Eating does not involve either bodily emissions or death, the principal sources of pollution, but like them it involves a transition from one ongoing state of being to another. Such transitions are sensitive states ritually, if not actually defiling.

Many villagers abbreviate or omit such daily rites of transition because they have neither time nor a change of clothes nor great concern with ritual niceties. Yet few ignore these daily transitions altogether; even poor villagers of the lowest jatis are sensitively aware of impure states. Harijans also guard, as best they can, against certain kinds of pollution. A Brahmin in this Bengal village does not omit certain ritual steps that others may omit. Thus he must change his clothes as well as wash after excretion. "Before changing clothes, a Brahmin may not enter his own room or touch any household objects, and if he touches even a low caste (untouchable) at such a moment, the latter will be defiled and will need a change of clothing" (ibid.).

The most dramatic emission of all is childbirth. After a birth, mother and child must remain in seclusion for a specified period, have the proper ritual acts performed for them and undergo purificatory rites to mark the end of the seclusion period. Thus purified, the mother may resume normal relations within her family and village; the child can emerge into society as he has into the world. Other members of the household are affected by the event of childbirth; they too must undergo some ritual restoration to their normal status.

Pollution is not the only reason given for seclusion after childbirth. The seclusion may be thought of as a means of protecting mother and infant during a period when both are particularly vulnerable to untoward influences, much as infants in a hospital nursery are secluded from unhygienic visitors. In other rites of transition also, the ritual acts are done for several reasons, but purification is always one of them.

Death in a family is the most traumatic transition and brings disabling effects upon the surviving kin. These effects must be expunged by ritual before the close relatives can reenter normal life. Proximity to death imperils a person from the supernatural sphere and disables him in the social sphere. Funeral rites are directed toward restoring all those who have been so imperiled and disabled to a condition of relative purity, of social safety and normality. Among the Kotas of the Nilgiris, for example, widows and widowers must undergo purificatory ritual and the whole lineage must be cleansed and restored. The very corpse and spirit of the deceased are not finally pure, able to take their proper place in the cosmos, until the proper rituals have been enacted (Mandelbaum 1954b, pp. 89–90). So is it generally in village India; all and everything that has been close to the event of death must be ceremonially restored to normalcy.

Every person thus must go through a cycle of impairment and restoration both regularly and sporadically. Bodily excretion imposes a daily cycle; other biological facts—of sex, of menstruation, of cutaneous growth, of birth, of death—entail recurrent disability and require periodic restitution. When a person is brushed by the death or birth of a close kinsman, the experience charges him with ritual disability, which must be discharged by the appropriate ritual acts. There are, to be sure, great differences in the purification practices of different jatis. But virtually all villagers, rich and poor, high and low, lackadaisical as well as orthodox, observe some such biologically-induced and ritually required purification.

A state of purity must be voluntarily induced, a state of pollution is usually involuntary or the consequence of biological processes. There are various degrees of both pollution and purity. One's normal state is neither especially pure nor defiled; "a mild form of impurity" is one description of it (Srinivas 1952a, p. 107; see also Stevenson 1954, p. 50; Harper 1964, pp. 152–155). From this mild state a person's ritual condition can be changed in either direction. The two stages of ritual purity that are recognized in the Telengana region of Andhra Pradesh are described by Dube (1955c). The most pure state is attained through protracted ablution procedures, including the cleansing of teeth and bathing. Clothes that have been washed and dried under conditions of complete ritual asepsis must be worn.

So sanctified, a man may perform a major rite of passage, such as the initiation ritual by which boys in the "twice-born" varnas assume full adult status. In this pure state, he may also celebrate the offering of the morning meal to deity. The state of high purity continues while the food is being cooked and served. As soon as the celebrant eats, his ritual condition is transformed. It then is at the lesser degree of purity, attainable through bathing and the wearing of silk and sufficient for such lesser rites as marriage ceremonies and the preparation of evening meals, which do not entail a sacred offering (Dube 1955c, p. 188). Those high degrees of purification are immediately dissolved by acts of urination, defecation, and sexual intercourse, by touching an impure animal or a person not ritually clean, by touching unclean objects, such as leather or even clothes that have not been specially washed.

Whenever any villager prepares for formal worship, he must make himself properly pure for approach to the supernatural. He abstains from polluting personal acts, he avoids contact with defiling persons and objects, he bathes and performs other preliminary acts. Even those of the lowest jatis, whose touch can temporarily disqualify others from entering the precincts of the high gods, are also careful to be in a fit state before entering their own sacred places. They usually have shrines of their own in a village, even though modern legislation has removed the legal bars to their entry into the great temples.

Roles That Require Special Purity

Certain kinds of people have to be particularly meticulous about
ritual purity. These include priests of all jatis and widows of the
higher varnas. Priests are ritual leaders and must observe more
stringent purification than do laymen since they approach close
and frequently to deity (cf. Harper 1964, p. 176). Among the
jatis of the Brahmin category, those whose traditional calling is
that of priest usually rank below those whose men traditionally
devoted themselves only to learning. Service in a temple, Baines
wrote, is not undertaken by the "better class" of Brahmin; it is
held to be degrading and is left to those Brahmin jatis that are lower
in station (1912, p. 27). Bhattacharya pointed out that while the
scriptures recommend "the performance of priestly functions for
the superior castes" as a proper vocation for a Brahmin, the work
of a priest is not esteemed. It involves "almost menial service" in
worship, it does not require knowledge, and those whose jati function it is to "study the original works that regulate these rituals, can
find fault with the priest at every step, and reserve for themselves
the higher functions of the critic and superintendent" (1896, p. 25).

Priests at large temples, through which flow a mixed concourse
of worshippers, are especially exposed to contamination from visitors of unknown habit. For this reason, among others, some of these
priests are not highly respected and are suspected of laxity in diet
and demeanor. A village priest is more under the public eye and
usually keeps himself more guarded ritually than do the laymen
whose rites he leads.

Not all, nor even most, members of a Brahmin jati of priestly
vocation need actually act as priests; they follow diverse occupations. There are also jatis of the Brahmin category in which the
men do not provide priestly services for others, but are landowners
and cultivators. Not all Brahmin jatis are vegetarian; K. N. Sharma
has pointed out that vegetarianism is more a value of the Vaishnava
practice of Hinduism than of "Brahmins as such" (1961a). But the
practices of jatis of the Brahmin category are expected to be purer
than those of other jatis of their local systems. None in a Brahmin
jati can practice such abominations as removing night soil or handling carcasses, which would tarnish their whole jati.

Widows of the higher varnas are also expected to be more stringent about ritual purity than other people need be. Such a widow is permanently debarred, by reason of her indissoluble link with a dead man, from many of the social and ritual functions she could perform as a wife. She must be more fastidious in ritual observance than she was while she was a wife because her widow-hood has altered her social and ritual position for the worse (Stevenson 1954, p. 59). Yet, paradoxically, widows may undertake defiling tasks that wives will not, perhaps because widows have less to lose by temporary defilement. One widow of high jati whom I knew assisted at the delivery of an untouchable woman having a difficult and dangerous time in childbirth. Among the Havik Brahmins of Mysore, widows help at childbirths because, it is said, it is less in-convenient for them to remove severe pollution (Harper 1964, p. 175). Widows of lower jatis are also under some ritual cloud, but they may remarry and resume the role of wife again.

These pollutions, both from biological functions and mortal demise, are temporary and personal. They bring about only tem-porary avoidances and isolations which can be lifted (Stevenson 1954, pp. 51–53). Their contagious qualities may be spread by physical contact, but they are personal to the defiled person or to those of a close kin-group; the contagion does not radiate more widely and more automatically than that. Such pollution does not directly affect the ranking of jatis.

Corporate Pollution and Jati Rank

The kind of pollution that does influence rank pertains to an entire jati. Lasting and pervasive disabilities fall equally on all members of a jati who, because of their traditionally ascribed practices, must deal with death or with bodily emissions. The defile-ment of death falls heavily upon those who have to do with animal carcasses and with the products of the carcasses. The residues of dead animals, like those of humans, contaminate.

The most sacred animal of all, the cow, carries special potency both for purification and for pollution. The products of a dead cow, its meat and hide, are more defiling than are the products of other animals (cf. Brown 1957). Those who are vegetarians by jati practice consider themselves ritually purer than those who eat such carcass products as mutton and venison. Most defiled of all are those Hindus who eat beef (or whose jati fellows are reputed to do so), or who will handle any product derived from dead cattle. Among animals, swine are highly defiling because they will eat excrement; those who keep swine are tarred by that defilement.

Those whose jati occupation is to wash clothes, who handle clothes that are not only soiled but soiled with the exudation of sweat, are therefore consigned to low jati rank. More defiling still than sweat-soiled clothes are clothes that have been stained with menstrual blood; washermen who launder the former may not want to touch the latter.

There are differing degrees of jati pollution. Those villagers who wash clothes usually are ranked above those who remove dead cows, eat their flesh, work with their hides. The degree of a jati's permanent pollution is a prime factor in ascertaining "who may cook for or eat with whom; who may work for whom, or work with whom, or worship with whom . . ." (Stevenson, 1954, p. 50; also see Ghurye 1961, pp. 1–27).

Permanent pollution is contagious and corporate within a jati. A barber incurs pollution when he attends to the bodily growths of others. Women of the barber jati, in many places, attend at confinements. A man who gets a shave bathes ritually afterward to cleanse the barber's touch. A new mother undergoes a longer purification but she too is restored to her previous ritual and social status. But those who provide the services for pay incur permanent social disability, and that stigma marks every person in their jati.

One born into that jati ranks with barbers and midwives even though he himself may never have given a shave nor his wife ever assisted at a childbirth. If a barber family takes to shaving men of a jati inferior to its own—perhaps leatherworkers who have prospered and are ready to pay well for services they have not hitherto been able to get—the other families of the barber jati may strongly object. They fear that their own jati rank may be further demeaned if one of their families puts itself in an inferior position to so low a group. But, as we shall see, some of these prospering groups eventually do secure the services of others, and not only of barbers but of Brahmin priests as well.

A jati's ritual pollution is not lessened by the ritual cleanliness of individuals within the group. Even if some members of a low-ranking jati lead lives of exemplary purity, people of higher rank must still keep them and all their jati fellows at the proper social distance. The lowest jatis either carry on defiling practices presently, or are alleged to have done so in the past, or are supposed to be descended from ancestors who incurred permanent pollution. In the middle ranges of a local order there may be jatis whose members have no such discrediting marks, real or alleged. The ritual criteria alone do not explain why they should be ranked lower than others who may in fact not maintain as high a degree of ritual purity as they do. Other factors enter into the ranking as we shall note later. However, ritual pollution is commonly used by villagers as a blanket explanation; they are likely to think of some pollution-related rationale when they feel pressed to tell why they should rate one jati as higher than another.

Ritual stringency also varies by jati. Scriptural edicts direct the "twice-born" to perform more sacraments, and those more austere, than the sacraments performed by people of the Shudra category. In actual practice, villagers of the highest jatis do commonly devote more time, wealth, and energy to ritual observances than do those of low rank. One reason is that the lower are often too impoverished to be able to spend much time or money on ritual performances (Dube 1955c, pp. 187–189; Mathur 1964, pp. 99, 106).

But this is only a general tendency. There are low-ranking jatis whose rituals are both elaborate and stringent. Some of the lowest in a local order may be more rigorous in ritual observances than are some of those ranked above them. In Totagadde village in Mysore, for example, untouchables are on the whole more strict about menstruation taboos than are a good many of the Shudra category. Harper suggests that this may be because of the greater familiarity with Brahminical customs which these Harijans acquired as indentured servants and also because they are now the most militant about improving their jati status (1964, p. 191).

Though there are many villages with similar instances of a low-ranked jati's being more meticulous than are some of the higher, it is generally true that people of the higher jatis are more guarded about personal and corporate purity than are those of the lower echelons. The concepts of purity and of pollution are basic features in the local systems of society and we examine them in some detail.

CHAPTER **II** The Social Relevance of
Ritual Pollution and Purity

Pollution is a well-defined and clinging state of being. Purity is more evanescent and fleeting. It is the achievement of a transient elevation rather than any lasting presence of grace. Pollution overcomes purity. A person who has purified himself is, as it were, in a precariously balanced state of being which is soon undone. Being in a pure state is a temporary holding off of inevitable encroachment—encroachment from one's own biological functions if from no other source. In both high purity and deep pollution a person must be insulated from social contacts and isolated from society.

Pollution and purity are central to worship in that participants in religious ritual must make themselves pure for such acts. The purpose of much of ritual behavior is to make persons, objects, and animals less defiled and more pure than they had been before. Villagers apply their concepts of purity and pollution ritualistically, in symbolic and compulsive ways.

An experience in one sphere of conduct is symbolically taken to influence and to represent the whole range of social relations. If a man must be avoided in the religious context, he must be avoided across a whole range of possible secular contacts. These concepts are compulsively applied in that a defect in a part compels men to treat the whole as defective. If only a few families of a jati handle ordure, all families in the jati are so categorized. This is so because all members of a jati are related in a kinship frame, they may eat together and generally have closer contacts with each other than with those outside their jati. Hence villagers hold that a regular and serious defilement of some in the jati inevitably spreads, by contact, to the whole—unless normal jati relations with the defiled ones are cut off.

The Contagion of Pollution

Pollution is lasting and contagious. Personal pollution is believed to last until it is removed with ritual ablutions and invocation. All pollution is transferable by physical contact between a person or object that is more defiled and a person who is less defiled until the moment of contact. The mere presence of a powerful source of pollution may transfer defilement to others. The most quoted historical example of this is that of the low jatis of Kerala, whose members were not supposed to approach closer than ninety-six paces to a person of high jati status lest their nearness pollute him. This was reported by early European travelers in the region but even in the 1930s Aiyappan noted that the Nayadis, beggars of southern Kerala, had to keep a distance of from seventy-four to one hundred feet from a local Brahmin. "But in practice the Nayadis keep themselves at a greater distance than the prescribed minima" (Aiyappan 1937, p. 18; Raghuvanshi 1966, pp. 157–158).

The Nayadis presented an extreme example of avoidance even in earlier centuries, but the contagion of ritual pollution is still a lively concern for many. This is illustrated in an incident from the autobiography of a man of a merchant jati in Rajasthan. He is in government service and was once invited to tea by an official superior. When he arrived, he discovered that eggs were being served. As a strict vegetarian, he would not eat them. He tells of his dilemma, not about refusing eggs but about drinking his tea. "I did not like to see others touching my teapot with hands of eggs but could not help" (Carstairs 1957, p. 281).

Two kinds of events, birth and death, radiate pollution, not only through contact or presence, but also through kinship bonds. In all jatis, the "happy" pollution of birth falls on a smaller grouping of kinsmen and for a shorter period than does death seclusion. The members of a dead person's family become ritually and socially incapacitated from the moment of his death. They must remain in seclusion and undergo purificatory ritual over a time and in a manner prescribed by the custom of their jati. Commonly the members of the deceased's lineage are also touched with death pollution and must also refrain from normal activities, though not for so long a period as the members of the bereaved household (Mathur 1964, pp. 106–108; Orenstein 1965a; pp. 3–10).

Among the Havik Brahmins of Mysore, these family members are treated as untouchables during the mourning period. Lesser degrees of seclusion are prescribed for other kinsmen, both agnatic and affinal. As we have noted previously, these Brahmins carry the ramifications of death pollution to an extraordinary length, at least in their theory. They stipulate that if a man is related to the deceased through a common patrilineal ancestor as much as twenty-one generations removed, he is supposed to bathe on receiving news of the death (Harper 1964, pp. 161–167).

Each jati in a village is likely to have its own phrasing of the pollution-purity rules and the observance of these rules marks out jati membership and helps to integrate the jati as a social unit. Mathur notes this about the jatis of Potlod village (Indore district) in Madhya Pradesh. "One of the main purposes of the rules of pollution then, is to contain a person within his caste or *jati* and to keep him well integrated with this natal status group" (1964, p. 114).

Purity is precarious while pollution is sure. It is nontransferable while pollution is highly contagious. A Brahmin in a state of high purity cannot transmit his purity to anyone, but he can be defiled by almost everyone. Only in very few contexts can ritual merit be transmitted. One such context is when a man performs certain rites before the high gods. His wife cannot directly participate in them but she stands by her husband, touching him, and so derives merit through him.

Pure things, however, can be used to set up a field of purity that may ward off evil influences. Amulets are so used, as are also the products of the living cow. Cow's milk cannot be defiled and does not transmit pollution. However, if one drop of water should be mixed in with the milk, that drop may defile a drinker of high jati. That drop may have been from water defiled by contact with a vessel touched by an untouchable (Harper 1964, pp. 173, 188).

Purity is a more relative condition than pollution. An untouchable can make himself pure for his own worship; he can never become pure enough so that an orthodox Havik Brahmin, say, will worship side by side with him. Yet such a Brahmin, polluted by a kinsman's death, temporarily bears the same degree of ritual defilement as does the untouchable (Harper 1964, p. 194).

Extrapolations of the Ritual Criteria

It is not only people who are graded on a scale of pollution and purity. The sides of the body, for example, have different degrees of pollution and purity. The right side is the more pure. The right hand is used in eating rather than the left which is used for more menial tasks, as in washing the body after defecation.

Similar rankings are made of the species of animals and plants. Even physical materials differ in the inherent qualities of pollution and purity attributed to them. The nonhuman ratings may be used in grading the varieties of men. For example, in some localities there are two different jatis whose members make pots. A potter jati that uses bullocks for transport is superior to one that uses the donkey, "that useful, but in India foulfeeding animal" (Baines 1912, pp. 58, 65; see also Ketkar 1909, p. 20; Stevenson 1954, pp. 50–51; Mathur 1964, p. 99).

It is not difficult to see why animals that feed on leavings and excreta, as do swine and donkeys, should be defiling, and why those who keep such animals should be socially demeaned. But it is more difficult to explain why a particular plant or material should be rated above another in purity. The general explanation may be that Indian villagers project hierarchical classifications on all their world, and tend to attribute graded ranks to most of what they perceive.

Many scriptural treatises are devoted to the explication of hierarchical arrangements of all sorts, in which the taxonomy of grading is extended, embroidered, and ramified with great care. The ordinary villager does not command such detail, but he does know that pollution affects much more than mankind and that hierarchy is a characteristic of every part of creation, including the Creators. The supernatural powers, too, are ranked in an order of relative purity. Gods can become defiled; this indeed is one of the frequent motifs of scriptural tales. The continuum in purity from higher to lesser gods extends through to the grades of men (Harper 1964, p. 195).

Ingestion as a Ritual and Social Act

Some of a person's daily acts are particularly vulnerable to pollution, especially the acts of ingestion—eating, drinking, and even smoking. Food and water are susceptible to ritual pollution and so each villager must take care about the purity of what he eats and drinks. What he eats must be an accepted part of his jati's diet and cuisine. From whom he will take food and with whom he will eat express his jati's status relative to that of cooks or fellow diners.

In most village households today, the rituals of mealtime follow the essentials of the pattern laid down in ancient and medieval scriptures (cf. Kane 1941, pp. 757–806). That ritual was remarked early in the sixteenth century by the Portuguese observer, Duarte Barbosa, the first of his nation to learn an Indian language.[1] He understood and spoke Malayalam. Barbosa described the "custom as to eating" of the Zamorin, the ruler of Calicut, in these words:

> . . . no one must be present while he is eating, nor must see him eat, saving only four or five servants who wait on him. Before eating he bathes in a very clean and large tank inside the palace, where he performs his observances quite naked, worshipping thrice towards the east wind, walking round and dipping thrice under water, then he attires himself in fresh garments, clean and washed, and he proceeds to seat himself in a house which is cleared for his meals, which is plastered [i.e., with a purifying cow dung paste]. . . . He takes no food with his left hand. Then they place before him a silver ewer filled with water, and when he wishes to drink he takes this in his left hand, and raising it into the air lets the water flow from above into his mouth without its touching the ewer. . . . And when he cleans his hands he makes no use of a napkin or any other cloth, and when he finishes his meal he washes himself (Dames 1921, pp. 22–23).

The modern editor of this account added the note that

> Barbosa's description of the Zamorin's ordinary rice meal is, excepting the appurtenances of state, an accurate description of any decent Malayali's mode of eating and drinking (Dames 1921, p. 22).

[1] Many travelers before Barbosa had noted the great concern of Indians about the act of eating. In the fifteenth century the Russian, Nikitin, observed that some Indians cover themselves with a kerchief when they eat so that no one may see them (Nikitin 1960, p. 114).

A householder of some leisure and of an orthodox bent still takes his main meal in much this pattern, having a preliminary bath, wearing ritually clean clothes, sitting in a ritually clean place, eating food untouched in its preparation by anyone of lower jati rank, and concluding with a final rinse.

Even a poor man of lowly jati follows certain of the main ritual precautions that Barbosa noted long ago for the ruler of Calicut. All eat with the right hand. Even among the Nimar Balahis, a very low-ranking jati of Madhya Pradesh, "Food is taken only with the right hand, while the left hand can be used to hold the cup when drinking. The left hand should not touch food because it is used for cleaning after a call of nature" (Fuchs 1950, p. 370). The left hand can be used to handle one's food, but it should not touch the lips. Water is poured into the mouth; its passage through air is considered, by those who expound the reasons for ritual acts, to be a purifying process (cf. Stevenson 1954, p. 54; Mathur 1964, pp. 135–136).

In every household, the place where food is prepared is a sensitive area, which must be specially safeguarded. The observance of ritual purity is particularly focused on the kitchen. Thus in a village close by Bangalore city and rapidly changing, "no caste permits any individuals other than close relatives of the same caste to enter the kitchen" (Beals 1955, p. 134).

All that concerns one's food and drinking water is important to personal purity because whatever is incorporated into the body has great potency for pollution. Such internal pollution is a more serious danger than that incurred externally by touch. Water that can be used for external ritual cleansing may not be pure enough for internal use (Stevenson 1954, p. 57).

Jawaharlal Nehru, in assessing the consequences of these standards of purity, saw them as both good and bad—good in their promotion of bodily cleanliness, bad in their "fantastic lengths" of "touch-me-notism" (1946, p. 251). But for those orthodox Hindus who are mainly concerned with the fate of their soul—in their view the only worthy concern—these standards and rituals enable a man to reach, as closely as he may, toward the true good and to avoid the false, the fleeting, and the worthless. Purity is not merely ceremonial purity, an Indian scholar has written, it is the principle of "the varying degrees of dominance of the soul over the senses, the

dominance of the real man or God in man over the animal in man"
(S. C. Roy 1934, p. 86).

For most villagers it is the social meanings of eating practices,
rather than the theological concepts, that are of main consequence.
The company in which one eats is of great social importance. Eating together is a sign of equality among individuals and groups,
second only to intermarriage. Those who take their meals side by
side, eating food from the same cook and kitchen, thereby show
that each has equal ritual status with his fellow diners. And those
who eat together are apt to act together and support each other,
whether as family group, faction, lineage, or jati.

Sheer physical proximity while eating is very important. At village feasts where diners are ranged in seated rows, those of a higher
jati will not tolerate those of much lower rank to sit in an unbroken
line with them. And guests of one jati are content to be in the same
row as those whom they acknowledge to be higher, even if they
must sit, as it were, below the salt (cf. Harper 1964, pp. 157–158).

Who handles the food while it is being prepared for eating is a
matter of high concern, because it is then in a pollution-vulnerable
state. How food stuff is handled while it is raw, dry, unpeeled, or
unmixed does not much matter. Directly it is taken in hand to be
made edible, it becomes imbued with the same degree of pollution
as inheres in the cook who touches it. Hence a person may not eat
from the hand of anyone who bears greater pollution, personal or
jati, than himself. That is why the cook for the King of Calicut
was a "Bramene" and why Brahmins are desirable as cooks for
households of most jatis. A cook's jati purity does not flow through
the food to the eater, but whatever pollution he bears can contaminate food. A Brahmin cook suffers no ritual hurt if the lowest
eat of his cooking.

Food can be ritually affected by other influences besides the
cook's touch. Polluted utensils can conduct defilement. A clay pot
is more easily polluted than a brass pot and is less readily reusable
after being dirtied. This, according to one explanation, is because
the more porous substance cannot be as thoroughly cleaned. In
some households, servants of low jati are allowed to handle the
brass utensils but not the pottery.

Drinking water may not be drawn by servants of the lowest jatis.
Even though water is purified by being poured through the air

from cup to mouth, water which has been carried by defiled hands is beyond such purificatory redemption. A chart of who will take water from whom, as given by Sharma for a village in Kanpur district, is a useful index for a local hierarchy. The acceptance of water there "is basic and most important" (1956a, p. 236). And Baines' comment holds true widely in India, that water is the element, above all, through which personal contamination can be conveyed (Baines 1912, p. 67).

Some foods have special purity, either inherent as in milk, or instilled as through frying. Food that has been fried, either in oil or, preferably, in ghee, is thereby made much less vulnerable to pollution (Mathur 1964, pp. 128–129). Such fried stuff, called *pakka* food, is usually taken by those of high jati in North India from the hands of people of quite low (though not the very lowest) rank. Thus a traveler will commonly eat fried food that he has bought from a roadside vendor, from whose hands he would never take *kachcha* food, that cooked in water, mixed with water, or baked. In South India this distinction between ghee-fried and unfried food is not as clearly made. Even in North India, frying only mitigates the cook's touch, it does not convert tabooed food. So even if meat were fried in ghee, it would be meat all the same to one of vegetarian jati.

Food that is left on a plate after a meal, as occurs at feasts, is tabooed to all but the lowest jatis, because it has been defiled by having been touched to the lips of another person. But leavings from the plate of one's father or husband, or leavings from offerings to the gods are in quite a different class (cf. Carstairs 1957, p. 80). It is good to eat them; in so doing one does not violate proper relations of subordination and authority but in some degree thereby partakes of the good qualities of his human guardians and divine mentors.

Harper discusses these practices as "respect-pollution." He mentions an extreme case of this among the Havik Brahmins whom he has studied. It is that of a widow who had become accepted as a *sadhu*, a holy person. When she visited the village of Totagadde, some of the Brahmins drank of the liquid in which her feet had been washed (Harper 1964, pp. 181–183). Such acts of respect-pollution seem to desecrate the deepest tenets of food and drink pollution but they symbolically affirm the larger order for which these rules are used. They affirm the proper hierarchical relations, both among people and between man and holy beings.

Villagers of all jatis accept these broad ritual criteria. Those who are disadvantaged by them do not usually deny that there should be such criteria although they do commonly deny that their own practices are really as demeaning as their neighbors contend. Those of a meat-eating jati do not argue that eating meat is ritually irrelevant; they usually have only vegetarian food on their most sacred occasions. They eat meat, partly because they are accustomed to do so, partly because their jati's station in society does not require the sacrifice of this taste. They may be from a jati of warrior tradition for whom the eating of boar flesh, say, is quite seemly, or they may be so poor that they cannot afford to forego any nourishment—even from a carcass no one else will touch. Non-vegetarian villagers can usually get meat only very occasionally, and the proportion of meat in their total diet is minute, but it is for them a welcome addition to the common grain-and-vegetable staple. Welcome as it is for a special meal, it is not a ritual asset.

The Balahis are meat-eaters; many are so poor as to be quite used to starvation-rations. They eat meat from slaughtered or diseased cattle when they can get it; it usually is cheaper than goat's meat or fowl. Their diet is a main reason why they are treated as untouchables, their practice of eating the leavings of others at a feast is something for which higher jatis have "equal revulsion as to the eating of beef" (Fuchs 1950, pp. 357–359).

Yet there are many kinds of food Balahis will not eat, including domestic pork and horsemeat. Moreover, even these lowly, bone-poor Balahis "consider taking a meal an important act," make suitable ritual preparation for a meal, and preserve certain ritual safeguards during it. Nor is the eating of beef taken as an indifferent act. "After eating beef, the Balahis feel polluted and must take a bath of purification. Such a bath is necessary if afterwards they want to worship their gods or perform any other act for which ceremonial purity is required" (Fuchs 1950, pp. 369–370). For men and women at all social levels, what is eaten affects their personal purity and therefore their roles in social interaction. With whom and from whom they take food has social consequences for their jati's place in the local order.

Alcohol is a special vector of pollution. The drinking of strong liquor is abhorrent in the Brahmin tradition, perhaps because a drunk man is apt to forget ritual precautions, to touch what should not be touched, to take in what should be kept out, and to trespass where he should not go. In other jatis, especially of the Kshatriya category, there is a more easy-going tolerance of liquor. People of lower jatis are more likely to drink liquor and may even make alcoholic libations to their deities. Those whose jati occupation is the making of liquor are thereby of low rank. Alcohol is thus doubly loaded against a man of higher jati, being defiling in itself and having been handled by polluting people (Mandelbaum 1965, pp. 283–284).

The Ritual and Social Bearing of Sexual Acts

Sexual relations also induce ritual impurity. After conjugal relations a purificatory bath should be taken though even the generally orthodox Havik Brahmins postpone this until the customary morning bath. In Totagadde village gleeful stories were told about one especially orthodox wife who rushed out to take a cold bath immediately after intercourse with her husband, thus announcing to village gossip the exact schedule of her sexual relations.

Abstinence from sex is prescribed before important ceremonies or before any approach to deities (cf. Srinivas 1952a, p. 103). Marital intercourse does not bring on a high degree of ritual pollution, but leaves a person in a bodily state that must nevertheless be purified. Intercourse between a man and a woman of different jatis, however, can have great social consequences. A man does not usually suffer great loss nor must he make ritual recompense if it becomes known that he has had an affair with a woman of a jati not very different in status from his own. His wife and relations may make him smart, but his jati fellows usually do not consider that they all have been defiled by his dereliction (cf. Dube 1955b, p. 144). Such jati taint is felt, however, if it becomes publicly known that a man of highest jati has consorted with a woman of the lowest. If a woman of high jati rank is discovered in sexual connection with a man of low jati, she may be cast out forever from her family, her jati, and her village.

Dire punishments, ranging from heavy fines to death are prescribed in Sanskrit scripture for sexual partners of unequal rank. "In general," Ketkar summarizes the texts on the subject, "the higher the varna of the woman contaminated the greater should be the punishment to the guilty man; the lower the varna of the man, the more severely he is to be treated" (1909, p. 153; Orenstein 1965a, p. 9). Sexual relations between a man of higher jati and a woman of somewhat lower jati are often deplored by village opinion but are not usually taken to undermine social structure as would cases of open interdining or intermarriage.

The usual distinction made between commensal and consexual relations is shown in the previously noted instance of the Nambudiri Brahmins of Malabar. Only the eldest Nambudiri son could marry, and younger sons established regular and recognized sexual relations with women of the Nayars, a group of warrior tradition whose kinship organization was strongly matrilineal. A Nambudiri man would visit the home and bed of his Nayar beloved regularly, but he would never eat of her food, nor would she eat with him (Rao 1957, p. 106; Miller 1954, p. 413; Mencher and Goldberg 1967).[2] Eating the same food would imply a marriage relationship, it would mean that the couple were of equal ritual status. The Nambudiri man would then suffer a permanent status loss rather than the temporary, removable incapacities that he incurred by contact with a non-Brahmin.

Means of Purification and Ideas about Pollution

Against pollution that is removable, certain agents of purification are available. Flowing water is a basic solvent for ritual impurity. Habits of ablution in India were noted in the seventh century by a

---

[2] Barbosa's account, written about 1516, notes an interesting qualification to a Nambudiri man's choice in establishing a relationship. "The brothers who remain bachelors sleep with the Nayre women, they hold it to be a great honour, and as they are Bramenes no woman refuses herself to them, yet they may not sleep with any woman older than themselves." The obligations of respect which a younger person owes those older affected even a man's relation with a woman of different rank. Nayar men, in their turn, could customarily carry on sexual relations with women of still another group. Of the jati who laundered clothes Barbosa observed, "Those born of this class do not mix with others, nor others with them, save only that the *Nayres* may take their women as concubines if they bathe and change their clothes" (Dames 1921, pp. 35, 58).

Chinese Buddhist pilgrim. "They are pure of themselves and not by compulsion. Before every meal they must have a wash . . . before they have finished ablutions they do not come into contact with each other; they always wash after urinating" (Watters 1904, p. 152).

Twelve centuries later, similar ablution habits are still practiced by villagers, especially those of the higher jatis and wealthier families. Very few Indian villages are models of hygiene and villagers are no more hygienically clean than are rural folk in impoverished circumstances anywhere. But the ritual wash is part of villagers' daily routine. In Potlod village, for example, Mathur observed that "every morning most of the Hindus of Potlod took a bath and changed into clean clothes." Being unwashed and physically dirty, Mathur comments, is generally considered to be an impure state, though being physically clean does not necessarily mean that one is ritually pure (1964, pp. 98, 103).

Villagers often try to get defiling tasks done during the early morning. They bathe during mid-morning and then are fit to take their meal. The morning ablution rite is commonly an abbreviated affair, though those who have the time and inclination can protract the rite for hours. Handbooks on ritual procedure are available in bookstalls for those who want to perform full purificatory devotions (cf. Diehl 1956, pp. 66–95; Harper 1964, p. 153).

Water and washing are necessary but not sufficient for purification. The washing must be done in a proper formal manner and must be accompanied by ritual acts of speech and gesture. Other agents of purification are also used; fire, sun, and Ganges water are among the most potent (Mathur 1964, pp. 100–103). Most commonly used for purification are the products of the living cow. Cow dung, usually mixed with water, is applied as a general means of ritual cleansing and prophylaxis. The housewife cleans her kitchen regularly, using that mixture. With it the priest purifies the places where he performs his rites. Such use of cow dung entails the respect-pollution which we have noted above. As Harper puts it, "The cow's most impure part is sufficiently pure relative to even a Brahmin priest to remove the latter's impurities" (1964, p. 183). The most potent personal purification of all is the ingestion of a mixture containing five products of the cow, namely milk, curds, ghee, dung, and urine.

These vectors of purity and of pollution are known among all villagers though each group has its own ritual idiom, its particular combination of the main elements and their interpretation. All believe that contacts with death and bodily emissions are polluting, beliefs which can be interpreted as their expressions of a general apprehension about transition states. Death and birth are, of course, major transitions. Menstruation and even the cutting of body hair can be seen as transitions from one state of physical being or of physical wholeness to another.

The impairment of previous wholeness can make objects as well as people vulnerable to pollution. Fruits and nuts, as long as they are whole, are not considered subject to ritual defilement. Thus even an orthodox Brahmin can take a whole plaintain or coconut from a person of lower jati. But once the coconut is broken or the plaintain cut, he cannot do so (Harper 1964, p. 156).

The transitions of the heavenly bodies create a parlous state for mankind. The days of the new moon and of the full moon are times when the immanent supernatural powers are more imminently present, and so are more powerful and more dangerous. The time of an eclipse, a visible transition, is a time of great vulnerability during which special precautions must be taken (Harper 1964, pp. 170, 188).

The ranking of jatis is explained, not only on the basis of their relative pollution and purity, but also by reference to the scriptural concepts of *karma* and of *dharma*. These concepts will be discussed again in later chapters, we need only note here that karma has to do with the transmigration of souls and with the supernal merit or demerit earned by a soul in its previous incarnations. One's station and jati in present life derive from one's conduct in previous existences. Further, to improve his soul's karma for future incarnations, a man is bound to fulfill properly the obligations of his current status, especially of his jati roles. Even the most polluting work, if selflessly done as a matter of jati calling, can enhance one's karma. "Because *karma* carried out in this manner, and this alone, does not pollute the individual soul, even though the *karma* (particular to one's caste) happens to be unclean or polluting" (Mathur 1964, p. 87).

That is the explanation commonly given by those of higher jati, and so a vast array of Hindu scripture and scriptural exegesis propounds. But villagers of the lower jatis may have a different under-standing of pollution, karma, and dharma. In the southern village of Kumbapettai, in Tanjore district, ". . . . the non-Brahmins, al-though they are aware of them, view the Brahmanical theories with nonchalance." The Pallans, landless laborers, "when questioned denied them with merriment" (Gough 1960, p. 54).

In the village of Khalapur near Banaras the sweepers know and accept these concepts. They also argue that their jati really deserves high status on the basis of these standards but that their ancestors had been tricked and cheated out of their proper rank (Kolenda 1964).

Many villagers of all jatis, whether or not they subscribe to the explanations of Hindu scriptures, agree that there is an order of rank in their locality and that the respective ranks have to do with a jati's pollution and purity practices.[3] The ideas about pollution and purity, as we have discussed them in this chapter, are character-istic of those who observe the indigenous religions. However, the followers of the introduced religions—Muslims, Christians, Jews, and Parsis—also share some of these ideas and practices, though in what degree will be known only after more studies of these groups are available.

The ritual criteria provide broad standards for esteemed conduct and general guides for rank assignment in villages through most of the land. But although the ritual criteria are indeed important fac-tors, they are not the only influences that determine jati rank. The order of jatis in a locality is also shaped by the influence of power and wealth as exerted within the local community.

[3] One questionnaire study found that the great majority of 100 subjects who were questioned believed that untouchability "was mainly due to the unlawful acts of the upper caste people, tradition, and other social factors" (Rath and Sircar 1960a, pp. 305–306). Such views may be increasing and may now be held by certain groups, such as university students, but the results of this study have not been confirmed by carefully conducted village studies.

CHAPTER 12   Secular Criteria and the
Attribution of Jati Rank

THE wealth that the members of a jati can mar-
shal and the number of men they can muster for their jati purposes
are not supposed to have great bearing on social ranking. In the
ideal of scripture, it is ritual purity that counts. When jatis joust
for precedence, each side invokes ritual reasons to justify their
respective claims. This norm is expressed by Ghurye in his comment that the status of a person in Hindu caste society depended
not on his wealth but on the traditional importance of the caste in
which he had the luck of being born (1961, p. 2). Similarly, Prabhu
writes that in Hindu India a dissociation was attempted, and even
achieved, between wealth and status (1954, p. 117).

The ritual standards are used as a reference frame for the social
order, but interaction among villagers of different jatis is strongly
influenced by secular considerations. The Abbé Dubois recognized
this in his classic account of South Indian peoples in the early
nineteenth century. "Thus the caste to which the ruler of a
country belongs, however low it may be considered elsewhere,
ranks amongst the highest in the ruler's own dominions, and every
member of it derives some reflection of dignity from its chief"
(1928, p. 23).

Villagers still apply the ritual criteria to mark broad limits within
which a jati may be ranked; they follow secular considerations to
determine the status a group receives within these limits. There is,
moreover, a difference to be noted between formal precedence
and actual influence. The members of a ritually high jati may elicit
overt gestures of respect, but its men may have little power in
village affairs. Those however who combine secular dominance
and ritual eminence possess authority that is doubly fortified.

The Application of Secular Influence

Secular influences are brought to bear on social ranking in several ways. Among several jatis of relatively similar ritual practice, the one whose people have the main power and wealth usually ranks highest. Secondly, the ritual shortcomings of a secularly dominant jati tend to be leniently interpreted by others in their locality. Finally, a low-ranking group that acquires wealth and power characteristically uses its strength to change its demeaning practices and to raise its jati rank.

The preeminence of the powerful among their ritual compeers is illustrated in Rampura village in Mysore. In Rampura the jati called Peasants by Srinivas are the dominant landowners, and their "local dominance gives the Peasants a high status among the castes in the middle division" (1955b, p. 25). Another group studied by Srinivas, the Coorgs of South India, illustrate how the ritual deficiencies of a powerful jati tend to be less harshly interpreted than are similar faults of a poor and weak group. The Coorgs ate pork, drank strong liquor, countenanced the remarriage of widows, did not practice menstrual seclusion—usages that might well degrade a group hopelessly in other parts. But the Coorgs were the dominant people in their territory, a strong and numerous set of landowners and warriors (1952a, pp. 32–37). Hence, they were accorded very respectable status among the peoples of their hill area.

In their warrior orientation, they resemble Rajputs and other North Indian groups that glory in their military traditions. The men of these jatis follow the martial, extrovert model for conduct rather than a ritual, ascetic model. They acknowledge the religious superiority of the Sanskritic ritual standards but do not themselves feel compelled to adhere to all Brahmanical injunctions. "The martial Rajput," writes Hitchcock, "regards it as a kind of warrior's dispensation that he is permitted to hunt, eat meat (except of course for beef), drink liquor and eat opium" (1958, p. 220).

In some places the families of martial style so far overshadow everyone else that the local Brahmin jati may count for very little in village life. This occurs in a village near Delhi where the dominant landowner-cultivators are Jats, belonging to one of the larger jati-clusters of North India. By ritual criteria, these landowners rank well below Brahmins, but here the Brahmins are few in number, tenants with shaky rights and generally subservient to the overlord group. The ownership of land, with the power of eviction, enables the landed jati to prevail over other villagers, including the Brahmins (Lewis 1958, p. 60).

An extreme example of the glossing over of the ritual deficiencies of the powerful is reported by Dube from a village of Adilabad district in Andhra Pradesh. The dominant landowners there are Raj Gonds, a jati of tribal origin. When Dube studied the village in the early 1950s, the Raj Gonds were still performing cow sacrifice and eating beef, traits that would have consigned them to the lowest depths of defilement among other Hindus. But in this village Hindus of all but two jatis took water from them and the lower jatis also took food from them. We will note, in a later chapter on tribal people, the special reasons for the unusually strong position of the Raj Gonds of this place, including their advantage in having been favored by the Muslim rulers of their territory, which had been part of the princely state of Hyderabad (Dube 1955a, pp. 189–190). The example of the Raj Gonds indicates that under especially strong conditions of power, even the most heinous of polluting acts can be overlooked by otherwise orthodox Hindus.

The third mode of secular influence, the use of wealth and power to bring about a rise in rank, is discussed in later chapters on social mobility. However high the people of a jati may aim, whatever righteous ritual they may observe, their aspiration for higher rank can scarcely be realized unless their claims are backed up with solid wealth and power.

The Sources of Power

Local power flows mainly from the land. Land is the prime good in this agrarian setting; land is the main source of wealth; land is a main need for a jati on the rise. "Of all village values, the most important and permanent is not money but land." So commented S. S. Nehru in his survey of 54 U.P. villages (1932, p. 47), and this is a common fact in village India to the present time. Land is the primary, scarce, productive resource; control of land means control of livelihood.[1] Under British rule, land became even more precious because population increased, because some artisans were forced into agriculture, and because cultivable lands—available even in the mid-Ganges valley in the first part of the nineteenth century—were quickly taken up (cf. Mandelbaum 1949). In a stable political regime, land is power because the landowner has a secure base for his livelihood and because he can control the livelihood of his tenants. Alternate sources of occupation and of power have greatly increased in recent decades but still are relatively few; hence having money is good, owning land is better (cf. Bailey 1957, pp. 239–246).

Any landowner's power is safeguarded if he belongs to a numerous and unified jati-group and jati. Then the force of many men can reinforce their economic and legal rights. Yet numbers alone do not guarantee jati power. A low-ranking jati in a village may include many people, but their loyalties may be so fragmented among their patrons and their poverty may be so deep and debilitating as to block joint action for self-improvement. Whenever a group—whether jati, jati-group, or lineage—is relatively numerous and is economically secure enough to call up concerted action, its members can forcefully argue the justice of their ritual claims. Such arguments become all the more persuasive to others when the strong, united voices are those of the landowners.

Power may also accrue to a jati when its members have effective connections with the power of the state. The Abbé Dubois noted that a jati's standing was enhanced if the ruler was one of their own. This was so even if the ruler's dynasty was founded by a gross marauder of low degree. A ruler had lands and favors to distribute and usually did not stint his jati kinsmen. He had his royal dignity to uphold and it was better upheld if his jati-fellows were also elevated.

When British officials became the paramount rulers, those who

[1] It has not always been so. In earlier centuries, good new lands were available to be brought under the plough. Especially after great famines or epidemics, the scarcity was that of cultivators or of cattle rather than of land. Even into the twentieth century, some groups in sparsely populated places, as the Wynad taluq of Kerala, are more concerned with another kind of scarce productive resource, ploughing oxen, than they are with land (Rooksby 1956).

had regular access to them benefited. Such access could be obtained by fulfilling local offices, as of headman or policeman. But this was a relatively minor way of tapping the power reservoir. More ample access could be obtained through acquiring Western education. Education is still a good avenue to local influence. A villager who can write a petition in English or in the literary version of the vernacular and who can speak with the administrator in the language of officials is much better off than one who has to make his way through a thicket of interpreters, scribes, and open-palmed underlings.

A person who qualifies for an administrative post or is elected to important office comes closest to governmental sources of power. Hence a jati that has Western-educated men in number is believed to have great advantage. It does not matter much that the actual favors granted by an official to his jati-fellows may be few and trifling. Most villagers are impressed; such achievements by the educated men of a jati usually shed luster, by a halo effect, on the local ranking of all in the jati.

These are some of the ways in which the secular forces of land, numbers, office, and education influence social ratings. The ratings are supposed to be based, according to both scriptural and vernacular theory, solely on ritual criteria. In theory also, the ratings are made by the ritual leaders, especially by the local Brahmin jatis. In practice, the men of a powerful jati have often been able to persuade their ritual superiors to bestow on them the prerogatives of high rank.

The Reciprocal Use of Ritual and Secular Resources

Yet such men cannot change ritual limits immediately or entirely. For one thing, there is a considerable inertia in ritual ratings. No matter how high a jati may rise, there is a long—sometimes a centuries-long—memory of jati origins. Secular power may elicit gestures of esteem; it is more difficult to command that unquestioned, implicit respect which is given to those who combine long-established ritual eminence with present power.

Moreover, even the more ambitious villagers do not want to upset the ritual standards completely. A man appraises himself and his jati by these standards. He usually tends to make the most favorable appraisal possible, but there are appraisals that are not possible for him to make. There have been rulers whose ancestors were of quite humble jati origin; such a Maharaja could wield firm power over a large dominion, but he might well have difficulty in finding a bride of suitably high rank for his son.

It is true that an able individual of quite low jati status can sometimes attain influence in village affairs. Thus in Rampura in Mysore a man of the toddy-tapper group has gained considerable wealth and power (Srinivas, 1955b, p. 17). But the jati affiliation of such men excludes them from the full measure of respect and of ritual participation that is attainable by able and successful men of the higher jatis.

A villager of Kishan Garhi in U.P., Marriott observes, can much more readily increase his *izzat,* his personal prestige, by his personal accomplishments than he can affect the status of his jati: "In Kishan Garhi, a man's caste rank counts for little more than seven annas in the sum of his prestige; wealth and political affiliation together count for nine annas. Thus although nearly everyone in the village would agree that the caste of Brahmins is to be ranked at the top and the caste of Chamars ranked far down toward the bottom, still most persons would rate certain well-to-do and respectable Chamars as higher in individual prestige than certain pious and impecunious Brahmins" (1959b, pp. 102–103).

Instances of men of very low jati attaining very high prestige are not common, but are more frequent now than before. However, it is still a limited prestige in village life because in such crucially important relations as interdining and intermarriage such a man's personal status must be subordinated to his jati's level. Seven annas is less than half of the old rupee of sixteen annas, a marked reduction of the traditional influence of jati rank on personal prestige. But it is still a large portion of a man's social worth in his present society.

The religious respect that was given to people of Brahmin jatis helped to bolster their secular wealth. Sanskrit scripture teaches that it is meritorious to give to Brahmins; many an unlettered potentate dutifully followed this scriptural injunction. William Ward reckoned that the greatest means of support of the Brahmins he saw in Bengal were the properties given directly to Brahmins or donated to the gods and managed by and for Brahmin families. Ward wrote, "The donors were former kings, and men of property, who expected heaven as the reward of their piety" (1822, p. 88). Ward was not the most sympathetic or reliable observer of Bengali life, nevertheless he was quite right that Brahmin families were often supported by the income from such gifts. And supplementing their direct and prebendary income, some Brahmins also receive fees or jajmani returns for services rendered as household priests and teachers.

In addition to lands so received and inherited, a Brahmin family may be given advantage in the ordinary acquisition of land. Thus a more recent observer, S. S. Nehru, noted that the Brahmin is generally a *persona grata* in the villages he surveyed (mainly in Rae Barelli district of U.P.). He reports that Brahmins there were able to buy land at lower prices and could lease land at lower rates than could other villagers (1932, p. 51). Sharma offers another instance, from Gamras village, Kanpur district, where twenty of the twenty-six Brahmin families made their living from cultivation at the time of his study, and have long been landowners. "Many of them received land as gifts from their *jajmans*, while some of them purchased land to maintain their social status in the village" (Sharma 1956a, pp. 103–104). In the discussion of social mobility below, it will be noted that Brahmins who became poor often had an alternate occupation open to them as priests for lower jatis. In taking such service they remained part of the Brahmin varna.

Sometimes, when Brahmin jatis exerted strong double hegemony, both spiritual and temporal, they roused bitter resentment and even retaliation from other villagers. In earlier history these protests often took a religious form; latterly there has been political counter-action. In Madras state especially, non-Brahmins have been politically successful in reversing what they consider to be undue Brahmin advantages (Irschik 1969).

In general, ritual and secular influences have been reciprocally used. High ritual status has often brought secular rewards which, in turn, helped maintain ritual eminence. More significantly, when the members of a jati could increase in secular resources, they could generally augment their ritual status.

The Attribution of Rank According to Jati Blocs

The ranking of jatis is thus a main feature of interdependence within local systems. How and by whom is ranking determined? The short answer is that a jati's rank is often set in a rough and ready way, as part of a lump classification. It is set by the members of a united, dominant jati-group, where there is one, whose men calibrate the local order in the course of the exercise of their dominance. But where there is no such authoritative group, no exact order of precedence is set. In such villages, and there are many, conflict about who outranks whom is common. Yet the people of these villages have been able to carry on their community functions without a consensus about the detailed order of rank. Moreover, social mobility has long been a recurrent feature of village society, so at any one time there is very likely to be considerable disagreement about the proper rank of a jati whose members are in the process of changing their rank.

The assessment of rank within a village has to be rough-hewn, just as the varna and jati-cluster assessments used across villages have to be gross classifications. Villagers would have to perform prodigious feats of calculation if every status-relevant trait of a jati's members had to be computed. The roster of a jati's practices often includes some of relatively pure and some of relatively defiling character; within any jati, members differ in their ritual stringency and secular affluence.

In Gaon village (Poona district) for example, one of the high jatis practices the low custom of widow remarriage. One of the Harijan jatis there has some prosperous families who have raised their status enough to acquire the services of Brahmin priests. Within all the larger jati-groups there is considerable variation in family wealth (Orenstein 1965a, pp. 120–149).

A villager of Gaon does not make an analysis of such multiple variables in order to decide what his proper relations with a person of a particular jati should be. Nor is there any clear consensus in the village about the precise order of rank. Indeed, the same villager may make different rankings on different occasions. But there is considerable consensus and consistency about the main blocs (as they are termed here) into which the village jatis can be classified.

There are four such blocs in Gaon, the jatis in each bloc are taken as of about equal status for most purposes. Some do not care for the way their neighbors classify them, but they too use the same bloc ordering (Orenstein 1965a, pp. 136–138).

A bloc is mainly a local classification, unlike such groupings as jati-cluster and varna. In Gaon, eight jati-groups are placed in the bloc called "the high castes," which comes just after the topmost bloc of Brahmin jatis in ritual precedence. One of the eight is the Maratha, the local representation of the jati-cluster widespread in Maharashtra. Marathas have a military tradition. Yet classed in the same bloc with them in Gaon are the barber and blacksmith jatis; neither of these is in the same varna tradition nor classed so high in most other regions.

Although there is no fixed table of social precedence jati by jati which holds good in all villages, the top and bottom of the local order in most villages are usually quite clear. A Brahmin jati is often given highest ritual rank by village consensus and the jatis of Harijans are at the other extreme. Some psychological reasons for this clarity of the extremes are suggested in a cross-cultural comparison of caste behavior by George DeVos (DeVos and Wagatsuma 1966, pp. 332–384). Harijans are examples of the pollution that each person must cope with in his own life. They are a living demonstration of the degrading effects of ritual defilement. Perhaps people of other jatis have insisted on keeping them so low because in so doing they have been proving that ritual pollution really is debasing and to be avoided and expunged. Brahmin jatis, by the same token, exemplify the rewards of ritual purity.

In between the blocs at each extreme, several blocs of jatis are ranked. The blocs are taxonomic devices; they tell nothing about cooperation among the jatis that are classed together. In fact, the most bitter rivalries may be between jatis of the same grouping. Nor are these groupings clear-cut, well-defined categories. They are rather divisions which villagers make in a rough way, often because the people in each bloc have similar standards of accepting food and water from others. And while two jatis may follow similar patterns of food acceptance, their jati customs may be quite distinct.

In sorting out the local jatis, villagers are influenced by the varna classification, especially in the ritual eminence of Brahmin jatis. Frequently, however, as in Gaon village, the classical categories do not fit well with the actual groupings that are used. Thus the people of Kishan Garhi village (Aligarh district, U.P.) generally agree that the twenty-four local jatis are placed in five or six ranked blocs labeled the highest, the high, the low, Muslim, the very low, the lowest of all. Marriott comments that this grouping of jatis in blocs is reflected in much interjati behavior, as in forms of greeting, arrangements for eating, smoking, and sitting. "Within each major bloc, the ranking of separate castes must be estimated by villagers according to minor ritual criteria; estimates of precise rank within the blocs are not consistent or well agreed" (1959b, p. 102).

Similar groupings within a local system have been reported from all regions.[2] Sharma's account of a village in Kanpur district, U.P., illustrates the kind of rough classifications that villagers tend to make. In that village, the Brahmin jati-group is the most numerous (104 out of the village population of 697 at the time of the study) and is without question ritually superior to the other jatis. Yet five of the Brahmin men will eat meat although most of their jati fellows do not. This is no sudden departure; some elderly Brahmins confided that this had been done in their father's generation also. These meat-eating Brahmins had had military service, and perhaps this had something to do with their deviance, or perhaps the military service was only another expression of a personal deviation from what is expected of a Brahmin. Sharma notes other divagations from high Brahmanical conduct (1956a, pp. 181, 241).

Yet some Brahmins continue to officiate as priests, and the whole jati does not appear to be degraded by the derelictions of some of its members. In theory, it should be; in practice, their priestly tradition plus their numbers override such deficiencies. As a jati-group they stand fifth from the top in average per capita income, and their numerical strength has been weakened by warring factions. The

[2] In a village of West Bengal, J. Sarma noted eight such grades (1955, p. 168). Among the villages with five such blocs are Gamras, Kanpur district (Sharma 1956a, p. 240), Potlod in Madhya Pradesh (Mathur 1964, pp. 68–71), Shamirpet in Madhya Pradesh, with Muslims a sixth grouping (Mayer 1956, pp. 121–124). Six are reported from a Telengana village (Dube 1955c, p. 182), four from Gaon in Poona district, with two jatis outside any bloc (Orenstein 1965a, pp. 136–139), three from Kumbapettai in Tanjore district (Gough 1955, pp. 82–83), six in Malabar villages (Miller 1954, p. 411).

next highest jati, the Thakurs, do not accept *kachcha* food from those Brahmins whom they consider to be of dubious personal purity. For all that, this Brahmin jati continues to command ritual eminence.

The four families of the Kayasth jati—scribes by traditional occupation—have been rich and influential in the village for a century, particularly because of their tenure in village administrative posts, such as in the keeping of the land records. But the local Brahmins and Thakurs still recall that the Kayasths were anciently reckoned among the Shudras. With only four families, the Kayasths are not a numerous band in the village. The jati's situation in this village is similar to that which Kayasths have had to struggle against in many other villages of North India. Despite their outstanding wealth, political influence, and respectable ritual practices, "the Thakurs do not concede them an equal or nearly equal social status" (Sharma 1956a, pp. 242–243). The Brahmin and Thakur jati-groups have long managed village affairs in this place, but their control has not prevented the Kayasths, or even some of the very low jatis, from claiming higher privileges than the managing groups are willing to concede.

Through much of the round of village activities, a precise, definitive order of precedence for all jatis is unnecessary. When disputes about jati rank do arise, they should be settled, in the ideal view of the higher jatis, according to scriptural precepts. Since the most learned in scripture are usually the men of the local Brahmin jatis, they ought to settle disputes about the relative rank of two lower jatis. Sometimes they do. But more often, as will be discussed in the chapters on councils, the facts of a case remain unclear or the learned men disagree or their opinion carries little weight or they are not consulted at all.

Consensus and Dissension About Rank Order

Where there is a strongly dominant jati whose members live up to respectable ritual standards, whose families are landed, numerous, and powerful, and whose men speak with one voice of authority, then the leaders of that jati judge a group's worth and define its ritual precedence. If such a dominant jati is not Brahmin, its men may listen to Brahmin advice on certain ritual matters.

Often, however, no single jati of a local system is strong and united enough to exert such rule. There need not be, and often is not, any compelling ritual authority in a local system. Brahmins have presumed first rights to such authority among Hindu villagers but the local Brahmins may not be allowed to exercise these rights.

A local system does not disintegrate in the absence of an authoritative, rank-allotting group. Villagers still distinguish among blocs of jatis and regulate their own relations with those of other jatis according to these blocs. Villagers of all levels hold to the belief in a social hierarchy based on ritual standards. The men of two higher jatis may be in bitter opposition, yet they will commonly unite to keep a ritually inferior jati in what they consider to be its proper place.

Disputes about precedence between two jatis of the same bloc are not uncommon. Thus in the account of Ramkheri in Madhya Pradesh we find that "one caste may say another caste eats from its hands, the second caste denying this" (Mayer 1956, p. 121). And Srinivas, in discussing the jati he calls Peasants in Rampura, Mysore, writes that it is alleged by some that the Peasants in neighboring villages eat the domestic pig, but any public statement to this effect before a Peasant would lead to unpleasantness. "It is also well known that the poorer Peasants in Rampura and around eat the field rat and water snake, but this again would be denied. Only a few of those who drink alcoholic beverages would admit to it" (Srinivas 1955b, p. 21).

Nor is there monolithic agreement about such matters within a jati. One man of the Peasant jati in a village may rank the blacksmith group, say, as higher in the scale than will his jati-fellows, perhaps because he has had unusually cordial relations with a blacksmith family. All jati-fellows are likely to share a complimentary opinion of their own jati, but, even in this, one man may have higher aspirations for his group than does another.

In the jockeying for better rating, the insignia of rank prerogative —trivial though they may seem to an outsider—can be given supreme importance. Many contemporary instances of this will be noted later; one example may be cited here from a seventeenth-century account by the Dutch missionary, Abraham Roger. He wrote (the English translation is by L. H. Gray) that among Shudras there are many and diverse groups "whereof each pretendeth to surpass the others; and therefore it doth ofttimes hap that great strife ariseth in the land, insomuch as one caste or another, be it in marriage or in burial of the dead, goeth beyond what is the custom."

In January 1640, he recalls, the city of Pulicat was in tumult "for that the Palijs, which is the caste of poulterers, spread a cloth upon the earth while burying one of their dead, to the end that the corpse might be covered thereover." This the "Cauwreaes" would not allow them to do because it was a privilege of their group. They obstructed the funeral, and the corpse remained unburied until the local governor had the body put away. His ruling incensed the "Palij" who began to attack the other side. Groups of artisans, such as carpenters, smiths, and goldsmiths "who must hold with them in time of parlousness" rallied to the aid of the Palijs. There were months of unrest in the locality," nor was the matter ended without effusion of blood, for in the month of March fifteen Palijs and Cauwreaes were slain in fight, so that ye may see how nicely each caste of Soudraes standeth on its own" (Jackson 1907, pp. 242–243).

The advantages of respectable rank, then and now, are considerable, hence the frequent struggles about the tokens of rank. A man of high jati is not so apt to be pushed around or brushed aside by others, whatever the situation, as is one of weak and low jati. For those at the lowest levels, improvement in status can mean the freedom to live in more desirable locations than those to which they are often confined or the freedom to use water points denied to the lowliest. "For others it is mainly a matter of self-respect—the Bhilala wishes to smoke freely with the great mass of upper castes, the Teli to eat on equal terms with Rajputs and so to have many eat from his hands who will not now do so" (Mayer 1956, p. 140).

The pulling and hauling about rank has made for a relatively labile social order of the jatis of a locality within a relatively fixed set of cultural standards. The disputes about rank probably helped to reinforce villagers' ideas that high rank was indeed very important. But along with the competition and dissension about local rank, there has also been a degree of consensus about jati endogamy and about the ritual criteria.

That necessary, minimum consensus allows for some quite wide variation, both by individuals and groups. In this general survey, individual life histories cannot be studied in detail. It may be well, however, to mention here the case of one woman who did not abide by the conventions, who manipulated the system for her own highly unconventional purposes, who has not followed the cultural script for her role as a woman, a Brahmin, and a widow.

She is a widow of a Brahmin jati in the village of Kanpur district U.P. studied by K. N. Sharma. She refused to accept the austere role prescribed for Brahmin widows and carried on an affair with a Thakur man. Becoming pregnant, she ran off with him, managed an abortion, and then returned to the village, where the two lived as man and wife though without benefit of clergy or approval of the respectable people. Well-to-do families in this region customarily send gifts of food, *sidha*, to Brahmins on certain occasions. About ten years after this widow's first escapade, a leading Kayasth, Lala Shiva Prasad, acting on the advice of Brahmin elders, stopped sending her this token of jati esteem. She objected violently to this lapse, arguing that her Brahmin birthright overrode her personal failings. "Then she began to abuse him and other Brahmins of the village. Lala Shiva Prasad gave a *sidha* to avoid unnecessary trouble" (Sharma 1956a, p. 433).

A less determined Brahmin widow would have slunk far off with her shame; a more determined Kayasth, especially if prodded by strong Brahmins, would have faced the woman with wrathful and righteous rejection. As it was, she violated tenets that must be inviolable for others if the system is to continue, transgressed in ways that bring drastic punishment to similar transgressors, yet she brazened it out, withstood disapproval, even insisted successfully on some of a proper Brahmin's due.

Such cases are exceptional. Villagers shrug them off as exceptional and carry on with the village order despite such individual contradictions. But it is important to take notice of them, not only because such abnormal instances help define the norm but also because the irregular, untypical, and contrasystemic cases may portend important social change.

A whole jati or a group of jatis may be treated as a special case by others in a locality. They are not fully incorporated into the local system but yet do not threaten its operation. For example, a jati's ranking may be held in abeyance for a time. In discussing the commensal order in Ramkheri village, Mayer observes that "the Ahirs are recent immigrants from the North, and at present eat from nobody; neither does any caste take food from them" (1956, p. 122). We shall see later how certain artisan groups of South India have for centuries acted as though they belonged in the Brahmin category, while most of the others in their villages did not accept their self-styled rank.

In some places, however, dissent about ranking has had to be periodically resolved. There were ceremonial occasions when the rank order was set forth plain for all to see. On such occasions there was a clear—if temporary—settlement of the rank order. Fewer villages now have such occasions, mainly because a settlement is more difficult to reach.

At a ceremony in which all the village jatis participate, the distribution of festal food symbolizes the order of local society. What groups eat next to what other groups and who is served before whom at the feast show agreement about the order of rank, or at least show how current disputes about rank have been settled for the time being. In the ordinary round of village life, villagers commonly use the acceptance of food and water as the best guide to the order of rank. A jati's place is thus defined at a feast in which all local jatis join—by where its members are seated, by what other jatis will take cooked food from its members and from whom they will accept food. But even when such clear ranking is publicly made at a village ceremony, some particulars of that order may be contravened in another context or at a different time, and ranking is likely to be somewhat different in other villages of the vicinity.

The order of rank, nevertheless, is a matter of great and continuing consequence to many villagers. Some studies have attempted to formulate a general scale of rank in a village by asking village informants to arrange in rank order a set of cards, each bearing the name of a jati of the village (Freed 1963b). The answers are mathematically combined to give a general result. But this mathematically derived listing, Berreman has commented (1965), may not be very relevant to actual behavior because it does not take into account the various criteria for ranking and the different contexts in which rank influences interaction. Another approach uses questions about actual situations to formulate ritual distances among jatis by a multiple scaling technique (Kolenda 1959). This does take contexts and criteria into consideration but is limited to a relatively few of the many that are actually used.

How a jati's practices are evaluated by other villagers, and the bloc in which a jati is classed, depend on such considerations as the power of its families and the popular stereotype of their conduct, as well as on the ritual quality of the practices. Though the appraisals of rank are full of fine nuances, they are made on the basis of a few generative principles. Purity and pollution, wealth and power are major considerations.

THE hierarchical order of jatis in a locality is further bolstered by cultural differences among the jatis. The higher groups characteristically follow domestic and religious practices that they hold to be far superior to those of the lower jatis. The people of the lower jatis do not necessarily agree that their own customs are abysmally inferior, but once they are able to do so they emulate the more prestigious ways of the higher jatis. The process of emulation is discussed in the later chapters on social mobility; we note here some common cultural differences within a local order.

Villagers expect that each jati will have some unique traits and that these will characterize all in the jati. In practice there can be considerable variation in customs within a jati. In some jatis, the traditional occupation is followed by very few of the jati members. Further, there may be only slight cultural differences between one jati and another in a locality. Nevertheless, the villagers' concept is in some degree borne out in practice; there are typically certain customary ways unique to each jati.

There are, moreover, cultural differences among the main grouping of jatis. The scriptural, ritual differences appear most clearly in the contrast between the topmost and the bottommost blocs in a locality. Brahmins and other high jatis are purer in their diet than are the lowest—who may not be able to forego the occasional dietary windfall of a carcass. The highest jatis tend, on the whole, to be more fastidious ritually than are the lowest—who may not be able to afford, or may not know about, all the ritual niceties. Diacritical details of costume, such as the sacred thread, usually distinguish the higher from the lower. Men of the Brahmin jatis are—or are supposed to be—familiar with some of the main scriptural concepts, or are linked in other ways with the great, sacred, literate tradition of Hinduism. This is in contrast to people of the lowest jatis who do not, and formerly could not, presume to sacred scriptural learning.

This learning is more appropriate for men of Brahmin jatis than for those of the two other "twice-born" categories, but jatis of all three higher varnas, as we shall note in discussing models for mobility, are expected to differ from those of lower rank in style of life, in daily ritual, in jati ceremonial, and particularly in conjugal relations. Among groups at the top of the social scale, a woman at marriage enters a permanent inviolable relationship that must endure through all the here and the hereafter. Widows must never remarry; divorce is prohibited. No such taboos lie upon women of the lower jatis, who may divorce and be divorced and who may remarry whether they are divorcees or widows.

Brahmins tend to put more emphasis on the rites performed by males for their ancestors, an emphasis that makes sons especially prized in a family. Writing about non-Brahmins in Mysore, Srinivas notes that though a son is preferred, a daughter is not unwelcome. Girls are in demand among them and there is no religious duty to get a girl married before puberty. The code under which a woman has to live is not so harsh among them as among the Brahmins (1956a, p. 485).

Not all the proprieties practiced by Brahmins have clear sanction in scripture. Sanskrit scripture is not a single, coordinated corpus of holy writ. Earlier texts differ from later ones; widely different interpretations have been made of the same text or of a particular directive. But scriptural exegesis is of small concern to a villager. The important and prevalent belief is that holy scripture is the font of purity-pollution concepts and related conduct. To most villagers who know anything at all about the literate tradition these concepts are now and forever established; they have been revered in all preceding generations; they are revered even in this untoward age.

Differences in Religious Practices

There are significant differences between the scriptural, transcendental aspects of religion, which are mainly in the keeping of the high jatis, and the pragmatic aspects, which are used by all but are kept up principally by people of the lower jatis. These differences are discussed below in the chapters on village and civilization and on the accretion of tribal peoples; to indicate the nature of the cultural separations in religion among social strata, some of the distinguishing features of the two aspects should be mentioned here.

Animal sacrifice is one of the contrastive traits; it is more commonly performed by the lower jatis than by those who follow the "twice-born" models. There are scriptural precedents for certain kinds of animal sacrifice, but these are considered irrelevant to present-day Sanskritic worship by the learned, quite as clergy in the Judeo-Christian tradition wave aside Old Testament prescriptions for blood sacrifice.

Possession is another differential trait. In many regions there are persons who regularly become possessed. When a man (or more rarely a woman) becomes possessed with a deity or a spirit, the voice of the supernatural speaks through him, answers questions about illness and personal problems, and gives commands or advice for remedying what has gone wrong. These shamans are mainly from the blocs below the highest; rarely does a Brahmin become possessed in this way (cf. Harper 1957b; Carstairs 1957, pp. 92–94).

A comparison of worship in various social levels of Kishan Garhi village shows clearly that scriptural deities figure more prominently in the devotions of the higher groups than in the worship of the lower. The rites of the lower jatis are more concerned with the local godlings. "Forty-five percent of the deities worshipped by Brahmins are Sanskritic; 35 percent of the deities worshipped by members of ten high castes below the Brahmins are Sanskritic; but only 15 and 19 percent, respectively, of the deities worshipped by members of the low and lowest castes are Sanskritic deities" (Marriott 1955b, p. 209).

These figures illustrate significant differences in religious emphasis and also show considerable overlapping, especially in that Brahmins worship a number of local spirits and godlings, as do women of all jatis. Although these figures are only about relative numbers and not about the relative importance attached to the different deities, it is significant that these Brahmins hold in reverence many deities unhallowed in scripture.

All in a village can appeal to local deities for certain specific purposes. Thus in Kumbapettai village, in the Tanjore district of Madras, the village deity is the spirit of a Konar (cowherd) woman who died of smallpox. Her priest is a non-Brahmin. Besides being a deity of the Konar, propitiated by them at their annual festival, this goddess is worshipped by both Brahmins and Adi Dravidas ("Original Dravidians," a more acceptable term than "untouchables") at specific times of the year. The shrine of the goddess stands on a boundary of the village and "is believed to protect the whole community from crop failure, infectious diseases, female barrenness and deaths in child-birth." People of any jati may propitiate the goddess when illness, barrenness, or insanity afflicts their households. The chief village festival is celebrated for this local deity (Gough 1955, p. 89).

Cultural Contrasts and Their Social Effects

In Kumbapettai village the cultural differences between the top and the bottom of the local order are especially marked. In the 1950s the local Brahmins were, as they had been for centuries, the ritual superiors and also the strongly dominant landowners. The two jatis of Adi Dravidas are mainly poor landless laborers (Gough 1956, pp. 826–827).

These Brahmins place great importance on the continuity of the lineage and on a man's tight nexus with his immediate ascendants and descendants. Lineal descent is highly important to them because it determines the control and inheritance of land. To the economic significance of lineal relations is added the great religious necessity for sons. A dead man's soul does not find secure place in any afterlife unless it is fed regularly with ritual offerings made by a son. After his death a father is supremely dependent in this way on the son; while he is alive the son should be greatly dependent on him. The asymmetrical relation, in which the father or father surrogate is in complete authority and in which the junior male is the obedient disciple, is one that is highly prized and idealized.

The Adi Dravidas, at the opposite end of the local social scale, have no land; inheritance is not of paramount interest to them. Grown sons must fend for themselves and they break away from the father's authority soon after puberty. They are not much con-

cerned with religious duties for departed souls. They do not stress
a long and close relationship between father and son, nor do they
idealize a state of dependency. Their emphasis is on the solidarity
of peers, on the equivalence of brothers and of sisters (cf. Mandelbaum 1941; 1955). It is on the ties that a man has among a wide
compass of his contemporaries rather than, as with the Brahmins,
within the narrow range of his immediate forebears and descendants. They find it feasible to act together as peers of a jati group
and to be represented by their headman. Conversely, the Brahmins
of this village find it much less feasible to take joint action and to
agree on a single chosen representative for all (Gough 1956, pp.
840, 846).

These different emphases are reflected in kinship terminology.
The Brahmin terminology makes plain a person's relation to those
of his lineage; there are relatively few terms for affinal relatives.
Adi Dravida kinship terms are laterally extended over a wide range
of affinal and cognate relatives (Gough 1956, p. 848).

A Brahmin woman in Kumbapettai works only in the home, does
not own land, and at marriage her social personality becomes
closely assimilated into that of her husband so that, for example,
she adopts her husband's terms in addressing his kin. A bride's family must transfer wealth to the groom's family to ensure a stable
marriage and the couple must live in the husband's natal household.
The scriptural ban on divorce and on widow remarriage transfers
the bride into her husband's social position for all her life.

Adi Dravida women are much more independent—economically,
socially, ritually. They work with the men in the fields and are paid
separately and individually. At marriage it is the groom's family
that transfers wealth to the bride's rather than the other way around
as with the Brahmins. Residence after marriage need not be strictly
patrilocal. A woman remains much more of an independent social
personality after marriage; she does not take over the same kin terminology used by her husband; she retains greater affiliation with
her natal family and its social ties. Marriage is not an irreversible
commitment. Adi Dravida women may divorce and remarry. They
have greater spatial and social mobility than do Brahmin women.
This is not to say that a wife rules the roost in these jatis; she must,
overtly at least, be relatively submissive. But she, much more readily than a Brahmin woman, can pick up her children and go home

to mother, leaving behind—perhaps permanently—an impossible husband.

The Adi Dravidas of Kumbapettai do not value sexual asceticism as do the Brahmins. Further, their men can more readily give vent to their aggressions, can trade blows and later forget the quarrel. Brahmin men may not explode into physical aggression in the same way; a physical fight among the men of a Brahmin family would be a most shameful, unforgettable event (Gough 1956, p. 847).

This comparison between the Brahmins and the Adi Dravidas of Kumbapettai village provides a particularly vivid contrast. In most villages there is not so great a disparity between highest and lowest, but some such differences are common. There are relative differences in culture and also certain sharper differences.

In the highest jatis there is relatively more worship of the scriptural deities, and among the lowest jatis relatively more assistance is sought from shamans. In families of top rank, as was noted in the chapters on family roles, there is relatively more deference to elders and less independent status for women than in families of lowest rank. A jati that is ritually highest in its local order may not be vegetarian, but its members are usually more meticulous about their diet, more selective than are their social inferiors. The local Brahmins may not be very learned, but they are more learned than their neighbors. Those who cherish a Kshatriya tradition take pride in being fiercer warriors than all others. Those of highest ritual status are relatively more scrupulous in ritual observance than are those of lowest rank.

The sharper differences are in such traits as *being* a shaman and *performing* an animal sacrifice. Those of superior status may willingly share the benefits of a seance or of the sacrifice of a goat, but it is rare for one of them to become possessed or actually to wield the sacrificial blade. And as between highest and lowest, a woman's lot in marriage has been different—no divorce, no widow remarriage, prepuberty weddings (though postpuberty nuptials and consummation) in the top rank; easier divorce, unquestioned remarriage of widows, postpuberty marriage at the lowest echelon.

Cultural differences have been the trigger and symbol of great social disturbances, as in the conflicts between right-hand and left-hand Hindu factions early in the nineteenth century or the riots between Muslim Sunnis and Shias early in the twentieth. But such upheavals have been limited in time and space; they have not been characteristic of the ordinary round of village life in which cultural differences are routinely accepted.

Certain understandings about society are shared by villagers no matter what their religion or jati status may be. There is usually implicit consensus in a village that there is and should be a hierarchy of ranked endogamous groups, that this hierarchy is very important, that it is based on criteria of ritual pollution and purity. These common beliefs form a broad, monistic frame for social organization. Within the limits set by this frame, cultural pluralism is allowed and expected.

Differences are not, in themselves, suspect. A Brahmin may abjure widow remarriage for Brahmins but he will not care whether the widow of his sweeper remarries. The Harijan shaman, when possessed by the spirit of a village godling, does not usually decry the gods worshipped in the great temple, nor do devotees of the scriptural deities ordinarily try to wipe out worship of the local spirits. The gods of the Sanskritic pantheon are held by Hindus to be universal deities, but they are not accorded monopoly over all the village, nor do the *dei loci* demand exclusive rights within their own locale.

In later chapters other cultural differences will be examined, such as those of sect, religion, and region. Within a village, differences between one sect and another may seem extraordinarily minute to an outside observer but may, on occasion, loom large in the view of villagers. Conversely, the differences in dogma that separate Islam from Hinduism may, in the ordinary round of village life, result in relatively little difference in the daily life of Muslims and Hindus of the same social level in the same locality. The premises of jati organization require some degree of differentiation in custom among jatis; villagers can tolerate quite wide cultural divergences within a local system so long as the basic tenets are not perturbed.

Résumé

"The institution of caste provides a common cultural idiom to Indians: wherever one may be in India one is in a universe of caste." Studies done in all parts of the land confirm this statement by Srinivas (1958, p. 573), yet as we noted in Chapter 1, students of caste have been mindful also of the problems involved in formulating the grammar (not to say the lexicon) of this idiom and of mapping the dimensions of this universe.

A scholar of an earlier generation, Émile Senart, asked in his book on caste, which appeared in 1896, whether we should abandon the difficult attempt to give a picture of the caste institution as a whole. Senart's answer, together with the fifteen chapters that follow it, asserts that the attempt should be made. Any such attempt, Senart said, will be incomplete, but will not necessarily therefore be false and misleading. "It will be enough to remember that no assertion should be regarded as absolute, that the relationship of facts leaves room for a multitude of fine shades of difference, and that only the most general characteristics are common to the whole domain" (1930, pp. 19–20). With due regard for the warning about absolute assertions, we review the characteristics of jatis and of relations among jatis that have so far been discussed.

Most of the peoples of the subcontinent have lived in jati-based social order, yet no single hierarchy has ever regulated all of Indian caste society. Caste organization has flourished as a vast series of local systems, each partially independent of others, each intricately related to others.

Each local system is centered in a village or a close set of villages. It includes those who come in from other villages regularly to perform jajmani or other functions. A person normally participates as village member in the local system that centers on the village of his residence. He participates as jati member in other localities where his kin and jati fellows live. In both capacities he perceives much finer social distinctions among those who are close to him than among those with whom he has less intimate relationships. Outside the marital and household sphere a person needs to recognize only broader social divisions. A landowner may be in frequent relation with his barber, washerman, and field hand for a lifetime without knowing much about their respective clans or the position of the jati of each within a jati-cluster of barbers, washermen, or laborers.

The broader social divisions are of several kinds. We have used the term jati-cluster for a grouping of several jatis under a common name with close enough ties of culture and communication to foster some feeling of mutual identity. Villagers also sort the jati-groups of their village into a series of blocs, groupings of different jatis lumped together and similarly treated. Sometimes the blocs are essentially the varna categories plus others, such as Muslims, who are not mentioned in the varna scheme. But a bloc may include jatis whose members follow quite different varna tradition, yet are similarly treated by other villagers. Nevertheless, villagers try to reconcile the main blocs with the varna classification, which not only transcends locality, but also is hallowed by the eternal and universal ambience of scripture.

Taken as an empirical formulation of Indian caste society, the varna outline is easily shown to be deceptively oversimplified, even misleading. Seen as the villagers' model of their social structure, it appears as a useful, even a necessary, social device. Using it, a person can maintain and establish relations with people belonging to a great diversity of groupings within his local system, and with the vaster diversity of jatis beyond this home locality.[1] Peoples of a complex civilization need a simple social theory; in India such theory is taken from Hindu scripture.

Groups that are divergent by reason of religion or sect are fitted, as will be seen below, into the local order of caste. The field of hierarchical force generated by a local system draws in and adapts groups of all sorts, even those that have been formed on the grounds of antagonism to caste. A villager does not necessarily feel threatened by cultural differences among his neighbors nor impelled to change their ways to his. He does object if others try to take on what he considers to be his jati's prerogative. The fact that there are regional differences in caste order and criteria does not disturb villagers, even if they are aware of such differences.

All the variations—among regions, within local systems, within a person's repertoire of caste roles, in his perception of social divisions—are played out in a kind of counterpoint to the constant

---

[1] The extent of that diversity can be judged from the various and incomplete census attempts to count the number of caste groupings. In the 1901 Census of India, the counted number of "main castes" (mostly jati-clusters in our terms) came to 2,378. Ten years before that there had been some counting of the subdivision within certain main castes; for Ahirs there were more than 1,700 entries, for Jats a similarly large number, for Kurmis there were nearly 1,500 names.

In the 1931 Census, more than 15 million Brahmins were returned. In the hill state of Tehri-Garhwal, with a total population of only 350,000, there were counted 387 "subcastes" of Brahmins and 1,025 of Rajputs (Davis 1951, p. 166).

themes of jati organization. These themes have to do with ritual pollution and purity and with their consequences for social relations, particularly for endogamy. They entail the ritual and secular attributes of jatis, their interdependence and order. Certain personal practices, especially those having to do with eating and other bodily functions, affect a person's ritual pollution and purity, and this regulates the relations that he may have with other people. Such regulation is made within the family when one member is temporarily more polluted or is more purified than are the others. These temporary, ritual inequalities within a household arise and are mitigated daily.

Permanently, all in a household are ritual equals because of, and by means of, their intimate interaction. Similar ritual equality prevails more widely for all families among whom intermarriage may occur. Endogamy bounds the jati, which is kept as a firm unit by the strong taboo on marrying out of the jati. If we coin the term excest for this taboo, we can say that the horror of excest in village India is almost as powerful as the horror of incest. Genetically, a jati is a breeding unit as well as a unit of social reproduction. The genetic aspects of jati organization remain a relatively unexplored part of the study of caste society.

Each person is born into a jati, into one and only one jati. He and all the others in his jati are considered by their neighbors to have certain attributes, commonly including a traditional occupation. These attributes affect the permanent pollution or purity of the jati members and therefore affect the kinds of relations they may have with people of other jatis, who carry greater or less permanent pollution-purity than their own. Villagers rank those jatis they consider to be the purer as higher and accord them greater jati prerogatives; those seen as more polluted are ranked lower, with greater ritual disabilities. The ritual criteria for rank are, in practice, combined with the secular factors of a jati's wealth and power in the overall assignment of jati rank. Commonly all in a village agree that there is a social hierarchy and that it has certain outlines, but there is often considerable disagreement concerning at least some details of the rank order.

The jatis are both independent and interdependent. The members of each are held apart from all others in certain matters, by jati differences and avoidances. All are bound together by their dependence on each other; typically no jati is sufficient to itself either economically or ritually. Although there have long been important fields of village life in which jati rank was largely irrelevant, and these activities are rapidly increasing in scope and in importance, most villagers still identify strongly with their jati and conduct many of their relations with their neighbors with consideration to jati rank.

These thematic patterns provide the basic rule of the social game in villages through most of the land. For many centuries they have been bolstered by the ideology of Sanskrit scripture and its vernacular versions, which encompassed diverse local orders in a common frame. Villagers of the lower ranks have had little formal acquaintance with doctrinal concepts, but they have shared in scriptural stories and concepts. In sum, people at all levels and in hundreds of thousands of villages, have shared a similar image of society as a whole. They also have shared similar ideas about relations within their jati.

PART **IV** *Relations within the Jati*

14 Alliances and Sections
within the Jati

Jati members cooperate in many ways, as kinsmen, as ritual equals in certain contexts, as political allies in others. Some aspects of this collaboration have already been noted, others will be discussed in the next few chapters. But there are also formal restrictions and implicit limits upon cooperation among the people of a jati.

The range of a person's relations within his jati depends on such matters as its size, his own social and economic status, and the formal subdivisions of the jati.

In a very small jati, such as the Gayawal (who number about one hundred twenty families in the town of Gaya), a man can know and relate to most others of his jati (Vidyarthi 1961, pp. 53–57). But many jatis are spread across scores or hundreds of villages, and a man can maintain jati relations with only a small part of the total. This part has been called his "effective jati," comprising those with whom he actually maintains such relations (cf. Mayer 1960, p. 151; Klass 1966, p. 954).

A villager's compass of jati relations usually varies according to his wealth and education. Srinivas notes that an elderly, uneducated Okkaliga of the Mysore and Mandya districts in Mysore State might not consider Okkaligas of other districts as belonging to his jati at all. His effective social span would include the Okkaligas within a radius of about twenty-five miles of his village. "But an Okkaliga lawyer or doctor would regard all the divisions as Okkaligas, and he might give his daughter in marriage to the son of an urbanized and educated Okkaliga from distant Shimoga in the west" (Srinivas 1966, p. 115). What the uneducated villager sees as separate jatis of the Okkaliga jati-cluster, the educated professional man now takes to be one jati.

In addition, the people of a jati commonly group themselves into subdivisions that limit the possibilities for full jati cooperation. Some jatis are formally subdivided on the basis of the marriage rules of hypergamy. Another kind of subdivision, one which is usually not formalized but which occurs frequently, is between opposing alliances. Jati members can be competitors and rivals for status as well as comrades and allies. Membership in a ranked section of a jati is inherited; joining an alliance is more voluntary.

Hypergamy and Hypergamous Sections

Women are generally expected to be more strict than men are about domestic ritual observances and niceties of domestic status. They are likely to feel more vulnerable than do men to breaches of such observances. Parents may be willing to arrange the marriage of a son to a girl from a family a bit lower than theirs in prestige and status but are usually unwilling to marry a daughter into a family of lower status within the jati. That course not only consigns their daughter to an inferior family but also lowers their own prestige in the eyes of their jati fellows.

This common preference to marry a daughter for better and not for worse is formalized in some jatis as a rigid rule of hypergamy. Under that rule, a woman must marry into her own section or into one that is higher but must not be married into a lower section of the jati. A man may take a wife from a lower section.[1] These ranked sections are hereditary, but section affiliation is reckoned in different ways. The sections of some jatis are made up of lineages; in others the ranked units are made up of clans or villages or territorial divisions.

Among Rajputs, the far-flung and numerous jati-cluster of northern and western India, clans are so classified and ranked in a complex fashion. There are four major sets of clans, named after the

---

[1] The rule is propounded in scriptural sources. Marriage between a man of higher position and a woman of lower is called *anuloma* ("with the hair"), and is, within certain limits, approved. The reverse, a woman marrying beneath her position, is called *pratiloma*, against the grain ("against the hair") and is strongly disapproved (Ghurye 1961, p. 54; Bouglé 1908, pp. 122–126).

Sun, Moon, Fire, and Serpents; for purposes of hypergamy, the sets are generally ranked in that order, though with some questions about the relative ranking of Fire and Serpents sets (Karve 1965, pp. 165–171).

A Rajput clan often is associated with a geographic region and there is a concomitant rating by region. Although a Rajput man, and especially a ruler, could marry into a clan far lower than his (or even take a non-Rajput wife), in practice hypergamous marriages are made mainly between Rajput families of clans that are not far apart in the clan ratings, as these are understood by the families contracting the alliance. (There may be much the same difference of opinion about the relative ranking of Rajput clans in a locality as there is about the relative rating of some of the jatis in the caste system of that locality.)

Hypergamous ranking by clans also occurs among the Marathas of western India. The highest, most exclusive set includes the smallest number of clans; a clansman of this set may take a wife from any of the other sets down to the one that is lowest in position and that includes the greatest number of clans. Dr. Irawati Karve describes five such sets of Maratha clans (1965, pp. 176–179).[2]

Among the Patidars of Charottar in Central Gujarat, sets of villages are ranked. "These circles are arranged in a hierarchy such that Six Villages at the top of the Charōttār Pātidārs will take brides from any other village if the father is able to pay a substantial dowry but they refuse to give their daughters outside the Six Villages" (Pocock 1957b, p. 21; also see Fukutake et al. 1964, p. 59). Patidar husband and wife must come from different villages.

Many North Indian jatis observe village exogamy, as was mentioned above in connection with rules of marriage, and in some places people of all jatis in a village follow the same pattern of hypergamy in arranging marriages with a family of another village. This occurs in Kishan Garhi (Aligarh district, U.P.). If a Kishan Garhi man—of any jati—has taken a wife from village A, then that village is deemed an inferior one for marriage alliances by all in Kishan Garhi. No father in Kishan Garhi will give his daughter in

---

[2] Arrangement into five sections is not found among all the jatis called Maratha. Thus in the villages of Poona district that Henry Orenstein has studied, clan hypergamy among Marathas is much more loosely arranged (1963, pp. 5–6; 1965a, pp. 126–128).

marriage to a man of village A. In this area, the northern villages are generally regarded as the superior, and brides at marriage usually go north to the groom's village.[3] "Marital relationships are formally one-sided and unbalanced: the boy's side is the high and demanding side, while the girl's side is the low and giving side" (Marriott 1955b, p. 176). The village from which the bride comes is inferior, for purposes of marriage arrangements, to the village into which she is married.

Often mentioned in discussions of hypergamy are the Rarhi Brahmins of Bengal. They are divided into four ranked sections, of which the Kulin is the highest. (The term "Kulin" is used widely for the highest unit in any ranking having to do with hypergamy.) A woman of the Kulin section may marry only a Kulin man, while a Kulin man may marry into one of the lower sections (Bhattacharya 1896, p. 38; Risley 1915, pp. 163–171; Hutton 1961, p. 53; Majumdar 1958a, p. 337).

The Kanyakubja Brahmins of Uttar Pradesh carry their internal jati stratification to a highly involuted extreme. A table listing forty-six sections of the jati is presented by Sharma as an illustrative but not a complete list. Each of these forty-six sections is characterized by a unique combination of attributes, such as *Upadhi* (surname), *gotra* (clan), grade (one of four categories), *Asami* (a famous person in the genealogical line), residence (traditional locality), and an evaluative order number called *biswas* (Sharma 1956b; Khare 1960).

The matrilineal Nayars of Kerala also followed the rule of hypergamy. The Nayars were classed into four ranked groupings, the royal and chiefly lineages, five groups of temple servants, five of commoner Nayars, and three of temple menials. A commoner woman could choose a temple servant man as her spouse and a temple menial woman could choose a commoner man. But royal and chiefly men had relations only with commoner women, not with women of either temple grouping.

A Nambudiri Brahmin man, as was noted in discussing family relations, could have an alliance with a Nayar woman of any status.

---

[3] In the Ganges-Jumna valleys, upstream is the superior direction in marriage alliances. This is north in the region of Kishan Garhi; it is west after the Ganges changes the main direction of flow.

At the other end of the local social scale, below the lowest Nayar jatis, were the "polluting" jatis of the locality; there was a sharp cleavage between them and all Nayars. No Nayar or Nambudiri man could have any kind of intimacy with women below this line. These hypergamous relations, Kathleen Gough comments, probably strengthened the unity among the ruling groups of an area against the lower jatis and also against external attack (Gough 1961c, pp. 319–321; 1965; Thurston 1909, vol. 5, pp. 300–303).

In general, hypergamy makes possible the internal stratification of a jati without completely ending endogamy.[4] It is a kind of qualified endogamy. Formal hypergamy has been used, as will be noted later, as a step in social mobility. Families of an upwardly mobile group begin to set themselves apart from the other, less fortunate families of the jati by establishing hypergamous relations between themselves and the others. They still will take brides from the other families but will not give their girls to them in marriage. The others may protest vigorously, but sometimes the wealthier, more powerful families have succeeded in establishing formal subdivisions of their jati. In time, the memory that there was such a struggle for higher status is forgotten and those of the high sections are likely to say that their eminence within the jati was ordained from on high.

Contests for advantage and status among jati fellows still go on. How a family's status is, in some degree, tested on the occasion of a marriage of a child of the family has been noted. There are many other occasions when the prestige of a family or of a lineage within the jati is felt to be in the balance.

Such contests frequently occur among the men of a jati-group who are dominant in their village. The dominant jati-group splits into two or more opposing sets of families. These subdivisions

---

[4] The principal distribution of formal hypergamy, according to W. H. R. Rivers' survey, is among Rajputs and other groups living close to Rajputs who have adopted the Rajput model. He attributes Maratha hypergamy to the example of the Rajputs. It is also characteristic of the Kulin (i.e., Rahri Brahmin of Bengal) and of those Bengal groups that have followed the Kulin pattern. Hypergamy occurs among some Punjabi Brahmins (Rivers 1921, pp. 12–16). It is found only sporadically in the former Central Provinces (Russell and Hira Lal 1916, vol. 1, p. 28). Apart from the Nayar and other Kerala cases, hypergamy is not common in South India.

within the jati are not formalized or freely acknowledged as are the hypergamous sections, but they are often more potent factors in the lives of the people so divided.

Alliances within a Jati-Group

The members of a jati-group are both kith and kin to each other. Day-to-day cooperation among jati fellows takes place mainly among those who live in the same village or cluster of villages. A villager's political activities are centered in his village; it is the scene of his livelihood and the daily stage for the enactment of his principal roles. Hence his relations with the people who are both neighbors in the village and kinsmen of the jati have a particular and a political importance to him (cf. Gould 1964, p. 26).

The political importance is likely to be especially marked in a jati-group whose people are numerous and economically strong enough to dominate their village. The common patterns of such domination are noted in the later discussion on the internal regulation of the village. But in their own jati affairs, the members of a large, dominant jati-group are likely to be split. In a small jati-group, solidarity can be enhanced by close interaction, as when all participate in each family's ceremonies. In less powerful jati-groups all can feel themselves confronted, and so consolidated, by their status rivals in the village. But the members of a large jati-group cannot interact as intimately as can a group of only a few families, and they confront only themselves in the village, since as a jati-group they are already in a paramount position. So with them the pervasive struggle for power and precedence is commonly carried on within the jati-group, among the several alliances of its families. They usually do unite solidly against a clear threat to their status as a jati, but ordinarily much of their competitive energy goes into competition among themselves. In the Bengal village of Govindapur (Midnapore district), for example, Mahisyas are dominant, having 63 percent of the population and 66 percent of the land. Ralph Nicholas notes that village politics are mainly carried on between opposing groups of Mahisyas; "political affairs in the village, on the whole, are *not* caste affairs" (1965, p. 31).

In a survey of the data on village disputes Cohn writes that splits in the "dominant-caste" group are reported for most villages so dominated (1965, p. 92; references there cited include Lewis 1958, pp. 114–154; Majumdar 1958a, pp. 114–123; Harper and Harper 1959, pp. 461–462; Bailey 1957, pp. 194–195; Opler 1959a; Mayer 1960, pp. 126–127).

These divisions within a jati-group have often been called factions; the term emphasizes their competitive, contentious functions. In this vein Nicholas has analyzed the characteristics of factions. He defines factions as conflict groups. The conflict is political competition for public power; factions are not corporate, enduring groups; members are recruited by a leader and are drawn in for diverse reasons and principles (1965, pp. 44–46; 1966, pp. 52–57). This is a useful analysis, but very often a group that may well be called a faction is also a cooperative group whose members help each other in ways that are not just the upshot of mutual opposition to rivals. The term "resource group" has been proposed in order to emphasize this collaborative function (Sharma 1963). Typically also, such a group has a hierarchical structure of authority and an acknowledged scope of influence; the word "domain" stresses this aspect (Hitchcock 1959). The terms "alliance" or "allied families" include both competitive and cooperative activities and they are used in that inclusive sense here. Several alliances may join forces for a particular purpose and for a limited period to form a coalition.

Within a dominant jati-group then, there generally are several alliances, each one a set of families who interact more often and more intimately with each other than with others of the jati-group and who act collectively in the internal competition for status and power. The family is the fundamental component of any alliance. Brothers occasionally join different alliances, but they do not thereafter long remain together in one family. Lineage is almost always relevant in an alliance. Commonly all in a lineage are in the same alliance and an alliance is often composed of one or more lineages. If a man joins an alliance different from that of his lineage, it is evidence of his estrangement from his close agnates.

An example of how seriously this can be taken is given in Scarlett Epstein's study of Wangala village in Mysore. Only one man of the dominant jati there had associated himself with a faction (the term Dr. Epstein uses) other than that of his lineage. He was the eldest of five brothers, Tupa by name, who wanted to be an independent farmer. But when the ancestral land was partitioned at his instigation, his share came to so little that he could not start cultivating independently.

He had hoped to get some of the land that his father had purchased separately from the ancestral lands, but the father refused to part with any of it, as was his legal right. Tupa then sought support from the faction to which his lineage is strongly opposed. He did get some financial aid and struck up a strong friendship with one of the leaders of this opposing faction. His own lineage excommunicated him. It would have been his ritual duty, at his cousin's wedding, to fetch sanctified water from the pond to the bridegroom's household. Tupa was not even asked to attend the wedding. His place in the ritual was taken by his younger brother (Epstein 1962, p. 130).

This instance parallels the kind of redressive action that is used at other levels of caste organization. To be sure, Tupa was not put out of his jati, but he was cut off from his lineage. No one approved his switch, not even those with whom he allied himself, and "his dereliction prevents him from achieving the prestige that he sought." Lineage ties are thus usually important but not imperative in the formation and maintenance of an alliance. A split in lineage alignment is not approved, but it can occur when divisive pressures in a lineage builds up.

An alliance is generally made up of a few core families and several dependent, client families. The core families are rich and powerful enough to generate a field of influence and to withstand challenges from other families. Their leaders can marshal unwavering support within the alliance and, importantly, the stronger family heads have reached an understanding so that they do not undermine each other. If these strong families falter, that particular alliance is likely to disintegrate. They can loan bullocks or money to the dependent families, offer them fields to cultivate on a share-crop basis, or give them honorable employment. Their leaders can dicker with an intrusive policeman, negotiate a government favor, or fight a court case.

Together, the core and the client families form a unit of power and manpower. Leaders of such groups in Khalapur say of their allies, "They are the real friends of the family; they would come to our support whether we were in the right or in the wrong." Hitchcock comments that the implication here is that the real friends of the family would come to its support either with quarter-staffs in the event of a fight or as witnesses in a court case (1959, p. 29). And in a serious contest, the allied families can usually mobilize assistance from some of their retainers of lower jatis. They may also find support from others in the jati and village whose interests at the moment and in the context of the particular struggle happen to coincide with their own.

The makeup of an alliance is visible when the men come in from the fields. In villages of the north, they cluster in small groups to share a hookah. The smokers who congregate in the same men's house or sitting platform are apt to be of one alliance. In South India, the allies gather on the verandah of a big house or under a special tree, talking, resting, looking, playing cards, passing their leisure time together. They are partners in recreation as in council, in the banter of the evening as well as in the heat of a quarrel. Their women too are close to each other but women's interchange is more limited and less visible publicly than that of the men.

In a village near Jodhpur in Rajasthan, the powerful Jats are split into two rival camps. The principal unit of alliance affiliation is the lineage; few men break with their lineage mates to join rival groups. The reasons given for associating one's lineage with a particular alliance are mainly those of kinship, especially because of affinal ties (Bose and Malhotra 1964, pp. 312–316).

A survey of the alignment of 255 families in two West Bengal villages (where Mahisyas are dominant) showed that for 28 percent of the families the alignment was based on kinship ties with alliance leaders and for 27 percent on economic dependence on them. Residential proximity to alliance leaders accounted for 21 percent, caste reasons 14 percent, and protection from a powerful enemy 10 percent (Nicholas and Mukhopadhyay 1962, p. 32; Nicholas 1966, p. 56).

In sum, an alliance within a dominant jati-group is commonly a federation of lineages but may also contain a few adherents who have split with their own lineage. The alliance is cemented by the patronage and protection of the stronger families and by the tacit concord among the stronger family leaders. Amity within an alliance is reinforced daily by intimate, informal relations, and its strength is mobilized from time to time for status defense or aggrandizement.

An alliance is more flexible but less perduring than a kinship sodality. An alliance may endure for decades but it may also be ephemeral or may alter suddenly, precisely because no formal and durable principle of allegiance binds its members together. It is not usually denoted by any special term, or if it is, the term is apt to be pejorative, fastening on the contentious functions. Nor is it a unit of society clearly recognized by the villagers as are lineage and jati. Yet it is a group of considerable importance in many villages, not only within a dominant jati-group but also, as will be noted later, among families of different jatis.

The Bases of Alliance Strength

The strength of the whole alliance rests on its resources in wealth and in manpower, and on its access to wider sources of power, especially those of government. Wealth, as we have seen, is still primarily wealth in land. With enough land a family can be assured of its own livelihood and can provide for dependent families, no matter what the factional opposition may be. With the money from the yield of the land, it can buttress its power and prestige. But although land is a chief component of wealth, other sources of wealth—whether from trade, religion, raids, or government—have on occasion been mainstays of alliance power. Modern enterprises are increasingly important, their yield often being used for alliance purposes in quite the traditional ways.

One set of Patidar families in Gujarat has formed a flourishing corporation that provides petrol and oil used in irrigation pumps. Through the company they also operate tube wells and pumps and sell water to farmers. The rise of this alliance illustrates how dynamic families may now increase their wealth and in so doing expand and strengthen the cohort of their allies.

The company of these Patidar families buys land on the outskirts of a village area that is not irrigated or only little irrigated because the cultivators cannot afford a tube well and pump. These lands usually belong to the poorest Patidars who are therefore willing to sell, especially since they know that the rest of their poor land, if irrigation is available, may become much more fertile. After the pump is in operation, all the village farmers want water from it, but they may not be able to pay immediately or may fall behind in their payments and go into debt to the company. Although water rates are supposedly fixed there are times in the year when a villager must either pay heavily for water or see his crop ruined. So once the company is established in a village, which is to say once the alliance is thus established, it extends its business and also its power. "Customers are also clients. Upon this socio-economic base a web of power is spun and if the need arises, shall we say in some future business project, the company has widened the army of its allies" (Pocock 1957a, p. 303).

Wealth, aggressively wielded, begets more wealth and power. In Khalapur village (Saharanpur district, U.P.) for example, there are many more families of the dominant Rajputs than of the service and retainer jatis. So a family of potters, say, serves a number of Rajput families, some affluent, others poor. The wealthier Rajput families can provide more favors for their retainers, fodder for their buffaloes, wood for their fires, and generous amounts of food on ritual occasions "and by the same token, of course, are in a position to threaten them with deprivation." Hence a wealthier family, provided that its men are militant, gets better service than does a poorer family and the benefits spread to its allies. It reaps economic benefits especially at harvest time when there is a shortage of labor. The powerful families usually can get the field workers they need when other cultivators cannot and moreover they can get them at the time when they most need them (Hitchcock 1959, p. 28).

Manpower is another fundamental resource of alliance power. It permits the rallying of hands for peak labor demands and putting on a brave display at festive occasions. Even more, it provides the capacity to mobilize fighters if blows are to be exchanged. The use of force is a constant possibility, even if a latent one, in the opposition among alliances. Men who seek to maintain and improve their position in the village must stand ready to defend or attack with force. Members of an alliance usually see their own use of force as defensive, even when some of their people set fire to a hayrick under cover of night, stealthily spoil an opponent's crop, or divert his cattle. In many villages, blows, beatings, and ambushes figure in the history of opposed alliances and in many, also, an occasional factional murder can be recalled. Even when the men of a dominant jati-group do not engage in violent acts themselves, they may not discourage their retainers or clients of other jatis from carrying out violence on their behalf.

Nonviolence has been an influential religious doctrine in certain places and contexts, especially as applied in Gandhian passive resistance. But in the context of most village struggles, violence is a stark fact of life that is partly controlled, partly exploited, partly manipulated, but always a potential factor with which a responsible man must reckon.

The third element of alliance strength is the ability to bring sources of influence from outside the village to bear in its behalf. Thus if the alliance leaders are eminent devotees of a religious sect, as is true of the Patidar magnates just mentioned, their fellow devotees will usually give them at least moral support in any dispute with others (Pocock 1957a, p. 302).

By far the most important source of power beyond the village is government. The holder of a village office, such as headman or revenue collector, gives advantage to his alliance. The villagers' presumption is that the higher officials with whom he deals will favor his cause and that of his alliance, or at least will give him the right of first hearing and the benefit of any doubt—provided that he has fortitude and skill to wield the tool of office. The ability to sway the police in one's favor is a prime asset in a dispute and is an immediate necessity in any serious outbreak of violence (cf. Epstein 1962, p. 289). In a protracted contest, the capacity to use the courts as a weapon and as a battleground of one's own choosing is an almost indispensable asset. Adversaries can be balked, their thrusts parried, their material resources exhausted through adept use of litigation. Many an alliance has prospered in its village because its leaders were skilled in the use of police and courts, and by the same token, many have fallen victim to these skills of their opponents.

An educated villager has considerable advantage in dealing with officials. He can fill out the myriad forms for himself; he can find out whom to see about what; he can speak to officials in terms they like to use; he can make his own way through bureaucratic procedure; and he feels less like an awkward bumpkin when facing officialdom. With government grants and aids becoming increasingly significant, those who aspire to respectable status usually find that they must have at least one educated member in their family or alliance in order to hold their own.

Education drains men from the village and the alliance. An educated son, if he has a secondary-school education—and all the more if he has a college degree—tends to make his career outside the village. But he is not entirely lost to his family and its alliance; whatever success he has redounds to their prestige, and he himself may remit cash and influence. A village family of wealth and power generally likes to have at least one son educated enough to deal with the officials and their papers. It is better if he lives in the household, but if he is employed in a place not too distant, he can still provide liaison services when they are urgently required.

An alliance is more apparent to an observer when its members strike out as a faction than when they interact as a cooperative group. When two powerful sides in a village are locked in struggle, each trying to defeat, forestall, and derogate the other, each trying to recruit as much help as possible in order to get its way, then villagers can scarcely avoid the subject of the contest, much as they may want to present a smooth face to a visitor. Even when the rivalries are less blatant, talk of them tends to come repeatedly to the attention of the observer after he has been in the village long enough to hear more than the *politesse* offered to a casual visitor from the city or from a foreign country. Cooperation among alliance associates goes on less obtrusively in such activities as the exchange of labor, the giving and taking of loans, and the choice of marriage partners.

Alliance Cohesion

The extent of collaboration within an alliance is illustrated in H. S. Dhillon's study of Haripura village, near Mandya in Mysore. This is a village of Vokkaligas (Okkaligas), the landowning cultivators who are dominant in many villages of this part of Mysore. Of one hundred thirty-five families in Haripura at the time of the study, one hundred twenty-six were Vokkaligas, sorted out into six alliances, which the author calls factions.

A main topic of Dhillon's inquiry was factional dispute, but he stresses the fact that hostility to other groups is seldom the only or even the major force that holds together the families. "The factors which bind members of a faction and enable it to function as a cohesive unit are the intensive kinship ties and the economic, social and ceremonial relations between faction members" (1955, p. 30). As elsewhere, members of a lineage generally belong to the same alliance and if some of them should line up with different alliances they seldom join sides that are bitterly antagonistic to each other. There are two strongly opposed sides in Haripura, each a coalition of two alliances. One of the six alliances is quite neutral, another is not fully engaged in the opposition between the main antagonists.

Dhillon looked closely at the amount of economic, social, and ceremonial interchange within an alliance as compared with that between alliances. He traced the major economic transactions (defined as sale or mortgage of land and major loans) within the village over a period of ten years. Of a total of 664 such transactions, 302 occurred within an alliance, only 30 were between members of two hostile alliances and in 22 of the latter the participants were linked by marriage ties. Most of the rest were between members of different but friendly alliances. In this total there were 22 mortgage transactions of which 12 were within an alliance; none were between members of opposed alliances. Of 55 land sales, 38 took place within an alliance and only one between members of two hostile alliances; in that one seemingly exceptional case, the men involved were married to full sisters. There were 205 intravillage loans in the list, of which 86 were negotiated within an alliance, only 10 between members of hostile alliances. The importance of affinal relations is reflected in the fact that of 222 loans between Haripura men and men of other villages, 80 percent were made with people of villages having numerous marital ties with Haripura. In sum, nearly half the major economic transactions were between members of the same alliance, and a great many in the other half were between members of friendly alliances (Dhillon 1955, pp. 59–65).

Ceremonial observances are also carried on mainly among alliance families although certain traditional obligations override factional cleavage. At a certain stage of a marriage celebration, for example, a Haripura family gives a feast for all in its division of the village. Those of a hostile faction who live in the same part of the village are invited and they do attend as tradition requires. However, they are not asked to help the hosts in the preparations, as with cooking. Such active participation is restricted to the host's alliance or those friendly to it.

Tradition further requires that on certain ritual occasions, in festivals for the village deity, all must participate together regardless of factional quarrels. This led to a stalemate in Haripura for several years. Animosities were so intense that the antagonists refused to let these rites be performed rather than join with their enemies in common worship. For several years the ceremonies were not held at all; then the hostilities were sufficiently mollified (though by no means erased) to allow the normal ceremonial cycle to be resumed (Dhillon 1955, pp. 67–75).

The most eloquent testimony of alliance cohesion lies in the arranging of marriages. Bride and groom may be of the same village, as is the South Indian custom, and 23 percent of the Haripura marriages studied (68 of 297 marriages) were intravillage matches. Among these 68 marriages, only 3 had been made between families that at the time had belonged to antagonistic factions and each of these three had resulted in a shift of alliance so that the families now linked through marriage were no longer separated by factional hostilities (Dhillon 1955, p. 74).

In other villages as well as in Haripura, cooperation among allied families has been noted in accounts that focus on factional dispute. Thus Lewis writes of the groups he calls factions among the dominant Jats of Rampur, near Delhi, "The small groups which we have delineated are held together primarily by cooperative economic, social, and ceremonial relations" (1958, p. 114). And in the hamlets of low-ranking cultivators in the Panchmahals highlands of Gujarat, Shah remarks that the faction (i.e., alliance) rather than the hamlet is the unit of all important social activities (1955b, p. 115).

A common feature of alliance affiliation is pressure for total commitment. Alliance leaders are usually not content only that a man have closer relations with the allied families than with others; they would prefer that he not have close relations with anyone outside the alliance. His social range in the village should be mainly within the alliance; his allegiance to and identification with others of the alliance should override any loyalties to those outside it.

Above all, they insist that he must support the allies completely and unswervingly in a quarrel.

When hostilities between two strong alliances of a dominant jati-group are very intense, the opposing sides tend to dichotomize the village on the principle that a friend of my enemy is my enemy. Still, hostilities have a way of flaring and diminishing in intensity over the years, so that not everyone need be aligned on every village issue and there are often some neutral alliances and families in a given factional quarrel. Even within a closely knit alliance, a person generally can have some friendly relations with others who are not of his family's allies so long as they do not belong to an enemy alliance.

A villager need not take sides in every issue. In Haripura, for example, two men who are married to sisters but belong to contending sides, need not take active part in a quarrel between their respective alliances. But they must not give support to the other side and even this passivity is not tolerated if the fight is a very serious one. Similarly, a man may support either side of a quarrel where his own allies are not involved unless the leaders of his alliance take a firm partisan stand and then he must back them with full support (Dhillon 1955, pp. 51, 80).

A whole alliance may keep relatively neutral. One of the less wealthy alliances in Haripura does not carry on any active opposition at all, perhaps because its men do not feel strong enough to leap into the status fray. They do have some influence, however, and they are preferred on occasion by other alliances just because they are not active contestants. In Wangala village certain of the wealthier and prestigious lineages are relatively aloof from rivalries within the jati-group, perhaps because they feel secure and as yet unchallenged in their position. They too are influential in local affairs because they are not committed in advance and so can back either one side or another (Dhillon 1955, pp. 53, 59; Epstein 1962, p. 132).

Even strongly antagonistic alliances within a jati-group stop short of being full enemies. Their members are usually outwardly civil to each other when they must come together at public ceremonies, they all stand as one against danger to the jati-group from forces outside it. But beyond that, members of hostile alliances generally try to avoid each other. Sometimes their meetings are used for factional advantage. Hitchcock describes some leaders in Khalapur who wage factional struggle as a kind of game. They continually engage each other in trials of strength, which involve various forms of chicanery but not violence. Even though one of them may just have come from the police station where he tried to have his opponent recorded as a dangerous and criminal character, the two men continue to meet one another, smoke the hookah, and talk. "Needless to say the verbal exchange is often full of indirect and humorous aggression" (Hitchcock n.d., MS. p. 40).

More often there is precious little humor in the situation and the opponents do not go beyond minimal public civility. They stay away from each other as much as possible. In the Delhi State village of Rampur they will not attend each other's ceremonies, will not visit each other's homes, and do not smoke the hookah together except when visiting the home of a neutral villager. They can be "counted upon to marshal vicious gossip about rivals" in council meetings. While direct attack is rare, indirect attack is highly developed (Lewis 1958, p. 116). In a Rajasthan village members of the rival alliances among the dominant Jats do not attend each other's weddings nor do they participate together in other domestic, clan, or village ceremonies (Bose and Malhotra 1964, pp. 319–320).

In Haripura, members of opposed alliances among Vokkaligas do not usually visit each other's houses and they normally avoid speaking to each other. As we have seen they do not intermarry even though they could do so as jati fellows. The factions in Haripura are described as not very tightly knit and interfactional relations are not so strong or so sharply defined as in Rampur, but they are sharp enough to keep opponents apart in all sorts of social relations they might otherwise have, from casual conversations to formal betrothals (Dhillon 1955, pp. 31–32).

In Wangala also, Epstein describes factions as not rigidly opposed and as coming into play only in certain situations. Wangala, like Haripura, is in Mandya district of Mysore State, and in both places Vokkaligas are dominant. At the time of Epstein's study, members of opposing groups mixed freely in everyday relations and, except for a few leading members who never spoke to each other, the others would sit together at night and chat. Yet the situations where members of hostile alliances avoided each other were not insignificant. They did not celebrate festivals and life-cycle rites together. At one wedding, children of a rival alliance swarmed around when a particular delicacy was being served "but their elders insisted that they stay away and impressed on them the deep enmity that existed between the factions." Moreover, there had been no intermarriage between members of the opposed sides for ten years (Epstein 1962, pp. 129–136).

Thus there is a tendency for hostile alliances within a jati-group to treat each other in certain respects almost as different jatis. Those on one side observe a measure of social avoidance toward the other, they restrict mutual participation in ceremonies, they do not arrange marriages with adherents of the other alliance. All this takes place within the same jati, in which the ritual criteria for group separation are not relevant. Because the contests between jatis have often been waged for symbolic prerogatives, such as the right to wear the sacred thread, the ritual symbols overshadowed and masked what was essentially a struggle for general power in the village. This mask does not apply to the oppositions within a jati-group; there the political power struggle, without ritual trappings, is plain to see.

CHAPTER 15

Opposition and Cohesion
within the Jati-Group

WHAT then is the opposition about? Why are there quarrels between alliances within the same jati-group? The manifest reasons are easily ascertained. There is a stock alliterative answer in Hindi which applies to conflict among men of different jatis as well as to our present concern with conflict among jati fellows. The causes of quarrels are said to be *Zamin, Zar, Zanani*—land, wealth, and women. Many fights do indeed spring from these sources of friction.

Land is the one main productive resource, scarce and costly. The possession of land gives independence and openings to power. Possession of land is schemed for, contrived, wangled, and disputed. Other kinds of wealth, like cattle or houses, are also sensitive matters, so that even a slight, perhaps an unintentional, infringement on a man's herd or house is likely to raise his hackles. Women are considered to be both submissive to and more highly sexed than men; the men, especially among the dominant jatis of the North, are supposed to be both personally venturesome and puritanically zealous of their women's honor. So Zanani really is a fertile source of trouble among men and alliances.

The old saying is borne out statistically in a tabulation of the causes of major quarrels over a period of forty-five years among the Vokkaligas of Haripura village. This count shows that land, women, and the inheritance of wealth were the leading causes. "Major" quarrels are defined by Dhillon as those fought between alliances and, we may infer, long and bitterly contested. Six of these major controversies were about land, five about illicit sex relations, five about inheritance. There were also four about procedure in festivals and three about adoptions. In "minor quarrels" land and inheritance were each involved in nine controversies; three were about illicit sex relations; three were over adoptions; and one was about festival observance (1955, p. 80).

The incidents that precipitate great contests in a village can be quite trivial in themselves—an argument about a scrap of land, a disagreement about minor details of a ceremony, a question of how a cow could have strayed into a standing crop. Such small and restricted disputes can blow up into great, bitter fights because, for one reason, the allies of the two immediate antagonists identify thoroughly with their respective partisan. So the one who wins brings victory to his whole alliance and the one who loses drags his whole coterie into defeat. Moreover, defeat even in a trivial matter can be taken to mean total submission, and the victory thus may be interpreted by the victors as a sweeping ascendency of their alliance. Such drastic, total interpretation conforms to the basic concept that most social action is hierarchically arranged. Ranked status is imputed to many contexts, and superior rank implies general, as well as specific, dominance over those of lower status.

Challenges and Realignments

Not every small village dispute escalates into a factional conflict. But when the people of two alliances are already poised as challengers and challenged, incidents that might otherwise sputter and fade become reasons for great quarrels. Such confrontations within a dominant jati-group recur because villagers usually accept subordination to men close in status only provisionally—even token subordination to others of the same jati. So families of lower status in a jati-group characteristically try for a higher as soon as their strength permits; those of higher rank oppose such attempts so long as their strength avails. Within a jati-group as among jatis, a family's gain in secular resources is often deployed for status rise. As Pocock comments in contrasting Patidars in Gujarat with those who settled in East Africa, "In Gujarat certainly wealth and power are important but there it is wealth and power for the purpose of standing in a particular system where, in a sense, it is status that makes life worth living" (1957a, p. 303).

As a family or a set of families gather resources, they first make symbolic assertions about themselves that do not directly threaten any specific group and so can scarcely become the subjects of argument. Such a crescive family among the Rajputs of Khalapur builds better houses, acquires showy bullocks (not necessarily efficient ones for farming), and gets fine clothes and jewelry. Such families now keep their sons in school. Because they are lavish in hospitality, more and more men come to spend time with them in their men's house. And they arrange good marriages and stage rich weddings for their children. Having prepared their base of power and prestige they can then challenge another alliance in local arguments, in court trials, or in elections. "In such quarrels the end sought is not so much material benefit—a few square feet of property, for instance—as the immaterial gains deriving from a demonstration of power which is relatively greater than one's rival" (Minturn and Hitchcock 1963, p. 256).

The more direct challenges are often about ritual prerogatives and village offices. These are usually in the possession of the lineage or alliance that was formerly supreme in the village. When others of the jati-group gain strength, they resent the disproportion between their economic and their ritual status. There are, for example, two prospering lineages of the dominant jati in Wangala whose men are relatively recent arrivals in the village and so do not hold any office in the traditional rites. "We find here an imbalance between economic, political and ritual status in the village and since ritual status is regarded as the ultimate criterion of social status, the 'progressive' faction is led continuously to bring its ritual status into line with its economic dominance." Whenever council meetings are held to discuss plans for a forthcoming ceremony, the leaders of the "progressives" try to get some formal place for their own lineages. The entrenched lineages resist this, all the more sharply because their own secular power has declined (Epstein 1962, p. 132).

In like manner, an imbalance of power and status among families within an alliance tends to disrupt previous relations. We have noted that an alliance characteristically includes core families and dependent families. But in time families may change in power. A talented, ambitious, driving man may come up in a dependent family and lineage. If he is additionally favored by the lottery of biology so that he inherits considerable land as sole son or survivor and yet has enough kinsmen to afford a firm base of support, he may gain quite rapidly in power.

Leaders of the core families do not joyously welcome a previous dependent as an alliance leader. Thus in Haripura village "the leading families within a faction do not tolerate any rise in the economic status of families which lie at its lower rungs and which depend on them for many of their needs" (Dhillon 1955, p. 32). These leaders treat a rising dependent in much the same way as lineage fellows or separated brothers treat each other. They are bound to help him when he is in clear and present danger and when his defeat would impair their interests, but when his difficulties do not threaten them they can be quite aloof.

The leaders who are expected to maintain unity in the alliance are not, however, "supposed to sacrifice their vested interests for other members of the faction." Thus when a man is involved in serious litigation, his alliance characteristically gives him moral encouragement, physical security, help in raising loans, and aid in marshaling court evidence. But if he loses the case and is financially ruined, they usually make no special effort to help him regain his previous economic position, as by giving him loans without charging interest (Dhillon 1955, pp. 32–33). The top families are generally interested in keeping up the power and ritual level of the whole alliance but otherwise they are more concerned with keeping their position in the alliance as it exists, knowing that a dependent family may well try to challenge their leadership if it can.

The cleavage of an alliance, as of a joint family, tends to be hastened if there is considerable increase in its numbers. Among the Mala and Madiga, the main Harijan jatis of Andhra, it has been noted that a hamlet of about fifty houses will split into two sets of allied families because, for one reason, a man celebrating a marriage cannot feed all in so large a hamlet (Reddy 1952, p. 258). Though our previous examples have mainly been of dominant, landowning jati-groups, Harijans also sort themselves into separate alliances of families within their segregated hamlets. There may be a certain critical range of size for an alliance.[1] Less than a certain number of families will be too few for the requisite self-sufficiency and more than a certain number will make it difficult to keep the alliance intact.

[1] In a survey of six U.P. villages, 175 "factions" were counted among 3,125 households. The average number of households in a faction was thus 17.8; the largest faction had 43 or 44 households (Baljit Singh 1961, p. 9).

To answer the question at the beginning of this chapter, recurrent conflicts within a jati-group, especially a large and dominant one, stem from the common quest for wealth and power. Like so many village people in the world, villagers in India are apt to see the supply of good things as limited and not susceptible of growth or expansion (cf. Foster 1965, 1966). Hence if one man gets more, another must get less. To be more, to get more, to possess more, one must contend always with others, even with one's jati fellows and neighbors. Underlying these contests is the pervasive drive for status that sharpens and accelerates competition not only in the economic arena but also in many other contexts. Status competition may be waged within a jati-group at the bottom of the social hierarchy as well as at the top, as witness the example of the Malas and Madigas of Andhra, but the alliance relations within dominant jati-groups are often politically central in their villages.

Alliances are formed because a man and his family need close interchange with others beyond the lineage. A family must have allies if it is to succeed at all in status competition; a strong family needs dependents, a weaker one needs a protector. Lineage bonds alone are usually insufficient for these purposes. The number of a man's agnatic allies is generally too small for his needs, even though there is some flexibility in amassing such allies. Moreover, lineage relationships cannot be assumed or abandoned as readily as political manipulation may require. Yet an alliance can be quite a stable group, lasting over years, sometimes decades; usually some of its members are bound together by lineage ties and others by mutual interest, mutual support, and continued interchange. But the very force of status competition and of protector-dependent relation that helps cement an alliance also works in time to disrupt it. As talents and resources are reshuffled, alliances split. New contestants and allies take the place of the former ones; new alignments and new arguments arise.

Alliance Development and Variations in Alliance Formation

The process of alliance combination and recombination, which on the village ground seems to be the result of merely local forces and personal motives, is actually shaped by large demographic, economic, and political movements. Thus the steady increase in population since the 1920s may well have unsettled previous alignments in many villages, making some of the former alliances too large to be viable. The introduction of irrigation, cash crops and other new sources of income has permitted ambitious and able men to become much more prosperous than their fathers were, and this also makes for rearrangement of allies. Land reform legislation and the electoral franchise have contributed to the reallocation of resources and so of alliance loyalties.

Some broad regularities in the history of alliances can be seen in three widely separated villages for which we have historical information. One is Radhanagar, a village in northern Bihar where a Brahmin jati is dominant; Brahmin families own 90 percent of the land though they are only 28 percent of the population. Another is Rampur in Delhi State where Jats are 60 percent of the population and own practically all the land. The third is Haripura, south of Bangalore, where the Vokkaligas are some 95 percent of the inhabitants and own all the land. The Jats of Rampur have much the same rank as do the Vokkaligas of Haripura, both are Sudras in the varna scheme and both brook no infringement on their sovereign status within their villages.

The historical record in all three villages begins with a dual division within the dominant jati-group in the late nineteenth century. Factional conflict existed, changes in alignment of families all occurred within a two-party frame. Then came a period of intensified conflict; there was a good deal of shifting about, and in recent years new alliances have emerged in addition to the original two.

In Radhanagar the old moiety arrangement, with two Brahmin alliances in contention, lasted until 1937. Then the Brahmin opponents were forced to unite against a challenge, inspired by the Kisan political movement, from the other jatis and from a few dissident Brahmins. The traditional overlords finally won this contest through a court case in 1942 but the dual alignment was disrupted. There followed a period of unstable alignments. By 1959 there seemed to be some stabilizing of factional alignments with a return to two or three alliances (Roy 1963).

In Rampur and Haripura the dual division was altered at about the same time; 1915 is the date given for the change in Rampur, 1919 in Haripura. In both places there followed several years of intense conflict and jockeying, after which each jati-group settled down to a number of new alliances. The realignment took place about 1939 in Rampur, about 1942 in Haripura (Lewis 1958, pp. 142–147; Dhillon 1955, pp. 82–94). The development suggested by these three case histories—from dual division through a period of intensified conflict and shifting alliances to fairly stabilized multiple alliances—may have wider application and should be tested when more evidence is available (cf. Cohn 1965, pp. 97–98).

The present evidence does indicate certain main variations in the nature of alliances within the jati-group. One variation is between North and South India, another between villagers who have been more affected by newer, urban influences and those less affected by them. The differences in alliance functions between Rampur in North India and Haripura in South India are noted by H. S. Dhillon, who was in a particularly good position to make the comparison because he had participated in the study of Rampur and then went south to conduct the study of factions in Haripura.

Dhillon observed that the factions in Rampur are more cohesive units than in Haripura and the hostilities between them are stronger and more sharply defined. The reasons are rooted in the differences between Northern and Southern social structure and particularly in affinal relations. In the South a woman maintains closer relations with her natal family after her marriage than she is able to do in the North and, since the men of her natal family are not total inferiors to her husband's family as they are in the North, they are more likely to take some part in her husband's affairs. A man's feminal kindred in Haripura do intercede in his relations with his brothers and with his lineage mates whereas in Rampur "such cognate relations are expected to have absolutely nothing to do with the affairs of a family" (Dhillon 1955, p. 77).

In Haripura hostilities are considerably reduced in duration and in vehemence, because adversaries usually have feminal relatives in common and these—true to the welfare functions of feminal kinsmen—often succeed in pacifying the angry ones. Moreover, Haripura women can take the initiative in restoring friendship within an alliance, while in Rampur women cannot take so active a part. Another difference is that in the southern village more disputes occur over festivals, perhaps indicating a greater weighting of religious and ritual matters.

The diminished bite of hostilities in Haripura decreases the num-

ber of coalitions and enmities across villages, as compared with the
situation in Rampur (Dhillon 1955, pp. 32, 77–82). But even though
alliance opposition in Haripura is less protracted and pervasive, alliance loyalties are still quite durable. Dhillon writes that although
most quarrels within a faction are settled in the course of time, "as
many as 12 cases of shifts from one faction to another as a result of
these quarrels were noticed during the period of the last 60 years"
(1955, p. 78). Twelve in sixty years is not very many.

Sometimes villagers are caught between loyalty to their agnates
and concern for their feminal kin. Dhillon learned of five such dilemmas in Haripura, in four of which the families involved remained
relatively neutral; in council meetings they showed preference for
their lineage allies but in private they helped their feminal kin with
loans and tried discreetly to recruit support for them in other villages. This was a reasonable compromise in view of the cultural
norms: agnates form more of a corporate, public body; feminal kin
are more concerned with private, personal matters. In the fifth case,
the man openly helped his sister's husband as against his own agnates
and he was forced out of his alliance. He did not go over to its chief
opponents but joined another alliance whose members were nevertheless favorable to the side of his sister's husband (Dhillon 1955,
p. 79). Although alliance cohesion is less strong and alliance hostilities are less bitter in the southern village than in the northern one,
among the Vokkaligas of Haripura a man's alliance still holds his
strong allegiance and gives him strong support.

A second variation in alliance formation occurs in South India.
Brahmins there are less inclined to form stable, cohesive alliances
than are villagers of other South Indian jatis. In North India, Brahmins do maintain staunch alliances, as we have seen from the example of Radhanagar in Bihar. But in the South, Brahmins tend to be
more atomistic, and opposition among them is more often between
strong individuals than between alliances.

This is exemplified among the Havik Brahmins, overlords in
Totagadde village of northwestern Mysore. Harper observes that
a Havik is likely to have very close relations with one or two other
men of his jati-group and hostile relations with perhaps one or two.
Such enmities are common and they are commonly long continued,
but they are more like feuds between two individuals than factional

struggles between two sides. In feud as in faction, the tactics can be rough. Though physical violence is not used by the opponents themselves, each may formally accuse the other of breaking the law and may try sorcery against him. These feuds arise between men of comparable status, in the usual focus of rivalry between two men (or two alliances or two jatis) who are close in rank within the local hierarchy. One of these feuds between two prominent men verges on factional alignment.

Each leader has some men who support him, but most Haviks are not aligned with either group and not all the close friends of each leader give him factional support. For the most part, quarrels among Haviks are between individuals; a man's kinsmen and friends do not feel bound to support him against his opponent (Harper and Harper 1959, pp. 460–463).

This social atomism arises from each man's strong sense of his independence and equality. Men have authority over other men of this jati only as their seniors in a joint family that owns property. In all other situations, Haviks fiercely cherish their equality with all other Havik men. "A junior male in one property-owning group is the equal of the senior male in any other." Alliances cannot solidify when no man is willing to be a follower or dependent (Harper 1963, p. 165).

The same individualism characterizes the dominant Brahmins of Kumbapettai village in Tanjore district. There also, quarrels are more often between individuals and families than between alliances. The men of a lineage may unite against another lineage, perhaps to secure some prerogative, "but in a short time, affinal and matrilateral ties between their members serve to mitigate the group-conflict" (Gough 1960, p. 37). As Gough analyzes the values of these Brahmins and the child-rearing practices that inculcate the values, it appears that their most prized personal relationship is a dyadic one, held with someone much senior in age and much superior in status. They do not attach great importance to solidarity among peers, as we have noted before, even though fraternal concord is extolled as a formal ideal. They do not maintain powerful leaders because so few Brahmins are willing to be in any way subordinate to another Brahmin. Therefore they do not display the kind of alliance cohesion that non-Brahmins do.

A third variation in the nature of alliances comes about because some villagers have adopted new status symbols and procedures that are not part of the traditional game of status rivalry. This is exemplified in Epstein's contrast between Wangala, where the traditional oppositions are carried on in traditional ways, and Dalena where they are not. Both these Mysore villages are chiefly populated and dominated by Vokkaligas.

Wangala, as has been noted before, has prospered through the advent of irrigation and sugarcane cultivation. Its prosperity was fostered by the managers of the local sugarcane factory, who laid down the rules and provided the main requirements for cane production; all that the Wangala farmers had to do was follow instructions, work hard, and reap a rich harvest. They did not have to venture abroad, choose among economic alternatives, or make contacts in town and government. Hence their way of life has developed into a prosperity-intensified version of what it was before.

The two principal alliances compete vigorously for symbols of ritual status, the "progressives" trying to redress the balance between their new power and lack of ritual office, the "conservatives" trying to prevent them from doing so by keeping the ritual offices in their own possession. In their heated opposition, both sides implicitly agree on what things are worth fighting for. The challenging alliance does not want to change the traditional ritual pattern but only to secure a better status position in it for its own people (Epstein 1962, pp. 129–137).

The irrigation canals stopped short of Dalena but a number of its men have prospered because of their own vigorous efforts. They have secured land and jobs outside the village and have established contacts in the nearest town. Here, also, the chief opposition is between "progressives" and "conservatives," and the conflict affects all village issues and every dispute. The leaders of the "progressives" are three enterprising men who have close knowledge of town manners and government officials. These innovators are more concerned with status symbols in the political and social spheres beyond the village, where their economic interests are now vested, than in the traditional signs of prestige within the village. They are not much interested in carrying on village rituals and so many of the traditional ceremonies are no longer performed at all in Dalena.

In Wangala, the clashing sides agree so thoroughly on the importance of village ceremonies that a duplicate set is performed because of factional disagreement. In Dalena even the "conservatives" do not fully carry on the traditional ceremonial cycle. In Wangala, all the villagers close ranks to face a common danger, as from drought or disease, but in Dalena there are now fewer threats that the villagers see as a common danger to be met by common defense. It is not at all that any leader in Dalena has lost interest in the status quest; it is only that some have shifted their sights from the traditional symbols of status to the new array in the wider social field of district and state (Epstein 1962, pp. 284–290). Although Dalena social life has been affected by this shift, it has not been disrupted by it. In some places, however, this shift has been quite disruptive because while the new standards of status have not yet been fully assimilated, their impact has undermined the worth of the traditional patterns.

Such an inchoate state of village affairs prevailed in Namhalli, a village near Bangalore, when Alan Beals observed it in 1952–1953 (Siegel and Beals 1960a, 1960b). Namhalli is not dominated by one jati-group, but there was discord within each of the main jati-groups of the village. Pervasive factionalism, as Beals calls it, prevailed. Few cooperative activities of any kind for the benefit of the village as a whole were carried on. All agreed that certain things badly needed doing; the village roads should be improved, irrigation facilities maintained, ceremonials and dramas conducted, government subsidies obtained. But all efforts to accomplish such projects failed.

The villagers would not and could not cooperate because they so mistrusted each other, and they nourished past enmities so zealously that even an attempt to settle a dispute was usually used as a way to resume waging an earlier dispute. The traditional ties of allegiance did not bind people together as they formerly had—it was not unusual to find brother ranged against brother in a public argument— and the traditional ways of healing social differences foundered. Villagers changed sides frequently. The victory of one faction over another generally accomplished nothing more than the temporary humiliation of those who were defeated. "Victory was usually followed by betrayal and renewal of hostilities along new alignments"

(Siegel and Beals 1960a, p. 397; Beals 1959, p. 433). A main reason for this disorganization, according to the authors, was an excessive degree of internal strain, uncertainty and conflict, about appropriate forms of behavior in situations that required cooperation or mediation.

When Beals returned in 1960 to have another look at Namhalli, he found a different state of village affairs (1962, pp. 92–97). In these few years, the strain had been mitigated, and the pervasive factionalism was quite abated. Villagers cooperated effectively for the common good. This happier condition came about mainly because a number of the villagers had secured jobs in the city, many of them in one of the largest of the new factories. They not only learned new skills, they also learned about new ways of organizing the village. The new financial technique of the "chit-fund" proved an effective way of launching both personal and community enterprises. It provides a farmer with capital for improved seed and fertilizer, and it is also used as a way of raising money for such enterprises as a bus trip for school children or the rebuilding of a village temple.

The people of Namhalli have come to have much easier relations with government officials than they did before. Membership in a labor union has given some of the villagers a sense of access to political power. Formerly they were wary of police and eager to keep them away from the village and out of village conflicts. It was not until 1959 that a complaint was lodged with the police by a Namhalli villager about the acts of neighbors. When a policeman visits now, the leaders chat with him as with an old friend. "If he threatened anyone or tried to collect bribes, he would be reported, and officials of the factory and the labor union would complain to the higher ranking police officials" (Beals 1962, p. 95).

The traditional way of life in Namhalli has by no means been abandoned but has been "reworked, reformulated, and enriched." Jati and jati-group are still important in matters of family, home, and religion, but are of less account now in livelihood. All social relations in the village are much more stable than they were in the period of pervasive factionalism. The Namhalli example illustrates a development from general disruption toward integration and also shows that urban influences can make for either condition, depending on how and to what purpose the urban forces are channeled.

Forces for Jati-Group Cohesion

Despite the common cleavages within jati-groups and the major variations among them, the members of a jati-group do maintain a unity and present themselves as a unit for certain important purposes. Their common ritual status provides a main cohesive force. All in the jati-group share a common dependence on other jatis for certain services. In that sense they must deal together with the people of the other jatis in the village and its vicinity. Their village neighbors, in turn, deal with all in a jati (and often of several jatis) as though they are all equal members of a ritually defined unit.

The rites performed by the members of a jati-group also foster their solidarity. Certain rites are explicitly intended to transcend secular antagonisms. Funeral rites are commonly so interpreted; antagonists will often participate together in the mourning rites of a lineage-mate or a jati-fellow. Certain jati festivals are quite manifestly rites of consolidation and affirmation in which enmities are formally laid aside.

Both funerals and festivals express a kind of defensive unity—of society against man's biological fallibility in funerals, of society vis-à-vis the supernatural powers in festivals. Such observances reaffirm the solidarity of the jati as a coherent and supportive entity. At a funeral, for example, the lineage fellows and the closer feminal kin of the dead person attend to carry out the general functions of mortuary rites (cf. Mandelbaum 1954b, 1959b). Commonly also at least one representative of every lineage or family of the jati-group must attend the funeral of a member to symbolize the sharing of the whole jati in the family's grief and the support of all in re-establishing normal social relations. Such consolidating mechanisms do not always work, of course, but many villagers still have the feeling that they should (cf. Dhillon 1955, pp. 69, 71, 87).

Conflict within the jati-group is not something paraded before an outsider. Others of the jati are not keen to marry their daughters into a jati-group that is a hot battlefield, just as they do not like to send daughters into a squabbling family. Further, a smoothly co-operative jati-group is a matter of pride and prestige while a plainly discordant one is not. So although it may not take long for a visitor to discover that there are real rifts in the ideal of jati solidarity, it is not something he can usually find out through the first question. Ralph Nicholas has written that it can be taken as a general principle for the parts of Bengal where he has worked that the statement "there are no factions (*dal*) in our village" means exactly the obverse. Furthermore, it is likely that those who make this statement are themselves intimately involved in the factions (Nicholas 1962, pp. 172–173).

Yet the unity of the jati-group is not merely a cosmetic cliché; it can be a vital reality under certain circumstances. Characteristically, when the people of a higher jati feel their status threatened by a lower or when those of a lower feel that their just rights are being axed by a higher, then internal conflict is summarily dropped and all stand as one against the menace. This immediate, united defense takes place in other social echelons, notably in the whole village when all in it feel threatened together, and also in a whole jati; but the tightening of defense is more common in a jati-group, since most challenges to status are laid down on the local ground. Thus when the lower jatis of Radhanagar in Bihar challenged the political dominance of the local Brahmins, the two Brahmin sides at once gave up their long and bitter enmity, joined together to fight a protracted court case and won (Roy 1963). In Senapur in eastern U.P., the ruling Thakurs several times dropped their factional opposition in order to suppress the leatherworkers' attempt to improve their social position (Cohn 1955, pp. 68–72).

In a Kota village of the Nilgiri Hills of South India, I found active hatred between the Kota reformers and conservatives. But when a leading light of the reform party was beaten up by men of a stronger jati because of his reformist ways, all his fellow villagers, the die-hard conservatives among them, rose up together to claim, and get, reparations from the jati of the assailants (Mandelbaum 1960).

An episode in Wangala illustrates the unified response of a dominant jati-group against an assertive gesture by a lower group. In dramas staged by the Harijans of the village, the actor in the role of king traditionally does not sit on a prop throne but squats, in order that his head may not be higher than those of the people of higher jati in the audience. When their drama company let it be known that in a forthcoming production a stage throne would be used, there was a strong reaction. All the Vokkaligas stopped employing

Harijan laborers. Eventually the Harijan headman sued for peace and his people had to pay a fine. The assertion and its purpose were defeated, at least for the time (Epstein 1962, pp. 183–189).

Not every altercation between jatis galvanizes jati-group unity. In Rampur, for example, the several Jat factions united when the Chamars first refused to pay the traditional house tax. But some years later when Chamars disputed the ownership of a plot of land with one of the Jat leaders, two of the Jat alliances openly supported the Chamars in the court case (Lewis 1958, pp. 74, 141). What rallies a jati-group at one period and under certain circumstances may not do so at others. But at any juncture there will usually be some kind of act that can impel members of a jati-group to drop internal quarrels, if only temporarily, and react together in joint defense.

Conflict within a jati-group is thus limited, but it is not formally channeled. Conflict is as inherent as is cooperation in a large, dominant jati-group, but while the cooperative functions of lineage and alliance groups are clearly and formally expressed in ritual, the competitive functions are not formally recognized or plainly avowed. This is one reason factional infighting so frequently seems to an outsider to be an anarchic hurly-burly. There are few, if any, occasions when latent conflicts between groups can legitimately be crystallized and expressed, as in competition in ritual games or in regular political engagements. The government law courts do serve on occasion as a means of resolving conflict but in general they have been used by villagers more to wage conflicts than to settle them.

An Indian anthropologist once remarked to F. G. Bailey that villagers are not in a face-to-face community; the more typical posture is back-to-back (Bailey 1965, p. 6). Each side in a major village dispute may attract some supporters who join in not because of kinship or alliance loyalty, but to get even for a loss in a previous and often quite unrelated tussle (cf. Atal 1963). Coalitions of alliances are quickly made and may be just as quickly unmade. A few men may hover around the edge of any major quarrel seeking whatever may be to their own gain. Free-lance advisers, usually claiming connections to higher powers, are ready to give help for the justice of the cause and for some kind of fee.

The contestants operate according to a game theory directed toward the same goal as that involved in making marriage alliances;

that is, higher status in the local hierarchy. But while in the making of marriages all are supposed to gain, in the exercise of internal jati-group conflict someone must lose if anyone is to win. In this winning and losing many are passionately involved. Even those men who stand apart from the contests usually follow them with enormous interest. For the principals, it is a most earnest game, sometimes acted out in dead earnest.

Though these struggles are seen by villagers as disruptive of the harmony that should prevail among jati brethren, they are not entirely disruptive for the jati-group. In the contests, a man of ability can gain coveted laurels; through them he can reaffirm the values of the jati. By means of such contests, the "moving oligarchy" of a dominant jati-group is maintained, with the jati remaining paramount in the village but with successive actors and alliances coming into control (cf. Hitchcock n.d., MS., pp. 51–55; Cohn 1965, p. 97).

In sum, the jati-group is a fundamental unit of village society, a category of attribution, a field for cooperation, and sometimes a unit of group action. Within a small jati-group, numbering only a few families, relations among the families are not much different from those within a lineage. But when a jati-group is larger, with perhaps a score or more families, alliance formation often begins to appear. And when a jati-group is both large and dominant in the village, then the relations among its alliances take on some of the feaures of relations among jatis, except that ritual criteria are not entailed. Thus there can be great status rivalry among alliances, avoidance of one by the other, totality of commitment to one's own group, and even the casting out of a transgressor. And this is done under the cover of an ideology that disparages competition within a jati much as the popular varna theory of caste discounts competition among jatis. Though the alliances of a dominant jati-group may be embattled against each other, together they control the village in the sense that they respond together to a challenge from villagers of other jatis.

Alliance rivalries, wide disparities of wealth and prestige, can occur within jati-groups at every level of village society. At every level also the families of a jati-group feel bound together by their common rites and traditions, their common ritual standards, their mutual economic interests and treatment by others. They acknowledge their cohesion and have agents and agencies for maintaining it.

CHAPTER **16** Maintaining the Jati:
Leaders and Panchayats

A JATI does not just hang together like the parts of a cat, it must be actively maintained. To do so, men assume certain roles and support certain agencies. Central to jati maintenance are the leadership roles and panchayat patterns that are used at every level from family and lineage to regional council. These roles and patterns are highly formalized in some jatis, as in those whose headmen are ceremoniously invested with the office and are given distinctive insignia and regular duties (cf. Blunt 1931, pp. 107–109). In other jatis there may be no formal headmen at all and such jati organization that exists may be quite informal. Organization need not be ineffective because it is informal; both formal and informal organizations have their respective advantages for social maintenance, as will be noted again below, and one task for future research on the subject is to sort out the conditions favorable for each in the Indian context.

The modern trend is for the traditional jati organization to become less formal and for the newer caste associations to become more formalized, with set parliamentary procedures and prescribed office bearers. Yet in many villages the traditional jati leaders and councils are still powerful means of jati maintenance. One anthropologist, S. C. Dube, was impressed with the power and skill of a jati-group headman in the Andhra village of Shamirpet whose handling of a recalcitrant young man Dube witnessed.

"You bastard," this headman stormed at one point, "You seem to have developed great notions about yourself." He went on to rake the offender in terms and for reasons noted later, ending with "If you have the cheek to answer me back I shall make life impossible for you in the village. You have a long tongue, but if you wag it against us we shall pull it" (Dube 1955b, p. 204).

Leaders: Tasks and Motives

Both rough and smooth methods are needed for effective leadership at all jati levels. In a family, the senior man is expected to see to it that family quarrels do not get out of hand, that family members behave properly, that the family gives the appearance of a reasonably harmonious household. Among the senior men in a lineage, there is commonly at least one who tries to keep the whole lineage on an even keel, who attempts to calm stormy encounters and is alert to signs of impending trouble. Such lineage leaders warn a wayward youth or admonish a negligent father or cajole an embittered woman or ridicule an idle kinsman. They encourage lineage fellows to help gather in a sick kinsman's crop; they collect for lineage festivals; they take the complaint of an aggrieved kinsman before a council. The more influential of the lineage chiefs do the same for their alliance or for the jati-group as a whole.

At each level the leaders or elders assume the maintenance functions of trying to avert difficulties within their group and of containing and settling disputes when they break out. They also see to it that the normal activities of the group are properly performed. If a lineage has to help stage a wedding or a funeral, the lineage leader commonly is in charge of the arrangements or finds someone who will take charge. If the jati-group is responsible for a special part in a village festival, its leader oversees the performance of that part. He is asked to help supervise certain critical acts in a ceremony; when a large sum of money is handed over in a marriage, for example, it is given first to respected elders who count it aloud, "thus making the transaction public and stamping it with the seal of their authority" (Minturn and Hitchcock 1963, p. 252).

Another function is that of protecting and defending the group's interests against outside encroachments. A lineage elder is expected to be mindful of his lineage's prerogatives and to ward off any usurpation from other lineages. An alliance leader guards his supporters from the sniping of opponents. The headman of a jati-group similarly protects the rights of all the group and comes to the defense of anyone in it who may be threatened or abused.

Yet another function expected of a leader or elder is to act as a link between his group and larger social echelons. Thus the more influential men speak for their lineage in a jati-group council. The eminent men of the jati-group represent it in the councils of village and jati. They also represent their groups before the highest echelon of all, the supernatural. The head of a family performs homage to the ancestors on behalf of all the family; an elder of the lineage leads in the rites for the lineage deities and clan rites in those jatis that have them. When a feast is given in expiation for ritual trespass, the leaders partake first, initiating the restoration of the offender.

These functions are intended to maintain and preserve the several groups, not to alter them. Leaders are not expected to be innovators, except when a change in practice will help raise jati status—and then the innovation is generally represented as a return to the jati's ancient custom. A leader is not usually able to commit his group to a new activity or decision. His capacity as representative is more to protect the group's interests and to communicate group sentiments than to launch a course of group action. The headman of a jati-group must first canvass the lineage and family heads for their approval before he can effectively consign them to an action. A leader tends to have more leeway when he acts in clear defense of his group or when he judges a weak dependent for a gross transgression. There are occasional leaders whose personal power is great enough that they can take decisive action for their group and make the decisions stick. But generally a leader's independent powers are not broad.

Why then do men take on these roles that carry heavy responsibilities and bear limited authority? Some inherit an office of leadership, many aspire to positions of prestige, others find themselves laden with responsibilities for the group in the course of striving for quite personal advantage. It sometimes happens, for example, that a younger brother is so markedly more energetic, able, and enterprising than his elder brother that he gradually takes over the management of the family's affairs despite the formal authority of the elder.

Three such families are mentioned in one account of a village of Delhi State. In each the elder brother was quite content to let his clever younger brother take charge as family head and as lineage leader, and the younger made the relationship easier by giving symbolic deference to the elder while he controlled the family affairs (Gangarade 1963, pp. 5–6). Initially such a man takes charge so that the family's fields will be better kept, the yield more abundant, and selling more profitable. Then he may look to enlarging the landholdings and securing good marriages. If he is notably successful, he becomes known as the effective head of the family. When lineage or alliance affairs are to be discussed he is asked by the other family heads to attend along with his elder brother, and when he gives his opinion on a matter involving the welfare of the lineage the others listen respectfully to what he has to say. As the family prospers under his direction, his lineage mates increasingly seek his help in lineage affairs. So the younger brother, who began by attending more carefully to the bullocks and the weeding and the hired labor than did his other brothers, finds himself involved, say, with collecting money for the temple of the lineage deity or asked to help soothe a set-to within another family of the lineage.

Any family head who prospers and acquires dependents in the course of building up his own fortunes is likely to be pressed into taking concern for a larger group whether he likes to do so or not. He generally likes to do so; he likes the esteem and power given to a responsible and effective person. Prestige and power grow with public acknowledgment of them. As he climbs in personal status and wealth, he is consulted on affairs of wider and wider social consequence. Elders and peers bring him in because they need the weight of his influence to firm up any decision that may be taken, because without his active participation and that of other powerful men, no decision is worth much. But a man's rise to leadership in the village community is normally limited to his own social level.

A woman can take virtually no overt leadership, though some women exert considerable influence through their men. A Harijan leader may be preeminent in his jati, but he can have only indirect influence, if any at all, in the affairs of the village. At any level, an able man presents a larger and more tempting target to detractors as he rises. He must assuage or cope with those who feel threatened by his rise in order to fulfill the functions of leadership.

Attributes of Leaders and Methods of Leadership

In their personal qualities, the leaders in a jati generally follow a characteristic pattern (cf. Dhillon 1955, pp. 118–126; Lewis 1958, pp. 125–130, 149–150). They need to have enough wealth and family support to back up their word. It is well if the man's family has an ancient and honored reputation, but it is even more necessary that his family be united behind him. One eminent leader in Khalapur lost his influence in part because he could not get his own nephew to obey him (Hitchcock MS. 1959, p. 41; Retzlaff 1962, p. 43). Further, a leader commonly has to have the time and the interest to keep himself closely posted on what goes on among his jati fellows. A man who keeps abreast of the gossip, rumors, and facts—and can skillfully distinguish among them—can anticipate and control trouble.

Unless a man has wealth enough to afford the leisure for this kind of participation, his interest in doing so will not avail. Moreover very few young men can spend their time in garnering local intelligence nor will the kinsmen and neighbors of a younger man give him the respectful attention that they give to an elder man. So the term "elder" is generally a valid synonym for leader. Age alone is not sufficient to qualify a man for leadership but youth is a disqualification and reasonable maturity as father and manager is necessary.

Similarly, wealth is necessary but is not in itself sufficient. To be an effective leader, a man must use his wealth properly in extending hospitality, in entertaining many visitors, and, as we have noted above, in staging generous family and jati rites. A wide net of connections with powerful people is an advantage, so too is some education, which presumably gives entree to holders of power. Because an effective leader must communicate effectively, fluency and cogency in public speech are great assets. In addition, the rising leader of a jati should demonstrate that he intends to use these assets for the general good before he is regularly, widely, and spontaneously invited to help maintain the whole jati.

As in many another society, a man who seeks to be a leader best presents himself as an unostentatious person, more interested in the welfare of his jati kin and neighbors than in personal aggrandizement. If he does not do so, his public judgments and acts will be suspected of being in his own selfish interest. That suspicion is usually not far distant in any case and a leader in the jati or village frequently has to make his way against a rolling drumfire of gossip and innuendo.

A main attribute of an effective leader is the ability to switch personal styles of conduct, to adapt readily to differing situational requirements. This is a hallmark of effective leadership everywhere; in the context of jati relations, it means that a man must be aggressive and selfishly partisan while he consolidates his wealth. But when, as a prominent man, he gives judgments in council on jati affairs, he is expected to be unaggressive, judicious, unselfish, seeking the jati's good rather than his own, upholding the values of the brotherhood (cf. Dhillon 1955, p. 107, Hitchcock MS. 1959, p. 44). Though he is not required to sacrifice the interests of his family, he should also not act as a fervent partisan of his kinsmen in jati council. In order to link different levels of society a leader should be able to change gear in this way, acting in terms of one pattern vis-à-vis the smaller group, using another in relation to the larger.

In addition to the active leaders, there may be more passive leaders in a village, men of moral prestige whose advice is sought at critical junctures. These men have influence and functions separate from those of the other leaders, as Orenstein has noted in Gaon village, Poona district.

Two of the leaders there are Brahmins who make no effort to interfere in the actions of others. Because they are esteemed for their high moral conduct, they are sought out as mediators and have influence in that capacity. The eight active leaders of Gaon are deeply occupied with status competition and do not feel impelled to live up to the ideal moral standards. There are also three "unsanctioned" leaders in this village, men of a higher jati who support and lead the Harijans against the higher groups and do so by strong-arm methods (1959, pp. 422–425).

Any jati-group of more than a few families usually has acknowledged leaders and, as was mentioned at the beginning of this chapter, the role is quite informal in some jati-groups while in others it carries a title, specific obligations, and special rewards. The advantage to the group of having a formal headman is that a particular person is thereby clearly and continually responsible for group maintenance. These headmen usually have ritual as well as secular duties so their secular leadership tends to be bolstered by their religious functions.

Such leaders are not the same as the so-called headmen who are arbitrarily selected to transmit messages from the rulers to the ruled (cf. Dumont 1957b, p. 293). A government official or a landlord may appoint someone from a Harijan hamlet to carry orders to his jati fellows. That man may or may not be the real leader of his jati-group. A main disadvantage of formalizing the maintenance roles, for jatis as for empires, is the problem of succession. Formal succession is usually hereditary; the inheritor may be quite incompetent and become an easy target for others to the detriment of group solidarity, so the actual influence of a formal headman of a jati or jati-group depends greatly on his personal ability.

An able man is in a favored position to wield influence, but one who is uninterested or inept will make little of the office he has inherited or will allow a kinsman to wield the power latent in the office. The latter course occurred in Wangala in Mysore where a younger brother took over authority from his elder brother, in this case the authority of hereditary headman of the dominant jati and so of the village. The elder was weak and incapable, the younger had, in abundance, the qualities expected of a headman. So the younger acted as the real leader; the villagers called him "chairman," using the English term. He headed the council discussions and was recognized as the chief arbitrator in village affairs. But the more formal duties of headman, as in collecting taxes (and retaining the fee) continued to be done by the elder brother. The son of the elder brother would succeed to the headmanship, and if there was no longer any need then to delegate the headman's authority, the new office and title of chairman might well disappear (Epstein 1962, pp. 126–127).

In Dalena, the contrastive village of the same district of Mysore, the hereditary headman has also allowed much of his traditional duty and authority to be taken over by another man, also called chairman. The reasons here arise not from the headman's failures but from his economic success. He is an extremely capable man who has a flourishing business outside the village. Hence he is not much interested in village affairs; the villagers, for their part, do not trust him, particularly because he does not veil his business success, as a leader should, by expressions of humility and of frequent concern for the general welfare. So the villagers give their confidence to another able man who better fulfills their requirements for a leader (Epstein 1962, pp. 280–283).

In these two villages the partial displacement of the hereditary headman has been accomplished with reasonable smoothness. But it does not always happen that an incompetent inheritor has a talented younger brother to whom he is willing to hand over effective authority. Even more rarely does an able man become so engrossed in affairs outside the village that he is content to let another perform his inherited duties within it. So although there is flexibility about hereditary succession, there have also been bitter struggles in many a village about the inheritance of the formal role of leader.

The jati-group headman of Shamirpet, whose deliberate tirade to a disobedient young man was quoted above, combines the prestige of hereditary office and the power of personal ability. The way such a leader operates is sketched in Dube's study of this village near Hyderabad (Dube 1955b, pp. 47–49). Each of the seventeen main jati-groups in the village has a hereditary headman who is held responsible for the good conduct of his jati-fellows. His authority is not clearly defined and he must depend on the force of his personality rather than on any consensus about his legitimate powers.

At the time when Dube studied the village, most of these hereditary headmen were not very effective. Some of them were only nominal members of the village council; others merely represented their jati-groups. But the man who was quoted, headman of a middle-ranking cultivator jati, was both the formal and the real leader of his jati-group. Though he was then only in his late thirties, other villagers listened respectfully to him. He had great influence in the village council as well as in his own jati. There was another able and influential man in his jati-group, and it is a measure of this headman's skill that their relations were quite cordial.

Dube tells that this headman intervenes when a son in his jati-group does not show due regard to his parents or a husband and wife quarrel too often and too publicly. Similarly, if one of his fellows fails to fulfill the terms of his obligations or in any other way brings dishonor to the group, or if boys get unmanageable, or girls earn an evil reputation for easy virtue, "he effectively enters the scene, gives suggestions and advice, admonishes people if they do not seem amenable to persuasion, and in the case of adolescents and young boys may even inflict light corporal punishment" (Dube 1955b, pp. 48–49).

One day while Dube was in the village this headman came to the aid of a younger brother who had quarreled with his elder brother. The two brothers were living alone together, their parents being dead, and the elder was one of a band of young men who had taken to gambling, drinking, and generally "planning mischief." He earned little from their land, spent most of it on himself, and was saving nothing for his brother's marriage. The younger brother had already complained about him to the jati elders and on this occasion ran to the headman for help.

When the headman went to their house and summoned the elder brother, he was greeted with this volley, in Dube's translation of the Telugu (the original was probably racier), "Have you nothing else to do? What brings you here? Is it because of jealousy that you cannot see our welfare and prosperity and you are instigating my brother to separate from me?" At this, the usually calm and sedate headman switched into another mode of address, which included, in addition to the charges quoted above, the rebuke that "After spending a few months in the city—and with the support of that band of rascals—you think that you can defy the authority of the village elders. I will show you what it means to be impertinent to me." A crowd collected, other leading men of the jati-group came up and supported the headman. The other elders then induced the young man to apologize, which he did rather reluctantly, and they set the sum that he would have to provide for his younger brother's wedding (Dube 1955b, pp. 203–204).

An able headman continually prompts cooperation within his group, soothes hurt feelings, calms cranky kinsmen, sniffs trouble and tries to divert it. His success, as with all leaders, depends on the willingness and cooperation of the followers, as well as on his own motivation and ability. This day-to-day influence is highly important for the group—whether lineage, alliance, jati-group, or village—but it is not particularly visible. It is exerted in private conversations (though the case above blossomed into a public affair), in incidental actions, in quiet but firm suggestions.

When, however, a transgression has been committed, when a dispute cannot be sidetracked, or when a group enterprise must be arranged, the leaders can no longer act privately and individually. Then they meet in council and act through the role formation called the panchayat.

Panchayat as Pattern of Action

The term "panchayat" literally means a group or council of five. In village usage it refers not only to the group that convenes but also to a set of processes for resolving conflict, for redressing transgression, and for launching group enterprises (cf. Cohn 1965, pp. 90–91). The pattern of panchayat action is triggered by a problem that people feel must be tackled and that cannot be handled by individuals acting singly. The issue may be one that touches only the families of a lineage or it may be one that concerns all in an alliance, a jati-group, or a jati. The responsible men of the group gather to discuss the issue. Their number, the timing of the meetings, the sanctions that may be imposed, all depend on the nature of the problem rather than on any fixed specifications or schedule.

It should be noted at once that this traditional panchayat pattern is quite a different thing from the recent, legislative use of the term panchayat. The recent usage refers to a statutory local body, recruited through elections, given legal powers, and charged with certain governmental functions. The relation between the traditional panchayats and the new institutions requires a separate analysis; the focus in this chapter is on the traditional panchayat as a means for maintaining the jati.

The panchayat pattern may be brought into play for so small an instance as the quarrel just described between the two brothers of Shamirpet. One brother appealed to the headman of the jati-group who hurried over to set things right. As voices were raised in anger, other elders gathered; such elders are usually of the same lineage and live within earshot of a family fracas. Together these elders assessed the case and made recommendations on the spot; their judgment was backed by the possibility of more formal and severe action if their recommendations should not be followed.

Such on-the-spot arbitration has been called an *ad hoc* panchayat and so it is; most other panchayat meetings are also *ad hoc* in the sense that they are called to deal with a particular problem. Some problems can be resolved by quick arbitration, as when a lane is blocked by a cart or a woman is slightly hurt in a quarrel; others, such as family arguments about partition, typically drag on for a long time, through many sessions, with changes of position by the disputants and changes of recommendations by the arbitrators (cf. Epstein 1962, pp. 120–122; Srinivas 1952a).

The scope of a panchayat meeting and the participants in it depend on the nature of the issue that brought on the session (cf. Cohn 1965, p. 100). A family quarrel is normally considered first in a meeting of the leaders of its lineage. Where strong alliances confront each other, as in Haripura, each side gathers its own panchayat to settle disputes among alliance members and to collect funds for village festivals and public works (Dhillon 1955, pp. 109–110).

For some problems a panchayat of the whole jati-group must be convened, including leading men of all lineages and alliances. Thus if a man is seen in town eating in low company or a woman of the jati is discovered with a man not her own, no time must be lost in gathering a jati-group panchayat to preserve all from the ritual peril raised by the delinquency of one. Or if village servants refuse to perform a traditional service for the overlords, a panchayat meeting of the patron jati-group is called to bring their power to bear on the recalcitrants. Conversely, if the privileges of a lower, serving jati are curtailed, their men gather in panchayat to determine how to bring their united strength to bear on the landowners.

Quarrels between jati fellows of different lineages or alliance are taken up in a panchayat of the jati-group. If a quarrel among brothers cannot be settled at the lineage level, any one of them can take the case before the jati-group panchayat, though he may risk decisive loss if opinion there goes against his claim. The planning of joint enterprises, as well as arbitration, may be the business of a panchayat meeting. The jati-group's participation in a village festival, its contribution to a jati temple, its share in village improvements are determined in a council of its elders and leaders.

In a village where one jati-group is strongly dominant, its council is, in effect, the village panchayat. But in a village where several jatis are strong, the leaders of each meet to take up problems affecting the village as a whole. Shamirpet is such a village; in it there is some overlap of jurisdiction between the panchayats of the village and of the jati-group. Serious offenses are laid before both panchayats; cases of incest or of beef eating so threaten both the jati-group and the entire village that they are taken up at once by both councils. Both give judgments to restore the whole community to its normal social status (Dube 1955b, p. 55).

Certain problems require elders and leaders from more than one village. If a betrothal is broken and one side feels injured by the break, its men look to a panchayat for satisfaction. That panchayat must include elders from the two villages. So also with divorce cases, not uncommon in the middle and lower jatis, when a council must adjudicate questions of return of marriage payments. When a particularly heinous transgression becomes known, as when a Hindu villager kills a cow (even if inadvertently), then more than his jati-group stand endangered by the deed. A council of his jati from a number of villages is convened. In some jatis the killer must be made outcaste, at least for a time, whatever the circumstances of the killing.

Any offense for which a person is likely to be cast out of his jati requires an intervillage council of the jati, so that the punishment can be widely known and totally supported. Councils of larger scope are also held for a variety of larger problems, disputes between jati-groups, promotion of jati festivals, reform of jati practices and, latterly, education for the jati's youth.

The number of villages represented in a jati panchayat varies by the organization of the jati and the gravity of the issue (cf. Cohn 1965, pp. 93–94, 99–100). Some jatis have quite well-defined panchayat circles and notices are sent to each village when a problem for the larger council arises. The Rajputs of Ramkheri, for example, are part of a tight set of five villages within a radius of four miles of the center village; their council meetings must be attended by elders from all five villages. The weavers of Ramkheri belong to a circle of fifteen villages; attendance from all fifteen is not compulsory in their meeting but the three hereditary leaders in this weavers' circle must be present.

The larger councils of most jatis in Ramkheri are held at any large gathering of jati-fellows, mainly at marriages or funerals. At such times, when many jati brethren have come together from a number of villages (from five to twenty-five or more), the elders assemble to judge a case that has been put before them (Mayer 1960, pp. 253–255). Occasionally a wealthy family will summon a special jati council to hear its complaint and will invite jati fellows from all the villages where their kinsmen live. But the summoners must be able to feed a large concourse and to bear other expenses of an extraordinary council.

The tale of such a grand council is told among the Balahis, who are Harijans in Nimar district of Madhya Pradesh. One of the sons of an important family had been most grievously insulted by his mother-in-law—she hit him with a shoe—and the family brought together Balahis from eighty villages to hear their complaint. The council excommunicated the whole jati-group of the offensive mother-in-law. Those who were outcast resisted the verdict for a while, but after a few months declared their submission and had to stage an expiatory feast for an equally large gathering, also from some eighty villages. Nearly a ton and a half of wheat cakes were required for this feast, Balahis say; other expenses were proportionally large (Fuchs 1950, pp. 41–42).

This unusual convocation was remembered vividly twenty years after the event, and it would be unusually large even for people of higher, wealthier jati. The geographic range represented in a traditional jati panchayat is usually limited by the means and speed of transportation as well as by the kinship radius of the conveners. The potters of a village in Lucknow district belonged to a formal jati circle that included more than fifty villages. This size was found too unwieldy and extensive so they regrouped into smaller circles (Majumdar 1958a, p. 98).

Some jatis support yet a higher council, of broader geographic scope, which usually is more concerned with the jati's external relations than with internal disputes. Thus several of the jatis in Ramkheri maintain temples in Ujjain, the sacred center of the Malwa region. The rites at such a temple are not specific to the jati that supports it nor are they offered particularly for its members, but there are pilgrim lodges attached to a temple to which jati fellows come from a wide territory during the main religious festivals at Ujjain. At such times and in the facilities provided by the pilgrim lodge, the temple committee may convene a large meeting to propose jati policies. At one such meeting of a barber jati, the assembly resolved to fine and, if necessary, outcast a jati fellow who poached another's clients, if the client had not paid all that he owed to his previous barber. The meeting also set a maximum fee for matchmakers who arrange a remarriage (Mayer 1960, pp. 255–256).

Such traditional centers and assemblies are not maintained by all jatis, but a jati that has developed from a sect is particularly likely to have such organization. This is partly because devotees feel special need for regular convocations of the true believers, surrounded as they normally are by a vast ocean of unbelief, and partly because sectarian jatis tend to maintain their own sacred centers to which believers come annually from far places. The regional center is also the seat of the spiritual head of the sect who may be endowed with temporal as well as spiritual powers. Before him are laid serious disputes and major transgressions. His decree is accepted as final, above any judgment of a council, though he may be assisted by a council. Some of the Jain and Lingayat jatis maintain such leaders, and certain jatis that are not of sect origin, such as the Havik Brahmins of Mysore, also revere a guru whose judgments are final in jati affairs (Sangave 1959, pp. 101, 111, 330–335; McCormack 1963, p. 63; Harper and Harper 1959, p. 465; Hutton 1961, pp. 97–98; Dubois 1928, pp. 284–285).

With the upsurge of political participation in the twentieth century, regional assemblies have been developed by a good many jatis, more rationalized and formalized than the originals, and made possible by great improvements in communication and travel facilities. The organization of these regional assemblies is usually modeled after the structures of Indian political parties and governmental agencies. Thus the Telis, oilmen, of Puri district in Orissa have an elaborate table of organization for the fourteen thousand Teli families in the district. They are organized into six "dominions," each dominion is further subdivided into a number of regions, each region into villages and each village into one or more wards.

The "dominion" assembly takes up the same kind of cases that a less formalized jati panchayat would consider, but it also discusses matters of wider policy as a council of traditional form and scope would not be likely to do. This modern, more elaborate organization of Telis thus performs traditional panchayat functions and also goes beyond them.

A still higher level of organization has now been added, the congress of oilmen from the various districts of Orissa. In 1959 an All-Orissa Teli Congress was held, including representatives from the three major Teli jatis of Orissa. Among the proposals suggested was that the Orissa Congress of Telis should enter into close relations with a still broader organization, the All-India Oilmen's Association (Patnaik and Ray 1960, pp. 76–77). At these conventions, as we shall discuss below, the main concern is for educational advance, economic improvement, jati reforms, and status elevation. This is far removed from the traditional functions of a jati panchayat, but these are still carried on, among Telis as among many other groups, by the more localized councils.

The Jats of Meerut Division did not have to create a new organization for these modern functions, they had only to revive their ancient regional council. Before 1850 that council had been maintained for centuries to provide for the common Jat defense, to collect revenue, and to administer some governmental affairs over the hundreds of villages within this Jat-dominated area. After a lapse of a century, this council was convened again in 1950 and has continued to meet, not for the old military, revenue, and administrative functions, but for the modern purposes of jati reform, lobbying, and regional welfare.

These Jats, as depicted by M. C. Pradhan (1965) have long had an unusually complex yet clearly conceived organization with a graded series of panchayats that have functioned continuously. There are other jatis in this Meerut region but the Jats are the dominant landowners, and their organization sets the style for and, in certain respects, includes the other jatis.

There are nine levels of Jat organization; a social unit at each level is made up of smaller units of the level just below it. Panchayats are assembled for groups of every kind. If a serious case cannot be settled by a panchayat of a smaller unit, it may be taken up by a panchayat of the next higher level. Issues between groups at one level are adjudicated by a panchayat of a unit at the next higher level.

A fundamental unit in this series is the lineage. As we have noted above, Jat lineages are strictly localized, in that a certain tract of land in every village is the property of a particular lineage. Only members of the lineage may own that land, no others may share in it. Because of this cohesion factor, these lineages are larger than those in most other parts. The minimal lineage is the same as the lineage we have previously discussed, a set of families whose men are closely related because of their common descent from a known ancestor, perhaps three to four generations removed from them. The maximal lineage among the Jats comprises all those families who have rights in a particular part of the village land. Their men are also descended from a common ancestor, but at a much greater generational distance (Pradhan 1965, pp. 1822–23).

A panchayat of the minimal lineage is convened to settle disputes of the kind that close relatives and neighbors are apt to get into. The partition of joint family property is a common issue before such a council. Other issues are quarrels about irrigation, borrowed farm implements, thefts, and repayment of loans. Several minimal lineages may together have common interests and so may assemble a panchayat of their elders to protect their interests. For example, the people of one set of minimal lineages became much annoyed with their genealogist and agreed in a panchayat session to fire him.

The panchayat of the maximal lineage takes up the more stubborn cases that the councils of its component minimal lineages have not been able to resolve. This panchayat is able to outcast an offender as the smaller units cannot do alone. And since the families of the maximal unit cultivate contiguous lands, that council also deals with land management problems, like the sale of their sugarcane or the voluntary building of roads. A maximal lineage is also a political unit, in that its men feel strong obligation to stand together against other lineages.

A village panchayat is convened to hear disputes between maximal lineages or between different jatis in the village. Since the village is an administrative unit, this panchayat deals also with representations to government or with activities related to the larger organization of the jati.

That larger organization includes units ranging from five to eight contiguous villages and, at the next higher level, units of as many as twenty villages. The principal higher unit is that of the clan-area; Pradhan mentions one clan tract that covers 84 villages. Elders and leaders from this clan-area assemble to consider serious problems—flagrant incest or adultery, difficult quarrels between maximal lineages or villages or between two jatis within the tract. An aggrieved man may appeal the judgment of a lower panchayat before this council (Pradhan 1965, pp. 1856–1857).

A range of enforcement sanctions are available to this council, provided always that there is strong and nearly complete agreement among the leaders sitting in council. Offenders may be fined and made to undergo expiatory rites. Sometimes they must express their repentance by touring the villages of the tract and asking the forgiveness of the elders in each village. To bring a recalcitrant offender to heel, a panchayat of influential men may assemble at his very door. They will discuss his case and refuse to accept any hospitality from him until he complies with their judgment. Few can resist such pressure.

Those who still hold out may be made outcaste. Even their whole lineage may be ostracized with them, if they support the defaulter. But in recent decades the outcasting has been almost always temporary. The transgressor asks for pardon and after suitable expiation is readmitted (Pradhan 1965, pp. 1859–1863).

Beyond outcasting, there is a greater, final penalty. It is the curse uttered by a panchayat. This may be inflicted by a council at any level, but when done by a high-level panchayat it is a particularly fearsome blow. Thus one man in his fifties entered into a marriage that had been forbidden by a high panchayat. That council then cursed him with the dread bane that he should have no sons. Twenty years later, in his seventies, he still had no son to his name. Pradhan comments that belief in the power of the curse is still fairly common even among educated and urbanized Jats; to a Jat villager it is a considerable inducement to bow to a given panchayat decision (Pradhan 1965, p. 1863).

In addition to the traditional functions, a panchayat of a clan-area now takes up such enterprises as the improvement of education for the children, the elevation of jati rites, the maintenance of communal harmony. And at the highest level of organization there is the revived regional assembly of eighteen clan-areas, which meets at intervals of several years. The modern effect of these Jat assemblies will be noted in later discussion of social mobility; like the grand congresses of Orissa oilmen, these assemblies pass resolutions for jati reform and political improvement. Enforcement of these resolutions devolves mainly on the lineages, but the regional assembly is increasingly a force for mobilizing jati strength in the halls of government, as its ancient prototype once mobilized jati armies for the field of battle (Pradhan 1965, pp. 1855–1864).

At every social level, panchayat action begins when leading men of a group, whether it is a lineage or a jati, meet to deal with a problem that affects that group. The meeting is convened by those who feel endangered or discomforted by the problem and it is attended by those who feel involved in it. Different kinds of issues induce councils of different kinds, from impromptu gatherings of lineage elders to planned convocations of people from many villages.

A vexing problem that cannot be resolved by a panchayat of first jurisdiction may be laid before a council of wider representation, often one gathered specifically for that purpose. There is usually no formal or regular mechanism of appeal from a judgment made at one level to a council of broader scope. A principal who is dissatisfied with a judgment, however, can bring his case to a larger council if he has influence enough to persuade elders to consider the case again and if he can afford to pay the costs of gathering and feeding them when they assemble.

Panchayat Participants and Procedure

The participants in a panchayat include those directly involved, either those accused of a transgression or both sides in a dispute. In an extempore meeting within a lineage, at least two or three elders should hear out the matter. For a summoned council meeting, all the effective leaders of the group involved should be present to concur in a judgment. If any are absent, by chance or by choice, a judgment may not be enforceable until they agree to enforce it.

There can be little electioneering for the position of indispensable elder because the position is a consequence of a man's power and influence. If he is influential, then everyone who is concerned with resolving the problem will be eager to invite him to sit on the council. His actively seeking the role implies that he may not be worthy of it, since a truly important man will know that the council cannot be effective without him.

A council meeting usually attracts a number of other men, some related to the principals, some who are particularly interested in the issue or who simply enjoy speaking in council discussions and listening to them. These come without special invitation. As jati fellows they have a right to hear and—if they are adult men—to be heard. Respected outsiders may be invited to attend in order to lend an aura of objectivity and authority to the proceedings. If it is an issue within a lineage, perhaps a wise elder of a friendly lineage will be asked to sit in; if it is a jati-group council, a respected man of another jati may be invited, often of a higher jati or of the dominant jati in the village (cf. Dhillon 1955, p. 106; Mayer 1960, p. 252; Minturn and Hitchcock 1963, p. 253).

The judges may be recruited on the spot, as when a sobbing woman rushes to an elder displaying the bruises from a beating by a neighbor. But in serious affairs, a council is summoned more formally and a date is set, perhaps for a time when many of the jati will gather to attend a festival or a wedding. Then messengers of a low jati are dispatched with written invitations and with a symbolic gift, perhaps of tobacco or areca nut. Within the village a crier—also of low jati—goes from place to place loudly announcing the meeting and its business. The venue is commonly in the vicinity of a temple, partly because it is an accustomed meeting place, partly to bring home the often quoted saying that where there is a panchayat, there also is God.

Elders demand respect for a council, whether it is an impromptu gathering or a jati conclave. Thus Srinivas tells that in the village near Mysore city that he studied, any house verandah will do as a place for settling ordinary disputes: "I have heard an elder, sitting in his verandah, sharply reminding a loose-tongued woman, party to a dispute, that she was in a *nyaya-sthana* (place of justice, court)." But when a serious dispute, one involving important people and several villages, is to be settled, the meeting is usually held before a temple, and every speaker begins and frequently ends his statement with a reference to his "soul as witness" or to "God as witness" (Srinivas 1954, p. 159).

No set agenda or order of presentation is required. The meeting usually goes on until every man has had his say and all are too tired or too replete with talk to add anything else. The session begins when the senior elders see that enough people are present, which is to say when all influential men who may be expected to come have arrived. There usually is no great concern about who shall preside. A particular man may take the lead on opening the council, either because he has a traditional right to do so or because he is the most senior or the most forward of the prominent men who are assembled. But any elder may take the lead in the discussions or interrogate as his interest prompts and as his fluency and pertinacity avail (cf. Dumont 1957b, pp. 293–294).

At the beginning there is apt to be an eloquent display by plaintiff and defendant and a heated exchange between them. An accused states his case and typically proclaims his innocence. Then the adherents and supporters of each side take part, offering whatever evidence and witnesses they can muster. The legal phrases and flourishes of government courts are so familiar that villagers commonly use them in panchayat discussions.

Now the men who take special interest in jural affairs also come in. They are self-appointed experts, but some of them are nonetheless trenchant, effective speakers (cf. Cohn 1965, p. 106). A panchayat is often the scene of impressive oratorical and legal performances. One ethnographer, describing a council meeting full of fine rhetoric in a case of suspected adultery in a Harijan group of Madhya Pradesh, waxes rhetorical himself, ". . . the men spoke with an eloquence and volubility, with a variety of superb gestures and suggestive change of voice, now pleading and imploring, then stern and firm, all of a sudden sarcastic and ironical, so that I could not but admire their oratorical talents" (Fuchs 1950, p. 35).

The place of council discussions in the life of many villagers cannot be grasped unless one understands that they are more than means for maintaining the peace and order of the group. As Dumont notes for the Kallar, a speaker often takes pleasure in unraveling a delicate and complicated case and in finding an elegant solution for it: "L'esthétique indigène est pour une bonne part verbale et juridique" (1957b, p. 293).

When the facts of a case are in dispute, each of the disputants is usually required to take a solemn oath attesting to his version of the story and invoking supernatural retribution if he speaks falsely. A crucial question of fact may be put before a deity in the temple. Lots may be drawn before the image, or some other method of finding the true facts may be used. An accused who protests innocence of a serious offense may be required to undergo an ordeal (cf. Dubois 1928, pp. 661–662; Hutton 1961, pp. 105–106). These oaths, omens, and ordeals do not always yield definitive answers, because both plaintiff and defendant may swear the same mighty oath to contradictory testimony, or the omen-taking may be inconclusive, or the ordeal subject to different interpretations.

The panchayatdars, the elders-in-council, usually do respond quickly and impartially when the ritual status of the whole jati is clearly in danger. Then they are likely to pin down the exact offense and the offender with objectivity and candor. But when there is a case involving two powerful alliances or two strong jati-groups within the jati, then their own interests may be drawn into the whirlpool of the dispute.

The role of the panchayatdar does not obliterate obligations of kinship; the panchayat member remains a kinsman though as councilor he should not join in partisan argument. Some sage councilors are above partisan involvement, others conform to Dube's comment on councils in Shamirpet. He says that outwardly all show an attitude of objectivity and impartiality, although in reality the rival factions within the council try to influence the procedure "so that the evidence may later be construed in such a way that it may prove advantageous to the client to whom they have already promised their support" (1955b, p. 202).

The most influential men ordinarily say little at the beginning of a council meeting. After others have had their say, the leaders start to put their points and questions, trying to steer the council into some compromise or course of action. Here, as Mayer notes, lies the value of a leader's flair for oratory and his firmness of temper and character. These qualities count more at this juncture than his hereditary position or wealth. The leaders size up the feeling of the council and estimate whether they can get a consensus. "If it is unlikely, they say less and less until the meeting peters out and it is understood that the matter will be taken up again later— there is not, in my experience, any formal postponement made" (Mayer 1960, p. 257).

A judgment is not usually reached unless there is unanimity or near unanimity among the presiding leaders. If they do not agree, the council meeting is dissolved with no decision taken; there is little point in pronouncing a decision unless it can be enforced, and it can be enforced only if the wielders of power determine to do so. Although some national leaders have written eloquently on the moral value of the striving for council consensus, F. G. Bailey has pointed out that councils in any society whose members have to implement their own decisions are impelled to search for such consensus. If the society provides a separate executive, then it is much more difficult for a disgruntled minority to block the majority decision in a council (Bailey 1965 pp. 8-9). But panchayats are not equipped with any separate executive officers. Hence in the village view it is generally more important to achieve broad agreement, even if it takes many meetings, much discussion, and considerable compromise, than it is to reach a decision quickly and to take action forthwith. There are, however, some kinds of cases in which decision and action follow in rapid succession.

The difference between protracted and speedy cases is illustrated in Scarlett Epstein's account of the formal panchayats that were held in Wangala during her year of residence there (1962, pp. 122-215). In that Mysore village the council of the dominant jati-group (Vokkaliga) is also the village panchayat. Among the protracted sessions were three that were held to discuss arrangements for village festivals. All three ended in a deadlock over how much food and firewood each household was to contribute and who was to prepare the food. One meeting was held to discuss the electrification of the village and the repair of the temple for the village deity; this too adjourned inconclusively because there was no agreement as to how much each household should contribute to the cost of these ventures.

Quickly decided, on the other hand, were two issues on which delay would have altered the circumstances. One was a straightforward medical emergency. An epidemic among the village buffaloes had in one day taken off twelve animals, more than ten percent of the total number. The panchayat met and decided on the steps to be taken immediately to prevent further deaths. Action was swift and effective. The other issue concerned a social emergency. It was the case, mentioned in discussing jati-group unity, in which the drama troupe of untouchables decided that the actor in the part of the king should sit on a prop throne rather than on the floor of the stage, as was customary for any untouchable actor (Epstein 1962, pp. 183–189). The Vokkaliga elders met this by declaring a boycott of the performance and a lockout of untouchable laborers. When the time came for the performance, the show was marred by a sudden rain as well as by the lack of a proper audience. The lockout was successful enough so that the village Harijans asked for relief and paid the fine decreed by the Vokkaliga council.

In all, this jati-group council effectively disposed of four of nine cases during the year. In the other five, factional differences came into play and each alliance blamed the other for unjustified obstinacy. Nevertheless these deadlocked meetings had an important societal function, Epstein points out, because panchayat meetings are one means of working out the relative strength of the respective alliances. The succession of seemingly inconclusive meetings served to demonstrate which men were now allied and which were in opposition. Although a particular plaintiff may not get his just due, the conduct of a case contributes toward clarifying the balance of alliance powers.

The egalitarian aspects of the traditional panchayat seem to pose a paradox. The need for unanimous consent and the right of every man to be heard appear dissonant to the leitmotif of hierarchy. If villagers are predisposed to view most social relations as being between superior and subordinate, why do they not implant a clear superior in the panchayat pattern? They might maintain a jati guru, as indeed some do, one chief who would pronounce a final ruling. The answer seems to be that most define a jati council as a council of peers. In it one family head usually feels himself quite the equal of any other, and so equally entitled to a voice in the discussions. It is true that a son will not contradict his father in open meeting, a young man will rarely ridicule or revile a respected elder, nor will a humble dependent readily stand up against his wealthy patron. Yet in the context of the panchayat meeting a family head tends to feel more as one among equals than as a subordinate. Therefore even a poor man will speak up if he feels moved to do so.

Any powerful man can ignore the wishes of the majority if he has not participated in a decision or has not agreed to it. He sees no more reason to subordinate himself to a particular number of his peers than to any one of them. Thus every issue must be extensively discussed until critical disagreements are eroded by the flow of talk and compromise becomes possible.

"The act of talking seems to relieve some of the aggression built up in a dispute," Cohn writes of the Chamars of Senapur, near Banaras, and this remark about Chamar councils applies to many others. A meeting may last for three or four hours; anyone can raise almost any problem without being cut off; issues that seem to have no bearing on the case are aired. When a meeting adjourns inconclusively, the leaders do more talking to the principals before the next meeting, trying to mediate. "Eventually a 'compromise' will be suggested, and even though it may be more favorable to one party, as long as it can be defined as a compromise in a rhetorical sense, both parties seem to be satisfied" (Cohn 1959a, p. 86).

Often a council meeting called to discuss one dispute will turn to adjudicate another that lies behind the antagonism and comes to the surface in the course of the discussion. The Chamars, Cohn observes, do not segment their lives into neat compartments and they see no point in trying to decide a dispute only on the basis of an immediate situation (1959a, pp. 85–86).

Quite a different pattern for group action, but also a traditional one, is used for certain other purposes. This pattern is more like committee procedure, with restricted membership, delegation of authority, and an expectation of firm decisions. It was commonly followed in the management of large temples, for looking after temple lands and endowments, for distributing temple perquisites, and in planning temple festivals. Mayer calls this the committee form (Samiti in the terminology of Ramkheri villagers) in contrast to the more common panchayat form (1960, p. 122). The committee model is the one now required for activities related to government, but the council procedure is still fruitful and congenial in many villages.

Dhillon's description of leaders (Yajmans) as councilors in Haripura applies widely. "Thus in this traditional panchayat, there is no delegation of powers for a specific period to an elected group. The Yajmans must make decisions in consultation with all concerned, and the confidence in them must be constantly reaffirmed by the people" (1955, p. 107). So panchayat procedure is a way of forming public opinion; through council discussions critical issues become known and sentiments crystallized. It is also a way of making public opinion effective for group maintenance.

Leaders have to be in close touch with their colleagues and followers if their leadership is to be effective. Leaders, whether lineage elders or jati headmen, help to hold their groups together; they help to overcome the social friction that is inevitable in any living group and to keep them functioning as groups. A leader's ordinary, daily efforts in these respects are not highly visible. When such quiet efforts become insufficient and leaders gather in council, their maintenance efforts then become necessarily and deliberately visible to their fellows.

CHAPTER 17   The Uses of Panchayats

THE common village saying, "Where there is a panchayat, there is God," might also add that where there is a panchayat, there also is the group. Because it is mainly in panchayat sessions that the nature of a group—whether lineage, jati-group, or jati—is made clear. There the group's boundaries are defined, its cohesion maintained, its standards set, its common action planned, its purposes shown. Panchayat meetings are a major means of assuring the internal order of a group, of correcting ritual transgressions and secular offenses, of smoothing the disturbance of disputes. Counterchange action within the system of village society is thus largely carried out through panchayats. They are also used in defense against external challenge.

The members of a lineage meet in panchayat when they must defend their group status within the jati; a jati-group protects its place in the village through its panchayat meetings; a jati guards or advances its standing in the local order through the jati panchayats. Further, the members of a group set up cooperative links with other groups and liaison with other social echelons in their panchayat discussions. A lineage council discusses its participation in jati affairs; a jati-group council plans its part in a village ceremony; a jati council takes up relations with agencies of the state. Finally, as described in the following chapter, panchayats are used to advance group enterprises and to adapt to changing conditions. We shall note the special features of village panchayats in later chapters on the village.

There is much variation among jatis in the degree to which the panchayat pattern is used. The people of some jatis—notably the very poor and the strongly dominated—traditionally made little or no use of panchayats; others used them frequently. The present trend is toward lesser reliance on panchayats for some purposes, especially for those in which government agencies have become increasingly influential. At the same time there is a tendency toward much greater reliance on the modern version of the jati panchayat, the jati association, for entrepreneurial and adaptive purposes.

Redress of Ritual Lapses

A panchayat function that is still of high importance for many villagers is the redress of ritual lapses, which is also the maintenance of ritual standards. The ritual integrity of the jati is most precious since a grave transgression by one individual can affect all in his jati. In this matter there is absolute equality, not hierarchy. Every member must equally adhere to the jati's minimal standards of ritual purity. These standards differ from one jati to another, and are generally more exacting among the higher ranks, but people of all jatis—even the lowest—try to maintain and enforce such standards.

Anything that defiles an individual so that he contaminates those who have normal relations with him as jati fellows, comes within the purview of a panchayat. This includes such acts as eating improper food or eating proper food in improper company. Incest discovered or endogamy openly violated are pressing matters for a panchayat. A man who takes up an occupation inexcusably beneath his jati's dignity must be checked or rejected by a council. One who is beaten with a shoe is so defiled, in the traditional view, that he cannot continue as a member of the jati until the pollution is dissipated. A Hindu who kills a cow is so debased that only long ritual restitution can redeem him to his jati.

In such serious cases of defilement the offender's intent or his innocence of motive do not dispel his deep pollution. Even though his involvement in the defiling act may have been involuntary, he is nevertheless contaminated and his corruption is contagious to all who treat him as a jati fellow. This is true even of one who inadvertently has social relations with an outcaste jati fellow. A Chamar of Mohana village near Lucknow was once visited by a Chamar from another village. The host hospitably shared his midday meal with the guest. The visitor had not told anyone in Mohana that he had been made outcaste and when this became known there, the panchayat of Mohana Chamars felt that they had to expel (even

though temporarily) the man who had merely acted with customary hospitality (Majumdar 1958a, pp. 94–95).

The contamination radiated by an outcaste can reach very far.
Thus one washerman in a Mysore village found himself charged
before a panchayat of his jati for arranging what he thought was a
perfectly suitable marriage for his niece. But the bridegroom's
mother's sister, it appeared, had been made outcaste some twelve
years before for living with an untouchable. The crucial question
before the panchayat was whether the bridegroom's mother had
resumed social relations with the outcaste woman, her sister. If so,
she was as defiling as the original culprit. Her son was as tarred as
his mother since he lived with her, and the man who gave a bride
to that son was also derelict, if the charge were true. The
panchayat was little interested in the accused's intent or knowledge
of the situation, the point at issue was whether there actually had
been a circuit of contamination (Srinivas 1954).

This case took a fresh turn when the bridegroom's mother threatened to beat the accuser with her sandals, "a great insult indeed,
involving both the aggressor and the victim in temporary loss of
caste" (Srinivas 1954, p. 155). In this jati, which is not one of the
higher, any one who is so beaten—a single slap on the face or head
with the sole of a shoe is sufficient—becomes ritually degraded, even
if he is the mistaken victim of a misguided attack. He must undergo
purification and readmission to the jati. The attacker may also be
thrown out of the group, but a desperate or vindictively determined
person may use the threat of shoe beating as a weapon.

The mere threat of being beaten with shoes can endanger a man
who is so threatened. This happened when a potter of Rampura
village in Mysore sat in a teashop one day angrily cursing Putta, a
Lingayat priest, for not repaying a loan. Finally he reached a
crescendo of anger and said, "May I sleep with the priest's wife.
May I sleep with his mother." Although this kind of abuse is not
uncommon, the potter then added something that is much more
rarely said and much more seriously taken. He said, "I am going to
beat him with my sandals, and I am going to beat him till five pairs
of sandals wear out."

The last bit was only added bravado but the utterance made the
matter a much graver affair and more difficult to settle than it
would have been otherwise. It could not be informally or quickly

adjudicated because a council of the priest's jati would have to consider him as ritually contaminated. "Putta is a priest and in an important temple at that, and the potter's threat to beat him with sandals was likely to be interpreted by the caste elders as equivalent to the act itself" (Srinivas 1959b, pp. 193, 205).

So whether a ritual breach has been committed deliberately or unwittingly, the culprit (or victim) is a continuing menace to all in his group. The group, acting through its panchayat, must protect itself. If the transgression is a minor affair, the councilors will assess a fine of a few rupees to be paid into the common fund and will require that the offender purify himself by a simple ritual ablution. He should also give assurance publicly that he will err no more.

If the offense is major, however, the group itself must first be purified by expelling the one who is polluted. This initial step for redressive action is also the ultimate sanction in the power of the traditional panchayat. If the offender then recants, pays the proper penalties, and undergoes the proper purification, he can usually be taken back into society. Some ritual crimes, however, can never be wiped away. For example, a Brahmin woman who goes to live with a Harijan is usually beyond redemption to her jati and is totally cut off from her former kinfolk. In many cases of outcasting, however, there is the possibility of subsequent incasting.

A person may be cast out of all sorts of groups; exclusion from one group does not necessarily mean total rejection by society. A family may sever relations with one of its members yet neither its jati-group nor jati need follow suit. In Ramkheri village, for example, a Rajput woman once openly lived with her Brahmin lover. Her family would have nothing to do with her but they did not demand that all similarly reject her. Though many in the village strongly disapproved, no formal judgment was made. The others were content to leave things as they were since the family had not demanded further action. If she had taken up with a man of lower jati, however, her jati-group could not have passed over the matter in the same way (Mayer 1960, p. 260).

Similarly, an offender may be cut off from normal relations with his jati-group and village but still be able to maintain relations with jati fellows in other villages. Thus in Totagadde of western Mysore one Havik Brahmin was so ostracized because he refused to make his married daughter return to her husband. Another Havik incurred this penalty when he refused to pay his share of road repair costs and of the costs of the guru's visit. In these cases the village council is said to "build a fence" around the offender. He then cannot hire local laborers; a priest will not perform domestic ceremonies for him; no one in the village will visit him; often he endures petty thefts and damage to his crops and fields. Yet such a person remains a member of the jati. He may resist for a while, but he is usually forced to give in and ask to be readmitted on the council's terms (Harper and Harper 1959, pp. 463–464).

Outcasting, expulsion from the jati, is the extreme form of group withdrawal, imposed for extreme ritual offenses. The Abbé Dubois, who lived among Tamil-speaking people, has a poignant passage on the fate of an outcaste: "It renders him, as it were, dead to the world, and leaves him nothing in common with the rest of society. In losing his caste he loses not only his relations and friends, but often his wife and children, who would rather leave him to his fate, than share his disgrace with him. Nobody dare eat with him or even give him a drop of water" (1928 edition, p. 38). Since this passage was written, in the early years of the nineteenth century, outcasting has become more rarely used; it is entirely obsolete in some jatis and even when it is imposed the one who is made outcaste can find some refuge, perhaps in a city or in a very low-ranking group. Yet in more than a few jatis the threat of the penalty still has the dread air of final social extinction about it that the Abbé expresses in his description.

Modern examples of outcasting are not lacking. When in 1955 a Havik Brahmin widow of Totegadde village was discovered to be pregnant, she was formally expelled from her jati (Harper and Harper 1959, p. 465). Social boycott is described for two Bengal villages in the 1960s. "Villagers will not speak with the offender; serving castes will be prevented from going to his house; daily laborers will not work for him, and he will receive no help at the time of marriage, death, or even starvation at his house" (Nicholas and Mukhopadhyay 1964, p. 22).

Outcastes who have no hope of readmission to their own jati may possibly join a Harijan jati, such as the Balahis of Madhya Pradesh, who take in people fallen from higher status. Such newcomers are in time enrolled on the register of a Balahi genealogist and may even found a new Balahi clan. But joining a Harijan group does not relieve or exempt an outcaste from jati requirements; it only changes some of the stringency and certain of the rules. The Balahis bear out Gandhi's saying that the untouchables have their untouchables; the Balahis have the Mehtars, who are sweepers. A Balahi may be expelled by his jati panchayat if he should sit with a Mehtar on the same bed or bullock-cart (Fuchs 1950, pp. 18, 61).

A panchayat can rejoin as well as reject. The sentiment of a panchayat does not usually incline to the social extinction of transgressors but to their redemption; the councilors generally want not to lose a jati fellow but to keep the jati intact. Hence there is provision for incasting as well as for outcasting. Among the Chamars of Senapur, Cohn notes, the longest period of outcasting was for twelve years, the penalty for incest.

During the time a Chamar is kept out of his jati all social relations with him are interdicted. No one will eat or smoke with him, allow him to use the well, lend him food or implements, or participate in domestic rites with him. Later, he and his family are allowed to pay a fine to the common fund and to give one or two feasts. They may then be under partial ostracism for a time—allowed to draw water from the hamlet well and to get fire from a neighbor's hearth but not to smoke a hookah in Chamar company or attend celebrations—until the full rituals of readmission have been completed (Cohn 1959a, p. 84; 1965, pp. 100–101).

A formula used in many jatis for setting the amount of the fine emphasizes the supremacy of jati over miscreant, of custom over aberration, of society over sinner. The council spokesman announces a fine much larger than the culprit is really expected to pay. The guilty one, who now accepts the verdict, prostrates himself—either literally or figuratively—before the panchayat and humbly begs that the amount be reduced. It is, but to a sum that is still much larger than the expected fine. This is repeated thrice or more until an acceptable and payable amount is reached. Each time there is public reaffirmation of the redressive action that has occurred. A surly or recalcitrant petitioner will not be let out of his troubles until he goes through this rite of submission (cf. Nicholas and Mukhopadhyay 1964, p. 22; Dumont 1957b, p. 298).

Such a rite on a grand scale was performed in 1961 by the Sikh leader, Master Tara Singh and by nine of his colleagues. He had vowed to fast until death unless his party's demand for a separate Punjabi-speaking state was granted (it was established in 1966). But government representatives persuaded him to stop his fast whereupon other Sikh leaders urged his expulsion from party and community because he had broken his vow. The matter was placed before five eminent Sikh religious leaders who decreed a five-part punishment for Master Tara Singh and lesser penalties for his colleagues. He had to arrange for scriptural readings and offerings at a temple. He himself had to recite certain prayers for a month and for five days he had to clean temple utensils and the shoes of the congregation. Further, the whole community had to be ritually purified through the gathering of a large congregation of Sikhs who recited prayers together. All this was duly done (*The Tribune*, Ambala, October 1–December 5, 1961; *Hindustan Times*, New Delhi, October 1–December 5, 1961).

Ritual readmission in any jati entails public expiation and purification. One means of purification described in Sanskrit scripture, is the ingestion of *panchgavya*, a mixture of the five products of the cow, milk, curds, ghee, cow dung, and cow urine (Ghurye 1961, pp. 92, 101; Hutton 1961, pp. 88, 108). The penitent may be required to travel to a holy center of pilgrimage there to purify himself in the most sacred precincts. There must also be a final rite of social restitution performed in the sight of the jati brethren (cf. Fuchs 1950, pp. 45–49). The pilgrimage may be omitted and the purification ablutions much curtailed, but the public drama of re-entry is not usually neglected. The final phase of readmission is a feast, given at the offender's expense, in which the former outcaste eats with his jati fellows, especially with those who hold hereditary offices. In this way they demonstrate that his sin has been properly expunged and that the jati's integrity has been successfully maintained.

Problems of Enforcement and Jurisdiction

Not all want to recant. Some resist the judgment of a panchayat, and a determined, strong man occasionally even defies formal expulsion from jati. I saw such a struggle going on for many years among the Kotas of the Nilgiris Hills in South India. As I have described elsewhere (1941, 1960), Sulli, the first Kota schoolteacher, was so set on reforming Kota custom that he had his long hair cut off. It was a portentous gesture since a Kota man's chignon was then the hallmark of being a man and a Kota. In response, the elders of the seven Kota villages met and made him outcaste. He remained in the village and kept fighting for his reforms even though he was for a time completely isolated from all his jati fellows. His brothers avoided him; his wife was whisked back to her father's house; his lineage mates deserted him. Because he had a job as a teacher he could continue to make a living. He was a vigorous entrepreneur and had saved money that he used in his defense, unshakable in his conviction that he was right.

After a time his wife returned, his close kin resumed relations, and a few supporters came to his side. He had powerful weapons with which he struck back. He released volleys of petitions to the local government authorities; he harried his chief opponents with endless litigation; he pried adherents loose one by one through various stratagems—a favor for one, a service for another, a loan for a third. After a few years he had collected an alliance and when I saw him last, nearly thirty years after the council's decision, only a few stubborn old men still considered him to be outside of Kota society. There are not many who are as determined and resourceful as Sulli. More commonly, when a large panchayat rules that a transgressor must be thrown out, the guilty one feels compelled to sue for mercy and restoration.

A firm and determined ruling by a jati panchayat will usually be respected by others of the locality. Villagers of other jatis, whether patrons or clients of the offended ones, will help enforce the judgment lest the wrath of the united jati be turned against them also. A landowner will not usually want to employ a sweeper who has been outcast lest he find himself without the services of other sweepers and embroiled in a series of annoying difficulties emanating from the sweepers' hamlet. The ruling of a council may be eroded, however, if it turns out that there is only indifferent support for its decision. The enforcement of panchayat judgments depends on united public opinion and action; enforcement is not assigned to specific officers who have legitimate recourse to force. The use of force is always a lurking possibility but it is rarely a deliberate, overt prescription for the carrying out of panchayat judgments.

Personal considerations figure largely in the making of a judgment and in its enforcement. In assessing the facts of a case, the character of a principal or of a witness is an important consideration. A villager has clear ideas about the worth of his jati fellows and, as Cohn writes of the Chamars of Senapur, he sees no reason why he should not include this knowledge in his evaluation: "Some come from honorable Chamar families, some are educated, some have travelled, some are loose morally, some are stupid, some lazy —all these personal characteristics are known, enter into the adjudicative process, and need not be made explicit" (1959a, p. 86).

The probable consequences of a ruling are also considered in making a judgment. A powerful man may be judged more leniently than a man who is poor and inconsequential, because the important man may resist or even nullify the decision. In two Bengal villages studied by Nicholas and Mukhopadhyay, there are three powerful men who are not even brought before a council for their offenses. One keeps a concubine, another lives with his elder brother's widow, a third has a mistress who is the wife of his sharecropper. All these sexual irregularities are well known and might well incur penalties if they were the acts of less influential men. These three, however, are exempted from panchayat scrutiny (Nicholas and Mukhopadhyay 1964, p. 22).

The same situation is noted in a decision of 1796 by a court of the East India Company in Bengal. Two powerful men openly kept mistresses, which theoretically should have caused them to be made outcaste by their jati fellows. "They dare not, however, take notice of their faults, nor even contradict them and much less expel them from their caste" (cited in Cohn 1965, p. 101).

Still there are limits to the leniency for mighty ones. The most wealthy and exalted personage of a jati could hardly get off scot-free if it became surely known that he had committed incest, or taken a woman of low jati to wife, or killed a cow. He might be readmitted to caste relations more readily than a poor man, but his jati fellows could not overlook his trespasses (cf. Fuchs 1950, p. 37).

A heavy weight of evidence can tell against a considerable weight of influence. Thus in a case in which one washerman accused another of having relations with an outcaste woman, the verdict went against the accuser, even though he was a powerful man. He was even fined for making a false accusation when it became clear in the council session that he had trumped up the charges (Srinivas 1954, p. 161). Similarly, in Khalapur a Rajput who was ordinarily quite immune from panchayat action was made outcaste and driven out of the village when it was proved that he had impregnated a village "sister," then tried to kidnap and sell her off to a distant place (Minturn and Hitchcock 1963, pp. 255–257).

All are held to be answerable for serious ritual and secular offenses, but all do not get equal treatment for equal offenses nor is this really expected. The councilors' first charge is to maintain the group. They cannot be oblivious of the facts of power because that is part of the makeup of the group.

Another relevant fact is the relation of the judged to the judges. When an elder is considering an affair in his own lineage that involves a culprit whom he knows well as a kinsman, his inclination is to smooth things over somehow and get the errant one back to normal relations with as little ado as possible. But when he sits on a jati council and judges a person whom he does not know personally and with whom he has no close ties, then he may be more of a stickler for the jati proprieties and press for a full measure of punishment and formal restitution.

The kinds of offenses for which a jati panchayat is summoned are usually the more blatant ones. In Ramkheri, for example, an inter-village council of a jati deals with the offenses "which are most easily apprehended and over which there is unanimity as to the appropriate punishment." The cases dealt with by the jati-group or village council "tend to be those which are harder to prove, over whose seriousness there can be varying opinions, and over which there is not much unanimous feeling about the correct punishment" (Mayer 1960, pp. 261, 262). In Shamirpet in Andhra Pradesh, the different panchayats tend to give different penalties; the jati-group council rarely outcasts a person, while a jati council often does. And in Rampura in Mysore the council of village elders is characterized as being more friendly and lenient than is a council of jati elders (Dube 1955b, p. 210; Srinivas 1959b, p. 207).

Different judgments are occasionally given by the two councils, that of the jati-group and of the jati. This happened in Ramkheri when a man of the farmer jati began living with a widow and cultivating her lands. Her deceased husband's kinsmen objected, ostensibly because of a jati rule that a dead man's brothers should not meet his widow's second husband—that is to say, he should not live in the same village as they do—but more importantly because they wanted her land. They called a jati-group council, which ordered the pair to separate or to move, and when they refused, the council declared them to be outcaste. A jati council should have been convened to reaffirm that decision, but the jati fellows of other villages kept aloof from this matter. They said that the jati rule had not been violated since the man was only the permanent lover and not the wedded husband of the widow. Whatever his relationship, he had friends and supporters in the other villages and was able to resist the boycott decreed by the jati-group council (Mayer 1960, pp. 263–264).

Another example of a divided opinion on a ruling comes from Gandhi's biography. After he returned from his studies in England he had to undergo ritual purification, as was then customary in many jatis. This was done not only because of the scriptural prohibition against travel over oceans but perhaps even more as a general prophylactic measure. One who had sojourned in places far from home might have been exposed to polluting influences and to unsuitable ideas. Expelling him from the jati and then, on his humble petition, readmitting him ceremonially, ensured that he was ritually fit and morally attuned for normal jati relations. On Gandhi's return from abroad his brother took him directly to the sacred center of Nasik where he performed the purification rites. His jati fellows in his home town received him back, but the jati leaders in Bombay and in Porbander (his birthplace) refused to accept him as one who had been reinstated into the jati (Gray and Parekh 1931, p. 8; Pyarelal 1965, pp. 223, 281–284).

Generally such disagreements between one part of a jati and the others are resolved or eroded in time but they can also lead, perhaps more as symptoms than as root causes, to sharp cleavages in a jati or even to the formation of a new jati by those who have split off. Thus in Ramkheri, a council of barbers was convened about the disappearance of jati funds that had been entrusted to a man who had recently died. His son disclaimed any knowledge of the money and any responsibility for it. Finally the men from the son's village and from half a dozen settlements near it got up and walked out of the council meeting without waiting to eat of the feast that had been prepared. This was doubly insulting; not only was the walk-out an affront to the council but it was also an insult to the host and a waste of his food. Thenceforth, at least for the several years that had intervened from the date of the council to the time of the study, each side formed separate jati councils and did not join in the same ceremonies (Mayer 1960, pp. 258–259).

When such quarrels involve serious differences about ritual matters, the split is likely to be more complete, so that the two sides no longer form a single endogamous entity. This has happened among Rajputs in the region of Ramkheri. The Rajputs of some twelve villages had together been adjudged guilty of a ritual infraction and all were cut off from the rest of the jati. They stood steadfast together and so have formed what is, from the point of view of the other local Rajputs, an outcast jati (Mayer 1960, p. 260). Such jati fission has been a common process in the recurrent change that we discuss later.

Withdrawal by an individual or a group is used as a weapon as well as a punishment at every level of village society. An important person can threaten to impair a ceremony by not participating in it. An important group can use this social leverage. Conversely, a group can exert pressure on an individual through various kinds of withdrawal, from not inviting him to a ceremony to cutting him off from society. In some of its uses, withdrawal is a political measure that entails the redefinition of groups and group action. Yet it is a political means that does not rest on the use of force. A person or a group declared outcaste is subject to social, not physical pressures and suffers through the withholding of interchange rather than from the inflicting of force.

Thus a panchayat of the Jats of Meerut Division may order beating as a punishment for certain offenses and offenders. For capital offenses there was never formal capital punishment even though these men reveled in their warrior traditions and fighting tempers. Their most severe punishment was not the taking of life but the taking away of social support and—through the curse of the panchayat—of supernatural support as well (Pradhan 1965, pp. 1862–1863).

Dispute Resolution and Government Courts

The secular matters that are laid before a lineage or jati panchayat are mainly about family and sex, land and livelihood, theft and assaults. Certain passages in a family's career are liable to be stormy. Cases of joint family partition are apt to be pending for council arbitration at almost any time in any village.

Betrothals sometimes run aground, perhaps because one family has discovered a hitherto unknown flaw in the other, or has uncovered the possibility of a better match, or is simply being difficult to make sure it is held in proper esteem. Disagreements between the contracting families at the wedding must be reconciled on the spot lest large damage ensue. Divorce and second marriages, inheritance and adoption, often require the ministrations of a council to calm domestic discord.

Certain sexual lapses are only secular, others require ritual redress. An irate husband complaining to a lineage panchayat that his wife has strayed with a lineage fellow presents a matter of only secular consequence. But if she were found with a man of her own natal lineage, then the affair smacks of incest and no simple patching up of marital relations will suffice.

Quarrels about land are often brought, at least at the outset, before a jati-group panchayat. The quarrel may be about the shifting of a boundary, or the encroachment of a path, or the trampling of a crop. Councilors try to keep such disputes from spreading to others in the village and to jurisdictions beyond the village. Water can be as bitter a subject of contention as is land; the use of a well, the diversion of irrigation flow are frequent causes of contention. Assaults and thefts committed by one jati member upon another are also taken before jati elders to the extent that outside authorities can be kept out of the affair. Among those jatis in which robbery was a regular source of income, a sharp distinction was made between the robbery of outsiders and of jati fellows. The latter crime was taken before a jati panchayat to be vigorously and righteously judged (cf. Dumont 1957b, p. 303).

Many of these secular problems also come under the cognizance of official governmental law. The government's laws and courts have influenced village life, but were generally viewed by villagers as adventitious forces which had to be coped with and manipulated. The intervention of state power in jati affairs, within certain limits, has long been accepted. In the ancient legal scriptures, the king is enjoined to maintain the social order, to prevent "the confusion of castes" (cf. Kane 1946, vol. 3, pp. 3, 57; Ingalls 1954, p. 42; Smith

1963, pp. 297–300). Even during the British regime, a Maharajah might settle disputes between jatis about precedence and might hear appeals from individuals who felt that they had been wronged by their jati councils (Hutton 1961, pp. 94–95; Cohn 1965, pp. 101–102).

There was a main difference, however, between the personal intervention of an Indian prince and the majesty of British law. The prince generally viewed his intervention as one element in a complex process of social maintenance. The British law for India did not take full account of that process or of the social order that was actually maintained. Soon after the British took control of large parts of India, they felt the need of using indigenous law in administering their new domains. At first they employed Brahmins to tell them what the Hindu law was. Later, when they discovered that Hindu law was very different in character from British law and that clear usage often was taken to outweigh written law, they tried to compile manuals of customary law. But this effort too, distorted the indigenous practices because British judges interpreted customary law much more rigidly than Maharajahs or village councilors ever did (Maine 1881, pp. 71–73; Cohn 1965, pp. 105–113; Galanter 1964). The distinctions that British Indian law did allow, such as those between Hindu and Muslim personal law, among several regional varieties of Hindu law, and the special customs of jatis, did not reconcile the fundamental differences in procedure between law as the British rulers thought of it and the actual jural practice of village society.

When a district officer on tour applied official law in the village, he might well understand and take tacit account of the real processes of social maintenance. But when the same officer was appointed as a judge and presided over court sessions in a headquarters town, he was then restrained from fully using his understanding of the unwritten village law by the rules of evidence, the formulae of legal procedure, and all the written and codified dicta that supported justice in England.

As the courts did not recognize most indigenous law-ways so, in their turn, villagers could scarcely accept the British legal apparatus as really relevant to justice and to the upholding of their society. British law assumed a social organization that villagers did not have and took little note of the organization they did have. It postulated values alien to village society and was conscientiously blind to some of the villagers' fundamental assumptions. It could not be ignored; the state and its police were, after all, very powerful and could be ubiquitous, but their actual jurisdiction could be held down to a certain minimal scope (cf. Cohn 1965, p. 105).

Cases of murder, of crippling assault, and of grand theft might be brought to the attention of the police in British times, especially if the attackers were of another jati or village than the victims. Alleged delinquencies of debt and breaches of contract were also brought to court, particularly when plaintiff and defendant were of opposed alliances or different jatis.

In most disputes internal to a jati, the villagers' inclination was to keep the matter out of the courts. Only large expenses and irrelevant judgments would be forthcoming there; most problems were better settled in council. While some villagers took to litigation early and avidly as a means of gaining personal advantage, many felt that courts could only hinder the settlement of important jati matters. Thus disputes about adoption in Haripura village were not taken to courts until about 1945. In Totagadde the first time a family of the middle jatis had recourse to a court was about 1949. In the 1950s no Harijan of that village had taken a case to court, having neither the knowledge, the money, nor the temerity to do so, although the Brahmins of the village had used the courts for longer than anyone in the village could remember. There was a "moving legal frontier." British law took hold more readily in some matters than in others and was used more quickly by some groups than by others (Dhillon 1955, p. 108; Harper and Harper 1959, p. 464; Galanter 1964).

Many jural issues could not be taken to a government court because the court could not assume jurisdiction over them.[1] Thus the redress of ritual offenses was—and still is—largely outside the official law. The social order of jati and village could not be maintained

---

[1] When persons who were made outcaste sued the outcasters in the courts, the courts tended to apply the English law relating to expulsion from a club. A Calcutta court, however, ruled that on grounds of "natural justice" legal protection was more necessary for expulsion from caste than for expulsion from a club, and therefore cases of outcasting were cognizable by the civil court. But when the matter was taken to the Privy Council, the analogy of the English law pertaining to clubs was upheld (McCormack 1959, pp. 34–38).

without provision for such redress. Government law offered no
such provision nor feasible alternatives. Villagers felt they had to
keep their own jural processes as free as possible from contamination by the government's legal system. They could not keep the
two entirely separate, partly because courts soon came to be used as
prime weapons in the status quest.

Four of the chief discrepancies between British law and village
law-ways are sketched by Bernard Cohn for North India (1959a,
pp. 90–92). They hold broadly true throughout India. The first
discrepancy is between the villagers' hierarchical view and the
basic precept of British-based law of the equality of the individual
before the law. When people appear in court they are to be judged
in terms of their stripped-down roles of plaintiff or defendant. Who
they are outside the court, what other roles they fulfill, how society
appraises their status—all this is not supposed to count, or at least
not very much. To villagers generally this is not quite nonsense—
legislators and judges naturally have their own jati customs—but it
is unsuitable for jati or village purposes. They know that in their
society men have widely different inherent worth. A man cannot
and should not divest himself of all but one narrow role. A Chamar
laborer knows that he is not equal to the Thakur landowner. "He
may want to be equal, but he knows that he is not. The Thakur
cannot be convinced in any way that the Chamar is his equal, but
the court acts as if the parties to the dispute were equal" (Cohn
1959a, p. 91). It renders its verdict on these grounds and frequently
the verdict is promptly negated by the actualities of village power.

A second discrepancy is between status and contract, as Sir
Henry Maine showed. In official law the relation between landlord
and tenant is a contractual one, limited to use of land and payment
of rent; actually it is a multiple relationship, involving many obligations. A judicial decision that deals only with the contractual
aspects must ignore such critical elements in the relationship as the
tenant's obligation to assist in the wedding of the landlord's daughter or the landlord's obligation to pasture the tenant's cow. "People
must continue to live and work together in the multiple society. So
decisions of the courts based on ideas of contract do not fit the
value system and social structure of the Indian village" (Cohn
1959a, p. 91).

A third disparity concerns the necessity for a decision. The procedure of official law requires a firm and reasonably quick decision; in any given case there should be a winner and a loser. The whole sense of the panchayat pattern is contrary to this. A common panchayat purpose is to delay, to talk, and to wear away the differences until a compromise satisfactory to all sides in a quarrel can be evolved. A man who feels that he has a strong case or who is overwhelmingly more powerful than his opponent may press for a quick decision in order to demonstrate his power, but a councilor should try to establish at least a fiction of compromise. The dignity of each disputant should appear to be preserved, so that the council promotes social maintenance rather than status victory.

Lastly, official procedure requires that in any legal case only that case is to be settled, related disputes are not directly relevant. In panchayat procedure nothing is irrelevant if it can bear in any way on the cause of the difficulty. The case that is ostensibly the crux of a dispute brought before a panchayat may turn out to be only a minor expression of a long-standing antagonistic relationship between two families. Elders in a panchayat believe that they must get to the root of the trouble if they are to judge effectively. An official court, on the other hand, can deal only with the case that is the symptom and is not allowed by its rules to probe from symptom to cause.

The official law could maintain the state, it could not and did not maintain the jati or the village. Governmental officials suppressed banditry, established better communications, ensured the collection of revenue, regularized land records, eliminated armed uprisings, and protected markets and trade. These consequences of the British regime had important effects on the whole system of caste and on its local manifestations.

Even though British officials did not want to get involved in caste matters and refused to allow caste questions to come formally to the government courts, they did in effect rule judicially on many caste issues. Among the cases in which they had to take jurisdiction were those involving varna classification, jati offices, and interjati relations (Cohn 1965, pp. 113–114). But for the most part government law could only set certain limits to social action. Within these very broad limits it either did not attempt to trespass or was kept out.

The Domains of Court and of Panchayat

The courts were well suited, however, to serve one aspect of village society, the waging of status competition. Individuals could gain superiority over their opponents, one alliance could establish supremacy over another, a jati could force advantage over others, if the rivalries could be framed as issues over which an official court could take jurisdiction. To succeed, the framers then had to win the court cases. Such use of the courts by individuals is illustrated from Totagadde village in Mysore, where courts are frequently used as tools in personal feuds. A man brings a case to court when he believes he can score better over his antagonist there than by laying the case before a panchayat, where the true facts are more likely to be ascertained and the record and personality of the disputants weighed in the balance (Harper and Harper 1959, p. 464).

Litigation figures also in the struggles between alliances in Kishan Garhi village (Aligarh district, U.P.) where, on the average, a new court case is entered each month. There were usually about three such cases pending at any one time when Marriott studied the village (1955b, p. 175). Struggles between jatis as well as alliances are waged through the courts by villagers of Senapur (Jaunpur district, U.P.). A landowner of the dominant Thakur jati who takes a case to court usually anticipates not just one quick case but a series of legal battles, adjournments, appeals and counterappeals, by which a poorer competitor can be ruined. "Since British procedure and justice appeared capricious to the Indians, someone with a bad case was as prone to go to court as someone with a good case." The prestige of a family was much enhanced by success in litigation and its power was heightened if it could ruin competitors through the agency of the courts (Cohn 1959a, p. 93).

Only the stronger competitors can afford a trial of strength at official law. Moreover, it is a more ruthless way to gain advantage, as Dumont points out in discussing courts and panchayats among the Kallar of southern Madras. A Kallar uses an official court when he seeks to ruin an adversary by any means, because the panchayat is too reasonable, too well informed, too careful of reconciliation "pour servir ce romantisme de la querrelle . . ." (1957b, p. 306).

Only the stronger families or alliances can purchase the legal
services needed to draw up charges and to steer a case through the
courts. Only they can mobilize the manpower needed to stage a
legally convincing scene and to supply suitably briefed and
staunchly unwavering witnesses. Occasionally a poor Kallar will
resort to the courts, but only if he is particularly stubborn and
foolhardy, and unusually convinced of the merits of his case.

Villagers sometimes fabricate a legal complaint as a means of
enforcing a panchayat ruling or of exerting pressure. In Sirkanda,
a hill village near Mussoorie, three of the disputes analyzed by
Berreman were so concocted. "In each case grievances which could
not be successfully brought to a court of law were resolved by
manufacturing a case which could be decided by the courts." In
one case a man involved in an illicit sexual affair was brought to
court on a charge of assault and rape and was punished by the court;
it was the only case of rape, either actual or alleged, ever known
in this locality. In another case villagers resented one man's prosperity; they hid liquor in his house and then told the police that he
was dealing in illegal liquor. The third case was of a villager of
lower jati who was considered to be intolerably insolent by men of
higher rank; he found himself in court charged with theft (1963,
pp. 270–272).

Civil proceedings are also staged for competitive advantage. Land
can sometimes be pried loose by litigation. In one West Bengal
village it is a main way of obtaining land. "Thus, a well-to-do man
who finds some claim, however ephemeral, to the land of a poorer
man, may consider it a wise investment to pursue the matter
through the courts." The poorer man, knowing he cannot sustain
a long legal struggle, may sell his land at a reduced price to another
man who does have the resources for a court fight. This sets two
prominent villagers at odds with one another or strengthens an
already existing rivalry (Nicholas and Mukhopadhyay 1964, p. 28).

The British judges who had to apply the official law were generally aware of its shortcomings. The author of one of the earlier
works on Hindu law examined the legal opinions delivered in every
court of the Presidency of Bengal from 1811 to 1828 and found
that "at least nine-tenths of the opinions were ascertained on
examination to be erroneous, doubtful, unsupported by proof or
otherwise unfit for publication" (quoted in Cohn, 1961c, pp. 624–

625). The author of a modern compendium of Hindu law comments that "a surprising amount of 19th century case-law is only partly competent, or even, frankly bad. The student should not look at any pre-1930 case in Hindu law which is not mentioned in this book; and even where one is cited he should approach it with reserve" (Derrett 1963, p. 6).

A former member of the Indian Civil Service, Penderel Moon, wrote about the puzzlement felt by a young officer when he recognized how the law actually worked: "Litigation has become a national pastime and the criminal law a recognized and well-tried means of harassing, imprisoning, and even hanging one's enemies." He found that every official who had anything to do with the criminal administration was aware that the courts were "a sham and a mockery," each one deplored it, and yet nothing could be done about it (1945, pp. 53–54).

The judges were honest and villagers could count on that. The judges could not be manipulated, but the law could be. Once the legal framework of a case was properly contrived, the judge had little or no alternative but to issue the verdict desired by the contrivers. It was too much to ask of government officials, whether British or Indian, that they give up the postulates and procedures of the official law and it was impossible for most villagers to accept postulates and procedures that were so incongruent with the realities of their society. Since independence, there have been notable changes in official law, but thoughtful and responsible officials still deplore the gap between the purposes of the law and the results of its use in the village milieu.

If the law has indeed been so ill-adapted to the maintenance of village society, how could it serve to maintain a state whose people are, in great majority, villagers? The answer is partly that the official law and the customary law have been used as parallel codes, each influencing the other, but each sovereign in a different domain and neither absolutely inimical to the other.

Just as individuals or alliances will wage the competitive struggle with their rivals through the courts, suitably transposing the issues into terms a court will comprehend, so a jati or an allied set of jatis may carry the struggle for higher status into the courts. During British rule, court rulings were handed down on the varna status of such jati groupings as those of the Kayasths and Marathas, and of such sect-based jatis as the Lingayats and Jains (McCormack 1959, pp. 23–30).

Fighting the jati's good fight in the legal battlegrounds is seen by villagers as an entirely proper thing to do, but hauling a jati fellow to court over an issue internal to the jati is not generally approved. It is done frequently enough, but usually in the face of social pressure against taking an internal affair into the external lists (cf. Cohn 1965, p. 107). This pressure is sometimes explicitly stated, as it was in an assembly of Mahanayaka Sudras, cultivators in Puri district, Orissa. At a meeting of this assembly in 1935, one of the recorded decisions was that no member should file legal proceedings in connection with caste observances. "In case one does so he will be outcasted till the Assembly of Nine-Regions decides one way or the other. No assembly of any single region or sub-region or an area will have the right to lift the boycott" (Patnaik 1960a, p. 88).

The difference between court and panchayat powers is illustrated in the account of a dispute between two Vokkaligas of Wangala village. The quarrel had been going on for five years when Scarlett Epstein observed it in 1954–1955. It was about the ownership of a quarter-acre of land. One claimant, Kempa, had strong support in the panchayat. The other, Timma, had won a number of legal appeals and was entitled to get police protection if anyone interfered with his cultivating the plot. But when Timma's wife began to plant seedlings, Kempa and his brothers stopped her. Timma brought a policeman from town who warned Kempa that he must not interfere. Yet after the police had gone Timma still did not dare to use the land. Police protection is a sometime thing; the danger from village antagonists is constant.

Shortly thereafter a compromise was suggested in a panchayat meeting: that the plot be equally divided between the two. Both men had already spent at least double the market price in legal fees, but neither was yet ready to compromise. Kempa belonged to a leading lineage and a strong alliance. Timma was of an inferior lineage and had to make recourse to the law because he had little power in the village. Kempa's strength had effectively blocked the legal writ. When Mrs. Epstein left the village, the case was still unsettled and the disputed land remained uncultivated (1962, pp. 123–124).

As a member of the jati, a man generally prefers to have disputes settled through the jati panchayat. But as a partisan in a contest, he feels he should avail himself of whatever means will advance his cause. If he believes that he can gain personal advantage through using the courts, he is likely to do so despite his contrary views when he is an interested onlooker rather than an engaged contestant.

Now that more villagers can use the law and government laws impinge ever more deeply into village affairs, the competition for status and power is increasingly staged in the arena of the courts. Nevertheless, much of the settlement of internal disputes and of the redress of ritual breaches continues to be handled by jati fellows through their own jural resources rather than by external legal agencies.

THE people of a jati do more collectively than regulate their internal affairs. They commonly carry on joint enterprises; they usually work together to advance and defend the jati's status in its local order. In addition, they take the jati as a prime focus of personal identification and as a primary cultural social unit.

Jati Enterprises

The annual rites for lineage or jati deities, among those who have them, require joint planning and preparation. If there is a jati temple, subscriptions may have to be collected for its upkeep. If the jati-group has a part to play in a village festival, its panchayat assigns the various roles and sees to the provision of needed materials and facilities. A feast is commonly a salient feature of such festivities. A panchayat arranges for the food and for the special cooking utensils that are needed. These utensils are group property; their care is entrusted to a respected and reliable member of the group. In such ceremonial activities people see their group physically defined; each one's place in it is made manifest in action. In a lineage rite only brethren of the lineage are active participants; all others are spectators. The boundaries of the lineage are then clearly defined and the hierarchy within the lineage clearly demarcated as elders, juniors, and women have their respective parts to play (cf. Mandelbaum 1954b). During village ceremonies in which several jatis cooperate each jati has its traditional assignment. Jati members can take pride in the honor of the assignment and in the merit of its performance. If there is argument between two jatis for a ritual privilege, each side gives battle in a spirit of jati solidarity.

Secular enterprises are occasionally undertaken by a jati-group or jati although they tend to be more in the province of the village council. The Harijans in a village generally use separate wells. Where there is more than one sizable jati-group of Harijans, each likes to have its own well. The sinking of such a well is the concern of the jati-group. Among the Balahis the decision to do so is made at a panchayat meeting. The headman is authorized to collect a share of the expenses from each family and he assigns the work to be contributed by each adult. "Whoever fails to pay his due or does not appear for work, is excluded from the use of the well after its completion" (Fuchs 1950, p. 40).

Among the Kotas, work parties would be organized to complete a specific task, as the laying of a roof, which needed more labor than a single family could muster at one time. Each family was expected to send a worker, usually one of the younger people. The work was done with singing and ribald repartee and was capped by a feast. This kind of mutual help has largely lapsed, labor is now mustered by wages rather than jati obligation, but many an old villager in the mid-twentieth century fondly remembered the good times he had, in retrospect at least, as a participant in the work parties of his youth.

Efforts to preserve or improve jati status are not matters of nostalgic reminiscence; they are lively, ongoing, common occurrences in village life. When a panchayat of a low-ranking jati meets to defend its rights, the principal weapon at its command is the boycott. The council may decree that all members of the jati should withdraw from jajmani relations, trusting that the need for their services will bring the other group to terms. Such strike action by a jati-group requires backing by a jati panchayat; otherwise the recalcitrant patrons may get the goods and services from other villages. It also presumes that the patrons cannot get along without these services. But as alternate sources of supply have become increasingly available, this power of the artisan and serving jatis has diminished. Thus in a village of Delhi State, the dominant Jats decided to reduce the fees paid to a family's barber for his part in the marriage arrangements. The local barbers refused to accept the reduction, whereupon the patrons entirely dispensed with the function of barbers at Jat weddings. At this the barbers stopped all their services to the Jats, including shaving and hair cutting. Some Jats began to shave themselves, others found willing barbers elsewhere, and the barbers' strike was broken (Lewis 1958, pp. 66–67, 82).

Another example of the breaking of a strike is from Khalapur in western U.P. There an untouchable group refused to perform their traditional task of removing dead cattle. The dominant Rajputs were inconvenienced, but, more important, "They saw the move as a threat to the social order." [1] There are deep factional cleavages among the Rajputs of this village, yet they stood together against the recusants. The Harijan house sites belonged to the Rajputs, and even though government rulings have set aside claims to this ownership, the villagers still feel that the Rajputs can evict others from their houses. Also the Rajput landowners can, if they like, prevent people of the lower jatis from using the fields for latrine purposes or for gathering fodder. The unified Rajput reaction quickly restored the traditional carcass-removal service by the Harijans (Minturn and Hitchcock 1966, p. 48).

The spur to much of a jati's joint enterprise is the pressure for advancing or defending jati status. Such efforts are examined in the later chapters on social mobility. Villagers of lower jatis commonly feel that their jati is inherently entitled to a higher place in the order than is generally assigned to it. As soon as they think they have the resources to do so, they try to make good their claims. From their viewpoint, they are not asserting any new status, but only restoring the rank that had been theirs in earlier times. So when Harijan villagers try to throw off debasing customs and to take on more elevated practices, they are not attempting to replace the highest jatis in their local systems and still less to do away with the hierarchical order, but rather to be accorded honorable place in one of the levels above the lowest.

The thrust for status rise is reflected in some of the early Buddhist writings concerning guilds of artisans. A guild had many of the functions of the later jatis. It fixed rules of work and wages, standards and prices; it had juridical authority over its members and that

---

[1] When the dominant Havik Brahmins of Totagadde in Mysore were confronted with the same kind of refusal, they did not interpret it as did the Rajputs of Khalapur. Although they seem to be as strongly dominant in their village as the Rajputs are in Khalapur, and more ritually meticulous, they found a scriptural passage that, as they interpreted it, permitted Brahmins to remove dead cattle. Therefore they did not take drastic steps against the recalcitrant Harijans (Harper 1968).

authority was upheld by king and government. Each guild was jealous of its prerogatives; each pressed its claims against competitors of other guilds, sometimes to the point of street battles and riots (Basham 1954, pp. 217–218). In more recent times, the records of the court of the Peshwas in the eighteenth century show that many jatis protested to government about being restricted to unduly low jati practices (Ghurye 1961, pp. 186–187).

The traditional methods of jati improvement have been expanded in modern times. Improved communications have contributed to the widening of social horizons, as have new economic opportunities and the new possibilities of political power. Education for the jati's youth has become an essential feature of a program for jati improvement. Jatis of a close cluster tend to merge and so give added strength to jati endeavor. In order to take advantage of the newer means of jati elevation, a different kind of organization is required, with elected representatives and empowered officials, regular meetings and jati publications, all usually fashioned after the models of government agencies or political parties. These modern jati enterprises are also discussed below in relation to social change.

Variations in Jati Organization

Jatis vary greatly in the extent and effectiveness of jati organization. We have mentioned this in connection with internal alliances; it applies as well to their external relations. Hutton reports, "It has frequently been observed that the lower the caste in the social scale, the stronger its combination and the more efficient its organization" (1961, p. 99). This generalization was based mainly on the observations of British administrators; it is borne out by some of the anthropological studies.

Thus in a village of Kanpur district (U.P.) the highest ranking jatis do not have intervillage panchayats while most others do (Sharma 1956a, pp. 298–301). Similarly, in Totagadde village in Mysore, the formal jati organization—both intravillage and intervillage—of the Harijans, "who are repressed by all other castes," is more tightly knit than that of the jatis of the Sudra category. Most loosely organized is that of the Havik Brahmins (Harper and Harper 1959, p. 461). The reason for the greater unity, the authors suggest, is that the lower jatis need to muster their strength against the

dominant landowners, while the men of the dominant jati, firm in
their power, do not have such a need. Yet in another Mysore village,
Wangala, the Harijans have no panchayat organization beyond the
village (Epstein 1962, p. 118), perhaps because they are even worse
off than are the Harijans of Totagadde.

When a jati-group is very poor and totally dependent, its people
cannot afford to organize at all beyond the village. This holds true
of whole villages where all the inhabitants are poor and quite completely at the mercy of outside landowners. In the parts of West
Bengal, for example, where village lands were owned by a few
dominant landowners or a single one, the landowners made most
decisions and panchayats of any kind were rare and feeble. In those
Bengal villages where land ownership was more widely shared,
there was a corresponding increase in panchayat activity and effectiveness (Nicholas and Mukhopadhyay 1964, pp. 36–38).

Rivalry, rather than poverty or dependence, is a main cause for
the looser cohesion of many higher jatis. For example, the Brahmin
landowners of Kumbapettai village (Tanjore district) maintained
little in the way of jati or jati-group organization at the time of
Gough's study of them. Quarrels between families of the strongly
dominant Brahmin jati "drag on in a desultory manner for months,
sometimes years, until both parties are weary or kinship or ceremonial obligations draw them together again" (Gough 1955, p. 44).
These Brahmins would gather in council to preserve a ritual norm
or to punish rebels of low jati, but this was not often necessary. As
for other matters, a Brahmin landowner does not particularly need
to cooperate with his peers, either economically or socially. He is
trained from childhood to value the dependent relation of son upon
father rather than the cooperative relationship among brothers. In
the low jatis, as we have noted, a father's authority is relatively
short-lived; it is broken shortly after a boy's puberty, when the boy
becomes an independent wage earner. In such jatis the main emphasis is on the equivalence and solidarity of peers and on the solidarity
of the jati-group and jati (Gough 1956, pp. 845–846).

Some social variations and cultural differences within a jati are to
be expected. Jati fellows do not always march as a close social company, hewing to a set direction, fulfilling given functions, and me-
chanically correcting deviations. Commonly there are differences in
wealth and power, in goals and ideals, in worship and occupation.

But in certain matters, particularly those that involve permanent pollution, the people of a jati impose sharp limits on possible deviation by any of their fellows.

Jati as Means of Identity and as Social Unit

Despite such variation within his jati, a villager typically holds strong feelings of jati identification and cohesion. He feels so strongly identified with his jati in part because there are few or no alternatives to claim his loyalty, but mostly because he has been identified as a jati member by others through all his life and he identifies himself as such. He does so because a very large part of all his social relations are within his jati. It is, first of all, the harbor of his kin; all his kinsmen are of the jati, none are outside it.

The valence of kinship helps to hold a jati together, despite the rivalries that beat at its unity. Men of one village may be at odds with their jati fellows in another village. Yet each side may well have affinal relatives in the other locality, and a man does not like to be long estranged from these kinsmen. So it goes through the intricate web of kinship. Thus disunity in the jati is diminished, if not always and for everyone, still often and for many of the jati.

There is, further, the bond of common interest in work and livelihood. A potter does not have the same economic concerns as does an astrologer, nor does a farmer find as close understanding with a merchant as he does with another farmer of his own jati. Even if only a few in a jati-group actually practice the traditional occupation, most are apt to be in a similar economic range of occupation. A man's friends in the village are most often of his jati; all the more so for a woman, whose movements and social contacts are more restricted.

The great ritual events of the life cycle, marriages and funerals, bring together gatherings of kin, that is, of jati fellows. When a person goes to another village he usually visits with his jati fellows there. Communication between villages is largely between people of the same jati. Within a village, different jatis or blocs of jatis may use different dialects as their home language (Gumperz 1958, 1961; Bright 1960; McCormack 1960).

A child learns quite early to discriminate between his jati fellows and those of other jatis. He absorbs the self-image of his jati in countless ways. A Rajput boy learns about the martial style and regal tradition of his group by the bearing of his elders, by their contemptuous references to lesser breeds, by the tales, proverbs, and ballads he hears frequently. He may later reject that ethos, but he is not often indifferent to it (cf. Hitchcock 1958). Similarly, one who was reared as an orthodox Brahmin may later deliberately leave behind his early training, but it does not usually leave him. He tends to prize learning, to disparage physical aggression, and to be personally fastidious, quite in the manner of his jati.

It is not only the higher jatis who entertain flattering views of themselves and have heroic tales to prove it. One of the great folk epics of northern India, the Lay of Lorik, is sung by Ahirs about one of their forebears. Ahirs are traditionally herdsmen and are not ranked among the higher jatis (Deva 1958, pp. 87–89). Even the very lowest jatis have explanatory tales telling how they fell from a higher state through no great fault of their own (cf. Reddy 1952, pp. 334–341; Fuchs 1950, pp. 235–237). The essential message of the origin legend of the tribal Konds, as summarized by Bailey, is duplicated in the origin myth of many lower jatis: "Konds belong to the same community as the rulers; Konds are a dominant caste; they have fallen because they are a little stupid and unlucky, and have had to come and live in the jungle, but in origin they are warriors and the associates of kings" (1960b, p. 161).

So a villager identifies closely with his jati because much of his social world is encompassed within it and because his concept of himself is part of his jati's idea of what kind of people they are. Coupled with this self-identification is his constant identification by others as one of his jati. Jati is a principal referent in village life and although one villager deals with another in terms of grosser categories jati is nonetheless at the basis of reference. Moreover, a villager's drive for higher status is tied to the status of his jati. He cannot rise much higher than its level and if his jati should fall in status he is bound to decline with it. From the inside view of the villager, his allegiance to jati is inevitable, necessary, and morally proper.

When jatis are surveyed from the observer's analytic view, the jati is seen as a main cultural and social unit in the larger system. On close examination many jatis turn out to be much less firmly bounded and distinctive than their members take them to be. Culturally, some jatis are indeed quite distinctive within their localities, but many more differ only slightly in ways of life from other jatis of the same level and vicinity. Whatever the actual degree of cultural difference may be, the salient factor for the system is that villagers think of jatis as culturally distinct from one another. This accords with their view that each jati is socially separate from all others in kinship matters. We have noted that jati boundaries are sometimes blurred in reality and that the exact range of jati membership is often unknown to its members. This does not impair the social system, however, principally because villagers assume that jatis are firm units. The fuzziness of jati boundaries has helped give flexibility to the system; because of it jatis could form and reform adaptively.

People use themes of behavior within the jati similar to those that they use in relations among jatis. Moreover, when a man acts to maintain a component of his jati, say his lineage or jati-group, he is thereby also helping to maintain the whole jati. Similarly, when he acts to uphold his jati, he is also contributing to the maintenance of the local system of relations among jatis. The main social context for these relations among people of different jatis is the village; it is another of the chief components of the social system.

Bibliography

AGARWALA, B. R.
  1955 In a mobile commercial community. *In* Symposium: caste and joint family. Sociological Bulletin 4:138–146.
AGGARWAL, PARTAP C.
  1966 A Muslim sub-caste of North India: problems of cultural integration. Economic and Political Weekly 1:159–167.
AHMAD, AZIZ
  1964 Studies in Islamic culture in the Indian environment. Oxford: Clarendon Press.
AHMAD, IMTIAZ
  1965 Social stratification among Muslims. The Economic Weekly 10: 1093–1096.
AHMAD, ZARINA
  1962 Muslim caste in Uttar Pradesh. The Economic Weekly 14:325–336.
AIYAPPAN, A.
  1937 Social and physical anthropology of the Nayadis of Malabar. Bulletin of the Madras Government Museum, n.s., Volume 2, No. 4.
  1944 Iravas and culture change. Bulletin of the Madras Government Museum, n.s., Volume 5, No. 1.
  1955 In Tamilnad. Sociological Bulletin 4:117–122.
  1965 Social revolution in a Kerala village: a study in cultural change. Bombay: Asia Publishing House.
ALLISON, W. L.
  1935 The Sadhs. London and Calcutta: Oxford University Press.
AMBEDKAR, B. R.
  1948 Remarks on draft constitution. Constituent Assembly Debates, Official Reports, Volume 7, No. 1, pp. 38-39.
ANAND, K.
  1965 An analysis of matrimonial advertisements. Sociological Bulletin 14:59–71.
ANANTAKRISHNA AYYAR, L. K.
  1926 Anthropology of the Syrian Christians. Eranakulam: Cochin Government Press.
ANSARI, GHAUS
  1955 Muslim marriage in India. Wiener Völkerkundliche Mitteilungen 3:191–206.
  1960 Muslim caste in Uttar Pradesh: a study of culture contact. The Eastern Anthropologist (special number) 13:5–80.

ATAL, YOGESH
1963   Short-lived alliances as an aspect of factionalism in an Indian village. The Journal of Social Sciences (Agra) 3:65–75.
n.d.   Trends of change in village politics: a case study. Mussoorie: Cultural Institute of Study and Research in Community Development. Mimeographed, 7 pp.

BACHENHEIMER, R.
1956   Theology, economy and demography: a study of caste in an Indian village. MS., 11 pp.

BACON, ELIZABETH E. (editor)
1956   India sociological background: an area handbook. New Haven: The Human Relations Area Files.

BADEN-POWELL, B. H.
1896   The Indian village community. London: Longmans, Green and Co. (Reprinted by HRAF Press: New Haven, 1957.)

BAILEY, FREDERICK G.
1957   Caste and the economic frontier: a village in highland Orissa. Manchester: Manchester University Press.
1958   Political change in the Kondmals. The Eastern Anthropologist 11: 88–106.
1960a   The joint-family in India: a framework for discussion. The Economic Weekly 12:345–352.
1960b   Tribe, caste and nation: a study of political activity and political change in highland Orissa. Manchester: Manchester University Press.
1961   "Tribe" and "caste" in India. Contributions to Indian Sociology 5:7–19.
1963a   Closed social stratification in India. European Journal of Sociology 4:107–124.
1963b   Politics and social change: Orissa in 1959. Berkeley: University of California Press.
1964   Two villages in Orissa (India). In Closed systems and open minds: the limits of naïvety in social anthropology, Max Gluckman, editor, pp. 52–82. Chicago: Aldine Publishing Co.
1965   Decisions by concensus in councils and committees. In Political systems and the distribution of power, F. Eggan and M. Gluckman, editors, pp. 1–20. London: Tavistock Publications; New York: Frederick A. Praeger.

BAINES, ATHELSTANE
1912   Ethnography (castes and tribes). Strassburg: Trübner Verlag.

BANNERJEE, HEMENDRA NATH
1960   Community structure in an artisan village of Pargannah Barabhum. Journal of Social Research (Ranchi) 3:68–79.

BANTON, MICHAEL
1965   Roles: an introduction to the study of social relations. London: Tavistock Publications.

BARANOV, I. L.
1965   "Kastovyi bunt" v Ramnade ("The caste revolt" in Ramnad) In Kasty v Indii (Caste in India), G. G. Kotovshii, editor, pp. 262–273. Moscow: Akademiia Nauk SSSR. Institut Narodov Azii.

BARNABAS, A. P.
1961   Sanskritization. The Economic Weekly 13:613-618.

BARTH, FREDRIK
1959   Political leadership among Swat Pathans. London School of Economics. Monographs in Social Anthropology, No. 19. London.
1960   The system of social stratification in Swat, North Pakistan. *In* Aspects of caste in South India, Ceylon and Northwest Pakistan, E. R. Leach, editor, pp. 113-146. Cambridge Papers in Social Anthropology, No. 2. Cambridge: Cambridge University Press.

BASHAM, A. L.
1954   The wonder that was India. London: Sidgwick and Jackson.

BASU, N. B.
1957   Gango (an instance of Hindu method of tribal absorption). Bulletin of the Tribal Research Institute (Chhindwara) 1:40-47.

BASU, TARA KRISHNA
1962   The Bengal peasant from time to time. London and Bombay: Asia Publishing House.

BEALS, ALAN R.
1955   Change in the leadership of a Mysore village. *In* India's villages, pp. 132-143. Calcutta: West Bengal Government Press.
1959   Leadership in a Mysore village. *In* Leadership and political institutions in India, R. L. Park and Irene Tinker, editors, pp. 427-437. Princeton: Princeton University Press.
1962   Gopalpur. New York: Holt, Rinehart, and Winston.
1964   Conflict and interlocal festivals in a South Indian region. The Journal of Asian Studies 23:95-113.
1965   Crime and conflict in some South Indian villages. Mimeographed, 23 pp.
        Dravidian Kinship and Marriage. Unpublished paper.

BEALS, ALAN R. AND BERNARD J. SIEGEL
1966   Divisiveness and social conflict: an anthropological approach. Stanford: Stanford University Press.

BEBARTA, PRAFULLA C.
1966   Family type and fertility. Economic and Political Weekly 1:633-634.

BEECH, MARY JANE, O. J. BERTOCCI AND L. A. CORWIN
1966   Introducing the East Bengal village. *In* Inside the East Pakistan village. (Asian studies papers. Reprint series, 2.) East Lansing: Michigan State University.

BEIDELMAN, THOMAS O.
1959   A comparative analysis of the jajmani system. Monograph of the Association for Asian Studies, No. 8. Locust Valley, New York: J. J. Augustin.

BENDIX, REINHARD
1960   Max Weber: an intellectual portrait. New York: Doubleday.

BERREMAN, GERALD D.
1960a   Caste in India and the United States. American Journal of Sociology 66:120-127.
1960b   Cultural variability and drift in the Himalayan hills. American Anthropologist 62:774-794.

1962a Behind many masks. Ithaca: The Society for Applied Anthropology.

1962b Caste and economy in the Himalayas. Economic Development and Cultural Change 10:386-394.

1962c Pahari polyandry: a comparison. American Anthropologist 64: 60-75.

1962d Village exogamy in northernmost India. Southwestern Journal of Anthropology 18:55-58.

1963 Hindus of the Himalayas. Berkeley and Los Angeles: University of California Press.

1965 The study of caste ranking in India. Southwestern Journal of Anthropology 21:115-129.

1966 Caste in cross-cultural perspective: organizational components. *In* Japan's invisible race, George De Vos and Hiroshi Wagatsuma, editors, pp. 275-324. Berkeley and Los Angeles: University of California Press.

1967a Stratification, pluralism and interaction: a comparative analysis of caste. *In* Caste and race, comparative approaches, A. de Reuck and J. Knight, editors, pp. 45-73. London: J. and A. Churchill.

1967b Caste as social process. Southwestern Journal of Anthropology 23: 351-370.

BÉTEILLE, ANDRÉ

1962 Sripuram: a village in Tanjore district. The Economic Weekly 14:141-146.

1964 A note on the referents of caste. European Journal of Sociology 5:130-134.

1965 Caste, class and power. Berkeley and Los Angeles: University of California Press.

BHARATI, AGEHANANDA

1961 The ochre robe. London: Allen and Unwin.

1963 Pilgrimage in the Indian tradition. History of Religions 3:135-167.

1966 The decline of teknonymy: changing patterns of husband-wife appellation in India. MS., 12 pp.

BHATT, G. S.

1958 Occupational structure among the Chamars of Dehra Dun. Sociological Annual 1:32-43. Dehra Dun: Sociology Association, D. A. V. College.

BHATTACHARYA, JOGENDRA NATH

1896 Hindu castes and sects. Calcutta: Thacker, Spink and Co.

BLUNT, E. A. H.

1931 The caste system of northern India. London: Oxford University Press.

BOSE, A. B. AND N. S. JODHA

1965 The jajmani system in a desert village. Man in India 45:105-126.

BOSE, A. B. AND S. P. MALHOTRA

1964 Studies in group dynamics (1): factionalism in a desert village. Man in India 44:311-328.

BOSE, NIRMAL KUMAR

1951 Caste in India. Man in India 31:107-123.

1953a   Cultural anthropology and other essays. Second edition. Calcutta: Indian Associated Publishing Company.

1953b   The Hindu method of tribal absorption. *In his* Cultural anthropology and other essays, pp. 156–170. Calcutta: Indian Associated Publishing Co.

1954   Who are the backward classes? Man in India 34:89–98.

1956   Culture zones of India. Geographical Review of India 18:1–12.

1957   The effect of urbanization on work and leisure. Man in India 37: 1–9.

1958a   East and west in Bengal. Man in India 38:157–175.

1958b   Some aspects of caste in Bengal. Man in India 38:73–97.

1958c   Types of villages in West Bengal: a study in social change. The Economic Weekly 10:149–152.

1960   The use of proceedings of caste panchayats. Journal of Social Research (Meerut) 1:98–100.

1964   Change in tribal cultures before and after independence. Man in India 44:1–10.

BOSE, N. K. AND SURAJIT SINHA

1961   Peasant life in India: a study in unity and diversity. Anthropological Survey of India. Memoir No. 8.

BOSE, SHIB CHUNDER

1881   The Hindoos as they are. London, Calcutta: Edward Stanford, W. Newman and Co.

BOUGLÉ, CÉLESTIN

1908   Essais sur le régime des castes. Paris: Felix Alcan.

BRASS, PAUL

1967   Regions, regionalism, and research in modern Indian society and politics. *In* Regions and regionalism in South Asian studies: an exploratory study, R. I. Crane, editor, pp. 258–270. Duke University Program in Comparative Studies on South Asia. Monograph No. 5.

BRIGHT, WILLIAM

1960   Linguistic change in some Indian caste dialects. International Journal of American Linguistics 26:19–26.

BROWN, W. NORMAN

1957   The sanctity of the cow in Hinduism. Journal of the Madras University 28:29–49.

1961   The content of cultural continuity in India. The Journal of Asian Studies 20:427–434.

BUCKLEY, WALTER

1967   Sociology and modern systems theory. Englewood Cliffs, New Jersey: Prentice Hall.

BURLING, ROBBINS

1960   An incipient caste organization in the Garo Hills. Man in India 40:283–299.

CARSTAIRS, G. MORRIS

1953   The case of Thakur Khuman Singh: a culture-conditioned crime. British Journal of Delinquency 4:14–25.

1955   Attitudes to death and suicide in an Indian cultural setting. International Journal of Social Psychiatry 1:33–41.

1957   The twice born: a study of a community of high caste Hindus. London: The Hogarth Press.

1961   Patterns of religious observance in three villages of Rajasthan. Journal of Social Research (Ranchi) 4:59–113.

CASTETS, J.

1931   L'église et le problème de la caste au XVIe siècle. Revue d'Histoire des Missions 8:547–565.

CHANANA, DEV RAJ

1961a   Caste and mobility. The Economic Weekly 13:1561–1562.

1961b   Sanskritisation, westernisation and India's Northwest. The Economic Weekly 13:409–414.

CHAUHAN, BRIJ RAJ

1960   An Indian village: some questions. Man in India 40:116–127.

CHHIBBAR, Y. P.

1968   From caste to class, a study of the Indian middle classes. New Delhi: Associated Publishing House.

COHN, BERNARD S.

1955   The changing status of a depressed caste. In Village India, M. Marriott, editor, pp. 53–77. Chicago: University of Chicago Press.

1957   India as a racial, linguistic and cultural area. In Introducing India in liberal education, Milton Singer, editor, pp. 51–68. Chicago: University of Chicago Press.

1959a   Some notes on law and change in North India. Economic Development and Cultural Change 8:79–93.

1959b   Madhopur revisited. The Economic Weekly 11:963–966.

1960   The initial British impact on India: a case study of the Benares region. The Journal of Asian Studies 19:418–431.

1961a   Chamar family in a North Indian village. The Economic Weekly 13:1051–1055.

1961b   The development and impact of British administration in India. New Delhi: Indian Institute of Public Administration.

1961c   From Indian status to British contract. Journal of Economic History 21:613–628.

1961d   The pasts of an Indian village. Comparative Studies in Society and History 3:241–249.

1962   Review of M. Marriott, caste ranking and community structure in five regions of India and Pakistan. Journal of the American Oriental Society 82:425–430.

1965   Anthropological notes on disputes and law in India. American Anthropologist 67:82–122.

1967   Regions, subjective and objective: their relation to the study of modern Indian history and society. In Regions and regionalism in South Asian studies: an exploratory study, R. I. Crane, editor, pp. 5–37. Duke University Program in Comparative Studies in Southern Asia. Monograph No. 5.

COHN, BERNARD S. AND MCKIM MARRIOTT

1958   Networks and centres in the integration of Indian civilisation. Journal of Social Research (Ranchi) 1:1–9.

COLE, B. L.

1932   The Rajput clans of Rajputana. Census of India, 1931, 27:134–141.

COLLVER, ANDREW
1963   The family cycle in India and the United States. American Socio-
        logical Review 28:86–96.
CORMACK, MARGARET L.
1961   She who rides a peacock. New York: Frederick A. Praeger.
CRONIN, VINCENT
1959   A pearl to India. New York: E. P. Dutton.
CULSHAW, W. J.
1949   Tribal heritage: a study of the Santals. London: Lutterworth
        Press.
DAHRENDORF, RALF
1966   Review of G. Lenski, power and privilege. American Sociological
        Review 31:714–718.
DAMES, MANSEL LONGWORTH (editor)
1918   The book of Duarte Barbosa, Volume 1 (Volume 2, 1921).
        London: The Hakluyt Society.
DAMLE, Y. B.
1963   Reference group theory with regard to mobility in caste. Social
        Action, April 1963.
DANDEKAR, V. M. AND KUMUDINI DANDEKAR
1953   Survey of fertility and mortality in Poona District. Poona: Gok-
        hale Institute of Politics and Economics.
DARLING, MALCOLM LYALL
1934   Wisdom and waste in the Punjab village. London: Oxford Uni-
        versity Press.
DAS GUPTA, BIWAN KUMAR
1962   Caste mobility among the Mahato of South Manbhum. Man in
        India 42:228–236.
DATTA GUPTA, JAYA
1959   A study on the Paundra Kshatriya of West Bengal. Bulletin of
        the Department of Anthropology, Government of India 8:109–
        130.
DATTA-MAJUMDER, NABENDU
1956   The Santal: a study in culture change. Department of Anthropol-
        ogy, Government of India. Memoir No. 2.
DAVIS, KINGSLEY
1951   The population of India and Pakistan. Princeton: Princeton Uni-
        versity Press.
DE, BARUN
1967   A historical perspective on theories of regionalism in India. In Re-
        gions and regionalism in South Asian studies: an exploratory study,
        R. I. Crane, editor, pp. 48–88. Duke University Program in Com-
        parative Studies in Southern Asia. Monograph No. 5.
DEMING, WILBUR S.
1928   Rāmdās and the Rāmdāsis. London, Calcutta: Oxford University
        Press.
DERRETT, J. DUNCAN M.
1960   Law and the predicament of the Hindu joint family. The Eco-
        nomic Weekly 12:305–311.

1961   Illegitimates: a test for modern Hindu family law. Journal of the American Oriental Society 81:251–261.
1962   The history of the juridical framework of the joint Hindu family. Contributions to Indian Sociology 6:17–47.
1963   Introduction to modern Hindu law. Bombay: Oxford University Press.

DESAI, I. P.
1955   An analysis. In Symposium: caste and joint family. Sociological Bulletin 4:97–117.
1956   The joint family in India: an analysis. Sociological Bulletin 5:144–156.
1964   Some aspects of family in Mahuva. New York: Asia Publishing House.

DESHPANDE, KAMALABAI
1963   Divorce cases in the court of Poona, an analysis. The Economic Weekly 15:1179–1183.

DEVA, INDRA
1958   The sociology of Bhojpuri folk-literature. Doctoral thesis, Lucknow University.

DEVONS, ELY AND MAX GLUCKMAN
1964   Conclusion: modes and consequences of limiting a field of study. In Closed systems and open minds: the limits of naïvety in social anthropology, Max Gluckman, editor, pp. 158–261. Chicago: Aldine Publishing Co.

DE VOS, GEORGE
1967   Discussion. In Caste and race: comparative approaches, A. de Reuck and J. Knight, editors, pp. 74–77. London: J. and A. Churchill.

DE VOS, GEORGE AND H. WAGATSUMA
1966   Japan's invisible race: caste in culture and personality. Berkeley: University of California Press.

DHILLON, HARWANT SINGH
1955   Leadership and groups in a South Indian village. Planning Commission, Programme Evaluation Organisation. New Delhi: Government of India. P. E. O. Publication No. 9.

DIEHL, CARL GUSTAV
1956   Instrument and purpose: studies on rites and rituals in South India. Lund: Gleerup.

DREKMEIER, CHARLES
1962   Kingship and community in early India. Stanford: Stanford University Press.

DRIVER, EDWIN D.
1963   Differential fertility in central India: Princeton: Princeton University Press.

DUBE, S. C.
1955a A Deccan village. In India's villages, pp. 180–192. Calcutta: West Bengal Government Press. (Second edition, 1960, M. N. Srinivas, editor, pp. 202–215. London: Asia Publishing House.)
1955b Indian village. Ithaca, New York: Cornell University Press.

1955c   Ranking of castes in a Telengana village. The Eastern Anthropologist 8:182–190.

1956   Cultural factors in rural community development. *In* The Indian village: a symposium. The Journal of Asian Studies 16:19–30.

1958   India's changing villages. Ithaca, New York: Cornell University Press.

1960   Approaches to the tribal problem. Journal of Social Research 3: 11–15.

DUBOIS, JEAN ANTOIN, ABBÉ

1928   Hindu manners, customs and ceremonies. (Translated by Henry K. Beauchamp.) Oxford: Clarendon Press.

DUMONT, LOUIS

1951   Kinship and alliance among the Pramalai Kallar. The Eastern Anthropologist 4:3–26.

1953   The Dravidian kinship terminology as an expression of marriage. Man 54:34–39.

1957a   Hierarchy and marriage alliance in South Indian kinship. Occasional Papers of the Royal Anthropological Institute, No. 12. London: Royal Anthropological Institute.

1957b   Une sous caste de l'Inde du sud. Paris: Mouton.

1959   Dowry in Hindu marriage as a social scientist sees it. The Economic Weekly 11:519–520.

1960   World renunciation in Indian religions. Contributions to Indian Sociology 4:33–62.

1961a   Les marriages Nayar comme faits indiens. L'Homme, Revue Francaise d'Anthropologie 1:11–36.

1961b   Marriage in India: the present state of the question. Contributions to Indian Sociology 5:75–95.

1962   "Tribe" and "caste" in India. Contributions to Indian Sociology 6:120–122.

1963   Le mariage secondaire dans l'Inde du nord. Paris: VIth International Congress of Anthropological and Ethnological Sciences 2: 53–55.

1964a   Marriage in India: the present state of the question; postscript to part one. Contributions to Indian Sociology 7:77–98.

1964b   A note on locality in relation to descent. Contributions to Indian Sociology 7:71–76.

1966   Homo hierarchicus. Essai sur le système des castes. Paris: Gallimard.

1967   Caste: a phenomenon of social structure or an aspect of Indian culture? *In* Caste and race, comparative approaches, A. de Reuck and J. Knight, editors, pp. 28–38. London: J. and A. Churchill.

DUMONT, LOUIS AND D. POCOCK

1957a   For a sociology of India. Contributions to Indian Sociology 1:7–22.

1957b   Village studies. Contributions to Indian Sociology 1:23–42.

1957c   Kinship. Contributions to Indian Sociology 1:43–64.

1960   For a sociology of India: a rejoinder to Dr. Bailey. Contributions to Indian Sociology 4:82–89.

DUTT, NRIPENDRA KUMAR
1931　Origin and growth of caste in India. London: Kegan Paul, Trench, Trübner.

EDGERTON, FRANKLIN
1952　The Bhagavad Gītā. Part 2: Interpretation and Arnold's translation. Cambridge: Harvard University Press.

EGLAR, ZEKIYE
1960　A Punjabi village in Pakistan. New York: Columbia University Press.

ELWIN, VERRIER
1964　The tribal world of Verrier Elwin. New York and Bombay: Oxford University Press.

EMENEAU, MURRAY B.
1956　India as a linguistic area. Language 32:3–16.

EPSTEIN, T. SCARLETT
1959　A sociological analysis of witch beliefs in a Mysore village. The Eastern Anthropologist 12:234–251.
1960　Economic development and peasant marriage in South India. Man in India 40:192–232.
1962　Economic development and social change in South India. Manchester University Press; New York: The Humanities Press.

FARQUHAR, J. N.
1920　An outline of the religious literature of India. London: Oxford University Press.

FERGUSON, FRANCES N.
1963　The master-disciple relationship in India. Research Reviews (University of North Carolina) 10:22–26.

FERNANDEZ, FRANK
1965　Indian tribal societies: tribal or peasant? MS., 13 pp. (Mimeo.)

FISCHEL, WALTER J.
1962　Cochin in Jewish history. American Academy for Jewish Research, Proceedings 30:37–59.
1967　The exploration of the Jewish antiquities of Cochin on the Malabar Coast: a historical-critical survey. Journal of the American Oriental Society 87:30–51.

FORTES, MEYER
1958　Introduction. In The developmental cycle in domestic groups, pp. 1–14. Cambridge Papers in Social Anthropology, No. 1. Cambridge: University Press.

FOSTER, GEORGE M.
1965　Peasant society and the image of limited good. American Anthropologist 67:293–315.
1966　Foster's reply to Kaplan, Saler and Bennett. American Anthropologist 68:210–214.

FOX, RICHARD G.
1967　Resiliency and culture in the Indian caste system: the Umar of U. P. The Journal of Asian Studies 26:575–587.

FREED, STANLEY A.
1963a　Fictive leadership in a North Indian village. Ethnology 2:86–103.

1963b An objective method for determining the collective caste hierarchy of an Indian village. American Anthropologist 65:879–891.

FREED, RUTH A. AND STANLEY A. FREED
1964 Spirit possession as illness in a North Indian village. Ethnology 3: 152–171.
1966 Unity in diversity in the celebration of cattle-curing rites in a North Indian village: a study in the resolution of conflict. American Anthropologist 68:673–692.

FREEDMAN, MAURICE
1962 The family in China: past and present. Pacific Affairs 34:323–336.

FRYKENBERG, ROBERT ERIC
1963 Traditional processes of power in South India: an historical analysis of local influence. Indian Economic and Social History Review 1:1–21.

FUCHS, STEPHEN
1950 The children of Hari: a study of the Nimar Balahis in the Central Provinces of India. Vienna: Verlag Herold.
1960 The Gond and the Bhumia of Eastern Mandla. New York, Bombay: Asia Publishing House.

FUKUTAKE, TADASHI, TSUTOMU OUCHI, AND CHIE NAKANE
1964 The socio-economic structure of the Indian village. Tokyo: Institute of Asian Economic Affairs.

FÜRER-HAIMENDORF, CHRISTOPH VON
1943 The Chenchus: jungle folk of the Deccan. London. Macmillan.
1945 The Reddis of the Bison Hills. London: Macmillan.
1967a Morals and merit: a study of values and social controls in South Asian societies. Chicago: University of Chicago Press.
1967b The position of tribal populations in modern India. In India and Ceylon: unity and diversity, P. Mason, editor, pp. 182–222. New York: Oxford University Press.

GADGIL, D. R.
1965 Women in the working force in India. Bombay: Asia Publishing House.

GAIT, E. A.
1913 Census of India, 1911, Volume 1, part 1. Report. Calcutta: Government Printing Office.

GALANTER, MARC
1963 Law and caste in modern India. Asian Survey 3:544–559.
1964 Hindu law and the development of the modern Indian legal system. Mimeographed, 32 pp.
1965 Legal materials for the study of Modern India. Appendix: Hindu law and the modern Indian legal system. Mimeographed. The College, University of Chicago.
1966a The modernization of law. In Modernization: the dynamics of growth, M. Weiner, editor, pp. 153–165. New York: Basic Books.
1966b The problem of group membership: some reflections on the judicial view of Indian society. In Class, status and power, R. Bendix and S. M. Lipset, editors, pp. 628–640. Second edition. New York: Free Press. (Reprinted from The Journal of the Indian Law Institute, 1962, 4:331–358.)

GANDHI. MOHANDAS K.
1940   An autobiography or the story of my experiments with truth. (Translated from the original in Gujarati by Madadev Desai.) Ahmedabad: Navajivan Publishing House.

GANGARADE, K. D.
1963   Dynamics of a panchayat election. Avard (Journal of the Association of Voluntary Agencies for Rural Development, New Delhi) 5:5–8.
1964   Conflicting value system and social case work. The Journal of Social Work 24:247–256.

GARDNER, PETER M.
1966   Symmetric respect and memorate knowledge: the structure and ecology of individualistic culture. Southwestern Journal of Anthropology 22:389–415.

GEERTZ, CLIFFORD
1960   The Javanese kikaji: the changing role of a cultural broker. Comparative Studies in Society and History 2:228–249.
1963   Agricultural involution: the process of ecological change in Indonesia. Berkeley and Los Angeles: University of California Press.

GHURYE, G. S.
1953   Indian sadhus. Bombay: The Popular Book Depot.
1959   The scheduled tribes. Second edition. Bombay: The Popular Book Depot.
1960   After a century and a quarter: Lonikand then and now. Bombay: The Popular Book Depot.
1961   Class, caste and occupation. Bombay: The Popular Book Depot.

GIDEON, HELEN
1962   A baby is born in the Punjab. American Anthropologist 64:1220–1234.

GIST, NOEL P.
1953   Mate selection and mass communication in India. Public Opinion Quarterly 17:481–495.
1954   Occupational differentiation in South India. Social Forces 33:129–138.
1955   Selective migration in South India. Sociological Bulletin 4:147–160.

GNANAMBAL, K.
1960   Ethnography of Gannapur. Cyclostyled, 127 pp.

GOODE, WILLIAM J.
1963   World revolution and family patterns. New York: The Free Press of Glencoe.

GOPALASWAMI, R. A.
1953   Census of India, 1951, Volume 1, India, part 1-A. Report. New Delhi: Government of India Press.

GORE, M. S.
1961   The husband-wife and the mother-son relationships. Sociological Bulletin 11:91–102.
1965   The traditional Indian family. In Comparative family systems, M. F. Nimkoff, editor, pp. 209–231. Boston: Houghton Mifflin.
1968   Urbanization and family change. Bombay: Popular Prakashan.

GOUGH, E. KATHLEEN
1955   The social structure of a Tanjore village. *In* Village India, M. Mar-
         riott, editor, pp. 36–52. Chicago: University of Chicago Press.
1956   Brahmin kinship in a Tamil village. American Anthropologist 58:
         384–853.
1960   Caste in a Tanjore village. *In* Aspects of caste in South India, Cey-
         lon, and North-West Pakistan, E. R. Leach, editor, pp. 11–60.
         Cambridge Papers in Social Anthropology, No. 2. Cambridge:
         Cambridge University Press.
1961a   Mappilla: North Kerala. *In* Matrilineal kinship, David M. Schnei-
         der and Kathleen Gough, editors, pp. 415–442. Berkeley and Los
         Angeles: University of California Press.
1961b   Nayar: Central Kerala. *In* Matrilineal kinship, David M. Schneider
         and Kathleen Gough, editors, pp. 298–384. Berkeley and Los An-
         geles: University of California Press.
1963   Indian nationalism and ethnic freedom. *In* The concept of freedom
         in anthropology, David Bidney, editor, pp. 170–207. The Hague:
         Mouton.
1965   A note on Nayar marriage. Man 65:8–11.
GOULD, HAROLD A.
1958   The Hindu jajmani system: a case of economic particularism.
         Southwestern Journal of Anthropology 14:428–437.
1959   The peasant village: centrifugal or centripetal? The Eastern An-
         thropologist 13:3–16.
1960a   Castes, outcastes and the sociology of stratification. International
         Journal of Comparative Sociology 1:220–238.
1960b   The micro-demography of marriages in a North Indian area.
         Southwestern Journal of Anthropology 16:476–491.
1961a   A further note on village exogamy in North India. Southwestern
         Journal of Anthropology 17:297–300.
1961b   Sanskritization and westernization: a dynamic view. The Eco-
         nomic Weekly 13:945–950.
1961c   Some preliminary observations concerning the anthropology of
         industrialization. The Eastern Anthropologist 14:30–47.
1964   The jajmani system of North India: its structure, magnitude and
         meaning. Ethnology 3:12–41.
1965a   Lucknow rickshawallas: the social organization of an occupational
         category. International Journal of Comparative Sociology 6:24–47.
1965b   Modern medicine and folk cognition in village India. Human
         Organization 24:201–208.
1965c   True structural change and the time dimension in the North
         Indian kinship system. *In* Studies on Asia, 1965, R. K. Sakai, editor,
         pp. 179–192. Lincoln: University of Nebraska Press.
GRAY, R. M. AND MANILAL C. PAREKH
1931   Mahatma Gandhi: an essay in appreciation (fourth impression).
         Calcutta: Association Press.
GRIGSON, W. V.
1949   The Maria Gonds of Bastar. London: Oxford University Press.
GROSS, NEAL, W. S. MASON, AND A .W. MCEACHERN

1958   Explorations in role analysis: studies of the school superintendency role. New York: John Wiley.

GUHA, UMA
1965   Caste among rural Bengali Muslims. Man in India 45: 167–169.

GUHA, UMA AND M. N. KAUL
1953   A group distance study of the castes of U. P. Bulletin of the Department of Anthropology 2:11–32. Calcutta: Department of Anthropology, Government of India.

GUMPERZ, JOHN J.
1957   Some remarks on regional and social language differences in India. In Introducing Indian in liberal education, Milton Singer, editor, pp. 69–79. Chicago: University of Chicago Press.
1958   Dialect differences and social stratification in a North Indian village. American Anthropologist 60: 668–682.
1961   Speech variation and the study of Indian civilization. American Anthropologist 63:976–988.
1964   Religion and social communication in village North India. The Journal of Asian Studies 32:89–98.

GUMPERZ, JOHN J. AND C. M. NAIM
1960   Formal and informal standards in the Hindi regional language area. International Journal of American Linguistics 26:92–118.
1964   Religion and social communication in village North India. The Journal of Asian Studies 23:89–97.

GUPTA, RAGHURAJ
1956   Caste ranking and inter-caste relations among the Muslims of a village in North Western U. P. Eastern Anthropologist 10:30–42.

GUPTA, T. R.
1961   Rural family status and migration: study of a Punjab village. The Economic Weekly 13:1597–1603.

GUPTE, B. A.
1919   Hindu holidays and ceremonials. Second edition, revised. Calcutta and Simla: Thacker, Spink and Co.

HARDGRAVE, ROBERT L., JR.
1964   Caste in Kerala: a preface to the elections. The Economic Weekly 16:1841–1847.
1966   Varieties of political behavior among Nadars of Tamilnad. Asian Survey 6:614–621.

HARPER, EDWARD B.
1957a   Hoylu: a belief relating justice and the supernatural. American Anthropologist 59:801–816.
1957b   Shamanism in South India. Southwestern Journal of Anthropology 13:267–287.
1959a   A Hindu village pantheon. Southwestern Journal of Anthropology 15:227–234.
1959b   Two systems of economic exchange in village India. American Anthropologist 61:760–778.
1961   Moneylending in the village economy of the Malnad. The Economic Weekly 13:169–177.
1963   Spirit possession and social structure. In Anthropology on the

march, Bala Ratnam, editor, pp. 165–197. Madras: The Book Center.

1964 Ritual pollution as an integrator of caste and religion. The Journal of Asian Studies 2:151–197.

1968 Social consequences of an "unsuccessful" low caste movement. In Social mobility in the caste system in India, James Silverberg, editor, pp. 36–65. Comparative Studies in society and history. Supplement III. The Hague: Mouton.

HARPER, EDWARD B. AND LOUISE G. HARPER

1959 Political organization in a Karnataka village. In Leadership and political institutions in India, Richard L. Park and Irene Tinker, editors, pp. 453–469. Princeton: Princeton University Press.

HARRISON, SELIG S.

1956a Caste and the Andhra communists. The American Political Science Review 50:378–404.

1960 India: the most dangerous decades. Princeton: Princeton University Press.

HAYE, CHOWDHRY ABDUL

1966 The Freedom movement in Mewat and Dr. K. M. Ashraf. In Kunwar Mohammed Ashraf: an Indian scholar and revolutionary, 1903–1962, Horst Krüger, editor, pp. 291–336. Berlin: Akademic-Verlag.

HAZLEHURST, LEIGHTON W.

1966 Entrepreneurship and the merchant castes in a Punjab city. Duke University Program in Comparative Studies in Southern Asia. Monograph No. 1.

HEIN, NORVIN

1958 The Rām Līlā. Journal of American Folklore 71:279–304.

HITCHCOCK, JOHN T.

1958 The idea of the martial Rājpūt. Journal of American Folklore 71: 216–223.

1959 Dominant caste politics in a North Indian village. Mimeographed, 59 pp.

1960 Surat Singh: head judge. In In the company of Man, J. B. Casagrande, editor, pp. 234–272. New York: Harper and Brothers.

HOCKINGS, PAUL

1965 Cultural change among the Badagas: a community of South India. Doctoral dissertation, University of California, Berkeley.

HOMANS, GEORGE C.

1950 The human group. New York: Harcourt, Brace and World.

HONIGMANN, JOHN J.

1960a South Asian research: a village of renown. Research Previews 7:7–14.

1960b Education and career specialization in a West Pakistan village of renown. Anthropos 55:825–840.

HOPKINS, EDWARD W.

1884 The ordinances of Manu. London: Trübner and Co.

HSU, FRANCIS L. K.

1963 Clan, caste, club. Princeton: D. Van Nostrand Company.

HUTTON, J. H.
  1941   Primitive tribes. *In* Modern India and the West, L. S. S. O'Malley, editor, pp. 417–444. London: Oxford University Press.
  1961   Caste in India: its nature, function and origin. Third edition. Bombay: Oxford University Press.

IBBETSON, DENZIL
  1916   Panjab castes. (Reprint of chapter in Census of the Panjab, 1883.) Lahore: Government Printing Press.

INGALLS, DANIEL H. H.
  1954   Authority and law in ancient India. Journal of the American Oriental Society, Supplement, No. 17:34–45.
  1958   The Brahmin tradition. Journal of American Folklore 71:209–215.

IRSCHIK, EUGENE F.
  1969   Politics and social conflict in South India: the non-Brahmin movement, Tamil separatism 1916–1929. Berkeley and Los Angeles: University of California Press.

ISHWARAN, K.
  1965   Kinship and distance in rural India. International Journal of Comparative Sociology 6:81–94.

ISAACS, HAROLD R.
  1965   India's ex-untouchables. New York: The John Day Company.

IYER, L. K. ANANTHA KRISHNA (ANANTAKRISHNA AYYAR, L. K.)
  1909–1912   The Cochin tribes and castes. Madras: Government Printing Press.

IZMIRLIAN, HARRY JR.
  1964   Caste, kin and politics in a Punjab village. Doctoral dissertation, University of California, Berkeley.

JACKSON, A. V. WILLIAMS, editor
  1907   History of India. Volume 9. London: The Grolier Society.

JAGALPURE, L. B. AND K. D. KALE
  1938   Sarola Kasar: Study of a Deccan village in the famine zone. Ahmednagar: L. B. Jagalpure.

JAY, EDWARD J.
  1959   The anthropologist and tribal warfare. Journal of Social Research (Ranchi) 2:82–89.
  1961a   A comparison of tribal and peasant religion with special reference to the Hill Maria Gonds. Mimeographed, 60 pp.
  1961b   Social values and economic change: the Hill Marias of Bastar. The Economic Weekly 13:1369–1372.
  1964   The concepts of 'field' and 'network' in anthropological research. Man in India 64:137–139.

KALIDASA
  1959   Shakuntala and other writings. (Translated by Arthur W. Ryder.) New York: E. P. Dutton.

KANE, PANDURANG VAMAN
  1941   History of Dharmaśāstra. Volume 2, part 1. Poona: Bhandarkar Oriental Research Institute.
  1946   History of Dharmaśāstra. Volume 3. Poona: Bhandarkar Oriental Research Institute.

KANNAN, C. T.
1963   Intercaste and inter-community marriages in India. Bombay: Allied Publishers.
KAPADIA, K. M.
1947   Hindu kinship: an important chapter in Hindu social history. Bombay: The Popular Book Depot.
1956   Rural family patterns. Sociological Bulletin 5:111–126.
1957   A perspective necessary for the study of social change in India. Sociological Bulletin 6:43–60.
1958   Marriage and family in India. Second edition. London: Oxford University Press.
1959   The family in transition. Sociological Bulletin 8:68–99.
1961   The growth of townships in South Gujarat: Maroli Bazar. Sociological Bulletin 10:69–87.
1962   Caste in transition. Sociological Bulletin 12:73–90.
1963   The passing of the traditional society. Fiftieth Indian Science Congress, Delhi.
1966   Marriage and family in India. Third edition. Bombay: Oxford University Press.
KARAKA, DOSABHAI FRAMJI
1884   History of the Parsis. Volume 1. London: Macmillan.
KARANDIKAR, S. V.
1929   Hindu exogamy. Bombay: Taraporevala.
KARIM, A. K. NAZMUL
1956   Changing society in India and Pakistan. Dacca: Oxford University Press.
KARVE, IRAWATI
1953   Kinship organization in India. Poona, Deccan College Monograph Series, No. 11. Poona: Deccan College.
1958a   The Indian village. Bulletin of the Deccan College 18:73–106.
1958b   What is caste? (1) Caste as extended kin. The Economic Weekly 10:125–138.
1961   Hindu society: an interpretation. Poona: Sangam Press.
1962   On the road: a Maharashtrian pilgrimage. Journal of Asian Studies 22:13–30.
1965   Kinship organization in India. Second revised edition. Bombay: Asia Publishing House.
KARVE, IRAWATI AND Y. B. DAMLE
1963   Group relations in village community. Deccan College Monograph Series. Poona: Deccan College.
KARVE, IRAWATI AND VISHNU MAHADEO DANDEKOR
1951   Anthropometric measurements of Mahārāṣhtra. Deccan College Monograph Series, No. 8. Poona: Deccan College.
KAUTILYA
1961   Kautilya's Arthaśāstra. (Translated by R. Shamasastry.) Seventh edition. Mysore: Mysore Printing and Publishing House.
KENNEDY, BETH C.
1954   Rural-urban contrasts in parent-child relations in India. Indian Journal of Social Work 15:162–174. (Reprinted by the Bureau of

Research and Publications, Tata Institute of Social Science, Chembur, Bombay.)

KENNEDY, MELVILLE T.
1925 The Chaitanya movement. London and Calcutta: Oxford University Press.

KETKAR, SHRIDHAR VENKATESH
1909 The history of caste in India. Ithaca: Taylor and Carpenter.

KHADDURI, MAJID AND H. J. LIEBESNY
1955 Law in the Middle East. Volume 1. Washington: The Middle East Institute.

KHAN, KHAN AHMAD HASAN
1931 Census of India, 1931, Volume 17. Punjab.

KHARE, R. S.
1960 The Kanya-Kubja Brahmins and their social organization. Southwestern Journal of Anthropology 16:348–367.

KHEDKAR, VITHAN KRISHNAJI
1959 The divine heritage of the Yadavas. Allahabad: Parmanand.

KLASS, MORTON
1966 Marriage rules in Bengal. American Anthropologist 68:951–970.

KOCHAR, V. K.
1963 Socio-cultural denominators of domestic life in a Santal village. The Eastern Anthropologist 16:167–180.

KOLENDA, PAULINE MAHAR
1958 Changing caste ideology in a North Indian village. Journal of Social Issues 14:51–65.
1959 A multiple scaling technique for caste ranking. Man in India 39:127–147.
1963 Toward a model of the Hindu jajmani system. Human Organization 22:11–31.
1964 Religious anxiety and Hindu fate. The Journal of Asian Studies 23:71–82.
1967 Regional differences in Indian family structure. In Regions and regionalism in South Asian Studies: an exploratory study, R. I. Crane, editor, pp. 147–226. Duke University Program in Comparative Studies in Southern Asia. Monograph No. 5.
1968 Region, caste, and family structure: a comparative study of the Indian "joint" family. In Structure and change in Indian society, M. Singer and B. S. Cohn, editors. Chicago: Aldine Publishing Company.

KOSAMBI, D. D.
1955 The basis of ancient Indian history (2). Journal of the American Oriental Society 75:226–237.
1965 The culture and civilization of ancient India in historical outline. London: Routledge and Kegan Paul.

KOTHARI, RAJNI AND RUSHIKESH MARU
1965 Caste and secularism in India: case study of a caste federation. The Journal of Asian Studies 25:33–50.

KRIPALANI, KRISHNA
1962 Rabindranath Tagore: a biography. New York: Grove Press.

KROEBER, A. L.
1944   Configurations of culture growth. Berkeley and Los Angeles: University of California Press.
1947   Culture groupings in Asia. Southwestern Journal of Anthropology 3:322–330.

KUDRYAVTSEV, M. K.
1964   On the role of Jats in North India's ethnic history. Journal of Social Research (Ranchi) 7:126–135.
1965   Musul'manskie kasty (Muslim castes). In Kasty v Indii (Castes in India), G. G. Kotovskii, editor, pp. 214–232. Moscow: Akademiia Nauk SSSR. Institut Narodov Azii.

LACEY, W. G.
1933   Census of India, 1931, Volume 7, part 1. Report, Bihar and Orissa. Patna: Government Printing Press.

LALL, R. MANOHAR
1933   Among the Hindus: a study of Hindu festivals. Cawnpore: Minerva Press.

LAMBERT, RICHARD D.
1958   Factory workers and the non-factory population in Poona. The Journal of Asian Studies 18:21–42.
1962   The impact of urban society upon village life. In India's urban future, Roy Turner, editor, pp. 117–140. Berkeley and Los Angeles: University of California Press.
1963   Workers, factories, and social change in India. Princeton, New Jersey: Princeton University Press.

LEACH, EDMUND R.
1960   Introduction: What should we mean by caste? In Aspects of caste in South India, Ceylon and North-West Pakistan, E. R. Leach, editor. Cambridge Papers in Social Anthropology, No. 2. Cambridge: Cambridge University Press.
1967   Caste, class and slavery: the taxonomic problem. In Caste and race: comparative approaches, A. de Reuck and J. Knight, editors, pp. 17–27. London: J. and A. Churchill.

LEACOCK, SETH AND DAVID G. MANDELBAUM
1955   A nineteenth century development project in India: the cotton improvement program. Economic Development and Cultural Change 3:334–351.

LEARMONTH, A. T. A. AND A. M. LEARMONTH
1958   The regional concept and national development. The Economic Weekly 10:153–156.

LENSKI, GERHARD
1966   Power and privilege: a theory of social stratification. New York: McGraw-Hill.

LEVINSON, DANIEL J.
1959   Role, personality and social structure in the organizational setting. Journal of Abnormal and Social Psychology 58:170–180.

LEWIS, OSCAR
1955   Peasant culture in India and Mexico: a comparative analysis. In Village India, M. Marriott, editor, pp. 145–170. Chicago: University of Chicago Press.

1958   Village life in Northern India: studies in a Delhi village. Urbana: University of Illinois Press.

LEWIS, OSCAR AND VICTOR BARNOUW
1956   Caste and the jajmani system in a North Indian village. Scientific Monthly 83:66–81.

LEWIS, OSCAR (assisted by Victor Barnouw and Harvant Dhillon)
1956   Aspects of land tenure and economics in a North Indian village. Economic Development and Cultural Change 4:279–302.

LOKANATHAN, P. S.
1965a   All India rural household survey. Vol. II. New Delhi: National Council of Applied Economic Research.
1965b   All India rural household survey, 1962. A summary statement on income distribution by rural and All India. Occasional Paper 13, National Council of Applied Economic Research. New Delhi.

LYNCH, OWEN M.
1967   Rural cities in India: continuities and discontinuities. In India and Ceylon: unity and diversity, Philip Mason, editor, pp. 142–158. London: Oxford University Press.

McCLELLAND, DAVID C.
1961   The achieving society. Princeton: D. Van Nostrand.

McCORMACK, WILLIAM
1956   Changing leadership of a Mysore village. Mimeographed, 9 pp.
1957   Mysore villager's view of change. Economic Development and Cultural Change 5:257–262.
1958a   The forms of communication in Vīraśaiva religion. Journal of American Folklore 71:325–335.
1958b   Sister's daughter marriage in a Mysore village. Man in India 38: 34–48.
1959   The development of Hindu law during the British period. Mimeographed, 65 pp.
1960   Social dialects in Dharwar Kannada. International Journal of American Linguistics 26:79–91.
1963   Lingayats as a sect. Journal of the Royal Anthropological Institute 93:59–71.

McCRINDLE, J. W.
1877   Ancient India as described by Megasthenes and Arrian. London: Trübner.
1901   Ancient India as described in classical literature. London: Constable.

McDONALD, ELLEN E.
1968   The modernization of communication: vernacular publishing in nineteenth-century Maharashtra. Asian Survey 8:589–606.

MacLACHLAN, MORGAN E. AND ALAN R. BEALS
1966   The internal and external relationships of a Mysore chiefdom. Journal of Asian and African Studies 1: 87–99.

MADAN, B. K.
1951   The economics of the Indian village and its implications in social structure. International Social Science Bulletin 3:813–822. Paris: UNESCO.

MADAN, T. N.

1962a The Hindu joint family. Man 62:88–89.
1962b The joint family: a terminological clarification. International Journal of Comparative Sociology 3:7–16.
1962c Is the Brahmanic gotra a grouping of kin? Southwestern Journal of Anthropology 18:59–77.
1965   Family and kinship: a study of the Pandits of rural Kashmir. New York: Asia Publishing House.
1968   Caste and development. Economic and Political Weekly 4:285–290.

MAHAJAN, MEHR CHAND
1963   Looking back. Bombay: Asia Publishing House.

MAHAR, PAULINE M. (see Kolenda, Pauline Mahar)

MAINE, HENRY
1861   Ancient law. London: J. Murray.
1881   Village-communities in the East and West. Fourth edition. London: John Murray.

MAJUMDAR, DHIRENDRA NATH
1944   The fortunes of primitive tribes. Lucknow: Universal Publishers.
1958a Caste and communication in an Indian village. Bombay: Asia Publishing House.
1958b Races and cultures of India. Bombay: Asia Publishing House.

MAJUMDAR, D. N., M. C. PRADHAN, C. SEN, AND S. MISRA
1955   Inter-caste relations in Gohanakallan, a village near Lucknow. The Eastern Anthropologist 8:191–214.

MAJUMDAR, R. C.
1960   The classical accounts of India. Calcutta: Firma K. L. Mukhopadhyay.

MALAVIYA, H. D.
1956   Village panchayats in India. New Delhi: Economic and Political Research Department. All India Congress Committee.

MANDELBAUM, DAVID G.
1938   Polyandry in Kota society. American Anthropologist 40:574–583.
1939a Agricultural ceremonies among three tribes of Travancore. Ethnos (Stockholm) 4:114–128.
1939b The Jewish way of life in Cochin. Jewish Social Studies 1:423–460.
1941   Social trends and personal pressures. In Language, culture and personality, L. Spier, A. I. Hallowell, and S. Newman, editors, pp. 219–238. (Reprinted in Anthropology of folk religion, C. Leslie, editor, 1960, pp. 221–255. New York: Vintage Books.)
1947   Hindu-Moslem conflict in India. The Middle East Journal 1:369–385.
1948   The family in India. Southwestern Journal of Anthropology 4:123–139.
1949   Population problems in India and Pakistan. Far Eastern Survey 18:283–287.
1954a Fertility of early years of marriage in India. In Professor Ghurye felicitation volume, K. M. Kapadia, editor, pp. 150–168. Bombay: The Popular Book Depot.
1954b Form, variation and meaning of a ceremony. In Method and perspective in anthropology, R. F. Spencer, editor, pp. 60–102. Minneapolis: University of Minnesota Press.

1955   The world and the world view of the Kota. *In* Village India, M. Marriott, editor, pp. 223–254. Chicago: University of Chicago Press.

1956   The Kotas in their social setting. *In* Introduction to the civilization of India, Milton Singer, editor. Chicago: University of Chicago Press.

1959a   Concepts and methods in the study of caste. The Economic Weekly Annual, Volume 2:145–149.

1959b   Social uses of funeral rites. *In* The meaning of death, H. Feifel, editor, pp. 189–217. New York: MacGraw-Hill.

1960   A reformer of his people. *In* In the company of man, J. Casagrande, editor, pp. 273–308. New York: Harper.

1962   Review of M. Marriott, caste ranking and community structure in five regions of India and Pakistan. Journal of Asian Studies 21: 434–436.

1964   Introduction: process and structure in South Asian religion. *In* Religion in South Asia, Edward B. Harper, editor, pp. 5–20. Seattle: University of Washington Press. (Also published in The Journal of Asian Studies 23:5–20.)

1965   Alcohol and culture. Current Anthropology 6:281–292.

1966   Transcendental and pragmatic aspects of religion. American Anthropologist 68:1174–1191.

MARRIOTT, McKIM

1955a   Western medicine in a village of Northern India. *In* Health, culture and community: case studies of public reactions to health programs, Benjamin D. Paul, editor, pp. 239–268. New York: Russell Sage Foundation.

1955b   Little communities in an indigenous civilization. *In* Village India, M. Marriott, editor, pp. 171–222. Chicago: University of Chicago Press.

1959a   Changing channels of cultural transmission in Indian civilization. *In* Intermediate societies, social mobility and communication, Verne Ray, editor, pp. 66–74. Seattle: American Ethnological Society.

1959b   Interactional and attributional theories of caste ranking. Man in India 39:92–107.

1960   Caste ranking and community structure in five regions of India and Pakistan. Poona: G. S. Press.

1962   Communication: rejoinder to Metraux. Journal of Asian Studies 21:263–265.

MARTEN, J. T.

1924   Census of India, 1921, Volume 1, part 1. Report. Calcutta: Government Printing Press.

MARTIN, MONTGOMERY

1838   The history, antiquities, topography and statistics of Eastern India. London: Allen and Co.

MATHUR, K. S.

1958a   Caste and occupation in a Malwa village. Eastern Anthropologist 12:47–61.

1958b   The Indian village: is it a structural unity? Journal of Social Research (Ranchi) 1:50–53.

1959   Caste and occupation in a Malwa village. Eastern Anthropologist 12:47–61.

1964   Caste and ritual in a Malwa village. Bombay: Asia Publishing House.

MAYER, ADRIAN C.

1952   Land and society in Malabar. London: Oxford University Press.

1956   Some hierarchical aspects of caste. Southwestern Journal of Anthropology 12:117–144.

1957   An Indian community development block revisited. Pacific Affairs 30:35–46.

1958a   The dominant caste in a region of Central India. Southwestern Journal of Anthropology 14:407–427.

1958b   Local government elections in a Malwa village. Eastern Anthropologist 9:189–202.

1960   Caste and kinship in Central India: a village and its region. Berkeley and Los Angeles: University of California Press.

1962   System and network: an approach to the study of political process in Dewas. In Indian anthropology, T. N. Madan and G. Sarana, editors, pp. 266–278. Bombay: Asia Publishing House.

MAYER, ALBERT AND ASSOCIATES

1958   Pilot project, India: the story of rural development at Etawah, U. P. Berkeley and Los Angeles: University of California Press.

MAYNARD, H. J.

1917   Influence of the Indian king upon the growth of caste. Journal of the Panjab Historical Society 6:88–100.

MENCHER, JOAN

1963   Growing up in South Malabar. Human Organization 22:54–65.

1965   The Nayars of South Malabar. In Comparative family systems, M. F. Nimkoff, editor, pp. 163–191. Boston: Houghton, Mifflin.

1966   Kerala and Madras: a comparative study of ecology and social structure. Ethnology 5:135–179.

MENCHER, JOAN P. AND HELEN GOLDBERG

1967   Kinship and marriage regulations among the Namboodiri Brahmins of Kerala. Man n.s. 2:87–106.

METCALFE, CHARLES T.

1833   Appendix 84 to the report of the Select Committee of the House of Commons on the affairs of the East India Company. III-Review, pp. 328–334. Minute on the Upper Provinces. London, 1833. (House of Commons sessional papers 1831–32. XI, superscribed enumeration pp. 692–698.)

MILLER, ERIC J.

1954   Caste and territory in Malabar. American Anthropologist 56:410–420.

1960   Village structure in North Kerala. In India's villages, M. N. Srinivas, editor, pp. 42–55. Second revised edition. London: Asia Publishing House.

MINTURN, LEIGH

1963   The Rājpūts of Khalapur, Part II, child training. In Six cultures: studies of child rearing, B. B. Whiting, editor, pp. 301–361. New York and London: John Wiley and Sons.

MINTURN, LEIGH AND JOHN T. HITCHCOCK
1963   The Rājpūts of Khalapur, India. *In* Six cultures: studies of child rearing, B. B. Whiting, editor, pp. 203–361. New York and London: John Wiley and Sons.
1966   The Rājpūts of Khalapur, India. New York: John Wiley. (Six cultures series, Volume 3.)

MINTURN, LEIGH AND WILLIAM W. LAMBERT
1964   Mothers of six cultures. New York: John Wiley and Sons.

MISRA, SATISH C.
1964   Muslim communities in Gujarat. New York: Asia Publishing House.

MITRA, A.
1965   Levels of regional development in India, being part 1 of General Report on India. Census of India, 1961, Volume 1, part 1-A (i). Delhi: Government of India Press.

MONGA, VEENA
1967   Social mobility among the Potters: report of a caste conference. Economic and Political Weekly 2:1047–1055.

MOON, PENDEREL
1945   Strangers in India. New York: Reynal and Hitchcock.

MORGAN, LEWIS H.
1871   Systems of consanguinity and affinity of the human family. Washington: Smithsonian Institution.

MORRIS, MORRIS DAVID
1960   Caste and the evolution of the industrial workforce in India. Proceedings of the American Philosophical Society 104:124–133.
1967   Values as an obstacle to economic growth in South Asia, The Journal of Economic History 27:588–607.

MORRIS-JONES, W. H.
1967   The government and politics of India. Anchor Books edition. New York: Doubleday and Co.

MORRISON, WILLIAM A.
1959   Family types in Badlapur: an analysis of a changing institution in a Maharashtrian village. Sociological Bulletin 8:45–67.

MUKERJI, A. B.
1957   The bi-weekly market at Modinagar. The Indian Geographer 2: 271–293.

MÜLLER, FREDRICH MAX
1868   Chips from a German workshop. Volume 2. Second edition. London: Longmans, Green and Co.

MULLICK, BULLORAM (BALARAMA MALLIKA)
1882   Essays on the Hindu family in Bengal. Calcutta: W. Newman and Co.

MURDOCK, GEORGE P.
1949   Social structure. New York: Macmillan.

MYRDAL, GUNNAR
1968   Asian drama: an inquiry into the poverty of nations. New York: Random House (Pantheon).

NADEL, S. F.
1951   The foundations of social anthropology. London: Cohen and West.
1954   Caste and government in primitive society. Journal of the Anthropological Society of Bombay, pp. 9–22.

NAIR, KUSUM
1963   Blossoms in the dust. New York: Frederick A. Praeger.
NANDI, PROSHANTA KUMAR
1965   A study of caste organizations in Kanpur. Man in India 45:84–99.
NANDI, SANTIBHUSHAN AND D. S. TYAGI
1961   Forms of villages. In Peasant Life in India, pp. 1–6. Anthropological Survey of India, Calcutta. Memoir No. 8.
NANDIMATH, S. C.
1942   A handbook of Virasaivism. Bangalore: Basel Mission Press.
NARAIN, DHIRENDRA
1957   Hindu character (a few glimpses). Bombay: University of Bombay. Sociology Series No. 8.
NARAYAN, JAYAPRAKASH
1958   Toward a new society. New Delhi: Congress for Cultural Freedom.
NATH, KAMLA
1965   Women in the new village. The Economic Weekly 17:813–816.
NATH, V.
1961   The village and the community. In India's Urban Future, Roy Turner, editor, pp. 139–154. Berkeley and Los Angeles: University of California Press.
1962   Village, caste and community. The Economic Weekly. 14:1877–1882.
NAVALAKHA, SURENDRA KUMAR
1959   The authority structure among the Bhumij and Bhil: a study in historical causations. The Eastern Anthropologist 13:27–40.
NAYAR, UNNI
1952   My Malabar. Bombay: Hind Kitabs.
NEALE, WALTER C.
1962   Economic change in rural India: land tenure and reform in Uttar Pradesh, 1800–1955. New Haven and London: Yale University Press.
NEALE, WALTER C., HARPAL SINGH AND JAI PAL SINGH
1965   Kurali market: a report on the economic geography of marketing in Northern Punjab. Economic Development and Cultural Change 13:129–168.
NEHRU, JAWAHARLAL
1941   Toward freedom: the autobiography of Jawaharlal Nehru. New York: John Day.
1946   The discovery of India. New York: John Day.
NEHRU, S. S.
1932   Caste and credit in the rural area. London:
NEILL, STEPHEN
1934   Builders of the Indian church. London: Edinburgh House Press.
NEWELL, W. H.
1963   Inter-caste marriage in Kuzti village. Man 63:55–57.
NICHOLAS, RALPH W.
1961   Economics of family types in two West Bengal villages. The Economic Weekly 13:1057–1060.
1962   Villages of the Bengal Delta: a study of ecology and peasant society. Doctoral dissertation, University of Chicago.

1963   Ecology and village structure in deltaic West Bengal. The Economic Weekly 15:1185–1196.

1965   Factions: a comparative analysis. In Political systems and the distribution of power, Max Gluckman and Fred Eggan, editors, pp. 21–61. London: Tavistock Publications; New York: Frederick A. Praeger. A. S. A. Monograph No. 2.

1966   Segmentary factional political systems. In Political anthropology, M. S. Swartz, V. W. Turner, and A. Tinden, editors, pp. 49–59. Chicago: Aldine Publishing Co.

1967   Ritual hierarchy and social relations in rural Bengal. Contributions to Indian Sociology, New Series 1:56–83.

NICHOLAS, RALPH W. AND TARASHISH MUKOPADHYAY
1962   Politics and law in two West Bengal villages. Bulletin of the Anthropological Survey of India 11:15–39.

NIEHOFF, ARTHUR
1958   A study of matrimonial advertisements in North India. The Eastern Anthropologist 12:73–86.

NIKITIN, AFANASY
1960   Khozhenie za tri moria Afanasiia Nikitina, 1466–1472. (Afanasy Nikitin's voyage beyond three seas, 1466–1472.) B. Kumkes, editor. Moscow. (Text in Russian, Hindi and English.)

O'MALLEY, L. S. S.
1913   Census of India, 1911, Volume 5, part 1. Report, Bengal, Bihar, Orissa and Sikkim. Calcutta: Bengal Secretariat Book Depot.

1934   India's social heritage. Oxford: Clarendon Press.

1941   Modern India and the West. London: Oxford University Press.

OPLER, MORRIS E.
1956   The extensions of an Indian village. In The Indian village: a symposium. The Journal of Asian Studies 16:5–10.

1958   Spirit possession in a rural area of Northern India. In Reader in comparative religion, W. A. Lessa and E. Z. Vogt, editors, pp. 553–566. Evanston: Row, Peterson.

1959a Family, anxiety and religion in a community of North India. In Culture and mental health, Marvin K. Opler, editor, pp. 273–289. New York: Macmillan.

1959b The place of religion in a North Indian village. Southwestern Journal of Anthropology 15:219–226.

1960   Recent changes in family structure in an Indian Village. Anthropological Quarterly 35:93–97.

OPLER, MORRIS E. AND RUDRA DATT SINGH
1952   Two villages of eastern Uttar Pradesh (U. P.), India: an analysis of similarities and differences. American Anthropologist 54:179–190.

ORANS, MARTIN
1965   The Santal: a tribe in search of a great tradition. Detroit: Wayne State University Press.

1968   Maximizing in jajmaniland. American Anthropologist 70:875–897.

ORENSTEIN, HENRY
1959   Leadership and caste in a Bombay village. In Leadership and political institutions in India, Richard L. Park and Irene Tinker, editors, pp. 415–426. Princeton: Princeton University Press.

1960   Irrigation, settlement pattern and social organization. *In* Selected papers of the fifth international congress of anthropological and ethnological sciences, Philadelphia, Anthony F. C. Wallace, editor, pp. 318–323. Philadelphia: University of Pennsylvania Press.

1961   The recent history of the extended family in India. Social Problems 8:341–350.

1962   Exploitation or function in the interpretation of jajmani. Southwestern Journal of Anthropology 18:302–316.

1963   Caste and the concept "Marāthā" in Maharashtra. The Eastern Anthropologist 16:1–9.

1965a   Gaon: conflict and cohesion in an Indian village. Pinceton: Princeton University Press.

1965b   Notes on the ecology of irrigation agriculture in contemporary peasant societies. American Anthropologist 67:1529–1532.

1965c   The structure of Hindu caste values: a preliminary study of hierarchy and ritual defilement. Ethnology 4:1–15.

ORR, W. G.

1947   A sixteenth-century Indian mystic. London and Redhill: Lutterworth Press.

PANIKKAR, K. M.

1956   Hindu society at the cross roads. Second revised edition. Bombay: Asia Publishing House.

1961   Hindu society at the cross roads. Third edition. Bombay: Asia Publishing House.

PARSONS, TALCOTT

1953   A revised analytical approach to the theory of social stratification. *In* Class, status and power, R. Bendix and S. M. Lipset, editors, pp. 92–128. Glencoe: Free Press.

1961   An outline of the social system. *In* Theories of society, Talcott Parsons *et al.*, editors, Volume 1, pp. 30–79. New York: Free Press of Glencoe.

PATNAIK, NITYANANDA

1953   Study of the weekly market at Barpali. Geographical Review of India 15:19–31.

1960a   Assembly of the Mahanayaka Sudras of Puri District, Orissa. *In* Data on caste: Orissa, pp. 81–118. Anthropological Survey of India, Calcutta. Memoir No. 7.

1960b   Service relationship between barbers and villagers in a small village in Ranpur. The Economic Weekly 12:737–742.

PATNAIK, NITYANANDA AND A. K. RAY

1960   Oilmen or Teli. *In* Data on caste: Orissa, pp. 9–80. Anthropological Survey of India. Memoir No. 7.

PATTERSON, MAUREEN L. P.

1958   Intercaste marriage in Maharashtra. The Economic Weekly 10:139–142.

PILLAI, N. KUNJAN

1932   Census of India 1931, Travancore Vol. 28, Part I. Trivandrum: Government Press.

PLANALP, JACK MILAN

1956   Religious life and values in a North Indian village. Doctoral dissertation, Cornell University.

POCOCK, DAVID F.
1954 The hypergamy of the Patidars. *In* Professor Ghurye felicitation volume, K. M. Kapadia, editor, pp. 195–204. Bombay: The Popular Book Depot.
1955 The movement of castes. Man 55:71–72.
1957a Bases of faction in Gujerat. British Journal of Sociology 8:295–317.
1957b Inclusion and exclusion: a process in the caste system of Gujerat. Southwestern Journal of Anthropology 13:19–31.
1962 Notes on jajmani relationships. Contribution to Indian Sociology 6:78–95.
1964 The anthropology of time reckoning. Contributions to Indian Sociology 7:18–29.

POFFENBERGER, THOMAS
1964 The use of praise. University of Baroda, Department of Child Development. Working papers in Indian personality. MS., 6 pp.

POFFENBERGER, THOMAS AND BIHARI J. PANDYA
n.d. The effect of the dowry system on endogamy among Leva Patidar in a low status village. MS., 8 pp.

PRABHU, PANDHARI NATH
1954 Hindu social organization. Bombay: The Popular Book Depot.

PRADHAN, M. C.
1965 The Jats of Northern India: their traditional political system. The Economic Weekly 17:1821–1824, 1855–1864.
1966 The political system of the Jats of Northern India. Bombay: Oxford University Press.

PRASAD, RAJENDRA
1957 Autobiography. Bombay: Asia Publishing House.

Pyarelal (Nair)
1965 Mahatma Gandhi, Volume 1: the early phase. Ahmedabad: Navajivan Publishing House.

RAGHAVAN, V.
1965 Variety and integration in the pattern of Indian culture. Far Eastern Quarterly 15:33–41.

RAGHUVANSHI, V. P. S.
1966 The institution and working of caste in the latter part of the eighteenth century from European sources. *In* Kunwar Mohammad Ashraf: an Indian scholar and revolutionary 1903–1962, Horst Krüger, editor, pp. 147–175. Berlin: Akademie Verlag.

RAJ, HILDA
1959 Persistence of caste in South India: an analytic study of the Hindu and Christian Nadar. Doctoral dissertation, American University, Washington, D.C.

RANADE, RAMABAI
1938 Himself: the autobiography of a Hindu lady. (Translated and adapted by Katherine van Akin Gates from a book wirtten in the Marathi language by Mrs. Ramabai Ranade.) New York, Toronto: Longmans, Green and Co.

RANGACHARI, DIWAN BAHADUR K.
1931 The Sri Vaishnava Brahmans. Bulletin of the Madras Government Museum. Volume 1, part 2. Madras: Government Press.

RAO, C. V. H.
1966   The fifth steel plant: Andhra's case. The Economic and Political Weekly 1:534.
RAO, M. S. A.
1955   Symposium on caste and joint family: in Kerala. Sociological Bulletin 4:122–129.
1957   Social change in Malabar. Bombay: Popular Book Depot.
1961   The jajmani system. The Economic Weekly 13:877–878.
1964   Caste and the Indian army. Economic Weekly 16:1439–1443.
RAO, V. L. S. PRAKASA AND L. S. BHAT
1960   Planning regions in the Mysore State: the need for readjustment of district boundaries. Calcutta: Indian Statistical Institute. Regional studies No. 1.
RAO, Y. V. LAKSHMANA
1966   Communication and development: a study of two Indian villages. Minneapolis: University of Minnesota Press.
RATH, R. AND N. C. SIRCAR
1960a The cognitive background of six Hindu caste groups regarding the low caste untouchables. Journal of Social Psychology 51:295–306.
1960b The mental pictures of six Hindu caste groups about each other as reflected in verbal stereotypes. Journal of Social Psychology 51:277–293.
REDDY, N. S.
1952   Transition in caste structure in Andhra Desh with particular reference to depressed castes. Doctoral dissertation. University of Lucknow, Lucknow.
1955   Functional relations of Lohars in a North Indian village. The Eastern Anthropologist 8:129–140.
1963   Spatial variance of custom in Andhra Pradesh. In Anthropology on the march, Bala Ratnam, editor, pp. 283–296. Madras: The Book Centre.
REDFIELD, ROBERT
1955   The little community: viewpoints for the study of a human whole. Chicago: University of Chicago Press.
RENOU, LOUIS
1953   Religions of ancient India. London: Athlone Press.
RETZLAFF, RALPH H.
1962   Village government in India. London: Asia Publishing House.
REYES-HOCKINGS, AMELIA
1966   The newspaper as surrogate marriage broker in India. Sociological Bulletin 15:25–39.
RISLEY, H. H.
1892   The tribes and castes of Bengal. Calcutta: Bengal Secretariat Press.
1915   The people of India. Second edition. London: W. Thacker and Co.
RIVERS, W. H. R.
1921   The origin of hypergamy. In The Journal of the Bihar and Orissa Research Society 8:9–24.
ROOKSBY, R. L.
1956   Status in a plural society: seminar on social and cultural problems

of India, School of Oriental and African Studies, University of
London. Mimeographed, 15 pp.

Ross, Aileen D.
1961   The Hindu family in its urban setting. Toronto: University of
        Toronto Press.

Rosser, Colin
1960   A "hermit" village in Kulu. In India's villages, M. N. Srinivas, edi-
        tor, pp. 77–89. Second revised edition. London: Asia Publishing
        House.

Rowe, William L.
1960   The marriage network and structural change in a North Indian
        community. Southwestern Journal of Anthropology 16:299–311.
1963   Changing rural class structure and the jajmani system. Human Or-
        ganization 22:41–44.
1964   Caste, kinship, and association in urban India. MS., 24 pp.
1968   The new Cauhāns: a caste mobility movement in North India. In
        Social mobility in the caste system in India, James Silverberg, edi-
        tor, pp. 66–67. Comparative Studies in Society and History, Sup-
        plement III. The Hague: Mouton.

Roy Burman, B. K.
1960   Basic concepts of tribal welfare and tribal integration. Journal of
        Social Research 3:16–24.

Roy, Ramashray
1963   Conflict and co-operation in a North Bihar Village. Journal of the
        Bihar Society 49:297–315.

Roy, Sarat Chandra
1934   Caste, race and religion in India: inadequacies of the current the-
        ories of caste. Man in India 14:75–220.

Rudolph, Lloyd I.
1965   The modernity of tradition: the democratic incarnation of caste
        in India. The American Political Science Review 59:975–989.

Rudolph, Lloyd I. and Susanne H. Rudolph
1960   The political role of India's caste associations. Pacific Affairs 33:
        5–22.
1967   The modernity of tradition: political development in India. Chi-
        cago: University of Chicago Press.

Rudolph, Susanne Hoeber
1965   Self-control and political potency: Gandhi's asceticism. The Amer-
        ican Scholar 35:79–97.

Russell, R. V. and Rai Bahadur Hīra Lāl
1916   The tribes and castes of the Central Provinces of India. Volume 1.
        London: Macmillan and Co.

Sachchidananda
1964   Culture change in tribal Bihar. Calcutta: Bookland Private Lim-
        ited.
1965   Profiles of tribal culture in Bihar. Calcutta: Firma K. L. Mukho-
        padhyay.

Sangave, Vilas Adinath
1959   Jaina community: a social survey. Bombay: Popular Book Depot.

SARMA, JYOTIRMOYEE

1951   Formal and informal relations in the Hindu joint household of Bengal. Man in India 31:51–71.

1955   A village in West Bengal. *In* India's villages, pp. 161–179. West Bengal Government Press.

1959   The secular status of castes. Eastern Anthropologist 12:87–106.

1960   A village in West Bengal. *In* India's villages, M. N. Srinivas, editor, pp. 180–201. Second revised edition. London: Asia Publishing House.

1964   The nuclearization of joint family households in West Bengal. Man in India 44:193–206.

SCHWARTZBERG, JOSEPH E.

1965   The distribution of selected castes in the North Indian plains. Geographical Review 55:477–495.

1967   Prolegomena to the study of South Asian regions and regionalism. *In* Regions and regionalism in South Asia studies: an exploratory study. R. I. Crane, editor, pp. 85–111. Duke University Program in Comparative Studies in Southern Asia. Mimeograph No. 4.

SEN, LALIT KUMAR

1965   Family in four Indian villages. Man in India 45:1–16.

SENART, ÉMILE

1930   Caste in India. London: Methuen.

SENGUPTA, SUNIL

1958   Family organization in West Bengal: its nature and dynamics. The Economic Weekly 15:384–389.

SHAH, A. M.

1955a   Caste, economy and territory in the Central Panchmahals. Journal of the Maharaja Sayajirao University of Baroda 4:65–91.

1955b   A dispersed hamlet in the Panchmahals. The Economic Weekly 7:109–116.

1959   Social anthropology and the study of historical societies. The Economic Weekly 11:953–962.

1964a   Basic terms and concepts in the study of family in India. Indian Economic and Social History Review 1:1–36.

1964b   Political systems in eighteenth century Gujarat. Enquiry (Delhi) 1:83–95.

SHAH, A. M. AND R. G. SHROFF

1958   The Vahāvancā Bārots of Gujarat: a caste of geneologists and mythographers. Journal of American Folklore 71:246–276.

SHAH, B. V.

1960   Joint family system: an opinion survey of Gujarati students. The Economic Weekly 12:1867–1870.

1964   Social change and college students of Gujarāt. Baroda: M.S. University of Baroda.

SHAHANI, SAVITRI

1961   The joint family: a case study. The Economic Weekly 13:1823–1828.

SHARMA, KAILAS N.

1956a   Urban contacts and cultural change in a little community. Doctoral dissertation, Lucknow University, Lucknow.

1956b   Hypergamy in theory and practice. The Journal of Research 3: 18–32.
1961a   Hindu sects and food patterns in North India. Journal of Social Research 4:47–58.
1961b   Occupational mobility of castes in a North Indian village. Southwestern Journal of Anthropology 17:146–164.
1963   Panchayat leadership and resource groups. Sociological Bulletin 12:47–52.

SIEGEL, BERNARD J. AND ALAN R. BEALS
1960a   Pervasive factionalism. American Anthropologist 62:394–417.
1960b   Conflict and factionalist dispute. The Journal of the Royal Anthropological Institute 90:107–117.

SILVERBERG, JAMES
1959   Caste-ascribed 'status' versus caste-irrelevant roles. Man in India 39:148–162.

SINGER, MILTON
1956a   Cultural values in India's economic development. Annals of the American Academy of Political and Social Science 305:81–91.
1956b   Introduction. In The Indian village: a symposium. The Journal of Asian Studies 16:3–5.
1958   The great tradition in a metropolitan center: Madras. Journal of American Folklore 71:347–388.
1963   The Radha-Krishna bhajans of Madras City. History of Religions 2:183–226.
1964   The social organization of Indian civilization. Diogenes, Winter issue 1964, pp. 84–119.
1966   The modernization of religious beliefs. In Modernization, Myron Weiner, editor, pp. 55–67. New York: Basic Books, Inc.
1968   The Indian joint family in modern industry. In Structure and change in Indian society, Milton Singer and Bernard S. Cohn, editors, pp. 423–452. Chicago: Aldine Publishing Co.
[1969] Modernization, ritual and belief among industrial leaders in Madras City. In Modernization in India: studies in social-cultural aspects, Amar Kumar Singh, editor. Bombay: Asia Publishing House.

SINGH, AMAR KUMAR
1967   Hindu culture and economic development in India, Conspectus 3:9–32.

SINGH, INDERA P.
1958   A Sikh village. Journal of American Folklore 71:479–503.
1961   Religion in Daleke: a Sikh village. Journal of Social Research (Ranchi) 4:191–219.

SINGH, BALJIT
1961   Next step in village India. Bombay: Asia Publishing House.

SINGH, INDERA P. AND H. L. HARIT
1960   Effects of urbanization in a Delhi suburban village. Journal of Social Research (Ranchi) 3:38–43.

SINGH, KHUSHWANT
1953   The Sikhs. London: George Allen and Unwin.
1963–   A history of the Sikhs. Two volumes. Princeton: Princeton University Press.
1966

SINGH, RUDRA DATT
1956   The Unity of an Indian village. In The Indian village: a symposium. The Journal of Asian Studies 16:10–19.

SINGH, YOGENDRA
1959   Group status of factions in rural community. Journal of Social Sciences 2:57–67.

SINHA, D. P.
1963   The role of the Phariya in tribal acculturation in a Central Indian market. Ethnology 2:170–179.
1967   The Phariya in an inter-tribal market. Economic and Political Weekly 2:1373–1378.

SINHA, SURAJIT
1957a   The media and nature of Hindu-Bhumij interactions. Journal of the Asiatic Society: Letters and Science 23:23–37.
1957b   Tribal cultures of peninsular India as a dimension of little tradition in the study of Indian civilization: a preliminary statement. Man in India 37:93–118.
1958a   Changes in the cycle of festivals in a Bhumij village. Journal of Social Research (Ranchi) 1:24–49.
1958b   Tribal cultures of peninsular India as a dimension of little tradition in the study of Indian civilization: a preliminary statement. Journal of American Folklore 71:504–518.
1959   Bhumij-Kshatriya social movement in South Manbhum. Bulletin of the Department of Anthropology, Government of India 8:9–32.
1962   Status formation and Rajput myth in tribal Central India. Man in India 42:35–80.
1963   Levels of economic initiative and ethnic groups in Pargana Barabhum. The Eastern Anthropologist 16:65–74.
1965   Tribe-caste and tribe-peasant continua in Central India. Man in India 45:57–83.
1967   Caste in India: its essential pattern of socio-cultural integration. In Caste and race: comparative approaches, A. de Reuck and J. Knight, editors, pp. 92–105. London: J. and A. Churchill.

SINHA, SURAJIT, BIMAR KUMAR DASGUPTA, AND HEMENDRA NATH BANERGEE
1961   Agriculture, crafts and weekly markets of South Manbhum. Bulletin of the Anthropological Survey of India. Volume 10, No. 1.

SMITH, DONALD EUGENE
1963   India as a secular state. Princeton: Princeton University Press.

SMITH, MARIAN W.
1952   The Misal: a structural village group of India and Pakistan. American Anthropologist 54:41–56.

SMITH, WILFRED CANTWELL
1957   Islam in modern history. Princeton: Princeton University Press.

SOVANI, N. V.
1961   The urban social situation in India. Artha Vijnana 3:85–224.

SOVANI, N. V., D. P. APTE AND R. G. PENDSE
1956   Poona: a re-survey: the changing pattern of employment and earnings. Poona: Gokhale Institute of Politics and Economics. Publication No. 34.

SPATE, O. H. K.
1954   India and Pakistan: a general and regional geography. New York: E. P. Dutton.

SRINIVAS, M. N.
1942   Marriage and family in Mysore. Bombay: New Book Co.
1952a   Religion and society among the Coorgs of South India. Oxford: Oxford University Press.
1952b   A joint family dispute in a Mysore village. Journal of the Maharaja Sayarijao University of Baroda 1:7–31.
1954   A caste dispute among washermen of Mysore. Eastern Anthropologist 7:148–168.
1955a   The social structure of a Mysore village. In India's villages, pp. 15–32. Calcutta: West Bengal Government Press.
1955b   The social system of Mysore village. In Village India, M. Marriott, editor, pp. 1–35. Chicago: University of Chicago Press.
1956a   A note on sanskritization and westernization. Far Eastern Quarterly 15:481–496.
1956b   Regional differences in customs and village institutions. The Economic Weekly 8:215–220.
1959a   The dominant caste in Rampura. American Anthropologist 61: 1–16.
1959b   The case of the potter and the priest. Man in India 39:190–209.
1962   Caste in modern India and other essays. Bombay: Asia Publishing House.
1965   Social structure. The National Gazeteer 1:1–77.
1966   Social change in modern India. Berkeley and Los Angeles: University of California Press.
SRINIVAS, M. N. AND ANDRÉ BÉTEILLE
1964   Networks in Indian social structure. Man 64:165–168.
SRINIVAS, M. N. AND A. M. SHAH
1960   The myth of the self-sufficiency of the Indian village. The Economic Weekly 12:1375–1378.
SRIVASTAVA, RAM P.
1962   Tribe-caste mobility in India and the case of Kumaon Bhotias. London: Department of Anthropology, School of Oriental and African Studies, University of London. Mimeographed, 80 pp.
SRIVASTAVA, S. K.
1963   The process of desanskritisation in village India. In Anthropology on the march, Bala Ratnam, editor, pp. 263–267. Madras: The Book Center.
STAAL, J. F.
1963   Sanskrit and sanskritization. The Journal of Asian Studies 22:261–275.
STEED, GITEL P.
1955   Notes on an approach to a study of personality formation in a Hindu village in Gujarat. In Villiage India, M. Marriott, editor, pp. 102–144. Chicago: University of Chicago Press.
STEIN, BURTON
1960   The economic function of the medieval South Indian temple. Journal of Asian Studies 19:163–176.
1967   Comment on Bernard S. Cohn's paper. In Regions and regionalism in South Asian studies, R. I. Crane, editor, pp. 41–47. Duke University Program in Comparative Studies in Southern Asia. Monograph No. 4.

1968   Social mobility and medieval South Indian Hindu sects. *In* Social mobility in the caste system in India, James Silverberg editor, pp. 78–94. Comparative Studies in Society and History, Supplement III. The Hague: Mouton.

STEPHEN, LESLIE

1921   Henry Sumner Maine. *In* The Dictionary of National Biography, Vol. 12. pp. 787–790. London: Humphrey Milford.

STEVENSON, H. N. L.

1954   Status evaluation in the Hindu caste system. Journal of the Royal Anthropological Institute 84:45–65.

STEVENSON, MRS. SINCLAIR

1920   The rites of the twice-born. London: Humphrey Milford.

STRIZOWER, SCHIFRA

1959   Jews as an Indian caste. Jewish Journal of Sociology 1:43–57.

STROOP, MILDRED LUSCHINSKY

1960   The impact of some recent Indian government legislation on the women of an Indian village. Mimeographed, 9 pp.

TANDON, PRAKASH

1961   Punjabi century, 1857–1947. London: Chatto and Windus.

THAPAR, ROMILA

1966   A history of India. Volume 1. Baltimore: Penguin Books.

THOOTHI, N. A.

1935   The Vaishnavas of Gujarat. Bombay, London: Longmans, Green and Co.

THURSTON, EDGAR

1909   Castes and tribes of Southern India. Seven volumes. Madras: Government Press.

TILAK, LAKSHMIBAI

1950   I follow after. (Translated by E. Josephine Inster.) Madras: Oxford University Press.

TRIVEDI, R. K.

1965   Fairs and festivals: Gujarat. Census of India, 1961, Volume 5, part 7-B.

TUMIN, MELVIN M.

1967   Social stratification. Englewood Cliffs, New Jersey: Prentice-Hall.

ULLAH, INAYAT

1958   Caste, patti and faction in the life of a Punjab village. Sociologus n.s. 8:170–186.

UNDERHILL, M. M.

1921   The Hindu religious year. Calcutta: Association Press.

UNNI, K. RAMAN

1956   Visiting husbands in Malabar. Journal of the Maharaja Sayajirao University of Baroda 5:37–56.

VAN BUITINEN, J. A. B.

1966   On the archaism of the Bhāgavata Purāna. *In* Krishna: myths, rites and attitudes. Honolulu: East-West Center Press.

VIDYARTHI, LALITA P.

1961   The sacred complex in Hindu Gaya. Bombay: Asia Publishing House.

1967   Some preliminary observations on inter-group conflict in India: tribal, rural and industrial. Journal of Social Research 10:1–10.

VOGT, EVON Z.
1960   On the concepts of structure and process in cultural anthropology. American Anthropologist 62:18–33.

VREEDE-DE STUERS, CORA
1962   Mariage préférential chez les Musalmans de l'Inde du Nord. Revue de Sud-est Asiatique 1962:141–152.
1963   Terminologie de parenté chez les Musalmans Ashrāf de l'Inde Nord. Bijragen tot de taal-, land- en Volkenkunde 119:254–266.

WALLACE, ANTHONY
1961   The psychic unity of human groups. In Studying personality cross-culturally, Bert Kaplan, editor, pp. 129–164. Evanston: Row, Peterson and Co.

WARD, WILLIAM
1822   A view of the history, literature and mythology of the Hindoos. London: Kingsbury, Parbury and Allen.

WATTERS, THOMAS
1904   On Yuan Chwang's travels in India, 629–645 A.D., T. W. Rhys Davids and S. W. Bushnell, editors. London: Royal Asiatic Society.

WEBER, MAX
1958   The religion of India. Glencoe, Illinois: The Free Press.

WEINER, MYRON
1967   Party building in a new nation. Chicago: University of Chicago Press.

WHEELER, MORTIMER
1953   The Cambridge history of India. Supplementary volume: the Indus civilization. Cambridge: Cambridge University Press.

WHITING, BEATRICE B.
1963   Introduction. In Six cultures: studies of child marriage, B. B. Whiting, editor, pp. 1–13. New York: John Wiley.
1965   Sex identity, conflict and physical violence: a comparative study. In The ethnography of law, Laura Nader, editor. American Anthropologist 67 (part 2):123–140.

WILLIAMS, A. HYATT
1950   A psychiatric study of Indian soldiers in the Arakan. The British Journal of Medical Psychology 23:130–181.

WINSLOW, J. C.
1923   Narayan Vaman Tilak: the Christian poet of Maharashtra. Calcutta: Association Press.

WISER, WILLIAM H.
1936   The Hindu jajmani system: a socio-economic system inter-relating members of a Hindu village community in service. Lucknow: Lucknow Publishing House.

WISER, WILLIAM H. AND CHARLOTTE VIALL WISER
1963   Behind mud walls. Berkeley and Los Angeles: University of California Press.

WOLF, ERIC R.
1966   Kinship, friendship and patron-client relations in complex societies. In The social anthropology of complex societies, Michael Banton, editor. London: Tavistock Publications.

WRIGHT, THEODORE P., JR.
1966   The Muslim League in South Indian since independence: a study in minority group political strategies. The American Political Science Review 60:579–599.

YALMAN. NUR
1962   The structure of Sinhalese kindred: a re-examination of the Dravidian terminology. American Anthropologist 62:548–575.
1967   Under the Bo tree: studies in caste, kinship and marriage in the interior of Ceylon. Berkeley and Los Angeles: University of California Press.

Index

Adi Dravidas, 47–48, 90, 225–227
adoption, 96–97
affinal relations. *See* marriage, kinship
Aga Khan, 555
Agarwala, B. R., 45, 51
Aggarwal, Partap C., 559
Aggarwals, 63, 644–645
"aggressive defense," 626
agnatic relations. *See* lineage, clan, kinship, brothers
agriculture: technology and social relations, 52, 409, 589–590; work in fields, 182. *See also* swidden agriculture
Ahirs, 219, 230, 322, 443–444
Ahmad, Aziz, 555
Ahmad, Imtiaz, 546–549
Ahmad, Zarina, 546, 550, 551, 554, 555
Ahmadiyas, 556
Ahupe village, 354–355
Aiyappan, A., 72, 91, 164, 193, 492, 502, 503, 653
Ajlaf, 549
alcohol, 201, 217; and distillers, 479–481, 569
Aliyabad village, 335
alliances: within jati groups, 235–252; lineage relevant to, 241–242; as federations of lineages, 243; bases of strength of, 244–247; cooperation within, 241, 243, 247–248; cohesion of, 247–252; neutrality of, 250; critical range of size for, 256; development of, 257–259; variations in formation of, 259–264; within the village, 373–377. *See also* factions
All-India Congress Committee, 368
All-India Sweepers' Association, 506
All-India Yadav Maha Sabha, 443–444
All-Orissa Teli Congress (1959), 283, 286, 504, 505
Allison, W. L., 533

Ambedkar, B. R., 350, 356, 495, 496, 656
Anand, K., 653
Anantakrishna Ayyar, L. K., *See* Iyer, L. K. Anantakrishna
Angadi village, 122
Ansari, Ghaus, 546, 549, 550, 551, 554, 555
Apte, D. P., (8), 35
Arnold, Edwin, 450
art and esthetic experience, 117, 387, 413
artisans: guilds, 318–319; mobility efforts of, 458–459
Arya Samaj, 334, 354, 450, 463, 544
"Ashrafization," 556–557
Ashraf, 549, 550, 551, 554, 556–557
associations and federations, 269, 282–283, 496–497, 500–520, 559, 598–599
astrology, 110–111
Atal, Yogesh, 267, 363, 576
authority: in family relations, 38–41, 46, 59, 87, 649–650; and deference in child-rearing, 121–123
Ayyar, L. K. Anantakrishna. *See* Iyer, L. K. Anantakrishna

Bacon, Elizabeth E., 88
Badagas, 20, 89, 469–470, 588, 600–603
Baden-Powell, B. H., 345
Baderi village, 577, 595–598
Bagdi, 183
Bai, Saraswati, 387
Bailey, Frederick G., 102, 126, 130, 139, 151, 165, 166, 209, 241, 267, 290, 322, 330, 346, 363, 365, 366, 368, 370, 371, 372, 406, 407, 422, 428, 430, 433, 479–482, 514, 578, 579, 580, 595–599, 663
Baines, Athelstane, 141, 162, 163, 188, 195, 199, 353, 358, 433, 435, 443, 459, 464, 488–489, 497, 540

Balahis, 61, 75, 76, 77, 197, 200, 281, 298–299, 317, 378
Balai, 476–477
Bamni village, 383–384
Banergee, Hemendra Nath, 383, 384
Banias, 21, 51, 461
Banton, Michael, 418
Baranov, I. L., 512
Barbosa, Duarte, 196, 202
Barias (Bariyas), 20–21, 463, 514, 515
Barnabas, A. P., 449
Barnouw, Victor, 173
Barth, Fredrik, 475, 663
Basham, A. L., 23, 319, 587
Basu, N. B., 453
Basu, Tara Krishna, 453
Beals, Alan R., 66, 69, 77, 105, 118, 128, 132, 149, 153, 171, 182, 197, 263–264, 331, 332, 336–337, 342–344, 345, 347, 354, 365, 375–376, 378, 395, 413, 477
Bebarta, Prafulla C., 53
Beech, Mary Jane, 549
Beidelman, Thomas O., 17, 21, 164, 171, 173
Bendix, Reinhard, 13, 528, 532, 638
Berreman, Gerald D., 64, 77, 87, 101, 103–104, 107, 137, 145, 146, 148, 174, 220, 312, 338, 353, 395–396, 662–664
Béteille, André, 340, 354, 397, 410, 420, 431–432, 435, 455, 458, 460, 471, 498, 524
Bhagavad Gita, 450
bhajan, 528–531
Bhakti, 182–183, 533, 539. See also religious movements
Bharati, Agehananda, 87, 402, 403, 416–417
Bhat, L. S., 385
Bhattacharya, Jogenda Nath, 12, 188, 238, 433, 438, 483, 484
Bhilalas, 476–477
Bhils, 514, 515, 584
Bhotias, 594, 610–612, 617
Bhumihars, 444
Bhumij, 594, 603–610, 617
Bhumij-Kshatriya Association, 608, 609
binary divisions, Hindu society as series of, 25–26
biological factors, 405–409. See *also* population
birth, 88, 119–120, 185–186. See also life-cycle observances, pollution
Bisipara village, 139, 150–151, 330, 363, 368, 369, 370–371, 372, 377, 422, 433, 479–482
Blunt, E. A. H., 120, 269, 489, 555

Bose, A. B., 171, 176, 177, 243, 251
Bose, Nirmal Kumar, 345, 391, 397, 417, 456, 457, 591, 594
Bose, Shib Chunder, 484
Bouglé, Célestin, 12, 23, 236
Brahmins, 40, 42, 47, 181, 188, 211, 212, 215–216, 219, 223, 225–227, 230, 232, 238, 239, 353–354, 366, 411–412, 437–439, 455–459, 482–484, 498, 506, 530, 605, 610, 625; of various linguistic regions, 18; legendary origin of, 23; conduct expected of, 24; as demonstration of rewards of purity, 214; in Gaon, 274; in Kumbapettai, 47–48, 261, 320, 347, 361–362, 363, 437, 577; in Radhanagar, 258, 266, 267; in Rampur, 112, 258; in Rampura, 336, 360–361; in Sripuram, 420, 431–432; Havik, 83, 90–91, 138, 145, 189, 194, 260–261, 282, 297–298, 308, 318, 436; Pandit, 79–80, 96, 146
Brass, Paul, 399
British rule, 209–210, 307, 435–436, 587–588, 629, 633, 641–642. See also law and courts
brothers, relations among, 64–66, 125–130, 139, 152–153, 271–272, 277
brother-sister relations, 67–71; relations to sister's children (and to mother's brother), 71–74, 148–149
Brown, W. Norman, 189, 421
Buckley, Walter, 660
Burling, Robbins, 575

Carstairs, G. Morris, 28, 61, 67, 68, 77, 131, 193, 199, 224, 330, 397, 415–416, 453, 456, 460, 464, 584
Castets, J., 567
caste, use of term, 3, 29; and political considerations, 12, 568
caste associations. See associations and federations
caste system: concept of, 4–6, 29, 663–665; flexibility in, 7–8; and astrological concepts, 111; processes of change in, 627–635, 636–638. See also hierarchical order of society, jati, pollution, purity, ranking, religion, system
Census of India, 44, 120, 446; (1867–1871) 446, 509, 601; (1883: Report on the Punjab) 488, 557; (1891) 52, 455, 509; (1901) 230, 446, 496, 587; (1911) 446, 489; (1921) 511–512; (1931) 230, 446, 452, 456, 461, 509, 555; (1941) 447; (1951) 614; (1961) 385, 549, 573, 574, 601

ceremonies and rites: family, 42; wedding, 67, 76, 115–118, 436–437; life-cycle, 71–72, 437–438 (see also life-cycle ceremonies); jajmani relations in, 165–166, 175–176; and conflict, 248–249, 263–264, 600–602; and social cohesion, 265–266; as jati enterprises, 316; and village unity, 333–334, 377
Ceylon: kinship in, 157
Chamars, 48–50, 51, 112–113, 142, 150, 181, 211, 267, 292, 295–296, 299, 302, 309, 371, 494–495
Chanana, Dev Raj, 449, 463
Chandipur village, 339, 347
Chenchus, 6, 580–581
Chetris, 583
Chhibbar, Y. P., 649
child-rearing, 82–83, 120–123, 131, 625–626; cross-cultural study of, 123–125. See also family
China, effect of military advance of on Bhotias, 549, 610, 612; traditional family in, 92
Chintanhalli village, 342–343
Christianity, 524, 545–546, 560, 564–571, 572, 630, 631
Christians, 546, 560, 564–571, 572, 625
Church of South India, 571
civilizations: problems of, 179–180, 405–409, 485; as concept, 421; links among, 570–571; styles of, 617–619. See also tribes
clan, 18, 134–135, 144–145; among tribals, 576, 578. See also gotra
Coats, Thomas, 641, 642
coercion: in jajmani relations, 172–174, 663–644; and panchayats, 305, 372
cognition, 419, 624–627. See also psychological factors
Cohn, Bernard S., 35, 47, 49, 50, 114, 132, 141, 142, 150, 240–241, 259, 266, 268, 278, 279, 280, 288, 292, 299, 302, 307, 308, 309, 310, 311, 314, 345, 377, 390–391, 392, 399, 403, 413, 474, 665
Cole, B. L., 146
Collver, Andrew, 34, 95, 96
colonialism and imperialism. See British rule, political factors
communications, channels of, 388
conflict: family, 61, 68, 77–78, 90–93, 125–130; and child-rearing, 123; within lineage, 139; among jatis, 167, 172–174, 213, 217–218, 472–480; within a jati-group, 239–247, 251–257, 267–268; within village, 332; of loyalties, 393–394; within a tribe, 595–599; as sys-

temic process, 627–628. See also panchayats
Congress Party, 509, 512, 513, 515, 516, 517, 608
Coorgs, 67, 157, 207, 389–390, 453, 455, 465, 473, 492, 538
Cormack, Margaret L., 122, 651
Corwin, L. A., 549
counterchange, 5, 6, 8, 21, 132, 242, 294, 372, 439–441, 633. See also social system
cow: special ritual potency of, 189–190, 203, 295, 442–443, 447, 586; and beef-eating, 200, 442–443, 447, 586
Cronin, Vincent, 566
Culshaw, W. J., 613, 614
cults. See religious movements
culture. See civilization
culture change and adaptation, 442–467 See also social systems

Dahrendorf, Ralf, 662
Daleke village, 541
Dalena village, 100, 114–115, 116, 262–263, 275–276, 344–345
Dames, Mansel Longworth, 196, 202, 415
Damle, Y. B., 174, 175, 354–355
Dandekar, Kumudini, 53
Dandekar, V. M., 53
Darling, Malcolm Lyall, 374
Das Gupta, Biwan Kumar, 383, 384, 606
Datta Gupta, Jaya, 489
Datta-Majumder, Nabendu, 614
Davis, Kingsley, 230
Day, Lal Behari, 453
Dayabhaga code, 36
De, Barun, 390, 393
death. See life-cycle observances, pollution
Dewara village, 18, 589
Deming, Wilbur S., 533
de Nobili, Roberto, 566–567
Derrett, J. Duncan M., 35, 60, 313, 449, 654
Desai, I. P., 35, 45, 46, 51, 53, 129, 130, 646
Deshpande, Kamalabai, 647
Deva, Indra, 322
Devons, Ely, 406
DeVos, George A., 214, 665
dharma, 204, 429
Dhillon, Harwant Singh, 113, 247–249, 250, 251, 253–254, 256, 259–260, 265, 273, 274, 279, 287, 292, 308, 341
Diehl, Carl Gustav, 203

dispute settlement. *See* panchayats
divorce, 48, 78, 223, 227. *See also* marriage, women
dominant jatis. *See* jatis
dowry, 107–109, 651–652
Dravidian: languages, 11; speaking people, 156–158, 445
Drekmeier, Charles, 410
Driver, Edwin D., 53, 79, 646, 648
Dube, S. C., 18, 63, 65, 70, 72, 73, 74, 77, 86, 92, 113, 166, 187, 191, 201, 208, 215, 269–270, 276–277, 280, 289, 303, 335, 347, 370, 432, 548, 576, 589
Dubois, Jean Antoine, Abbé, 206, 209, 282, 289, 298, 431, 455, 459, 538, 569
Dumont, Louis, 29, 45, 48, 56, 59, 60–61, 62, 67, 69, 71, 78, 83–84, 86, 117, 131, 139, 143, 146, 149, 157, 275, 288, 299, 306, 311, 327, 365, 366, 417, 526–527, 578, 665
Dutt, Nripendra Kumar, 22, 23

ecological factors, 343–344, 405–409, 575
economic factors: in family relations, 41–42, 46–54, 128–129, 149; in marriage arrangements, 100, 105–109, 115–118; in lineage cooperation, 139–142, 329; and kinship, 153–154; in jajmani relations, 161–164, 167–179; in jati rank, 209–212, 225–226, 432–435, 439–441, 475; in alliances, 244–248, 251–255, 262; in leadership, 273; in village organization, 342–345; roles, 410–411; in Vaishya model, 460–461; in jati fission and fusion, 488–490, 498; in religious movements, 535; in gift giving, 552; in tribal organization, 578–582, 586, 596–597, 612; in social change, 638–641. *See also* markets and trade
Edgerton, Franklin, 450
educated people, 112, 235–236, 247, 470, 471–472, 484–485, 494, 507–509, 530, 655
education: for girls, 108–109, 647–648; as source of power, 210, 246–247; as part of religion, 413–414, 456; as means of jati improvement, 500–508, 518–519. *See also* elite (new)
Eglar, Zekiye, 99, 149, 547, 551, 552
Elephant village, 343–344
elite (new), 636, 651
Elwin, Verrier, 579, 584
Emeneau, Murray B., 390
endogamy, 101–104 *passim*, 231, 239, 547, 577–578, 653. *See also* jati

evidence and sources, nature of those used herein, 8–9
Epstein, T. Scarlett, 70, 96, 98, 100, 106, 113, 115, 116, 130, 137, 143, 241–242, 246, 250, 251–252, 255, 262–263, 266–267, 275–276, 279, 290–291, 314, 320, 335, 344–345, 352, 379, 422, 439, 459
"excest", 231
exogamy, 101–104 *passim*, 134, 144, 146–148, 331; "four-gotra rule" for, 147; village, 87, 102–103

factions, 161, 241, 247–248, 249–252. *See also* alliances
family, 33–158; as social system, 5, 6; ideal and actual, 17, 34–37, 125–126; as fundamental social unit, 33, 41; conflict in, 61, 66, 77–78, 90–93; changes and continuities in, 34, 36, 39, 43, 45–47, 642–654; hierarchy in, 38–41, 120–121; as economic unit, 41–42, 47–54, 131; as religious unit, 42; as reproductive unit, 43; as socializing agency, 43, 131; as village unit, 43; role composition of, 43–44; use of term, 45; nuclear and joint, 34, 36–37, 44–45, 52–54, 125–130, 642–644; regional variations in, 54–56; affectionate relations in, 62, 74, 83; formation and maintenance of, 95–118; growth and completion of, 119–125; dispersal of, 125–130; as module and model, 130–133; and jati, 161–180, 181; processes widely shared, 626. *See also* jajmani, kinship, solidarity (filial-fraternal)
family cycle, 34–37, 46, 95–133
family roles: male, 58–81; female, 82–94
Farquhar, J. N., 538
feminal kin, 80, 135, 148–151, 259, 260
Ferguson, Frances N., 527
Fernandez, Frank, 580
fertility: fear of barrenness, 86; rewards of bearing children, 88–89
fictive kin, 135–136, 151–152, 183, 331
fields of action, 418–420
Fischel, Walter J., 561
food. *See* religious practices, vegetarian diet
Fortes, Meyer, 34
Foster, George M., 257
Fox, Richard G., 506
Freed, Stanley A., 65, 150, 220, 333–334, 353
Freed, Ruth S., 65, 333–334
Freedman, Maurice, 92–93
friendship, 354–356, 383–384

Frykenberg, Robert Eric, 431
Fuchs, Stephen, 61, 75, 76, 77, 197, 200, 281, 288, 299, 300, 302, 317, 322, 378, 473
Fukutake, Tadashi, 86, 97, 107, 127, 237
Fürer-Haimendorf, Christoph von, 416, 580, 583, 588, 589, 594

Gadgil, D. R., 649
Gait, E. A., 52, 120
Galanter, Marc, 307, 308, 449, 574, 654
Gamras village, 72, 212, 215, 359
Gandhi, M. K., 22, 59, 65, 246, 304, 327, 368, 473, 610
Gangrade, K. D., 65-66, 272, 416
Gannapur village, 354
Ganjam distillers, 480-481
Gaon village, 107, 139, 140, 213-214, 215, 274, 454, 475, 476
Gardner, Peter M., 577
Gayawals, 235, 438
Geertz, Clifford, 387, 407, 579
Ghurye, G. S., 7, 12, 14, 22, 190, 206, 236, 300, 319, 415, 459, 508, 574, 641, 642, 653
Gideon, Helen, 120
gift giving, 109, 552
Gist, Noel P., 653, 656
Gluckman, Max, 406
Gnanambal, K., 59-60, 92
Goldberg, Helen, 72, 202
Gonds. See Hill Maria Gonds, Raj Gonds
Goode, William J., 52, 53, 112, 120, 644, 646, 647, 648, 651, 652, 653
Gopalaswami, R. A., 44
Gopalpur village, 69, 118, 132, 149, 153, 331, 337, 343-344, 347, 354, 365, 376, 378, 477
Gore, M. S., 34, 38, 63, 83, 644, 647, 653
gotra, 28, 101, 145-146, 238. See also clan
Gough, E. Kathleen, 42, 47, 48, 56, 60, 62, 64, 70, 173, 205, 215, 225-227, 239, 261, 320, 340, 347, 361-362, 416, 437, 458, 460, 503, 514, 548, 577
Gould, Harold A., 102-103, 112, 119, 129, 171-172, 174, 178, 179, 182, 240, 353, 382, 402, 414, 449, 465, 645-646, 650, 662
government and administration, 264, 334-335, 345-352, 385, 411, 629-630; influence on jati rank, 209-210; and alliance strength, 246; and social change, 636-638
Govindapur village, 240

Gray, L. H., 217, 431
Gray, R. M., 304
Grewal, B. S., 349-350
Grierson, George, 400
Grigson, W. V., 590
Gross, Neal, 418
Guha, Uma, 549
guilds of artisans, 318-319
Gujarat, 141, 149, 244-245, 249, 254, 439-440, 446, 453, 460, 462, 464, 472, 493, 501, 514-516, 517, 526
Gujars, 397, 462
Gumperz, John J., 182, 321, 356, 399, 400, 451
Gupta, Raghuraj, 550
Gupte, B. A., 69
gurus, 282, 526-527, 532, 537-538, 595, 597, 607-608, 615; Gurus of Kumbakonam, 529

Hardgrave, Robert L., Jr., 503, 512, 513, 518
Hariana (Haryana), 39, 543
Harijans, 22, 23, 116, 185, 191, 214, 240-241, 256, 266-267, 272-274, 281, 298-299, 308, 317, 318, 319-320, 339-340, 355, 377-379, 451, 472, 476-477, 495, 515, 532, 542, 581, 626, 656. See also Untouchables
Haripura village, 113, 247-249, 250, 251, 253-254, 256, 258-260 passim, 279, 292, 308
Harper, Edward B., 61, 79, 83, 91, 116, 138, 145, 162, 165, 170-171, 176, 187, 188, 189, 191, 194, 195, 198, 199, 203, 204, 224, 241, 260-261, 282, 297-298, 308, 311, 318, 319, 353, 410-411, 436, 477
Harper, Louise G., 241, 260-261, 282, 297-298, 308, 311, 319
Harrison, Selig S., 391, 401, 431, 516, 518
Haye, Chowdhry Abdul, 559
Hazlehurst, Leighton W., 652
Hein, Norwin, 387
Hill Maria Gonds, 588, 589-590, 619
hierarchical ordering of society, 6, 29, 180, 183-184; in family relations, 37-40; exceptions to, 182-183, 291, 624; based on ritual standards, 217; common understanding of, 228; as assumption, 624; reinforced by religion, 624-625. See also caste system, jati, pollution, ranking, religion
Hindu Code, the, 654
Hindu Gains of Learning Act (1930), 42

Hinduism. *See* religion, religious movements
Hira Lal, Rai Bahadur, 239
Hitchcock, John T., 42, 83, 89, 119–122, 126, 128, 137, 150, 156, 207, 241, 242–243, 245, 251, 255, 268, 270, 273, 274, 287, 303, 318, 322, 356, 359, 362–363, 369, 452–453, 464, 649
Hockings, Paul, 588, 602
Holerus, 436–437
Homans, George C., 660
Honigmann, John J., 148, 553
Hopkins, Edward W., 453
Hsu, Francis L. K., 115, 128–129
husband-wife relations, 74–79, 85–87; wife's relatives, 69–70
Hutton, J. H., 12, 146, 238, 282, 289, 300, 307, 319, 584
hypergamy and hypergamous sections, 236–240, 439–440, 472

Ibbetson, Denzil, 8, 435, 437, 488, 557
identity and identification, 124, 322, 329–330, 401–404, 632–633
incasting, 297, 299
Ingalls, Daniel H. H., 306, 456
interchange, 5, 6, 21
Iravas (Ezhavas, Tiyyas), 500, 502–503
irrigation, influence of, 344–345, 434. *See also* Wangala
Irschick, Eugene F., 212, 399
Isaacs, Harold R., 471–472
Ishwaran, K., 69, 127–128
Islam, 524, 545–559, 630, 631
Islamization, 557–559
Isma'ili, 555
Iyer, L. K. Ananthakrishna, 397, 402, 565
Izmirlian, Harry, Jr., 126, 542
izzat, 468, 627

Jackson, A. V. Williams, 218, 431, 459
Jagalpure, L. B., 182
Jainism, 533, 534–536
Jains, 282, 314, 534–536
jajmani, 161–180, 352–354, 382, 410; associates help in family ceremonies, 98; of Muslims, 547, 551–552, 558–559
Jangamas, 537
Jatavs, 385–386, 472, 482, 493–496, 517
jati-cluster, 19–22, 229–230, 517
jati-groups, 15, 18, 229–230, 240–244, 249–268, 279–280, 316, 317, 320, 330, 365–369
jatis: as systems of social relations, 5; definition of, 14–15; occupations of,

114, 164–167; boundaries of, 15, 16–17, 33, 419, 487; flexibilities in, 16–19; "effective", 113, 235; and families, 161–180; dominant, 172–173, 207–208, 240–244, 358–367, 391–392, 562–564, 582, 589, 605; criteria for ranking of, 181–205; sources of power of, 206–213; blocs of, 213–216, 230, 541; evaluation of rank order of, 216–221; cultural differences among, 222–232; alliances and sections within, 235–252; leaders of, 270–278, 484–486; *panchayats* of, 278–293; enterprises and functions of, 316–323; regional influence of, 391–392; mobility of, 427–441, 627; cultural adaptation of, 443–467; change of name of, 445–447; mobility tactics of, 468–486; fission of, 488–496, 555, 634; fusion of, 496–499, 634; associations and federations of, 500–516; and education, 500–520 *passim*; compared to tribes, 576–585. *See also* jajmani, status competition
jatras, 331–332
Jats, 51, 112–113, 140–141, 207–208, 230, 243, 249, 251, 267, 283–284, 286, 305, 317–318, 354, 359, 391–392, 500–502, 507, 540, 541, 542, 552, 579
Jay, Edward J., 420, 576, 590
Jews, 491–492, 546, 560–563, 625
Jharkhand Party, 608, 615–616
Jitpur village, 648–649
joint family. *See* family
joking relations, 65, 87–88
Jodha, N. S., 171, 176, 177
Judaism, 545–546, 560–563
Julahas, 554
Justice Party, 512

Kaibartta (Hali Kaibartta), 446
Kale, K. D., 182
Kalidasa, 84–85
Kallars (Pramalai Kallars), 52, 60, 61–62, 86, 139, 149, 157, 288, 311–312
Kallas, 458
Kamaraj Nadar, 512
Kamas, 431
Kane, Pandurang Vaman, 184, 196, 306, 448
Kannan, C. T., 648, 652
Kanyakubja (Kanya Kubja), Brahmins, 238, 506
Kapadia, K. M., 35, 41, 45, 53, 56, 60, 73, 97, 126, 145, 642, 646, 647, 648, 650, 652, 653, 656
Kapp, K. William, 638

Karal village, 354–355
Karandikar, S. V., 146
Karim, A. K., Nazmul, 549
Karimpur village, 76–77, 91, 348–349, 350, 351, 359
karma, 204, 412, 429
Karve, Irawati, 14, 18, 19, 20, 28, 38, 46, 47, 56, 62, 64, 65, 67, 70, 78, 83, 85–86, 88, 89, 92, 103, 104, 106, 112, 114, 128, 133, 145, 146, 147, 157, 158, 174, 175, 237, 330, 337, 338, 340, 354–355, 389, 390, 392, 393, 397, 402, 415, 429, 433, 446, 450, 451, 452, 454–455, 462, 525, 526
Kautilya, 410
Kayasths, 62, 216, 433
Kennedy, Beth C., 122
Kennedy, Melville T., 533
Kerala, 55–56, 238–239, 455
Ketkar, Shridhar Venkatesh, 195, 202
Khadduri, Majid, 555
Khalapur village, 51–52, 68, 82–83, 89, 119–125, 150, 156, 242–243, 245, 251, 255, 273, 318, 356, 359, 362–363; 365, 399, 452, 649
Khan, Khan Ahmad Hasan, 524
Khare, R. S., 238
Khatis, 51, 363–364, 491
Khatris, 539–540
Khedkar, Vithan Krishnaji, 442, 443, 485
Khojas, 555
kinship, 33–158, 289; fundamental to jati, 33; agnatic, 63–64, 132–144; wider ties of, 134–158; feminal, 80, 135, 148–151, 259, 260; fictive, 135–136, 151–152, 183, 331; lineage, 136–144; clan, 144–145; terms, 145–148; uses of, 152–156; in North and in South India, 156–158; résumé of, 158; and pollution, 193–194; and tribes, 576; tribal and jati view of, 591. *See also* family
Kisan political movement, 258
Kishan Garhi village, 28–29, 211, 215, 224, 237, 311, 357
Klass, Morton, 97, 102, 105, 113, 146, 235
Kochar, V. K., 614
Kolenda, Pauline Mahar, 51–52, 171, 174, 205, 220
Kolis, 462–463, 472
Kolmel village, 600
Konds, 322, 422, 577, 578, 579–580, 585, 594, 595–598, 616–617
Kosambi, D. D., 587
Kotas, 20, 64, 78, 91, 186, 266, 300–301, 317, 469–471, 484–485, 575, 586, 594, 599–603, 617

Kothari, Rajni, 514–515, 516
Kripalani, Krishna, 483–484
Kroeber, A. L., 390, 421
Kshatriya Sabha, 500, 514–516
Kshatriyas, 23, 24, 25, 201, 207, 227, 434, 435, 446–447, 451, 452–455, 455–464 *passim*, 477, 478, 500, 514–516, 588, 594, 603–604, 606–609, 610
Kudryavtsev, M. K., 546, 579
Kui Samaj, 598–599
Kumbapettai village, 47–48, 90, 91, 205, 215, 225–227, 261, 320, 347, 361, 363, 437, 577
Kunbis, 20, 446
Kurmis, 230
Kurumbas, 600–601

Lacey, W. G., 444
Lall, R. Manohar, 68
Lambert, Richard D., 52, 344, 658
Lambert, William W., 68, 82–83, 122, 124
land, as source of power, 208–209; as source of conflict, 253
land ownership. *See* economic factors, jatis (dominant)
law, Hindu, 35, 307
law and courts, 35, 36, 42, 111, 246, 305–315, 449, 653–654
Lay of Lorik, 322
Leach, Edmund R., 25–26, 430, 665
Leacock, Seth, 410
leadership, 220–278, 484–486
leaders and leadership, 251, 256, 261, 270–278, 383, 484–486, 487
Learmonth, A. M., 391
Learmonth, A. T. A., 391
Lenski, Gerhard, 662
Levinson, Daniel J., 418
Lewis, Oscar, 65, 69, 88, 103, 105, 109, 113, 114, 117, 137, 146, 169, 173, 208, 241, 249, 251, 259, 267, 273, 318, 348, 349, 350, 354, 359, 382
Liebesny, H. J., 555
life-cycle ceremonies, 42, 71–72, 137, 138–139, 185–186, 225–226, 321, 437–438; jajmani relations in, 165–166
lineage, 134–144; as system of social relations, 5, 6; definition of, 17–18; localized, 134, 140; deities, 137–138; ritual functions of, 137–139, 316; members as allies, 139; in economic and jural affairs, 139–144; political functions of, 141–142; federations, 243; and alliances, 241–242; leaders, 270–

271; among tribals, 576; in group challenges, 627

Lingayats, 282, 296–297, 314, 343, 360, 450, 532, 536–539, 588

Lingayatism, 533, 536–539

linguistic regions, 392–401 *passim;* as outer boundary of bride search, 113; mapping of, 400

Linguistic Survey of India, 400

Lohars, 167–169, 171

Lokanathan, P. S., 637

Lony (Lonikand), 641–642

Lynch, Owen M., 386, 482, 493

McClelland, David C., 125

McCormack, William, 70, 71, 83, 282, 308, 314, 321, 449, 537, 538

McCrindle, J. W., 3

McDonald, Ellen E., 399

McEachern, A. W., 418

MacLachlan, Morgan E., 395

Madan, T. N., 40, 42, 43, 45, 46, 61, 66, 72, 75, 79, 80, 82, 83, 89, 91, 92, 96, 97, 102, 105, 117, 126, 127, 136, 139, 144, 145, 146, 149, 640, 647

Madigas, 256, 257, 340, 431

Madhupur village, 342, 604–610

Mahabharata, 35, 133

Mahabrahmans, 437–438

Mahajan, Mehr Chand, 110–111

Mahatos, 605–606

Mahavira, 534–536

Mahisyas, 240, 243, 367, 374, 392, 446

Mahuva, 53

Maine, Henry, 161, 307, 309, 327, 345

Majumdar, Dhirendra Nath, 46, 88, 98, 165, 166, 238, 241, 281, 296, 344, 576

Majumdar, R. C., 3

Malas, 256, 257, 340, 431, 432

Malaviya, H. D., 368

Malhotra, S. P., 243, 251

Mallika, Balarama. *See* Mullick, Bulloram

Mandelbaum, David G., 13, 35, 64, 78, 86–87, 112, 186, 201, 209, 226, 265, 266, 300–301, 316, 392, 395, 410, 411, 412, 469, 491, 547, 548, 558, 560, 576, 583, 586, 599–603, 626

Manu, 22, 23, 429, 453, 629

Marathas, 20, 147, 214, 237, 239, 445, 446, 454, 462, 476

maravars, 511, 512

markets and trade, 383, 385, 397–398, 410

marriage: and jati boundaries, 16–17, 33; preferential uncle-niece, 70, 91–92; cross-cousin, 70–71; and family

growth, 96–97; as test of status, 98–101; rules and procedures for, 101–109; to improve status, 104–109; gifts, 109, 651; precautions for, 110–112; prepuberty, 110, 111–112, 227; range for alliances, 112–115; ceremony, 115–118, 651, 652; affinal ties, 148–151; status variations in, 223, 226–227; and alliance cohesion, 249; jati intermarriage, 497, 653; changes in pattern of, 651–654. *See also* family, hypergamy, ceremonies and rites

Marriott, McKim, 22, 54, 69, 99, 114, 147–148, 151, 158, 211, 215, 225, 238, 311, 337, 356–357, 363, 391, 403, 412, 413, 447, 485

Marten, J. T., 443–444

Martin, Montgomery, 548

Maru, Rushikesh, 514, 515, 516

Marx, Karl, 327, 662

Mason, W. S., 418

matrilineal groups. *See* Nayars

Mathur, K. S., 139, 146, 182, 185, 191, 194, 195, 197, 199, 203, 204, 215, 656

Maya, 412

Mayer, Adrian C., 22, 25, 29, 40–41, 44, 46, 47, 51, 63–64, 65, 67, 73, 74, 79, 80, 89, 100, 113, 114, 115, 128, 131, 136, 137, 141, 144, 145, 146, 147, 153–155, 215, 217, 218, 219–220, 235, 241, 281–282, 287, 289, 292, 297, 303–304, 331, 332, 340, 347, 364–365, 373, 392, 398, 419, 420, 440, 453, 455, 457, 458, 471, 476–477, 491, 493, 532

Maynard, H. J., 435

Mazhbis, 541

Megasthenes, 3, 16

Mehtars, 299, 378

Memons, 555

Mencher, Joan, 56, 72, 122, 202, 337, 339, 408, 409

Meos, 558–559

Metcalfe, Charles T., 327, 328, 356

military traditions. *See* Kshatriyas

Miller, Eric J., 112, 202, 215, 337, 338, 370

Minturn, Leigh, 42, 68, 82–83, 89, 119–122, 123, 124, 126, 128, 137, 150, 156, 255, 270, 287, 303, 318, 356, 359, 362–363, 369, 464, 649

Misra, Satish C., 165, 166, 434, 546, 547, 551, 554, 555, 556

missionaries: Christian, 564–571 *passim,* 594, 614; Hindu, 611

Mitakshara, 35, 43

Mitra, Ashok, 391

models: family as, 130-133; regions as, 395-396; for mobility, 447-467; of tribals, 594
modernization: role of in status rise, 464-467, 491-497, 500-520; Parsis leaders in, 564; and tribals, 617-619
Mohana village, 295-296, 344
Moka Dora tribe, 574
Monga, Veena, 507, 508
Moon, Penderel, 313
Morgan, Lewis H., 156-157
Morris, Morris David, 640
Morris-Jones, W. H., 658
Morsralli village, 71
motivation, 418-419, 623-627, 639. See also psychological factors
Mughals, 550
Mukerji, A. B., 384
Mukhopadhyay, Tarashish, 243, 298, 299, 302, 312, 320, 338, 341, 374, 446
Müller, Frederich Max, 568
Mullick, Bulloram (Balarama Mallika), 88
Murdock, George P., 148
Muslims, 10, 228, 413, 434, 546-559, 571, 572, 575
Myrdal, Gunnar, 639-640
myths, origin, 429-430, 443, 445

Nadars, 71, 500, 510-514, 517, 569-571
Nadel, S. F., 660
Naim, C. M., 399
Nair, Sankaran, 435
Nais, 112-113
Nakane, Chie, 86, 97, 107, 127, 237
Nalli village, 542
Nambudiris, 55-56, 72, 202, 238-239, 370
Namhalli village, 127, 263-264, 343-344, 375-376, 377
Nanak (Guru), 539-540
Nandi, Proshanta Kumar, 506
Nandi, Santibhushan, 338
Nandimath, S. C., 538
Narayan, Jayaprakash, 638
Nath, Kamla, 648-649
Nath, V., 334, 340, 363
national identification, 401-404
national independence movement, 608-609, 610
Navalakha, Surendra Kumar, 607
Navsari, 53
Nayadis, 72, 91, 164, 193
Nayar, Unni, 55-56
Nayars, 35, 55-56, 64, 72, 122, 202, 238-239, 370, 455

Neale, Walter C., 169, 385
Nehru, Jawaharlal, 63, 68, 197, 415, 525, 638
Nehru, Motilal, 63
Nehru, S. S., 208, 212
neighborhood, social ties of, 341
Neill, Stephen, 568
networks. See social networks
Newell, W. H., 653
Nicholas, Ralph W., 70, 91, 128, 137, 240, 241, 243, 266, 298, 299, 302, 311, 320, 337, 338, 339, 341, 347, 367, 374, 392, 407, 446, 459
Niehoff, Arthur, 653
Nikitin, Afanasy, 196
Noniyas, 112, 150, 167, 172, 434, 477-478, 634
nonviolence, 246, See also Gandhi
"North India": definition of, 11; in contrast to South, 69-70, 89-90, 101-104, 106, 111, 141, 156-158, 199, 259, 390-391
Nrusingh, 422, 595-596

oaths, omens, and ordeals, 288-289
Okkaligas. See also Vokkaligas, 235, 247-249, 359-361, 363, 498
O'Malley, L. S. S., 12, 336, 489, 568, 613
Opler, Morris E., 42, 84, 90, 132, 241, 328, 329, 342, 438, 647-648
Orans, Martin, 175, 581, 585, 613, 614, 615, 616
Orenstein, Henry, 40, 52, 61, 62, 66, 69, 105, 107, 127, 136, 139, 140, 147, 155, 162, 163, 171, 173, 174, 175, 194, 202, 213-214, 215, 237, 274, 350, 408, 445, 446, 454, 459, 475,
Oriya, 422, 579, 585, 595-598
Orr, W. G., 533
Ouchi, Tsutomu, 86, 97, 107, 127, 237
outcasting, 284, 285, 295-305 passim, 483, 491, See also jatis

Padayachis, 455, 471
Pahari, 395-396
Pakistan, 10, 551-553
Paliyans, 6, 577
Pallas, 471
Pallans, 205
Panchala, 458-459
panchayats: lineage, 129, 137, 284; definition of, 278; pattern of action of, 278-286; social and geographic scope of, 280-286; powers of, 284, 285; participation and procedure of, 286-293; uses

of, 294–315; and the courts, 311–315; in the village, 367–373; as vehicle for reform, 503–505, 657–658
panchgavya, 300
Pandya, Bihari J., 107
Panikkar, K. M., 27, 435, 454, 653–654
Pans, 480–482
Parekh, Manilal C., 304
Parsis, 545, 563–564
Parsons, Talcott, 418, 660, 662
"passing," as mobility tactic, 471–472
Pat village, 553
Pathans, 550; *Swat Pathans*, 474–475
Patidars, 20–21, 51, 107–108, 237, 244–245, 246, 254, 439, 440, 446, 460–461, 463, 472, 493, 515, 516
Pativrata, 38
Patnaik, Nityananda, 166, 283, 314, 384, 460, 461, 466, 503–505
patrilineality. *See* family, lineage, clan
Patterson, Maureen, L. P., 653
Pendse, R. G., 53, 54
percolation, as mobility tactic, 472–473
pilgrimages, 401–402. *See also* religious centers
Piralis, 483–484
Planalp, Jack Milan, 65
Plato, 23
Pocock, David F., 20–21, 45, 146, 157, 164, 171, 237, 244–245, 246, 254, 327, 365, 366, 417, 430, 440, 446, 463, 473, 493, 647
Pods, 489–490
Poffenberger, Thomas, 107, 122
political factors: in lineage relations, 141–143; within the jati-group, 240–244, 252; and settlement patterns, 339; and village panchayats, 367–368; duality of politics and administration, 411; and jati mobility, 428–429, 435–436, 493–496, 633–634, 658; and caste associations, 500–520; in tribal organization, 578, 586, 603–610, 612–616
pollution, 14, 42–43, 184–187, 192–205, 231, 300–305, 537; of birth, 120, 138, 185–186, 193–194; rules of learned in childhood, 131; lineage 138; of death, 138, 184–186 *passim*, 193–195; and ritual specialists, 164; personal, 184–189; transition states as vector of, 185, 204–205; the contagion of, 189–191, 193–195; through ingestion, 196–201; corporate, 189–191; cows and, 189–190; "respect-pollution," 199–200; and alcohol, 201; through sexual relations, 201–202; Muslim view of, 547, 550;

concept reinforces hierarchy, 624. *See also* purification, purity, religion
Poona, 52, 53
population, 258, 636; and infant mortality, 120; and village size, 374–375; and migration, 490
possession, 224, 227
Potlad village, 194, 203, 215
potters, 296–297, 507–508
power, social and political: and kinship, 155–156; symbols of, 181–182; application of, 207–208, 252, 302, 428–429; sources of, 208–211, 244–247; limits of secular factors in, 210–211; imbalance of and status, 255, 439; shifts of in village, 373–380
Prabhu, Pandhari Nath, 23, 206
Pradhan, M. C., 141, 165, 166, 283–285, 286, 305, 392, 501, 502, 579
Prasad, Rajendra, 62
pratiloma, 236
psychological factors and personality, 414–417, 419–420, 425–428, 583–585, 623–627. *See also* identity and identification
purdah, 38, 62, 554
purification: ritual procedures for, 164, 165–166; means of, 202–205
purity, 14, 24–25, 42–43, 184–187, 192–205, 231, 537; as a concern of women, 77; in certain roles, 188–191; and the cow, 189–190; as nontransferable, 194; relative nature of, 194–195; significance of, 197–198; of certain foods, 199; and social mobility, 479–480; reinforces social hierarchy, 624
Pyarelal (Nair), 304, 473

Radha-Krishna bhajan, 529–531
Radhanagar village, 258, 260, 266, 339, 367
Raghavan, V., 421
Raghuvanshi, V. P. S., 193, 431, 462, 464, 488, 528
Raj Gonds, 208, 588, 589, 609
Raj, Hilda, 71, 511, 512, 568, 570, 571
Rajasthan, 193, 243, 251, 464, 472, 488–489
Rajputs, 51, 68, 82–83, 89, 113–114, 119–125, 141, 143, 146, 147, 150, 207, 218, 230, 236–237, 239, 245, 255, 280–281, 297, 305, 318, 322, 331, 359, 362–365 *passim.*, 373, 392, 444, 452–453, 457–458, 462–463, 464, 476, 477, 491, 493, 514–516, 526, 532, 550, 558, 609, 610, 649

Raksha Bandhan (*rakhi-bandhan*), 68, 557
Ram Lila, 132
Ramakrishna Mission, 416
Ramapur village, 342, 437-438
Ramayana, 132
Ramkheri village, 22, 25, 46-47, 51, 52, 63-64, 73, 89, 99-100, 113, 114, 115, 143, 144-145, 146, 147, 153-155, 217, 219, 280-282 *passim.*, 292, 297, 303-305 *passim*, 330-331, 332, 341, 346, 347, 363-364, 373, 398, 440, 457, 464, 476, 491-492, 492-493, 497, 532
Rampur village, 51-52, 103, 112, 114, 249, 251, 258-260 *passim*, 267, 348, 350, 359, 382
Rampura village, 128, 146, 170, 207, 211, 217, 296-297, 303, 334, 335, 336, 340-341, 349, 359-361, 362, 363, 365, 369, 377, 388, 485
Ranade, Ramabai, 83, 85
rank and ranking ritual criteria for, 14, 24-25, 181-191, 195, 206-208; secular criteria for, 14, 181-191, 206-221; of families, 18-19; within families, 41-45, 120-121; individual manipulation of, 218-219. *See also* hierarchical ordering of society, jati, caste system
Rao, M. S. A., 164, 174, 202, 442, 444, 466, 485
Rao, V. L. S. Prakasa, 385
Rao, Y. V. Lakshmana, 388
Rarhi (Rahri) Brahmins, 238, 239
Rath, R., 205
Ray, A. K., 283, 460, 467, 503-505
recurrent change. *See* social systems, social change
Reddis (tribe), 416, 588-589
Reddis, 431
Reddy, N. S., 65, 143, 167, 168, 169, 256, 322, 375
Redfield, Robert, 660
reference groups and reference categories, 447-467, 492, 594
"regionalism," 398-401
regions: differences in family form among, 54-57; jati blocs among, 215; assemblies of, 282; and market economy, 328; definition of 389; as delineated by observers, 389-393; as perceived by residents, 389, 393-397; linguistic identification of, 392-393, 395-396, 399-401; changes in over time, 397-399; dialects of, 399; functions of in economics, politics, and religion, 409-414

religion: linked to social concepts, 13, 23-24, 523; deities, 195, 223-225; transcendental and pragmatic aspects of, 223-224, 410-413; and social reform, 523-524; conversion for status gain, 524, 543-544; provides variety of choices, roles, experience, 525-527; Hinduism and Islam, 546-548. *See also* ceremonies and rites
religious centers, 281-282, 385, 398, 402, 403, 448
religious associations, 502-503, 526, 533-543
religious movements: 488, 502-503; cult and sect, 528, 531-533, 544, 555-557, 607-608, 614-615; indigenous, 523-544; introduced, 545-572
religious practices (ritual), 187; link lineages, 137-139; in eating and drinking, 197-201; jati differences in, 223-228; transgression and redress in, 295-300; for village solidarity, 331-334; of Muslims, 347-348; among tribals, 582-583, 586-587, 590, 615. *See also* pollution, purity
Renou, Louis, 533, 536, 537
residence. *See* family, marriage, lineage
Republican Party, 496
"resource group," 241
Retzlaff, Ralph H., 273, 365, 371
Reyes-Hockings, Amelia, 653
Rig-Veda, 22
ritual criteria for rank. *See also* pollution, purity, rank and ranking
ritual services, 164, 165-166. *See also* pollution, purification, purity
Risley, Herbert H., 238, 483, 489, 571, 576, 587-588, 607, 609
Rivers, W. H. R., 239
Roger, Abraham, 217, 430-431
roles: variety of social, 4, 381, 418-420, 657, 663; women's, 42, 43, 46, 47-48, 418; family, 58-94, 626; of special purity, 188-189; link, 386-388; dual, 409-414; special, 414-417; expansion of, 419-420; choice in, 422
Rooksby, R. L., 209
Ross, Aileen D., 39, 40, 45, 61, 67, 80, 84, 90, 129, 647, 648, 651, 652, 653
Rosser, Colin, 394
Rowe, William L., 67, 112, 114, 145, 150, 167, 172, 359, 434, 478, 651
Roy Burman, B. K., 576
Roy, Sarat Chandra, 198, 258, 266, 278
Rudolph, Susanne Hoeber, 59, 510, 511, 513, 516

Rudolph, Lloyd I., 510, 511, 513, 514, 516, 519
Russell, R. V., 239

sabhas. See associations and federations
Sachchidananda, 591
sacred thread. *See* "twice-born," symbolism
Sagar Rajputs (Sagar Dhangar), 445, 446, 454
Saibaba, 527; cult of, 527
samiti (committee form), 292
Sangave, Vilas Adinath, 536
sanskrit and sanskritization: ritual standards of, 207, 222-224, 412-413
Santals, 575, 581, 585, 594, 613-616
sanyassin, 415, 526, 527
Sapinda relations, 101
Sarma, Jyotirmoyee, 40, 50, 53, 59, 65, 67, 80, 86, 88, 92, 127, 131, 133, 183, 185, 215
Sayyads (Sayyids), 549-550, 553, 555
"scheduled" castes and tribes, 495, 574, 591-592, 594, 610, 612. *See also* Harijans, untouchables, tribes
Schwartzberg, Joseph E., 389, 391, 392
scripture (Hindu) 223-224; as basis of social order, 13, 23-24, 230; concepts from, 13, 23-24, 204, 205, 230, 412, 429; variations among texts, 223; origin myths of jatis in, 429-430, 443. *See also* Vedas, *Mahabharata, Ramayana,* sanskrit and sanskritization, religion
secular criteria for rank. *See* pollution, purity, rank and ranking
Sen, C., 51, 165, 166
Senapur village, 48-49, 51-52, 84, 112, 142, 150, 167-169, 171, 172, 205, 266, 292, 299, 302, 311, 328, 329, 332-333, 359, 371, 377, 434, 477-478, 647-648, 651
Senart, Émile, 12, 26, 229
Sengupta, Sunil, 52, 126
settlement patterns. *See* village
sexual relations, 62, 65-66, 75-76, 77, 111, 201-202, 253, 369-370, 491
Shah, A. M., 43, 44, 141, 146, 328, 338, 410, 446, 461, 462-463, 473, 493, 643
Shah, B. V., 653
Shahani, Savitri, 51
Shaikhs, 550, 554, 555
shamans, 227, 411-412, 582-583. *See also* religion, pragmatic aspects of
Shamirpet village, 72, 92-93, 113, 166,

215, 269-270, 276, 278-279, 289, 303, 335, 347, 370, 377
Shanti Nagar village, 151, 353
Sharma, Kailas N., 16, 72, 73, 74, 162, 181, 188, 199, 212, 215, 216, 219, 238, 241, 319, 359, 420, 456, 656
Sherurpur village, 171-172, 178-179, 352-353, 402, 414, 465
Shias (Shi'ahs, Shi'as), 227, 550, 555. *See also* Muslims
Shroff, R. G., 141, 146, 461, 462-463, 473
Shudras, 23, 26, 191, 217-218, 314, 319, 451, 455, 461-462, 477. *See also* varnas
Siegel, Bernard J., 66, 77, 105, 128, 263-264, 375, 376
Sikhs, 298-299, 524, 539-543, 568
Sikhism, 533, 539-543
Silverberg, James, 182
Singer, Milton, 335, 387, 421, 449, 528-531, 638-639, 640, 642, 644, 645-646
Singh, A. K., 640
Singh, Gobind, 540
Singh, Harpal, 385
Singh, Indera P., 166, 256, 375, 524, 541, 542
Singh, Jai Pal, 385, 615
Singh, Khushwant, 539, 540, 543, 568
Singh, Ranjit, 540
Singh, Rudra Datt, 333, 342, 438
Singh, Tara, 299-300
Sinha, D. P., 387
Sinha, Surajit, 12, 383, 384, 391, 578, 580, 583, 585, 589, 603-610, 665
Sircar, N. C., 205
Sirkanda village, 51-52, 87, 145, 146, 148, 312, 338, 353, 395-396
Smith, Donald Eugene, 306-307
Smith, Marian W., 341, 382
Smith, Wilfred Cantwell, 546, 556
social change, 427-432, 636-659; through religious movements, 523-544; aspects of, 594-595. *See also* jatis, social systems, status competition
social mobility, 427-467, 468-486, 553-555, 630-633; models for, 448-467; passing and percolation as means of, 471-473; and caste associations, 500-520; of tribal peoples, 593-619. *See also* family, lineage, jati, social change, social system, status competition
social networks, 114, 420
social organization: concept of, 4-6; ideal and real, 13-17, 23-25, 26-27, 268; family as unit of, 33, 41; wide acceptance of, 228, 623; of tribes, 578, 591; forces and processes for continu-

ity and change in, 623-635; trends of change in, 636-659. *See also* social systems

social perceptions, 17-22, 294-295, 599-603

social reforms and reformers, 12, 444-445, 466-467, 468-471, 500-520, 523-544

social stratification, 239, 634, 661-663. *See also* jati, social systems, hierarchical ordering of society

social structure, 428. *See also* social systems, social organization

social systems, 4-7, 658-659, 660-665; recurrent and systemic change within, 7-8, 427, 441, 523-544, 573-592, 619, 623, 628-635; subsystems, 381, 422, 661. *See also* jatis

solidarity, filial-fraternal, 34-35; advantages and disadvantages of, 36-37; women and, 49-50; effects of urban life on, 54, 650-655

"South India": definition of, 11; in contrast to North, 69-70, 89-90, 101-104, 106, 111, 141, 156-158, 199, 259, 390-391

Sovani, N. V., 53, 54

Spate, O. H. K., 340, 391, 398, 556

Sri Narayana Guru, 502

Srinivas, M. N., 8, 12, 23, 26, 64, 67, 78, 84, 86, 92, 93, 101, 106, 112, 117, 128, 141, 169, 170, 185, 187, 201, 207, 211, 217, 223, 235, 279, 287, 296, 297, 303, 328, 334, 335, 340-341, 350, 359, 360-361, 365, 369, 387-388, 389-390, 393, 399, 401, 403, 410, 420, 428, 429, 433, 435, 446, 447, 449, 450, 452, 453, 455, 459, 460, 461, 465, 466, 467, 472, 473, 475, 478, 482, 485, 490, 492, 493, 496, 498, 520, 523, 524, 525, 527, 538, 636, 651

Srivastava, Ram P., 610-612

Srivastava, S. K., 454-476

Staal, J. F., 450

status competition: among families through marriage, 98-101; among jatis, 217-218, 318, 429-432, 439-441, 468-486; among alliances, 254-264; through associations, 500-520; and the social system, 623

Steed, Gitel P., 143, 453, 464, 526

Stein, Burton, 393, 430, 435

Stephen, Lesie, 161

Stevenson, H. N. L., 29, 187, 189, 190, 195, 197, 448

Steward, Julian H., 408

stratification. *See* social stratification

Strizower, Schifra, 563

Sudras. *See* Shudras

Sulli, 469-471, 484-485, 600, 603

Sunnis, 227, 550, 555. *See also* Muslims

Swat Pathans, 474-475

Swatantra Party, 516

swidden agriculture, 407, 579-580, 590, 591

symbolism: in seating arrangement, 181-182, 220, 331; of rank, 217-218, 378-379, 477-478, 631-632, 634

Syrian Christians, 565, 568

systems. *See* social system, caste system

Tagore, Rabindranath, 483-484

Tagores, 438-439, 482-484

Tandon, Prakash, 432

Telengana, 215

Telis, 282-283, 364, 460, 466, 476, 477, 497, 500, 503-505, 562-563

terminology, 11, 28-29, 143-144, 145, 147-148

Thakurs, 48-50, 51, 165-166, 167-168, 180, 215, 266, 309, 311, 359

Thoothi, N. A., 21

Thurston, Edgar, 239, 459, 460, 509, 511, 538

Tilak, Lakshmibai. 117-118, 569

Tilak, Narayan Vamen, 569

Tiyyas, 370. *See also* Iravas

Todas, 157, 600-601

Totagadde village, 138, 145, 162, 170, 176, 191, 260-261, 297-298, 308, 311, 318, 319, 353, 410-411, 436, 630

trade centers, 383-386

tribes: characteristics of, 180, 575-576; and kinship, 180, 591, 596; "scheduled," 495, 574, 591-592, 594; transfer of into jati systems, 573, 585-619; compared to jatis, 576-585; political organization of, 578; direction of change of (examples), 593-616; and modernization, 617-619

Tumin, Melvin M., 662

Tyagi, D. S., 338

Tyagis, 550

Ullah, Inayat, 552

Underhill, M. M., 69

Unni, K. Raman, 56

untouchables, 429, 577. *See also* Harijans

Upadhi, 238

Upanayanam, 448

Uralis, 576

urban centers, 27–28, 385–386; influence of, 344, 395–398, 644–646, 650–651; religious movements in, 528–531
urban life: and families, 54, 650–655; and status, 100; influence on village organization, 264

Vaishyas, 23–25, 446–447, 451, 460–462, 506
Van Buitinen, J. A. B., 449–450
Vanniyars, 500, 508–510
varnas, 13, 22–26, 268, 625; as scriptural categories, 13, 23–24, 230; uses of, 24–25, 230; as reference models, 24, 25, 448–451; "twice-born," 24, 26, 187, 191, 223, 447–451, 585
Vedas, 7, 22, 145, 456
vegetarian diet, 89, 193, 455–456. See also religious practices, pollution, purity
Vellalas, 458, 460
Vidyarthi, Lalita P., 235, 438, 576
village: as social unit, 5, 6, 9, 14, 35, 327–329; interdependence within, 27; as social locale, 27; relation to government agencies, 28; solidarity of, 329–335, 376; and settlement patterns, 335–341; organization of, 342–345; officers, 345–352; economic and ritual transactions in, 352–354; social relations in, 354–357; internal regulation of, 358–380; outside ties of, 381–421; and social change, 421–423
villagers: as principal subjects of this study, 9–10, 356–357; identity of, 13–13, 329–330, 393–394; and townsmen, 382–386; link roles among, 386–388; in relation to biological and ecological factors, 405–409; local and regional connections
Virashaivism, 536
Vogt, Evon Z., 660
Vohras, 555
Vokkaligas, 251–252, 253–254, 258, 260, 262, 266–267, 290–291, 314, 379. See also Okkaligas
voluntary associations, 526, 544. See also associations and federations
Vorkate village, 354–355

voting, 126
Vreede-de Stuers, Cora, 551, 556

Wagatsuma, H., 214
Wallace, Anthony, 26
Wangala village, 113, 114, 115, 116, 241–242, 250, 251, 255, 262–263, 266–267, 275, 290–291, 314, 320, 334–335, 344–345, 351, 379, 422, 439
Ward, William, 211–212
Warner, Lloyd, 662
Watters, Thomas, 203
Weber, Max, 12, 525, 576, 578, 638
wedding. See ceremonies and rites
Weiner, Myron, 513, 515, 516, 517
"western India," definition of, 11
"Westernization," 467
Wheeler, Mortimer, 410
Whiting, Beatrice B., 123, 124, 125
widows: remarriage of, 78, 223; and purity, 189, 198–199, 219, 298
Williams, A. Hyatt, 390
Winslow, J. C., 568
Wiser, William H., 76–77, 91, 162, 167, 169, 348, 349, 351, 353
Wiser, Charlotte Viall, 76–77, 91, 348, 351, 353
Wittfogel, Karl A., 408
Wolf, Eric R., 33
women: legal rights of, 35; family roles of, 38–41, 42, 43, 46, 82–94, 120, 236; economic and status factors in roles of, 47–48, 223, 226–227; as source of family conflict, 49–50, 127, 253; and education, 108–109, 648; among tribals, 576; shift in roles of, 646–648. See also husband-wife relations, feminal kin
wrestling matches, 182–183, 331–332
Wright, Theodore P., Jr., 559

Yadav, B. N. S., 443
Yadavas, 442–443, 466, 485, 514, 517
Yalman, Nur, 55, 70, 89, 106, 157, 158, 548
Yogis, 456–457

zemindar, 604
Zoroastrianism, 545, 560, 563–564

Place-Names and Group Names
A SELECTION OF THOSE MENTIONED IN THE TEXT.

	Name	State	Author
1.	Aggarwals	Har.	(Gore)
2.	Ahupe	Mah.	(Karve and Damle)
3.	Badagas	Mad.	(Hockings)
4.	Baderi	Or.	(Bailey)
5.	Badlapur	Mah.	(Morrison)
6.	Bhotias	U. P.	(Srivastava)
7.	Bhumij	Bih., W. Ben.	(S. Sinha)
8.	Bisipara	Or.	(Bailey)
9.	Bolpur	W. Ben.	(N. K. Bose)
10.	Chandipur	W. Ben.	(Nicholas)
11.	Chenchus	A. P.	(Fürer-Haimendorf)
12.	Cochin Jews	Ker.	(Fischel, Mandelbaum)
13.	Coorgs	Mys.	(Srinivas)
14.	Daleke	Pun.	(I. P. Singh)
15.	Dalena	Mys.	(Epstein)
16.	Deoli	Raj.	(Carstairs)
17.	Dewara	A. P.	(Dube)
18.	Dimiria	Or.	(Patnaik)
19.	Gamras	U. P.	(K. L. Sharma)
20.	Gannapur	Mys.	(Gnanambal)
21.	Gaon	Mah.	(Orenstein)
22.	Garos	Assam	(Burling)
23.	Gayawals	Bihar	(Vidyarthi)
24.	Gopalpur	Mys.	(Beals)
25.	Haripura	Mys.	(Dhillon)
26.	Hijalna	W. Ben.	(Sarma)
27.	Iravas	Ker.	(Aiyappan)
28.	Jatavs of Agra	U. P.	(Lynch)
29.	Jats	U. P., Har.	(Pradhan, Kudryavtsev)
30.	Jhabiran	U. P.	(R. Gupta)
31.	Jitpur	Pun.	(Nath)
32.	Kadduhalli Nad	Mys.	(Beals and MacLachlan)
33.	Kanchanpur	W. Ben.	(Basu)
34.	Karimpur	U. P.	(Wiser)
35.	Karul	Mah.	(Karve and Damle)
36.	Kasandra	Guj.	(Steed)
37.	Khalapur	U. P.	(Hitchcock, Minturn, J. Gumperz, P. Kolenda)
38.	Kishan Garhi	U. P.	(Marriott)
39.	Kotas	Mad.	(Mandelbaum)
40.	Kothuru	A. P.	(Y. V. L. Rao)
41.	Kugti	H. P.	(Newell)
42.	Kumbapettai	Mad.	(Gough)
43.	Lamepur	Delhi	(M. S. A. Rao)
44.	Lonikand	Mah.	(Ghurye)
45.	Madhupur	W. Ben.	(S. Sinha)
46.	Mahuva	Guj.	(Desai)
47.	Malana	H. P.	(Rosser)
48.	Maroli Bazar	Guj.	(Kapadia)
49.	Mayur	Ker.	(Aiyappan)
50.	Meos	Raj.	(Aggarwal)

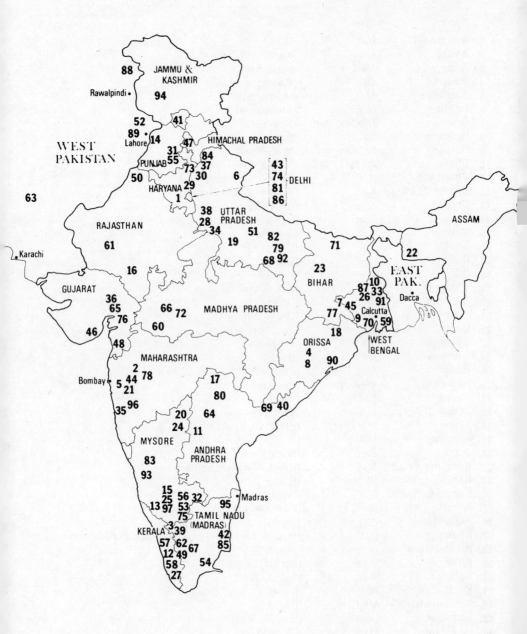

Place-Names and Group Names
A SELECTION OF THOSE MENTIONED IN THE TEXT.

Name	State	Author
51. Mohana	U. P.	(Majumdar)
52. Mohla	W. Pak.	(Eglar)
53. Morsralli	Mys.	(McCormack)
54. Nadars	Mad.	(Hardgrave, Raj)
55. Nalli	Pun.	(Izmirlian)
56. Namhalli	Mys.	(Beals)
57. Nayadis	Ker.	(Aiyappan)
58. Nayars	Ker.	(Gough, Unni Nayar)
59. Nehalpur	W. Ben.	(U. Guha)
60. Nimar Balahis	M. P.	(Fuchs)
61. Palana	Raj.	(Bose and Malhotra)
62. Paliyans	Mad.	(Gardner)
63. Pat	W. Pak.	(Honigmann)
64. Pathuru	A. P.	(Y. V. L. Rao)
65. Patidars	Guj.	(Pocock)
66. Potlod	M. P.	(Mathur)
67. Pramalai Kallars	Mad.	(Dumont)
68. Ramapur	U. P.	(Opler and R. D. Singh)
69. Reddis of Bison Hills	A. P.	(Fürer-Haimendorf)
70. Radhanagar	W. Ben.	(Nicholas)
71. Radhanagar	Bihar	(Roy)
72. Ramkheri	M. P.	(Mayer)
73. Ram Nagar	Har.	(Hazlehurst)
74. Rampur	Delhi	(Lewis)
75. Rampura	Mys.	(Srinivas)
76. Samiala	Guj.	(Fukutake, Ouchi, Nakane)
77. Santals	Bihar, W. Ben.	(Orans, Culshaw, Datta-Majumdar, Kochar)
78. Sarola Kasar	Mah.	(Jagalpure and Kale)
79. Senapur	U. P.	(Opler, Cohn, Planalp, Rowe, Reddy)
80. Shamirpet	A. P.	(Dube)
81. Shanti Nagar	Delhi	(Freed)
82. Sherurpur	U. P.	(Gould)
83. Shivapur	Mys.	(Ishwaran)
84. Sirkanda	U. P.	(Berreman)
85. Sripuram	Mad.	(Béteille)
86. Sungpur	Delhi	(Gangrade)
87. Supur	W. Ben.	(Fukutake, Ouchi, Nakane)
88. Swat Pathans	W. Pak.	(Barth)
89. Tararwala	W. Pak.	(Ullah)
90. Telis	Or.	(Patnaik)
91. "Ten Villages"	W. Ben	(Klass)
92. Tezibazar	U. P.	(Fox)
93. Totagadde	Mys.	(Harper)
94. Utrassu-Umangiri	Kash.	(Madan)
95. Vanniyars	Mad.	(Rudolph)
96. Varkute	Mah.	(Karve and Damle)
97. Wangala	Mys.	(Epstein)